O9-CFT-978

Bulgaria
a country study

Federal Research Division
Library of Congress
Edited by
Glenn E. Curtis
Research Completed
June 1992

On the cover: Alexander Nevsky Cathedral, Sofia

Second Edition, First Printing, 1993.

Library of Congress Cataloging-in-Publication Data

Bulgaria : a country study / Federal Research Division, Library of
   Congress ; edited by Glenn E. Curtis — 2d ed.
       p.   cm. — (Area handbook series, ISSN 1057-5294)
   (DA pam ; 550-168)
       "Research completed June 1992."
       "Supersedes the 1974 edition of Area Handbook for Bulgaria,
   edited by Eugene K. Keefe"—T.p. verso.
       Includes bibliographical references (pp. 287-295) and index.
       ISBN 0-8444-0751-8
       1. Bulgaria.   I. Curtis, Glenn E. (Glenn Eldon), 1946-   .
   II. Library of Congress. Federal Research Division. III. Series.
   IV. Series: DA pam ; 550-168.
DR55.B724   1993   93-10955
949.77—dc20   CIP

Headquarters, Department of the Army
DA Pam 550-168

For sale by the Superintendent of Documents, U.S. Government Printing Office
Washington, D.C. 20402

Foreword

This volume is one in a continuing series of books prepared by the Federal Research Division of the Library of Congress under the Country Studies/Area Handbook Program sponsored by the Department of the Army. The last page of this book lists the other published studies.

Most books in the series deal with a particular foreign country, describing and analyzing its political, economic, social, and national security systems and institutions, and examining the interrelationships of those systems and the ways they are shaped by cultural factors. Each study is written by a multidisciplinary team of social scientists. The authors seek to provide a basic understanding of the observed society, striving for a dynamic rather than a static portrayal. Particular attention is devoted to the people who make up the society, their origins, dominant beliefs and values, their common interests and the issues on which they are divided, the nature and extent of their involvement with national institutions, and their attitudes toward each other and toward their social system and political order.

The books represent the analysis of the authors and should not be construed as an expression of an official United States government position, policy, or decision. The authors have sought to adhere to accepted standards of scholarly objectivity. Corrections, additions, and suggestions for changes from readers will be welcomed for use in future editions.

Louis R. Mortimer
Chief
Federal Research Division
Library of Congress
Washington, D.C. 20540

Acknowledgments

The authors are indebted to numerous individuals and organizations who gave their time, research materials, and expertise on Bulgarian affairs to provide data, perspective, and material support for this volume.

The work of Violeta D. Baluyut and William Giloane, coauthors of the previous edition of the Bulgaria area handbook, provided an important factual base from which to develop new chapters. Thanks also go to the Bulgarian National Tourist Office in New York, the United States Embassy in Sofia, the Embassy of the Republic of Bulgaria in Washington, and Scott Thompson of the United States Department of State for assistance in locating illustration material. The expert photography of Charles Sudetic and Sam and Sarah Stulberg provided vivid new images of Bulgaria for users of the handbook.

Thanks also go to Ralph K. Benesch, who oversees the Country Studies/Area Handbook Program for the Department of the Army. In addition, the authors appreciate the advice and guidance of Sandra W. Meditz, Federal Research Division coordinator of the handbook series. Special thanks go to Marilyn L. Majeska, who supervised editing and managed production, assisted by Andrea T. Merrill; to Wayne Horne, who designed the book cover and the illustrations on the title page of each chapter; to David P. Cabitto, who provided graphics support and, together with Harriett R. Blood and the firm of Greenhorne and O'Mara, prepared maps; and to Tim Merrill, who compiled geographic data and adapted maps. The following individuals are gratefully acknowledged as well: Sharon Costello, who edited the chapters; Barbara Edgerton and Izella Watson, who did the word processing; Cissie Coy, who performed the final prepublication editorial review; Joan C. Cook, who compiled the index; and Malinda B. Neale of the Printing and Processing Section, Library of Congress, who prepared the camera-ready copy under the supervision of Peggy Pixley.

Contents

Chapter 3. The Economy 115

William Marsteller

Appendix. **Tables** 275

Bibliography 287

Glossary 297

Index 301

List of Figures

Preface

Beginning in 1989, Bulgaria passed through a time of political, social, and economic transition that changed many of its basic institutions and subjected society to stresses unknown in the forty-five years of totalitarian communist rule. Events that occurred after the ouster of Todor Zhivkov in 1989 demanded a new and updated version of *Bulgaria: A Country Study*. Although Bulgaria was one of the most closed communist societies until 1989, subsequent relaxation of tensions and restrictions has made available an increasing amount of reliable information about both the communist and the post-Zhivkov eras. Scholarly articles and periodical reports have been especially helpful in compiling this new treatment of the country. The most useful of those sources, together with a smaller number of key monographs, are cited at the end of each chapter.

The authors of this edition have described the changes in Bulgaria occurring in the last twenty years, with special emphasis on the last three. They have used the historical, political, and social fabric of the country as the background for these descriptions to ensure understanding of the context of the important recent events that have shaped the Bulgaria we see today. The authors' goal was to provide a compact, accessible, and objective treatment of five main topics: historical setting, society and its environment, the economy, government and politics, and the military and national security.

In all cases, Bulgarian personal names have been transliterated from Cyrillic according to a standard table; place-names are rendered in the form approved by the United States Board on Geographic Names; in the case of Sofia, the conventional international variant is used instead of the transliterated form (Sofiya). Unlike the previous edition of the Bulgaria study, this volume adds the diacritic (˘) to the letter ''ŭ'' to distinguish the distinctive Bulgarian vowel from the conventional ''u'' also used in Bulgarian. On maps, English-language generic designations such as *river, plain,* and *mountain* are used. Organizations commonly known by their acronyms (such as BCP, the Bulgarian Communist Party) are introduced first by their full English names.

Measurements are given in the metric system; a conversion table is provided in the Appendix. A historical chronology is provided at the beginning of the book, and a glossary and bibliography appear at the end. To amplify points in the text of chapters 2 and 3, tables in the Appendix provide statistics on performance and trends in the economy and various aspects of Bulgarian society.

The body of the text reflects information available as of June 1992. Certain other portions of the text, however, have been updated. The Introduction discusses significant events that have occurred since the completion of research, and the Country Profile includes updated information as available.

Table A. Chronology of Important Events

Period	Description
SEVENTH CENTURY	
ca. 630	First federation of Bulgar tribes formed.
681	Byzantine Empire recognizes first Bulgarian state.
NINTH CENTURY	
811	First Bulgarian Empire defeats Byzantine Empire, begins expanding.
870	Tsar Boris I accepts Christianity (Eastern Rite Orthodox) for Bulgaria.
893–927	Reign of Tsar Simeon, first golden age; maximum size of First Bulgarian Empire.
TENTH CENTURY	
924	Simeon defeated by Byzantines; first empire begins decline.
ELEVENTH CENTURY	
1014	Byzantines inflict major military loss on Tsar Samuil.
1018	Bulgaria becomes part of Byzantine Empire.
TWELFTH CENTURY	
1185	Asen and Peter lead revolt against Byzantine Empire, reestablishing Bulgarian state with capital at Tŭrnovo.
THIRTEENTH CENTURY	
1202	Tsar Kaloian makes peace with Byzantine Empire, achieves full independence, and begins Second Bulgarian Empire.
1204	Treaty with Rome recognizes pope and consolidates western border of Bulgarian Empire.
1218–1241	Reign of Ivan Asen II, second golden age of Bulgaria and period of territorial expansion.
1241	Tatar raids and feudal factionalism begin, causing social and political disorder.
1277	Peasant revolt; "swineherd tsar" Ivailo takes power.
ca. 1300	Tatar raids end.
FOURTEENTH CENTURY	
1323–1370	Under Mikhail Shishman and Ivan Aleksandŭr, territorial and commercial expansion resumes.

Table A.—Continued

Period	Description
1385	Sofia captured by Ottoman Empire.
1389	Turks defeat Serbs at Kosovo Polje, exposing remaining Bulgarian territory to Ottoman occupation.
FIFTEENTH CENTURY	
1453	Constantinople falls to Ottoman Empire, ending Byzantine Empire.
SIXTEENTH CENTURY	
ca. 1600	Ottoman Empire reaches peak of its power and territorial control.
SEVENTEENTH CENTURY	
1688	Suppression of Bulgarian revolt against Ottomans at Chiprovets ends Catholic influence in Bulgaria.
EIGHTEENTH CENTURY	
1741	Hristofor Zhefarovich completes his *Stematografia,* seminal work on Bulgarian cultural history.
1762	Paisi of Hilendar writes a history of the Bulgarian people, using vernacular Bulgarian.
NINETEENTH CENTURY	
1804	Serbia is the first Slavic land to take arms against Ottoman Empire.
1806	Sofroniĭ Vrachanski publishes first book printed in Bulgaria.
1815	Bulgarian volunteers join Serbian independence fighters.
ca. 1820	End of *kŭrdzhaliĭstvo,* anarchic period precipitated by breakdown of Ottoman authority in Bulgarian territory.
1835	Neofit Rilski opens first school teaching in Bulgarian, using Petŭr Beron's secular education system.
1840	First girls' school teaching in Bulgarian opens.
1844	First periodical printed in Bulgaria.
1856	First *chitalishte* (public reading room) opens.
1860	Bishop Ilarion Makariopolski declares Bulgarian diocese of Constantinople independent of Greek Orthodox patriarchate.

Table A.—Continued

Period	Description
1862	Georgi Rakovski forms first armed group for Bulgarian independence.
1870	Bulgarian Orthodox Church declared a separate exarchate by Ottoman Empire.
1875	September Uprising, first general Bulgarian revolt against Ottoman rule, crushed.
1876	April Uprising spurs massacres of Bulgarians by Ottomans and European conference on autonomy for Christian subjects of Ottoman Empire.
1878	Russo-Turkish War of 1877–78 ends in Treaty of San Stefano, creating an autonomous Bulgaria stretching from Aegean Sea to Danube.
1878	In Treaty of Berlin, Western Europe forces revision of Treaty of San Stefano, returning area south of Balkan Mountains to Ottoman Empire; a smaller Bulgaria retains autonomy within the empire.
1879	Tŭrnovo constitution written as foundation of Bulgarian state; Alexander of Battenburg elected prince of Bulgarian constitutional monarchy.
1886	Alexander deposed by army officers.
1887	Stefan Stambolov begins seven years as prime minister, accelerating economic development; Ferdinand of Saxe-Coburg-Gotha accepts Bulgarian throne.
1891	Social Democratic Party, later Bulgarian Communist Party, founded.
1899	Bulgarian Agrarian Union founded to represent peasant interests.
TWENTIETH CENTURY 1903	Suppression of Ilinden-Preobrazhensko Uprising sends large numbers of Macedonian refugees into Bulgaria and inflames Macedonian issue.
1908	Ferdinand declares Bulgaria fully independent of Ottoman Empire and himself tsar.
1912	First Balkan War pushes Ottoman Empire completely out of Europe; Bulgaria regains Thrace.

Table A.—Continued

Period	Description
1913	In Second Balkan War, Bulgaria loses territory to Serbia and Greece; Bulgarian nationalism on the rise.
1915–18	Bulgaria fights in World War I on side of Central Powers; decisive defeat at Dobro Pole (1918) forces Ferdinand to abdicate in favor of his son Boris III.
1919	Treaty of Neuilly-sur-Seine awards Thrace to Greece, Macedonian territory to Yugoslavia, Southern Dobruja to Romania, sets Bulgarian reparations, and limits Bulgarian army.
1919	Under Prime Minister Aleksandŭr Stamboliĭski, agrarians become dominant political party; socialist parties also profit from postwar social unrest.
1923	After four years of drastic economic reform and suppression of opposition, Stamboliĭski assassinated by Macedonian extremists.
1923–1931	Coalition Tsankov and Liapchev governments suppress extremists; social tensions rise with world economic crisis of 1929.
1934	In Balkan Entente, Greece, Romania, Turkey, and Yugoslavia reaffirm existing Balkan borders; Bulgaria refuses participation, is isolated.
1934	Right-wing coup by Zveno coalition begins dictatorship, abolishes political parties; Macedonian terrorism ends.
1935	Boris III deposes Zveno and declares royal dictatorship that remains in effect until 1943.
1941	Bulgaria signs Tripartite Pact, allying it with Nazi Germany in World War II; Bulgaria refrains from action against Soviet Union for duration of war.
1943	Boris III dies, leaving three-man regency to rule for his underage son Simeon II.
1943–44	Allied air raids damage Sofia heavily; activity of antiwar factions in Bulgaria increases.
1944	As Bulgarian government seeks peace with Allies, Red Army invades; temporary Bulgarian government overthrown by communist-led coalition.

Table A. —Continued

Period	Description
1946	Georgi Dimitrov of the Bulgarian Communist Party (BCP) becomes prime minister of the new Republic of Bulgaria.
1947	Dimitrov constitution goes into effect; remaining opposition parties to BCP silenced; state confiscation of private industry completed.
1948–49	Muslim, Orthodox, Protestant, and Roman Catholic religious organizations restrained or banned.
1949	Joseph V. Stalin chooses Vŭlko Chervenkov to succeed Dimitrov; period of Stalinist cult of personality, purges of Bulgarian BCP, and strict cultural and political orthodoxy begins.
1950	Large-scale collectivization of agriculture begins, continuing through 1958.
1953	Death of Stalin begins loosening of Chervenkov's control, easing of party discipline.
1956	Todor Zhivkov becomes first secretary of BCP.
1957–58	After Soviet invasion of Hungary, Bulgaria cracks down on nonconformism to party line in culture and politics.
1962	Nikita S. Khrushchev annoints Todor Zhivkov as successor to Chervenkov; Zhivkov becomes prime minister and is unchallenged leader for the next twenty-seven years.
1968	Soviet invasion of Czechoslovakia tightens government control in Bulgaria.
1971	New constitution specifies role of BCP in Bulgarian society and politics. '
1978	Dissident Georgi Markov assassinated in London.
1981	Economic restructuring in New Economic Model brings temporary economic upswing, no long-term improvement.
1981	Under direction of Liudmila Zhivkova, Bulgaria celebrates its 1,300th anniversary.
1984	First program of assimilation of ethnic Turkish minority begins.
1987–88	Dissident groups begin to form around environmental and human rights issues.

Table A. —Continued

Period	Description
1989 Summer	Second Turkish assimilation program brings massive Turkish emigration, increased dissident activity, and international criticism.
1989 Fall	Massive antigovernment demonstrations trigger party dismissal of Zhivkov.
1990	Three BCP-dominated governments are formed and dissolved; round table discussions between BCP and opposition parties begin to formulate reform legislation.
1990 June	First multiparty national election since World War II gives majority in National Assembly to Bulgarian Socialist Party (BSP, formerly BCP) with large opposition block to Union of Democratic Forces (UDF), which has refused participation in government.
1990 July	Tent-city demonstrations begin in Sofia, continue through summer.
1990 August	UDF leader Zheliu Zhelev chosen president.
1990 September	Zhelev meets with French and American leaders, receives pledges of economic support.
1990 November–December	General strike forces resignation of government of Prime Minister Andreĭ Lukanov; interim coalition government formed under Dimitŭr Popov.
1991 January	Initial phase of economic reform, including price decontrol on some commodities, goes into effect.
1991 Spring	Arable Land Law begins redistribution of land to private farmers.
1991 July	New constitution approved by National Assembly; national elections set for October.

Country Profile

Country

Formal Name: Republic of Bulgaria.

Short Form: Bulgaria.

Term for Citizens: Bulgarian(s).

Capital: Sofia.

Geography

Size: Approximately 110,550 square kilometers.

NOTE—The Country Profile contains updated information as available.

Topography: Mostly hills interspersed with plateaus, with major flatlands in north (Danubian Plateau, extending across entire country) and center (Thracian Plain). Main mountain ranges Balkan (extending across center of country from west to east, forming central watershed of country) and Rhodope (west to east across southern section of country); Rhodope includes two major groups, Pirin (far southwest) and Rila (west central).

Climate: Divided by mountains into continental (predominant in winter, especially in Danubian Plain) and Mediterranean (predominant in summer, especially south of Balkan Mountains). Rainfall also variable, with largest amounts at higher elevations.

Society

Population: 1990 estimate 8,989,172; 1990 growth rate negative 0.35 percent; 1989 population density eighty-one per square kilometer.

Languages: Official state language Bulgarian; main national minority language Turkish.

Ethnic Groups: In 1991, Bulgarians (85.3 percent), Turks (8.5 percent), Gypsies (2.6 percent), Macedonians (2.5 percent), Armenians (0.3 percent), Russians (0.2 percent).

Religion: In 1991 Bulgarian Orthodox (85 percent), Muslim (13 percent), Jewish (0.8 percent), Roman Catholic (0.5 percent). Significant increase in public worship and observance of religious holidays beginning 1990.

Health: In post-World War II era, state health care facilities became available to large part of population through polyclinic system, with all medical services free. In 1990 state control removed to promote diversity and specialization and reduce bureaucracy. Serious shortages of medical supplies and treatment, early 1990s.

Education and Literacy: Education compulsory between ages seven and sixteen. Complete literacy claimed 1990. Extensive growth in education system in post-World War II era, with rigidly Marxist ideological curriculum; complete restructuring, modernization, and depoliticization program begun 1990.

Economy

Gross National Product (GNP): Estimated at US$47.3 billion, or US$5,300 per capita in 1990. Growth rate of gross domestic product (GDP) 2.8 percent 1985–89, after continuous shrinkage through 1980s. Economic growth slowed in 1991 because of large-scale restructuring of economy from centralized planning to privatized market system.

Energy: Critical shortage of conventional fuels beginning with interruption of supplies from Soviet Union in 1990; heavy reliance on nuclear power from Kozloduy Nuclear Power Plant. Some small hydroelectric power plants. Main coal source Maritsa Basin (low-calorie, high-pollutant lignite); little domestic natural gas, oil, or hard coal.

Industry and Mining: Dramatic postwar growth in chemical, electronics, ferrous metals, and machinery industries, at expense of light industries such as food processing and textiles. Relatively narrow industrial base concentrated in several industrial centers, with inefficient use of fuels and raw materials. Major mining centers confined to lignite, iron ore, zinc, copper, and lead.

Agriculture: Redistribution of land from large-scale state farms to private ownership begun 1991; private plots, much more productive per hectare, vital to domestic food supply. Major crops: corn, tomatoes, tobacco (fourth largest exporter in world), attar of roses (world's largest exporter), grapes, wheat, barley, sugar beets, oilseeds, soybeans, and potatoes. Most numerous livestock: pigs, sheep, and chickens.

Exports: US$16 billion in 1989, of which 60.5 percent machinery and equipment, 14.7 percent agricultural products; 10.6 percent manufactured consumer goods; 8.5 percent raw materials, metals, and fuels. Largest export markets in 1989 Soviet Union, German Democratic Republic (East Germany), Czechoslovakia, Iraq, Libya.

Imports: US$15 billion in 1989, of which raw materials and fuels 45.2 percent, machinery and equipment 39.8 percent, manufactured consumer goods 4.6 percent, agricultural products 3.8 percent. Largest import suppliers in 1989 Soviet Union, German Democratic Republic (East Germany), Federal Republic of Germany (West Germany), Austria.

Balance of Payments: Hard currency trade surpluses maintained through 1985, when hard currency shortage caused recurring major trade deficits. Economic crisis of 1990–91 caused moratorium on hard-currency interest payment on foreign debt (US$10 billion in 1990).

Exchange Rate: Floating exchange rate established 1990, ending limitation of conversion to within Council for Mutual Economic Assistance (Comecon). First conversion tables issued by Bulgarian National Bank in 1991; official conversion value in 1991, 18 leva to U.S. dollar.

Inflation: Removal of price controls on selected categories of goods in 1991 led to severe but uneven price rises. On average, housing rose by 3.7 times, clothing three times, food six times in 1991 compared with 1989.

Fiscal Year: Calendar year.

Fiscal Policy: Governmental economic planning system remained centralized under noncommunist administration in 1991. Profit taxes (50 percent on profits of nonagricultural enterprises in 1990) most important state revenue source. Also turnover taxes on retail sales, excises on tobacco and alcohol, and individual income tax (less than 10 percent of total state revenue). Extensive state subsidies remained on selected economic activities in 1991.

Transportation and Communications

Railroads: Total freight carried 83 million tons in 1987; total passengers carried 110,000,000 in 1987. In 1987, 4,300 kilometers of track, of which 4,055 kilometers standard gauge, 245 kilometers narrow gauge, 917 kilometers double track, 2,510 kilometers electrified.

Civil Aviation: National line, Balkan Airline, carried 2,800,000 passengers and 24,213 tons of freight in 1987, using eighty-six major transport aircraft. International flights to major European cities and Algiers, Damascus, Baghdad, Kuwait, and Tunis. Usable airports 380, of which 20 with runways longer than 2,400 meters, 120 with permanent-surface runways. Major airports at Burgas, Khaskovo, Pleven, Plovdiv, Ruse, Silistra, Sofia, Stara Zagora, Tŭrgovishte, Varna, Vidin, and Yambol.

Highways: In 1987, 36,908 kilometers total, 33,535 kilometers hard surface, of which 242 kilometers motorway (highway); 940,000,000 passengers and 917,000,000 tons of freight transported in 1987.

Inland Waterways: In 1987, 470 kilometers; Danube River, along northern border, major commercial waterway.

Ports: Burgas and Varna on Black Sea; Lom, Ruse, Svishtov, and Vidin on Danube.

Pipelines: For crude oil, 193 kilometers; for refined petroleum products, 418 kilometers; for natural gas, 1,400 kilometers in 1986. Conveyed 21,000,000 tons in 1987.

Telecommunications: In 1987, 4,053 postal and telecommunications offices, 2.23 million telephones, 80 radio and 43 television transmitters; in 1990, 1,980,000 radio and 2.1 million television receivers. Two television networks broadcast to nineteen stations in 1991, with amplification to rural receivers. Three radio networks. Membership in Intervision East European television network and access to French satellite broadcasts.

Government and Politics

Government: Strong central government, with system of nine provinces (consolidated in 1987 from 28 districts), run by people's councils with limited autonomy and authority over local services, publicly owned enterprises, and administration. After ouster of Todor Zhivkov in 1989, communist party retained control of government but titles of head of state and party chief were separated. First noncommunist government elected 1991. Since 1990, president was head of state, prime minister was chief executive and head of fourteen-member Council of Ministers (cabinet). Unicameral legislature (National Assembly, Narodno sŭbranie) with 400 delegates; election law simplified in 1991 for direct representation by district. Legislative decision making slowed by distribution of seats between Union of Democratic Forces (UDF) and Bulgarian Socialist Party (BSP; formerly Bulgarian Communist Party, BCP).

Politics: Until 1989, BCP had complete control in one-party system with only nominal opposition. Opposition parties legalized after Zhivkov ouster in 1989. In 1990 BCP/BSP lost control of Council of Ministers when internal splits and strong opposition forced resignation of its last government, replaced by caretaker coalition government representing major parties. UDF, coalition of over twenty parties and movements, assumed leading role in 1991; with Movement for Rights and Freedoms, it formed working legislative majority after 1991 election and controlled Council of Ministers. Numerous smaller parties, notably Bulgarian Agrarian National Union and Bulgarian Social Democratic Party, remained active.

Foreign Relations: After collapse of Soviet-dominated Warsaw Pact and Comecon in 1991, sought acceptance into European community and improved relations with Balkan neighbors. In absence of Warsaw Pact protection, national security sought through detente with former enemy Turkey and Western support. International image improved by major reform in diplomatic corps in 1991.

International Agreements and Memberships: Member of United Nations and most of its specialized agencies. Also member of International Monetary Fund (IMF), World Bank, and General Agreement on Tariffs and Trade (GATT).

National Security

Armed Forces: Included army, air force, and navy; until 1990 under complete control of BCP. Administered in three military districts with president as commander in chief, advised by National Security Council, and chain of command through Ministry of National Defense to General Staff. Commission on National Security provided legislative oversight of national security decisions. In 1990 army had 97,000 active-duty personnel, including 65,000 conscripts; the air force 22,000, of which 16,000 were conscripts; the navy 10,000 active-duty personnel, half of which were conscripts. In 1991 total active-duty personnel reduced to 107,000, over 80 percent of which conscripts. Significant manpower reductions and organizational streamlining continued in 1992.

Major Military Units: In 1990, army organized in eight motor rifle divisions and five tank brigades. Major force structure change in 1991–92, reducing tank and mechanized infantry in favor of defensive systems (antitank, air defense). In 1991 navy, also being downsized, had small diesel submarines, small frigates, corvettes, missile craft, patrol vessels, coastal and inshore minesweepers, administered from Varna with bases at Atiya, Balchik, Burgas, and Sozopol. Air force had three MiG interceptor regiments, two MiG fighter regiments, limited numbers of fighter and other helicopters. Soviet SS–23 missile launchers remained in Bulgaria in 1992.

Military Budget: In 1990 defense expenditures estimated as equivalent of US$1.7 billion, about 3.6 percent of GNP.

Internal Security Forces: Drastic reform of State Security forces undertaken after ouster of Todor Zhivkov in 1989, to end their role as independent state enforcers of social discipline. In 1991 National Service for the Defense of the Constitution charged with identifying subversive or terrorist activities. Ministry of Internal Affairs reorganized, and its domestic and foreign surveillance arms cut deeply and put under strict civilian control in 1991. Power of militia (national police force, formerly chief enforcer of totalitarian rule) greatly reduced in 1990.

Figure 1. *Administrative Divisions of Bulgaria, 1991*

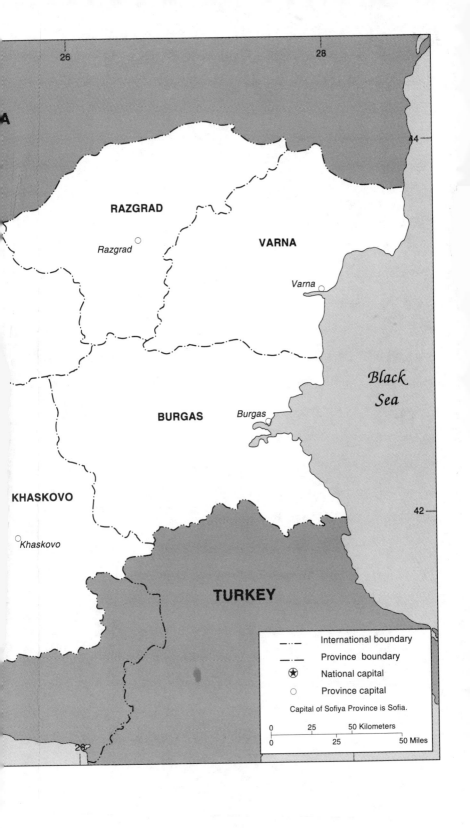

Introduction

FOR MOST OF ITS HISTORY, Bulgaria has been a small, agricultural nation whose location at the nexus of the European and Asian continents brought strong cultural and political influences from both east and west. Because of its location in the Balkans, on the border of Asiatic Turkey, and just across the Black Sea from the Russian and Soviet empires, Bulgaria received much attention from the commercial, political, and military powers surrounding it. Some of that attention was beneficial; much of it was harmful. In spite of foreign influences, which included centuries of occupation by the Byzantine and Ottoman empires and absolute loyalty to the Soviet Union in the twentieth century, Bulgarian cultural and social institutions maintained a unique national identity that was again struggling to reemerge after the collapse of the Soviet Empire in 1989.

When Bulgaria achieved autonomy within the Ottoman Empire in 1878, it was completely without modern political and social institutions with which to govern itself and deal with the outside world. Over the next seventy years, the process of inventing those institutions was rocky and uneven, both internally and in foreign relations. In spite of a very progressive constitution, Bulgaria's constitutional monarchy was plagued by frequent changes of government and governmental philosophy until World War II. The impact of a world depression and being on the losing side of both world wars also hindered Bulgaria's development before another expanding power, the Soviet Union, incorporated it into another empire as a result of Soviet victory in World War II. Then, when it emerged from the shadow of the Soviet Union in 1989, Bulgaria was faced again with inventing institutions that would enable its society, its economy, and its government to prosper in a world that had been evolving apart from them for many years.

The Byzantine and Ottoman occupations eclipsed the significant cultural developments of two golden ages (in the tenth and thirteenth centuries) when independent Bulgarian kingdoms dominated their region. Despite the centuries of occupation, village cultural and church life retained basic elements of ethnic identity that fostered a national revival as Ottoman power dwindled in the eighteenth and nineteenth centuries.

After finally regaining its independence at the end of the nineteenth century, modern Bulgaria stood in the shadow of European power politics through the first nine decades of the twentieth century. In that period, three successive major geopolitical antagonisms largely determined Bulgaria's place in the world: the Ottoman Empire versus Slavic Europe, the Axis powers versus the Allies, then the Warsaw Pact (see Glossary) opposing the North Atlantic Treaty Organization (NATO—see Glossary). In all three cases, Bulgaria stood as a minor player placed at the critical frontier separating the sides. Besides those conditions, Bulgaria's location amid the constant turmoil of the Balkans also shaped domestic life and foreign policy, even in the relatively uneventful postwar totalitarian years.

For the first forty-five years of the post-World War II era, Bulgaria was the East European country most closely allied to the Soviet Union, as well as the Warsaw Pact member most dependent economically on Soviet aid. During that time, all aspects of life that a totalitarian government could control were redrawn according to the Soviet model—from overemphasis on heavy industry to the content of works of literature. When the totalitarian era ended in 1989, it left behind many of the rigid structures and stereotypes formed by such imitation. Although Bulgaria had strayed from the prescribed Soviet path in noncontroversial areas such as glorification of the nation's 1,300-year history and token decentralization of economic planning, the machinery of independent national policy making was decidedly rusty when the post-Soviet era suddenly dawned.

At that point, Bulgaria was seemingly more independent of the power struggles of stronger neighbors than ever before in its history. But this liberation also deprived the nation of the economic and military security those neighbors had provided. The early 1990s saw a major reshaping of the economic power balance on the European continent. Because most of Eastern Europe emerged from the economic and political dominance of the Soviet Union at the same time, competition among the former Soviet client states for new economic and political positions was very keen. In this new context, Bulgaria, a nation of about 9 million persons located at the periphery of Europe, required particular energy and leadership to establish itself as an integral part of Europe. At the same time, energy and leadership were necessarily diverted to solving internal ethnic and political problems—most notably the integration into society of a substantial and vocal Turkish minority and the cultivation of an efficient government structure based on coalitions among Bulgaria's traditionally numerous political parties. In the background of those issues was an economy impoverished by decades of dependence on resources from the Soviet-led Comecon (Council for Mutual Economic Assistance—see Glossary) and poorly balanced Soviet-style central economic planning.

Before World War II, Bulgarian society was overwhelmingly agricultural, supported by rich farmland that grew a variety of grains, vegetables, fruits, and tobacco for domestic use and export. Well into the twentieth century, rural life remained steeped in village traditions that had not changed for many centuries, even under Ottoman rule. Cities such as Sofia and Plovdiv were islands of commercial activity and points of contact with other cultures. The fast-paced industrialization and agricultural collectivization programs of the postwar communist regimes brought four decades of intense migration into urban areas; in 1990 two of every three Bulgarians lived in a city or town. The migration process also reduced the isolation of remaining rural populations, which maintained contact with friends and relatives in the cities. Despite this process, however, the traditional dichotomy between cities and villages was still quite visible in the national elections of 1990 and 1991: Bulgaria's urban population largely supported economic and political reform platforms, whereas the rural regions expressed skepticism about reform by supporting the more conventional programs of the Bulgarian Socialist Party (BSP, formerly the Bulgarian Communist Party (BCP)).

Besides speeding urbanization, postwar industrial policy put most means of production under central BCP control. The state also took over the Bulgarian financial system, and agriculture underwent a series of collectivization phases between 1947 and 1958. Following the standard recipe for centralized economic planning, heavy industry received a high proportion of state investment compared with agriculture and consumer production. The ever-increasing quotas of five-year plans for all those sectors, however, reflected unrealistic expectations. Although later five-year plans aimed at more realistic goals, the centralized Bulgarian economic system failed consistently to increase output, although it devoted huge amounts of resources to the effort. Throughout the communist era, heavy industries lacked incentives because of state subsidies, and state-run agriculture never matched the productivity of small private plots. The Zhivkov government trumpeted major economic reform programs in the 1960s, 1970s, and 1980s, but they all remained within the restrictions of the centralized system, contributing nothing to Bulgaria's economic advancement.

As in the other East European countries, central planning of the economy produced severe environmental damage in Bulgaria. Damage was more localized in Bulgaria because its designated role in Comecon required fewer "smokestack industries" than that of Poland, Czechoslovakia, or the German Democratic Republic (East Germany). Nevertheless, cities such as Ruse, Dimitrovgrad, and Srednogorie suffered severe environmental deterioration from manufacturing activities under the communist regimes, which disregarded pollution in the name of progress. In 1988 public concern over environmental quality spawned the first Bulgarian protest groups, which played a central role in the overthrow of Zhivkov and then evolved into permanent opposition parties with strong public support.

In October 1991, the Grand National Assembly passed a Law on Protection of the Environment, and the next cabinet included a member of the Ekoglasnost environmental group as minister of the environment. Despite these measures, however, the critical need for economic growth in the postcommunist era hindered environmental recovery efforts. In 1992 auto emissions, heavy industry emissions, and power plants remained beyond government control although they contributed heavily to air pollution; excessive use of chemicals in agriculture polluted many Bulgarian lakes and streams; and reliance on nuclear power generated by unsafe equipment threatened a major radiation crisis.

Besides industrialization and urbanization, other important changes had occurred under the conventional communist totalitarian dictatorships that ruled Bulgaria under Georgi Dimitrov (1947–49), Vŭlko Chervenkov (1949–56), and Todor Zhivkov (1956–89). Centuries before, the Russian Empire had fought the first in a long series of wars with the Turks. Those wars conferred on Russia the stature of protector of the Slavs in the Ottoman Empire. In 1944, as Axis power retreated in Europe, a strong Russophile element remained in Bulgarian society. Accordingly, Bulgarians welcomed the arrival of the Red Army, whose presence ended Bulgaria's participation as an Axis ally in World War II and laid the foundation of the postwar political system. Interwar commercial and cultural relations with Western Europe (especially Germany and Italy) were curtailed when the postwar communist regimes intensified Bulgaria's traditionally close ties with the Russian Empire/Soviet Union. In 1949 this policy shift was codified by Bulgaria's membership in Comecon, which created a new network of East European trade relationships and subsidies dominated by the Soviet Union.

Between 1947 and 1989, Bulgarian foreign and economic policy followed scrupulously the policies of the Soviet Union. Intermittent periods of rapprochement and hostility between the Soviet Union and the West were mirrored in relations between Bulgaria and the NATO countries of Europe. Thus, for example, Zhivkov pulled back from newly invigorated relations with Western Europe in order to lend vigorous support to the Soviet invasions of Czechoslovakia in 1968 and Afghanistan in 1979. Bulgaria also followed the Soviet lead in assisting developing nations and supporting wars of national liberation.

The Bulgarian constitutions of 1947 and 1971 borrowed heavily from Soviet constitutional models, and, especially in its early stages, the Bulgarian centrally planned economy followed Soviet guidelines. Periods of economic experimentation also coincided in the two countries; Zhivkov's first large-scale restructuring of the Bulgarian system occurred in the early 1960s, at the same time that Nikita S. Khrushchev experimented with unorthodox economic methodology in the Soviet Union. Zhivkov was able to experiment more freely because the Bulgarian system was much smaller and more homogeneous and because Bulgaria had earned a place as the most trusted and loyal of the Comecon member nations. By the mid-1980s, economic imitation of the Soviet Union had turned earlier skepticism into cynicism in large parts of the Bulgarian public.

The communist regimes of the postwar era did accomplish significant improvement in national education and health care. Although the basic structure of prewar Bulgarian education remained intact after 1947, the primary goal of centralized education planning was to bring Marxist theory to as many Bulgarians as possible; hence promotion of literacy and expansion of primary and secondary education proceeded much more rapidly under the communist regimes. On a basic level, those goals were reached through a combination of rapid urbanization of the population and mandatory training for children and adults. But the state education program was a carefully regimented, technology-oriented imitation of the Soviet Union's system. After Zhivkov, the public education system and universities officially banned political indoctrination and activity in their institutions. Because many teachers and textbooks remained from the era when only the party line was acceptable, however, transition efforts encountered stubborn resistance in some quarters.

The communist era had provided very basic health care in state regional clinics available to most Bulgarians. Under the socialist health system, indicators such as average life expectancy, infant mortality rate, and physicians per capita improved steadily between 1947 and 1989. Nevertheless, post-Zhivkov governments embarked on decentralization and modernization programs to improve specialized care and raise the incentives for health care personnel and entrepreneurs in private facilities. In the early 1990s, the new programs underwent a difficult transition period that yielded uneven results. The overthrow of Zhivkov's orthodox communist regime in 1989 produced especially dramatic changes in Bulgarian political and economic life. By the mid-1980s, the Zhivkov regime already had wielded power for thirty years; by that time, the regime's inability to deal with new political and economic realities was obvious to many Bulgarians, especially the educated classes. Zhivkov took token political restructuring measures in the late 1980s, but by 1988 formidable opposition groups were forming around such issues as environmental standards and the chronic failure of the economic system to raise the standard of living. In 1989 Zhivkov's heavy-handed campaign to assimilate or exile Bulgaria's large Turkish minority depleted the labor force and evoked strong protest from the international community and many groups within Bulgaria. Shortly after an all-European environmental conference in Sofia provided an international audience for protesting groups, the Bulgarian Communist Party (BCP) ousted Zhivkov to avoid losing power entirely.

Although the BCP strategy succeeded in the short run, Zhivkov's communist successors were unable to meet the multitude of demands that society unleashed upon them once the symbol of monolithic state power had disappeared. Having lost the solid support of the Communist Party of the Soviet Union by 1990, the BCP hesitated between full commitment to political and economic reform and maintaining its still formidable grip on such sectors of Bulgarian society as management of heavy industry and administration of provincial government. A few months after Zhivkov's ouster, the party had changed its name to the Bulgarian Socialist Party (BSP) and introduced a series of government reform programs. But opposition groups, combined in the Union of Democratic Forces (UDF), refused to form a coalition government with the BSP or to support BSP reform proposals. Because the UDF represented a growing majority of Bulgarian society, by the end of 1990 the UDF strategy of non-participation had forced a political stalemate and resignation of the last communist-dominated cabinet, headed by Andreĭ Lukanov. This development negated the broad 100-day economic reform plan that Lukanov had proposed in the fall of 1990.

The old central planning system that remained in place in 1990 had included excessive emphasis on heavy industry, distorted pricing, declining agricultural productivity, and isolation from foreign markets. By the end of 1990, those failures had brought the Bulgarian economy to a severe crisis that included a drop of 11.5 percent in net material product (NMP—see Glossary), drastic increases in unemployment, curtailment of all payments to foreign creditors, and a drop in the standard of living.

The period following Lukanov's fall was one of extreme crisis; social unrest was very high, but political factions could not find an acceptable compromise course. Finally, Dimitŭr Popov, a judge with no political affiliation, became prime minister of a coalition cabinet that would run the government until the 1991 national elections chose a new National Assembly. Resolution of this crisis was due in large part to the negotiating skills of President Zheliu Zhelev.

In 1991 Bulgaria experimented with government coalitions to promote major reform programs. Important legislative packages included depoliticization of the army, the police, courts, state prosecutors, and the Ministry of Foreign Affairs; amnesty for political prisoners; restoration of property to political émigrés and victims of repression; and reform of the local government system that remained a stronghold of socialist bureaucrats. In 1991 such reform legislation encouraged loans from the World Bank (see Glossary) and other Western sources.

In mid-1991, all political factions agreed that economic reform was the government's top priority, but BSP members of parliament obstructed reform proposals that would bring temporary but severe economic dislocation. Instead, they favored a more gradual approach that would not threaten party members still entrenched in state industrial policy making. Although the National Assembly passed major legislation in 1991 on land redistribution, private commercial enterprises, and foreign investment, the key step of enterprise privatization remained unresolved in early 1992, and the land act required wholesale revision.

Privatization brought many difficult dilemmas for a system that until recently had been centrally planned. The new government had to distinguish state enterprises worth rehabilitation from those that should be replaced by totally new private enterprises. Restitution was needed for Bulgarians whose capital property had been seized by the communist state, but resolution of claims proved extremely complex. And rapid privatization inevitably displaced large numbers of workers from former state enterprises, damaging productivity, national morale, and earning power. In February 1992, the World Bank cited the lack of privatization legislation in delaying a loan of $US250 million. Both the Popov government and the government of Filip Dimitrov that followed spent months in fruitless debate of redistribution and regulation of large industries formerly operated by the state.

A vital economic support element, energy supply, became a critical problem in late 1991 when the Soviet Union first ended coal supply and later when Russia ended subsidized electric power supply to Bulgaria following the dissolution of the Soviet Union. Because Bulgaria's domestic energy base was quite inadequate to support an industrial system designed when outside energy supplies were plentiful and cheap, economic recovery depended on the single nuclear power plant at Kozloduy—a facility judged unsafe by both domestic and international authorities in 1991. Lacking foreign currency to import fuels, however, Bulgarian policy makers placed their hopes on Kozloduy's shaky technology to provide as much as half the country's electricity throughout the 1990s.

Political developments in 1991 made accelerated economic reform more likely. Remaining Zhivkov-era officials finally lost some of their power to obstruct the transition away from authoritarian government and a centrally planned economy. After considerable delay, in July the Grand National Assembly, which had been elected specifically to draft a new constitution, produced a document approved by a majority, but far from all, of its legislators. Some constituent groups in UDF refused to sign because they believed the constitution defended interests of the BSP, which was still the majority party at that point. Among vital innovations in the constitution were government by separation of powers, specification of the principles of a market economy, and full protection of citizens' private property rights.

The constitution also set conditions for election of a new National Assembly under reformed election laws. The new laws simplified the extremely cumbersome system used in 1990 and reduced the size of the National Assembly from 400 to 240. In the national election of October 1991, Bulgarian politics followed its long tradition of fragmentation when forty-two parties and other groups posted candidates. Of that number, thirty-five failed to receive enough votes for representation in the legislature. UDF candidates, running on three separate tickets, together won a plurality but not a majority of seats. The BSP held the next largest block of seats, making the twenty-four-vote block of the Movement for Rights and Freedoms (MRF) capable of swinging majority votes for the UDF or obstructing reform legislation. Because the MRF represented the substantial ethnic Turkish minority, many Bulgarians feared that the UDF would be coerced into pro-Turkish positions. The MRF blunted some criticism by announcing support of most of the UDF reform platform, however, shortly after the election.

The fourteen-member cabinet formed by Prime Minister Dimitrov, leader of the UDF, was young (average age forty-nine), professional, and included no BSP or MRF members. Among Dimitrov's structural reforms in the cabinet (reduced from seventeen to fourteen members) was abolition of the Ministry of Foreign Economic Relations, formerly a stronghold of Zhivkovite officials. For the first time, a civilian was named minister of defense. Key cabinet figures were Minister of Defense Dimitŭr Ludzhev, Minister of Foreign Affairs Stoian Ganev, and Minister of Internal Affairs Iordan Sokolov. As in previous cabinets, economic policy was divided among several ministries. Dimitrov, who introduced no formal program when he was appointed, listed ending inflation, raising productivity, and stabilizing the economy as his chief goals.

Despite the triumph of nonsocialist factions in the October elections, however, the Bulgarian government remained unsettled in the winter of 1991-92. Key constituent groups such as labor unions and the Turkish population continued to be somewhat aloof from the UDF coalition as 1992 began, and the coalition itself was constantly strained by the diversity of its membership. In 1992 the former communists remained the country's largest party, and the oversized government bureaucracy created by the communist regimes still controlled many parts of the national administration. But, unlike his predecessor, Dimitrov had no opposition ministers in his cabinet, and the UDF possessed a legislative majority if it could avoid internal fragmentation and keep the loyalty of the MRF.

With the environmental demonstrations of 1988, Bulgarian society renewed a long-dormant tradition of public protest, and such activities continued during the crisis years of 1990-92. The volatile ethnic issue of Turkish minority rights evoked many boycotts and protests by both Turks and Bulgarians between 1990 and 1992. And industrial strikes, most organized by the Podkrepa labor union, protested working conditions and unemployment throughout 1991 and early 1992.

Although Bulgarian society was ethnically relatively homogeneous, especially compared with neighboring Yugoslavia, the Turkish minority of about one million (estimates varied from 900,000 to 1.5 million in 1991) continued to present a delicate political problem in 1992. Bulgarian-Turkish animosity was based on the indelible Bulgarian memory of five centuries of occupation and cultural suppression by the Ottoman Empire. On the Turkish side, hostility was based on more recent memories of forced assimilation and restriction of human rights by the Zhivkov regime. The Zhivkov government had justified repression of the Turkish minority by appealing to ethnic Bulgarian fears that empowering Turks within Bulgaria would once again threaten Bulgarian security.

When Zhivkov fell, restoration of long-withheld civil rights became a central issue in the newly open political atmosphere. Minority rights found expression in the new political order; the MRF was formed to advance those rights, and the UDF somewhat cautiously advocated full use of the Turkish language in schools and full civil rights for all Turkish citizens of Bulgaria. Especially in eastern Bulgaria where the Turkish population was largest, a strong undercurrent of hostility grew in 1991 and 1992 between ultranationalist Bulgarians and their Turkish neighbors. Only a Supreme Court decision allowed the MRF to post candidates in the 1991 election, and the issue of restoring the teaching of Turkish in Bulgarian schools remained quite sensitive in 1992. In late 1991, the BSP, shorn of its parliamentary majority, accelerated its attacks on the MRF as a subversive organization working for Turkey—a desperate effort to build new support among Bulgarians fearful of new foreign domination.

In early 1992, the political situation left Turkish citizens with only partially restored civil rights, and school boycotts were called in some areas where the use of Turkish remained restricted. On this issue, the Bulgarian court system, which had been a purely political institution under the Zhivkov regime, was unable or unwilling to exercise fully the independence granted the judiciary in the new constitution. This was partly because the new antidiscrimination language of that document had never before been tested and partly because of the lingering tradition of judicial dependency on political officials. Meanwhile, politicians generally treated the Turkish issue with great caution in 1991 and early 1992. Nationalist factions attacked the governing UDF for its legislative "alliance" with the MRF, suggesting that UDF compromises would jeopardize national security. These conditions lessened the likelihood that the National Assembly would finally attack and resolve the "national question."

Bulgarian foreign policy also changed markedly in the years following 1989. As in domestic affairs, a strong body of opinion favored maintaining pre-1989 policy, in this case continuing to cultivate the Soviet Union as protector and economic benefactor. Actual policy sought a compromise that would not only change political relations but also ensure continued supply of raw materials, especially fuels. Negotiations with the Soviet government yielded promises of continued supply, but by 1991 the Soviet republics responsible for delivery were able to ignore the commitment. This situation deteriorated further when the Soviet Union dissolved into constituent republics in the fall of 1991. By January 1992, Bulgaria had established relations with Belarus, Russia, Ukraine, and the Baltic states in an effort to reestablish supply lines. In November 1991, Bulgaria joined a new economic association for East European cooperation and trade, formed by economic organizations in most of the former East European Comecon member countries, as well as in Russia, Kazakhstan, and Ukraine. The aim was to restore economic relations among those countries on a new basis.

A top foreign policy priority of the Dimitrov government was dismantling the bureaucracy of the Ministry of Foreign Affairs, which was still dominated by BSP functionaries under Prime Minister Popov. Shortly after his appointment, Minister of Foreign Affairs Ganev secured the recall of several ineffectual senior diplomats. In early 1992, he reviewed the performance of all ministry personnel in order to streamline the organization and purge remaining members of Zhivkov's state security establishment, which had been notorious for conducting espionage from diplomatic outposts.

Beginning in 1990, President Zheliu Zhelev and other Bulgarian officials met with Western officials to stress Bulgaria's commitment to economic and political reform and cement relations with the United States and the European Community (EC—see Glossary). The EC was the primary focus because Bulgarian policy makers saw acceptance into the European federation as the best way to avoid isolation and hasten internal reform. With this goal in mind, top-level diplomatic attention was divided among many West European countries, while overtures to Eastern Europe declined noticeably. In late 1991, France, Germany, Greece, and Italy promised to support Bulgarian membership in the EC, although at that point at least seven countries were ahead of Bulgaria on the list of prospective EC members. In 1991 Bulgaria did achieve associate status in the EC, together with Czechoslovakia, Hungary, and Poland. From the Western viewpoint, a stable Bulgaria offered a calming influence on the turbulent Balkans, where the disintegration of Yugoslavia in 1991 threatened to trigger wider conflict over ethnic and economic issues.

Bulgaria viewed the Yugoslav crisis of the second half of 1991 as a serious threat to regional stability. President Zhelev reiterated Bulgaria's policy of nonintervention and the right of self-determination for all people in Yugoslavia. This declaration was mainly to reduce accusations and fears in Serbia that Bulgaria would assume a direct role in weakening the Yugoslav Federation (now reduced to Serbia and Montenegro) and renew century-old claims on Macedonian territory. Zhelev's reassurances were also aimed at Greece, which feared annexation of its part of Macedonia into a state of Greater Macedonia. Following its advocacy of self-determination for Balkan states, Bulgaria recognized the four former Yugoslav secessionist republics, Bosnia and Hercegovina, Croatia, Macedonia, and Slovenia, in the winter of 1991. In late 1991, Bulgaria strongly backed mediation of the conflict between Serbia and Croatia by the EC and the United Nations, and Bulgaria embargoed military supplies and arms bound for Yugoslavia.

Meanwhile, relations with Turkey improved after the triumph of the UDF in the fall 1991 election. The UDF–MRF coalition pursued a treaty of friendship, cooperation, and security to match the treaty signed with Greece in October 1991. By early 1992, high-level military talks had substantially eased tension with Turkey, which maintained troops in eastern Thrace close to the Bulgarian border. Meanwhile, Foreign Minister Ganev was seeking a trilateral summit meeting with Turkey and Greece to enhance regional security as well as a "mini-Helsinki" conference of Balkan states, to enhance regional security. Cultivation of Turkey had the strategic role of counterbalancing Greece and Serbia, two regional powers potentially allied against Bulgaria over the Macedonia issue in 1992.

The overthrow of Zhivkov revealed a deep fascination in Bulgarian society with the culture and ideals of the United States, and a desire for closer relations. Although United States aid to Bulgaria remained quite small compared with aid given to Poland, Hungary, and Czechoslovakia in the early 1990s, high-level official contacts in that period were more friendly and frequent than ever before. President Zhelev stated Bulgaria's position very forcefully on two visits to Washington (1990 and 1991), and Prime Minister Dimitrov had a productive stay in March 1992 that gained a promise that the United States would accord Bulgaria the same status as the three major East European aid recipients. In November 1991, the United States officially granted Bulgaria most-favored-nation status.

The demise of the Warsaw Pact in 1991 left Bulgaria without the military protection of the Soviet Union and its allies. To bolster its security position, Bulgaria obtained NATO assurances about Turkey's military ambitions and established a special relationship with NATO headquarters in 1991. Meanwhile, the Bulgarian military establishment underwent reforms comparable to those elsewhere in society. A central aim of the Dimitrov government was to bring the military under civilian control, to end the separate, elite status that followed the Soviet model, and to make the military an open institution integrated into society. An immediate stimulus for this reform was the role of national military establishments in Yugoslavia's bloody internal conflict and in the failed coup in the Soviet Union in 1991. (The Bulgarian military had taken no part in any of the political turmoil of 1989–91.) The depolitization of the military decreed by the Bulgarian government in 1990 reduced BSP influence in the ranks. As in other phases of Bulgarian life, positions of power remained for some time thereafter in the hands of reactionaries from the Zhivkov era. By the end of 1991, however, about 85 percent of generals active in 1989 had retired voluntarily or under pressure. The resignations resulted in a net reduction of ninety-three generals from a top-heavy officer corps. The military reform campaign also sought to lift the status of the military as a profession and to foster positive relations between the civilian and military communities. In 1992, however, a shortage of army officers was partly attributed to the military's negative image in society.

Arms and spare-part supply to the Bulgarian military suffered greatly when the overthrow of Zhivkov caused the Soviet Union to abandon long-term contracts. At the same time, the disproportionately large Bulgarian arms industry, a pillar of the centrally planned economy, was hit hard by the loss of its Soviet market. The new government limited the activities of Kintex, Bulgaria's notorious arms export agency, by prohibiting sales to terrorists and totalitarian regimes. A long-term conversion program begun in October 1991 gave new civilian production assignments to many arms plants.

The Bulgarian military had a long history of cooperation with its Soviet counterpart. Weapons systems, doctrine, and training were interchangeable throughout the postwar era, and the Bulgarian military relied on Soviet fuel supplies even more heavily than the civilian economy. The sudden end of the Soviet partnership in 1990, followed shortly by removal of the communist symbols and dogma that had supported military morale, caused considerable turbulence and confusion.

New international responsibilities also affected the Bulgarian military establishment. To abide by the Treaty on Conventional Armed Forces in Europe signed by the Warsaw Pact and NATO in 1990, Bulgaria also faced reductions in military manpower and armaments beginning in 1991. Bulgaria sought to retain the Soviet SS–23 missiles installed in the 1980s, however, on the grounds that they predated the relevant nuclear disarmament treaty and were vital to national defense.

As the 1990s began, Bulgaria was in a completely new phase of national existence. For this phase to succeed, Bulgaria needed both a substantive new self-image and a believable new international posture. The postwar communist period had changed society by forcible industrialization and urbanization; those processes were accompanied by regimentation that suppressed cultural and economic individuality, and by isolation from influences and challenges outside the Soviet sphere. Then, in keeping with the wave of democratization that had swept most of Eastern Europe in 1989, Bulgaria made an abrupt about-face and began experimenting with democratic institutions in a manner unprecedented in the country's political history. After nearly fifty years of totalitarianism, and having had marginal success with democratic institutions prior to World War II, Bulgaria's experimentation was quite cautious at first. By 1992, however, a new generation of capable leaders had instilled impressive momentum in the transformation process. Although the slow pace of economic restructuring promised continued hardship, a large part of Bulgarian society was committed to reform, and hard-line revisionism and social unrest had declined in early 1992.

Besides adapting Western-type political and economic institutions to unique domestic requirements, Bulgaria's most difficult task was to overcome its Cold-War image as an obscure and somewhat sinister nation whose total loyalty to the Soviet Union had led it to support terrorists and assassins. By 1992 progress in that direction was significant; Western approval raised Bulgaria's status closer to that of Poland, Hungary, and Czechoslovakia, the three former Soviet client states whose democratization had given them a head start toward integration into the fabric of Europe. As it strengthened its connections to the West in 1992, Bulgaria finally had an opportunity to develop social and political institutions appropriate to its needs under reduced pressure from large-power European politics.

December 31, 1992

*   *   *

In the months following completion of this manuscript, Bulgaria underwent serious political upheaval, and its economy failed to move toward reform nearly as fast as planners had hoped. The Dimitrov government elected in late 1991 showed early promise in promoting economic reform and democratization. By mid-1992, however, Dimitrov's leverage was reduced by shifting factions in his political coalition and by rising public skepticism that Bulgaria's painful reform program would yield a better standard of living.

In 1992 Dimitrov's UDF coalition dominated political dialogue and enjoyed a narrow majority in the National Assembly. This position required that the coalition remain unified within itself and allied with the much smaller MRF. But in the second half of 1992,

UDF policies increasingly alienated influential parts of Bulgarian society such as the Orthodox Church, parts of the media, trade unions, and private businessmen. An atmosphere of escalating confrontation was the result.

Meanwhile, the MRF was taking increasingly independent stands on many issues, using the influence provided by the party's swing-vote position in parliament. In October 1992, judging the UDF response to its demands inadequate, the MRF finally joined the Bulgarian Socialist Party and dissident UDF members in a parliamentary vote of no confidence in the Dimitrov government. By destroying the Dimitrov coalition, the vote created another crisis period in which Bulgaria was unable to choose a government. Nearly two months later, Liuben Berov, an unaffiliated economics professor, was approved as prime minister after both the UDF and the BSP had failed to form governments.

The fate of the leading parties thus changed drastically at the end of 1992. The BSP, which had remained aloof from political struggle during the UDF's dominant period, found itself with the political influence of a parliamentary plurality as the new government took office. This happened in spite of the continued split between BSP conservatives allied with former communist party chief Aleksandŭr Lilov and the reformist branch of the party. Observers questioned whether the BSP would use its new influence to promote reform or to preserve the remaining Zhivkov-era party bastions in state industry and provincial government. In early 1993, BSP support of the Berov government was decidedly pragmatic, and experts saw a strong likelihood that support would be withdrawn (and the government automatically toppled) if policies displeased the BSP or if a new election would be advantageous to the BSP.

Meanwhile, the disparate membership of the UDF wrote another chapter in the acrimonious history of the coalition. The group again split formally when one faction of constituent parties formed a new coalition, the New Union for Democracy. Although Berov had pledged to continue the UDF reform program, UDF members of parliament refused all support for the Berov government. Relations between the UDF and its former allies in the MRF remained hostile. Several attempts at forming new coalitions and alliances failed for various reasons in early 1993. The most notable coalition was the Bulgarian Democratic Center, whose loss of two key member parties left a void in the center of the political spectrum.

Besides the confusion of a fragmented political base, the Dimitrov government left unforeseen financial woes. According to one estimate, Bulgaria's internal debt doubled in 1992. The reasons were inflation (which reached 6.6 percent per month in early 1993), the Dimitrov government's concealing of budget deficits by withholding funds from certain industries, and government assumption of the debts of state companies. After the government had borrowed heavily from the Bulgarian National Bank to pay its debts, only an estimated 5 percent of domestic credit remained for private investment. Experts forecast the same figure for 1993, leaving no prospect of meaningful support for a larger private sector.

In April 1993, Berov's coalition government was able to draft a budget bill containing the same deficit as in 1992, despite the debt left by Dimitrov. To do this, spending on education, health care, culture, and national defense were reduced significantly; the Ministry of National Defense would receive only half the money it requested. Nevertheless, the proposed deficit, 7.9 percent of the gross national product (GNP—see Glossary), caused concern among international lenders.

Economic reform in 1992 had limited success. The amended land redistribution law passed in March 1992 effectively abolished collective farms; nominally, nearly 80 percent of Bulgaria's total arable land had been reclaimed by individual owners by midyear. Although the legislative machinery was in place, however, by mid-1993 less than 20 percent of designated land had actually been restored, and Zhelev criticized the Berov government for neglecting this aspect of economic policy. In April 1993, farmers demonstrated in Sofia against inequities they perceived in the land law.

The political crisis stopped vital privatization legislation in late 1992, delaying the pilot privatization of 100 companies. Berov had called privatization the top priority of his government when he took office, and adjustments were made in existing laws to make conversion easier. Nevertheless, almost no privatization activity took place in the first four months of 1993. In early 1993, President Zhelev recommended that privatization be delayed until a large-scale national program, similar to those used in the Czech Republic, Hungary, and Poland, could be prepared. Meanwhile, inefficient state industries went deep into recession, cancelling the effects of what had been a rather successful economic stabilization plan in 1991.

International lenders, whose assistance was considered a vital ingredient in restructuring Bulgaria's economy, responded unevenly to the events of 1992. Lenders demanded faster progress toward a market system, but Bulgarian policy makers were wary of losing public support by further cutting state subsidies for social programs. In late 1992, Bulgaria agreed to repay part of the interest overdue to its international commercial creditors, as a good-faith step toward a 1993 debt settlement agreement. The additional expense, however, promised to exacerbate the budget deficit.

Prospects for Bulgaria's commercial relations with Western Europe improved in late 1992 and early 1993. In March 1993, Bulgaria signed an agreement with the EC to establish a free-trade zone with that group over a ten-year transition period. A strong incentive for the Europeans was bolstering Bulgaria as a stabilizing influence in the chaotic Balkans. In an April resolution on its relations with Bulgaria, the European Parliament (the legislative assembly of the EC) declared that no further guarantees of reform were needed because Bulgaria was on an irreversible line toward a market economy—a judgment likely encouraged by Balkan geopolitics. The new EC-Bulgarian accords were to go into effect in June 1993.

In March 1993, Bulgaria also signed a free-trade agreement with the European Free Trade Association (EFTA). Although at that point only 3.5 percent of Bulgaria's exports went to EFTA member nations (Austria, Finland, Iceland, Liechtenstein, Norway, Sweden, and Switzerland), the terms of the agreement made substantial expansion possible. Were the agreement ratified, 95 percent of Bulgarian industrial exports would have tariff-free access, while agricultural exports would be governed by bilateral arrangements.

Besides the drive for inclusion in West European economic groupings, the primary issue of Bulgarian foreign policy in early 1993 was preventing expansion of the Yugoslav crisis. In keeping with its own consistent policy of nonintervention, Bulgaria warned the other Balkan states to refrain from military involvement that might return the entire region to the chaos that preceded World War I. Bulgaria opposed lifting the arms embargo on Bosnian Muslims, predicting that such a move would expand the conflict between Muslims and Serbs. Meanwhile, Bulgarian diplomats remained in constant contact with Greece and Turkey while reiterating Bulgarian support for the independence of all four former Yugoslav republics: Bosnia and Hercegovina, Croatia, Macedonia, and Slovenia. Berov traveled to Moscow in March to discuss the Balkan situation, trade, repayment of Russian debts to Bulgaria, and economic cooperation. No concrete decisions were made, although the Bulgarian and Russian representatives noted their nations' harmony on the Balkan question. In early 1993, Bulgaria confirmed its intention to rely on Russia and Ukraine as primary military suppliers, choosing to maintain longstanding relations rather than incur the greater expense of refitting Bulgarian forces with Western equipment. According to official Bulgarian statements, no security threat was perceived from instability in any former Soviet republic.

Ethnic minority issues remained without solution in 1992, although no major open conflict resulted from continued tension between minorities and Bulgarian nationalists. Although 1992 human rights legislation improved the legal status of minorities, unemployment hit them especially hard, and as many as 40,000 Turks left Bulgaria in 1992. In the fall of 1992, the Roma (Gypsies) formed their first-ever national political organization in response to their dire economic conditions. Prime Minister Berov, whose government was nominally based on the ethnic-Turkish MRF, openly discussed pressure tactics used by both Turks and Bulgarian nationalists to influence ethnic self-identification in ethnically mixed regions. In 1993 those tactics still included campaigns against restoration of Turkish names (following Zhivkov's mass renaming campaign) and campaigns against use of Turkish in schools with Turkish populations, as well as forcible Turkicization of Bulgarian Muslims preferring to live as Bulgarians. Berov pledged to prevent human rights abuses on both sides, but little concrete change occurred in the first half of 1993.

Bulgaria began the fourth year of the post-Zhivkov era with prospects less optimistic than in the previous years. The momentum of economic reform was slowed significantly by continued high unemployment, rising inflation, low productivity, the resistance of Zhivkov-era holdovers in large state industries, and, increasingly, the cynicism of the Bulgarian public toward the usefulness of short-term sacrifice on the road to a market economy. The ominously growing shadow of the former Bulgarian Communist Party hung over the country, whose political system again collapsed into chaos in late 1992. International prospects seemed somewhat better, mainly because Bulgaria's designated role as a Balkan island of stability prompted increased Western support even when internal political and economic conditions failed to match Western expectations. But in 1993, the road from communism was proving much more rocky than most Bulgarians had anticipated; for many Bulgarians, living standards were lower than under the Zhivkov regime, and patience was wearing thin.

May 15, 1993   Glenn E. Curtis

Chapter 1. Historical Setting

Tsarevets Hill in Veliko Tŭrnovo, capital of the Second Bulgarian Empire

THE HISTORY OF THE LAND now known as Bulgaria has been determined by its location between Asia and Europe, by its proximity to powerful states competing for land and influence at the junction of trade routes and strategic military positions, and by the strong national territorial drive of various Bulgarian states. Before the Christian era, Greece and Rome conquered the region and left substantial imprints on the culture of the people they found there. The Bulgar tribes, who arrived in the seventh century from west of the Urals, have occupied the region continuously for thirteen centuries. Over time Bulgarian culture merged with that of the more numerous Slavs, who had preceded the Bulgars by one century. After converting to Christianity and adopting a Slavic language in the ninth century, the Bulgarians consolidated a distinct Slavic culture that subsequently passed through periods of both expansionist independence and subordination to outside political systems.

From the ninth until the fourteenth century, Bulgaria was a dominant force in the Balkans because of its aggressive military tradition and strong sense of national identity. The chief rival and neighbor, the Byzantine Empire, left a lasting political imprint on two Bulgarian empires as it competed with them for regional domination. Marking the deterioration of both the Byzantine and the Bulgarian political structures, the fall of Constantinople to the Ottoman Turks in 1453 began four centuries of Turkish suppression of Bulgarian cultural and political institutions.

By the eighteenth century, however, weakening Ottoman control allowed a Bulgarian cultural revival. In the next century, Western political ideas gradually combined with the reborn Bulgarian national consciousness to form an independence movement. The movement was complicated by internal disagreement on aims and methods, the increasing weakness of the Ottoman foothold in Europe, and the conflicting attitudes of the major European powers toward Bulgaria. Russia gained distinction as Bulgaria's protector by driving out the Turks in 1877, but France and Britain curbed Russian power in the Balkans by forcing establishment of a limited autonomous Bulgarian state under Turkish rule. The instrument of that limitation, the Treaty of Berlin, revived longstanding Bulgarian territorial frustrations by placing the critical regions of Macedonia and Thrace beyond Bulgarian control. Both of those disputed regions had substantial Bulgarian populations. During the next sixty years, Bulgaria would fight unsuccessfully in four wars, in a variety of alliances, to redress the grievance. None of the four wars brought substantial new territory to Bulgaria.

Beginning in 1878, Bulgaria was nominally ruled by members of West European royal houses under a parliamentary form of government. Prime Minister Stefan Stambolov unified the country during its first decade, but extremist political parties exerted substantial influence from the beginning. Between 1878 and the declaration of full independence in 1908, Bulgaria passed through a period of peaceful modernization with expansion in industry, science, education, and the arts. Modernization and industrialization sowed the seeds of class conflict, however, nurturing strong socialist and agrarian opposition parties in the decades that followed independence.

The period between 1912 and 1944 was full of irredentist wars and internal political turmoil. By 1900 Serbia and Greece were the major territorial rivals, but a World War I alliance with Germany gained Bulgaria little advantage over them. After the war, the agrarian reform government of Aleksandŭr Stamboliĭski had failed to unite the country by 1923. The series of unstable factions and forms of government that followed Stamboliĭski was broken only by Bulgaria's participation as an Axis ally in World War II. Again no territory was gained, but World War II brought Soviet occupation, the end of the monarchy, and forty-one years of unbroken communist rule beginning in 1948. During that entire period, Bulgaria was the closest East European imitator of Soviet internal and foreign policy. The years 1948 through 1989 were a time of collectivization, heavy industrialization, drastic restriction of human rights, and close adherence to Soviet Cold-War policy.

Early Settlement and Empire

The land now known as Bulgaria attracted human settlement as early as the Bronze Age. Almost from the first, however, existing civilizations were challenged by powerful neighbors.

Pre-Bulgarian Civilizations

The first known civilization to dominate the territory of present-day Bulgaria was that of the Thracians, an Indo-European group. Although politically fragmented, Thracian society is considered to have been comparable to that of Greece in the arts and economics; these achievements reached a peak in the sixth century B.C. Because of political disunity, however, Thrace then was successively occupied and divided by the Greeks, the Persians, the Macedonians, and the Romans. After the decline of the Macedonian Empire of Alexander the Great, a new Thracian kingdom

4

Thracian burial mound near Shipka Pass, central Bulgaria
Courtesy Sam and Sarah Stulberg

emerged in the third century B.C. Occupied by the Romans, it remained a kingdom within the Roman Empire until the emperor Vespasian incorporated it as a district in the first century A.D. Roman domination brought orderly administration and the establishment of Serditsa (on the site of modern Sofia) as a major trading center in the Balkans. In the fourth century A.D., when the Roman Empire split between Rome and Constantinople, Thrace became part of the Eastern, or Byzantine, Empire. Christianity was introduced to the region at this time. Both the Latin culture of Rome and the Greek culture of Constantinople remained strong influences on ensuing civilizations.

The Slavs and the Bulgars

Waves of Huns, Goths, Visigoths, and Ostrogoths invaded and plundered the Balkans beginning in the third century A.D. None of these invaders permanently occupied territory. Small Slavic groups began settling outlying regions in the fifth century, and by the seventh century the Slavs had overcome Byzantine resistance and settled most of the Balkans. The Slavs brought a more stable culture, retained their own language, and substantially slavicized the existing Roman and Byzantine social system.

The immigration of the first Bulgars overlapped that of the Slavs

5

in the seventh century. Of mixed Turkic stock (the word *Bulgar* derives from an Old Turkic word meaning "one of mixed nationality"), the Bulgars were warriors who had migrated from a region between the Urals and the Volga to the steppes north of the Caspian Sea, then across the Danube into the Balkans. Besides a formidable reputation as military horsemen, the Bulgars had a strong political organization based on their khan (prince). In A.D. 630 a federation of Bulgar tribes already existed; in the next years the Bulgars united with the Slavs to oppose Byzantine control. By 681 the khan Asparukh had forced Emperor Constantine V to recognize the first Bulgarian state. The state, whose capital was at Pliska, near modern Shumen, combined a Bulgarian political structure with Slavic linguistic and cultural institutions.

The First Golden Age

The First Bulgarian Empire was able to defeat the Byzantine Empire in 811 and expand its territory eastward to the Black Sea, south to include Macedonia, and northwest to present-day Belgrade (see fig. 2). The kingdom reached its greatest size under Tsar Simeon (893–927), who presided over a golden age of artistic and commercial expansion. After moving deep into Byzantine territory, Simeon was defeated in 924.

Meanwhile, Rome and Byzantium competed for political and cultural influence in Bulgaria. The Eastern Empire won in 870, when Bulgaria accepted Eastern Rite (Orthodox) Christianity and an autocephalous Bulgarian Church was established. This decision opened Bulgaria to Byzantine culture (and territorial ambitions) through the literary language devised for the Slavs by the Orthodox monks Cyril and Methodius. Establishment of a common, official religion also permanently joined the Bulgarian and Slavic cultures.

After reaching its peak under Simeon, the First Bulgarian Empire declined in the middle of the tenth century. Byzantine opposition and internal weakness led to a loss of territory to the Magyars and the Russians. Bulgaria remained economically dependent on the Byzantine Empire, and the widespread Bogomil heresy (see Glossary) opposed the secular Bulgarian state and its political ambitions as work of the devil. Seeking to restore a balance of power in the Balkans, the Byzantines allied with the Kievan Russians under Yaroslav and invaded Bulgaria several times in the late tenth century. Although the Bulgarians expanded their territory again briefly under Tsar Samuil at the end of the tenth century, in 1014 the Byzantines under Basil II inflicted a major military loss. By 1018 all of Bulgaria was under Byzantine control. For nearly two centuries, the Byzantines ruled harshly, using taxes and the political power of the church to crush opposition. The first and second Crusades passed through Bulgaria in this period, devastating the land.

The Second Golden Age

By 1185 the power of the Byzantine Empire had again waned because of external conflicts. The noble brothers Asen and Peter led a revolt that forced Byzantine recognition of an autonomous Bulgarian state. Centered at Tŭrnovo (present-day Veliko Tŭrnovo), this state became the Second Bulgarian Empire. Like the First Bulgarian Empire, the second expanded at the expense of a preoccupied Byzantine Empire. In 1202 Tsar Kaloian (1197–1207) concluded a final peace with Byzantium that gave Bulgaria full independence. Kaloian also drove the Magyars from Bulgarian territory and in 1204 concluded a treaty with Rome that consolidated Bulgaria's western border by recognizing the authority of the pope. By the middle of the thirteenth century, Bulgaria again ruled from the Black Sea to the Adriatic. Access to the sea greatly increased commerce, especially with the Italian Peninsula. Tŭrnovo became the center of Bulgarian culture, which enjoyed a second golden age.

The final phase of Bulgaria's second Balkan dominance was the reign of Kaloian's successor, Ivan Asen II (1218–41; see fig. 3). In this period, culture continued to flourish, but political instability again threatened. After the death of Ivan Asen II, internal and external political strife intensified. Sensing weakness, the Tatars began sixty years of raids in 1241, the Byzantines retook parts of the Second Bulgarian Empire, and the Magyars again advanced. From 1257 until 1277, aristocratic factions fought for control of the Bulgarian throne. Heavy taxation by feudal landlords caused their peasants to revolt in 1277 and enthrone the "swineherd tsar" Ivailo. After 1300 Tatar control ended, and a new period of expansion followed under Mikhail Shishman (1323–1330) and Ivan Aleksandŭr (1331–1370). As before, however, military and commercial success paralleled internal disorder; the social chaos of the previous century continued to erode the power of Bulgarian leaders. Meanwhile, Serbia had risen as a formidable rival in the Balkans, and the Ottoman Turks had advanced to the Aegean coast. In the late fourteenth century, Bulgaria was weakened by the division of its military defenses between the two perceived threats.

Ottoman Rule

The Ottoman Empire was founded in the early fourteenth century by Osman I, a prince of Asia Minor (see Glossary) who began

Source: Based on information from Christ Atanasoff, *The Bulgarians,* Hicksville, New York,
1977, 36; and Hermann Kinder and Werner Hilgemann, *The Anchor Atlas of World
History,* 1, Garden City, New York, 1974, 130.

Figure 2. The First Bulgarian Empire under Simeon, A.D. 893–927

pushing the eastern border of the Byzantine Empire westward toward
Constantinople. Present-day European Turkey and the Balkans,
among the first territories conquered, were used as bases for expansion far to the West during the fifteenth and sixteenth centuries. The capture of Constantinople in 1453 completed Ottoman
subjugation of major Bulgarian political and cultural institutions.
Nevertheless, certain Bulgarian groups prospered in the highly ordered Ottoman system, and Bulgarian national traditions continued
in rural areas. When the decline of the Ottoman Empire began about
1600, the order of local institutions gave way to arbitrary repression, which eventually generated armed opposition. Western ideas
that penetrated Bulgaria during the 1700s stimulated a renewed concept of Bulgarian nationalism that eventually combined with decay
in the empire to loosen Ottoman control in the nineteenth century.

Introduction of the Ottoman System

Ottoman forces captured the commercial center of Sofia in 1385. Serbia, then the strongest Christian power in the Balkans, was decisively defeated by the Ottomans at the Battle of Kosovo Polje in 1389, leaving Bulgaria divided and exposed. Within ten years, the last independent Bulgarian outpost was captured. Bulgarian resistance continued until 1453, when the capture of Constantinople gave the Ottomans a base from which to crush local uprisings. In consolidating its Balkan territories, the new Ottoman political order eliminated the entire Bulgarian state apparatus. The Ottomans also crushed the nobility as a landholding class and potential center of resistance. The new rulers reorganized the Bulgarian church, which had existed as a separate patriarchate since 1235, making it a diocese under complete control of the Byzantine Patriarchate at Constantinople. The sultan, in turn, totally controlled the patriarchate.

The Ottomans ruled with a centralized system much different from the scattered local power centers of the Second Bulgarian Empire. The single goal of Ottoman policy in Bulgarian territory was to make all local resources available to extend the empire westward toward Vienna and across northern Africa. Landed estates were given in fiefdom to knights bound to serve the sultan. Peasants paid multiple taxes to both their masters and the government. Territorial control also meant cultural and religious assimilation of the populace into the empire. Ottoman authorities forcibly converted the most promising Christian youths to Islam and trained them for government service. Called *pomaks,* such converts often received special privileges and rose to high administrative and military positions. The Ottoman system also recognized the value of Bulgarian artisans, who were organized and given limited autonomy as a separate class. Some prosperous Bulgarian peasants and merchants became intermediaries between local Turkish authorities and the peasants. In this capacity, these *chorbadzhi* (squires) were able to moderate Ottoman policy. On the negative side, the Ottoman assimilation policy also included resettlement of Balkan Slavs in Asia Minor and immigration of Turkish peasants to farm Bulgarian land. Slavs also were the victims of mass enslavement and forcible mass conversion to Islam in certain areas.

Bulgarian Society under the Turks

Traditional Bulgarian culture survived only in the smaller villages during the centuries of Ottoman rule. Because the administrative apparatus of the Ottoman Empire included officials of many nationalities, commerce in the polyglot empire introduced Jews,

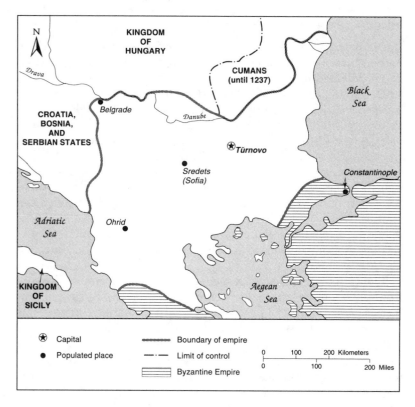

Source: Based on information from Christ Atanasoff, *The Bulgarians,* Hicksville, New York,
1977, 37; and Hermann Kinder and Werner Hilgemann, *The Anchor Atlas of World
History,* 1, Garden City, New York, 1974, 204.

Figure 3. The Second Bulgarian Empire under Ivan Asen, 1218–41

Armenians, Dalmatians, and Greeks into the chief population
centers. Bulgarians in such centers were forcibly resettled as part
of a policy to scatter the potentially troublesome educated classes.
The villages, however, were often ignored by the centralized Ottoman authorities, whose control over the Turkish landholders often
exerted a modifying influence that worked to the advantage of the
indigenous population. Village church life also felt relatively little
impact from the centralized authority of the Greek Orthodox Church.
Therefore, between the fourteenth and seventeenth centuries, the
villages became isolated repositories of Bulgarian folk culture,
religion, social institutions, and language.

Early Decay and Upheaval in the Empire

Notable Bulgarian uprisings against the Ottomans occurred in the 1590s, the 1680s and the 1730s; all sought to take advantage of external crises of the empire, and all were harshly suppressed. Beginning in the 1600s, local bandits, called *hajduti* (sing., *hajdutin*), led small uprisings (see fig. 4). Some writers now describe these uprisings as precursors of a Bulgarian nationalist movement. Most scholars agree, however, that *hajdutin* activities responded only to local misrule and their raids victimized both Christians and Muslims. Whatever their motivation, *hajdutin* exploits became a central theme of national folk culture.

By 1600 the Ottoman Empire had reached the peak of its power and territorial control. In the seventeenth century, the empire began to collapse; the wealth of conquest had spread corruption through the political system, vitiating the ability of the central government to impose order throughout the farflung empire. For the majority of people in agricultural Bulgaria, centralized Ottoman control had been far from intolerable while the empire was orderly and strong. But the growing despotism of local authorities as the central government declined created a new class of victims. Increasingly, Bulgarians welcomed the progressive Western political ideas that reached them through the Danube trade and travel routes. Already in the 1600s, Catholic missionaries in western Bulgaria had stimulated creation of literature about Bulgaria's national past. Although the Turks suppressed this Western influence after the Chiprovets uprising of 1688, the next century brought an outpouring of historical writings reminding Bulgarian readers of a glorious national heritage.

National Revival, Early Stages

For Bulgaria the eighteenth century brought transition from static subservience within a great Asian empire toward intellectual and political modernization and reestablishment of cultural ties with Western Europe. The monasteries of an increasingly independent Bulgarian church fostered national thought and writing; Western influences altered the nature of commerce and landholding in the Balkans; and the forcible assimilation of Bulgarian culture into a cosmopolitan Asian society ended, allowing Bulgarian national consciousness to reawaken. At the same time, social anarchy inhibited the liberation process. These developments set the stage for a full national revival.

The Written Word

In the eighteenth century, all Slavic cultures moved away from the formal Old Church Slavonic language that had dominated their literatures for centuries. The literary language that emerged was

11

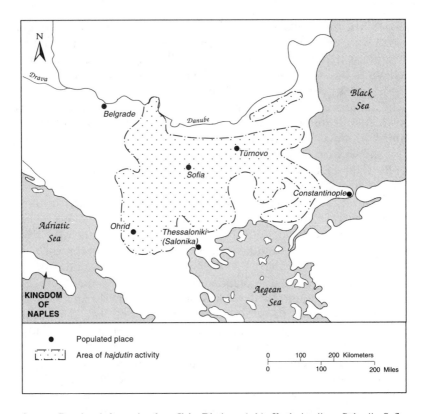

Source: Based on information from Ilcho Dimitrov (ed.), *Kratka istoriia na Bŭlgariia*, Sofia, 1981, 153; and Hermann Kinder and Werner Hilgemann, *The Anchor Atlas of World History*, 1, Garden City, New York, 1974, 208.

Figure 4. Hajdutin Activity in the Ottoman Empire, 1600-1800

much closer to the common vernacular, eventually making books accessible to a much wider readership. In 1741 Hristofor Zhefarovich published his *Stematografia*, a discussion of the cultural history of the Serbs and the Bulgarians. The book displayed the Bulgarian coat of arms and praised the glorious past of the Bulgarian people. In 1762 Father Paisi of Hilendar wrote a history of the Bulgarian peoples in a mixture of Old Church Slavonic and vernacular language. Circulated in manuscript form for nearly one hundred years, the book was a lively, readable celebration of the Bulgarian past and a call for all Bulgarians to remember their heritage and cultivate their native language. Paisi's history inspired generations of writings on Bulgarian patriotic themes. In part, its influence was strong because Paisi wrote at a monastery on Mt. Athos, the largest spiritual center in the Balkans and an early receptacle of ideas of the European Enlightenment (see Glossary). Paisi's follower Sofroniĭ Vrachanski further developed the literature by using a much more vernacular language to advance secular ideas of the Enlightenment in translations of Greek myths and his original *Life and Tribulations of the Sinner Sofroniĭ.* Sofroniĭ also published the first printed book in Bulgaria in 1806.

Commerce and Western Influences

Under the Ottoman Empire, the Mediterranean and Asian trade routes met in Bulgaria. Fairs and regional markets eventually brought tradesmen into contact with their foreign counterparts. After centuries of exclusion from population centers by Turkish policy, Bulgarians began migrating back to the towns, establishing an urban ethnic presence. By the eighteenth century, trade guilds included many workers in cloth, metal, wood, and decorative braid. The estate holders of Macedonia also profited from growing European cotton markets. Some Bulgarian merchants assumed positions as intermediaries between Turkish and European markets, grew rich from such connections, and established offices in the major European capitals. As the Bulgarian cultural revival spread from the monasteries into secular society, these newly wealthy groups promoted secular art, architecture, literature, and Western ideals of individual freedom and national consciousness. Of particular impact were the ideals of the French Revolution, introduced through commercial connections at the start of the nineteenth century.

The end of centralized Ottoman power over Bulgarian territory brought several decades of anarchy, called the *kŭrdzhaliĭstvo,* at the end of the eighteenth century. As at the end of the Second Bulgarian Empire four hundred years before, local freebooters controlled small areas, tyrannized the population, and fought among themselves. Political order was not reestablished in Bulgaria until 1820. Meanwhile, large population shifts occurred as Bulgarians fled the taxation and violence inflicted by this anarchic condition; the new communities they founded in Romania and southern Russia were important sources of cultural and political ideas in the nineteenth century.

The Bulgarian national revival took place in the larger context of Christian resistance to Turkish occupation of Eastern and Central Europe—a cause whose momentum increased as the Ottoman Empire crumbled from within. Russia fought a series of wars with the Turks between 1676 and 1878, and was given the right to protect Christians living under Ottoman rule in treaties signed in 1774 and 1791. Those treaties granted semiautonomy to the Romanian regions of Wallachia and Moldavia, which gave hope that Russia might provide similar help to Bulgaria during the *kŭrdzhaliĭstvo*. Intellectual ties between Bulgaria and Russia promoted the adoption of Russian revolutionary thought along with Western influences. In 1804 Sofroniĭ offered the help of the entire Bulgarian people to Russian armies fighting the Turks and moving toward Bulgarian territory. By 1811 a special volunteer army of several thousand Bulgarians had been formed, in the hope that Russian success against the Turks would liberate Bulgaria. Although the Russians did not aid the Bulgarians directly at that time, Russia remained crucial to Bulgarian foreign relations from that time to the late twentieth century.

European and Russian Policies, 1800

By 1800 the Ottoman Empire was universally labeled "The Sick Man of Europe." The empire was precariously near total collapse and ready to be dismantled by a powerful neighbor, just as the Byzantine Empire had been dismantled by the Ottomans. In this case the logical successor was Russia, an expanding empire with strong religious and cultural ties to the captive Slavic groups. Russia also had a continuing desire to achieve access to the Mediterranean Sea. Russian military power reached its peak with the defeat of Napoleon's invading army in 1812, but throughout the nineteenth century France and Britain used diplomatic and military means to counterbalance Russian influence in the Balkans and the Bosporus. This implicit defense of the Ottoman Empire delayed Bulgarian independence, but the intellectual basis of revolution grew rapidly in the nineteenth century.

The Bulgarian Independence Movement

Revolution in the Balkans

In 1804 Serbia began a series of uprisings that won it autonomy within the Ottoman Empire by 1830. Especially in the campaigns of 1804 and 1815, many Bulgarians in areas adjacent to Serbia fought beside the Serbs. When the Greeks revolted against Turkish rule in 1821, Bulgarian towns provided money and soldiers. Several hundred Bulgarians fought in the six-year Greek uprising, some of them as commanders, and some became part of the government of independent Greece. Bulgarians also fought the Turks in Crete; in addition, they fought with the Italian revolutionary Giuseppe Garibaldi and with other nationalist uprisings against the Habsburgs in 1848–49. In spite of Bulgarian sympathy for national liberation movements nearby, and although the ideals of those

Turkish mosque, Kyustendil
Courtesy Sam and Sarah Stulberg

movements permeated the Balkans from 1804 on, the anarchy of the early 1800s confined expression of Bulgarian national feeling primarily to the cultural realm until the 1860s.

Cultural Expressions of Nationalism

In 1824 Dr. Petŭr Beron, a member of the Bulgarian emigrant community in Romania, published the first primer in colloquial Bulgarian. His book also explained a new system of secular education to replace the outdated precepts of monastery pedagogy, and Beron's suggestions strongly influenced the development of Bulgarian education in the nineteenth century. In 1835 a school was opened in Gabrovo according to Beron's design. Under direction of the monk Neofit Rilski, it was the first school to teach in Bulgarian. Similar schools opened in the ensuing years, and in 1840 the first school for girls opened in Pleven. Education grew especially fast in trading towns such as Koprivshtitsa and Kalofer in the foothills of the Balkans, where textiles and other trades created a wealthy merchant class. In the 1840s, the first generation of Western-educated Bulgarians returned home. Forming a cosmopolitan intelligentsia, they diversified and expanded Bulgarian schools in the following decades.

In the first half of the 1800s, special educational and cultural ties developed with Russia and France. In 1840 the Russian government began awarding grants for Bulgarian students to study in Russia. The total number of students in the Russian program was never high, but several graduates were leaders in the independence drive of the 1870s. Several notable Bulgarians of that generation also were educated in France and at Robert College, founded as a missionary institution in Constantinople.

Parallel with educational advancement, Bulgarian book printing advanced substantially after 1830. Before that date only seventeen original Bulgarian titles had been printed; but by mid-century, printing had replaced manuscript copying as the predominant means of distributing the written word. The first periodical was printed in Bulgarian in 1844, beginning an outpouring of mostly ephemeral journals through the nineteenth century. Censorship before 1878 meant that the majority of such journals were printed in the Romanian emigrant centers, outside the Ottoman Empire. Most Bulgarian-language periodicals printed within the empire came from Constantinople, showing the cultural importance of that city to the Bulgarian National Revival. After 1850 Bulgarian émigré periodicals, supporting a wide variety of political views toward the national independence movement, played a vital role in stimulating Bulgarian political consciousness.

In the mid-1800s, a number of cultural and charitable organizations founded in Constantinople supported and directed Bulgarian national institutions that resisted Ottoman and Greek influence. The social institution of the *chitalishte* (literally "reading room") played an important cultural role beginning in 1856. Established in population centers by adult education societies, the *chitalishte* was a center for social gatherings, lectures, performances, and debates. Because it was available to the entire public, this institution spread national cultural and political ideals beyond the intelligentsia to the larger society. By 1878 there were 131 such centers.

The Bulgarian National Revival also stimulated the arts in the nineteenth century. Dobri Chintulov wrote the first poetry in modern Bulgarian in the 1840s, pioneering a national literary revival that peaked in the 1870s. Translation of Western European and Russian literature accelerated, providing new influences that broke centuries of rigid formalism. Painting and architecture now also broke from the prescribed forms of Byzantine church art to express secular and folk themes. Bulgarian wood-carving and church singing assumed the forms that survive today.

Religious Independence

The Bulgarian church achieved new independence in the nineteenth century. The Ottoman Empire had left the Bulgarian church hierarchy under the Greek Patriarchate of Constantinople for four centuries, disregarding the differences between the two Orthodox churches. (The last separate Bulgarian church jurisdiction, the archbishopric of Ohrid, was absorbed in 1767.) Early in the 1800s, few of the Bulgarian church leaders most closely connected with Enlightenment ideas sought separation from the Greek Orthodox Church. But in 1839, a movement began against the Greek Metropolitan of Tŭrnovo, head of the largest Bulgarian diocese, in favor of local control. In 1849 the active Bulgarian community of Constantinople began pressing Turkish officials for church sovereignty. Other large Bulgarian dioceses both inside and outside Bulgaria sought a return to liturgy in the vernacular and appointment of Bulgarian bishops. The first concession came in 1848, when the Greek patriarch of Constantinople allowed one Bulgarian church in that city.

Because a decade of petitions, demonstrations, and Ottoman reform suggestions had brought no major change, in 1860 Bishop Ilarion Makariopolski of Constantinople declared his diocese independent of the Greek patriarchate. This action began a movement for ecclesiastical independence that united rural and urban Bulgarians and began a bitter Greek-Bulgarian dispute. The Turks and the Russians began to mediate in 1866, seeking a compromise that would ensure the security of each in the face of increasing regional unrest. In 1870 the Ottoman sultan officially declared the Bulgarian church a separate exarchate. The Greek patriarchate, which never recognized the separation, excommunicated the entire Bulgarian church; but the symbolism of the Ottoman decree had powerful political effect. The new exarchate became the leading force in Bulgarian cultural life; it officially represented the Bulgarians in dealing with the Turks, and it sponsored Bulgarian schools. The novel administrative system of the exarchate called for lay representation in governing bodies, thus introducing a note of self-government into this most visible institution.

Early Insurrections

The social and cultural events of the National Revival moved parallel to important political changes. Bulgarian aid to the Russians in the Russo-Turkish wars of 1806–12 and 1828–29 did nothing to loosen Ottoman control. Then the Ottoman Empire ruthlessly quelled major Bulgarian uprisings in 1835 (in Tŭrnovo), 1841 (in Niš), and in 1850–51 (in Vidin). Those uprisings still bore the disorganized qualities of the *hajduti*, but, together with smaller movements in intervening years, they established a tradition of insurrection for the next generation. Meanwhile, beset by European

17

enemies and internal revolutions, the Turks entered a reform period in 1826. They replaced the elite but increasingly untrustworthy Janissary forces with a regular army and officially abolished the feudal land system. These changes reduced oppression by the local Turkish rulers in Bulgaria. In the 1830s, Sultan Mahmud II recentralized and reorganized his government to gain control over his corrupt officials and follow European administrative models. Although these changes had little direct effect on Bulgaria, they clearly signaled to the Slavic subjects of the empire that reform was now possible.

Balkan Politics of the Mid-Nineteenth Century

By 1850 the emerging Bulgarian nationalist movement had split into two distinct branches. The moderates, concentrated in Constantinople, favored gradual improvement of conditions in Bulgaria through negotiations with the Turkish government. This was the approach that created a separate Bulgarian exarchate in 1870. The moderates believed that the protection of the Ottoman Empire was necessary because a free Bulgaria would be subject to Balkan politics and great-power manipulation. The radical faction, however, saw no hope of gradual reform. Following their understanding of European liberal tradition and Russian revolutionary thought, the leaders of this faction aimed first for liberation from all outside controls. Liberation, they believed, would automatically lead to complete modernization of Bulgarian society.

The crushing of the large-scale Vidin peasant revolt in 1851 brought intervention by Britain and France, who bolstered and protected the Ottoman Empire throughout the nineteenth century as a counterweight to Russian expansion. To prevent destabilizing unrest, Britain and France forced the Turks to introduce land reform in western Bulgaria in the early 1850s and a series of major social reforms in 1856 and 1876. Nominally, those measures included equal treatment for non-Muslims in the empire and parliamentary representation for Bulgarians and Serbs. These changes, however, were the cosmetic product of Turkey's need for Western support in major wars with Russia. They did nothing to blunt the nationalist drive of the Bulgarian radicals.

The First Independence Organizations

In 1862 Georgi Rakovski assembled the first armed group of Bulgarians having the avowed goal of achieving independence from the Ottoman Empire. Rakovski, well-educated and experienced in the 1841 uprising and the drive for ecclesiastical independence, envisioned a federal republic including all Balkan nations except

Greece. His fighters were to stir a full-scale national uprising after crossing into Bulgaria from assembly points in Romania and Serbia. But the Serbs, who had supported the Bulgarians while they were useful in opposing the Turks, disbanded the Bulgarian legions in Serbia when they no longer served that purpose. Although Rakovski died in 1867 without achieving Bulgarian independence, he united the émigré intelligentsia, and the presence of his army influenced Turkish recognition of the Bulgarian church in 1870.

The Bulgarian Secret Central Committee, founded by émigré Bulgarians in Bucharest in 1866, continued Rakovski's mission under the leadership of Vasil Levski and Liuben Karavelov. These ideologues refined Rakovski's idea of armed revolutionary groups, creating a cadre of intellectuals who would prepare the people to rise for independence. Beginning in 1868, Levski founded the first revolutionary committees in Bulgaria. Captured by the Turks, he became a national hero when he was hanged in 1873. In 1870 Karavelov founded the Bulgarian Revolutionary Central Committee (BRCC) in Bucharest. The death of Levski temporarily shattered the group, but the committee resumed its activities when Georgi Benkovski joined its leadership in 1875. By this time, the political atmosphere of the Balkans was charged with revolution, and the Ottoman Empire looked increasingly vulnerable. Britain, Russia, and Austria-Hungary were growing concerned about the implications of those trends for the European balance of power. In 1875 Bosnia and Hercegovina revolted successfully against the Turks, and the next year Serbia and Montenegro attacked the Ottoman Empire.

The Final Move to Independence

In the early 1870s, the BRCC had built an intricate revolutionary organization, recruiting thousands of ardent patriots for the liberation struggle. Finally, in 1875 the committee believed that external distractions had weakened the Ottoman Empire enough to activate that struggle. Local revolutionary committees in Bulgaria attempted to coordinate the timing and strategy of a general revolt. Armed groups were to enter Bulgaria from abroad to support local uprisings, and diversionary attacks on Ottoman military installations were planned. Despite these efforts at coordination, the BRCC strategy failed. Although planned as a general revolt, the September Uprising of 1875 occurred piecemeal in isolated locations, and several local revolutionary leaders failed to mobilize any forces. The Turks easily suppressed the uprising, but the harshness of their response attracted the attention of Western Europe; from that time, the fate of Bulgaria became an international issue.

Following the failure of the September Uprising, Benkovski reorganized the BRCC and made plans for a new revolt. The April Uprising of 1876 was more widespread, but it also suffered from poor coordination. Poor security allowed the Turks to locate and destroy many local groups before unified action was possible. Massacres at Batak and other towns further outraged international opinion by showing the insincerity of recent Turkish reform proposals. The deaths of an estimated 30,000 Bulgarians in these massacres spurred the Bulgarian national movement. An international conference in Constantinople produced proposals to curb the Muslim fanaticism responsible for the Bulgarian massacres and give local self-government to the Christians on European territory in the empire. Two autonomous Bulgarian regions were proposed, one centered at Sofia and the other at Tŭrnovo. When the sultan rejected the reforms, Russia declared war unilaterally in early 1877. This was Russia's golden opportunity to gain control of Western trade routes to its southwest and finally destroy the empire that had blocked this ambition for centuries. Shocked by the Turkish massacres, Britain did not oppose Russian advances.

San Stefano, Berlin, and Independence

In eight months, Russian troops occupied all of Bulgaria and reached Constantinople. At this high point of its influence on Balkan affairs, Russia dictated the Treaty of San Stefano in March 1878. This treaty provided for an autonomous Bulgarian state (under Russian protection) almost as extensive as the First Bulgarian Empire, bordering the Black and Aegean seas. But Britain and Austria-Hungary, believing that the new state would extend Russian influence too far into the Balkans, exerted strong diplomatic pressure that reshaped the Treaty of San Stefano four months later into the Treaty of Berlin. The new Bulgaria would be about one-third the size of that prescribed by the Treaty of San Stefano; Macedonia and Thrace, south of the Balkans, would revert to complete Ottoman control. The province of Eastern Rumelia would remain under Turkish rule, but with a Christian governor (see fig. 5).

Whereas the Treaty of San Stefano called for two years of Russian occupation of Bulgaria, the Treaty of Berlin reduced the time to nine months. Both treaties provided for an assembly of Bulgarian notables to write a constitution for their new country. The assembly would also elect a prince who was not a member of a major European ruling house and who would recognize the authority of the Ottoman sultan. In cases of civil disruption, the sultan retained the right to intervene with armed force.

The final provisions for Bulgarian liberation fell far short of the

Statue of Iane Sandanski, nineteenth-century revolutionary, Melnik
Courtesy Sam and Sarah Stulberg

21

goals of the national liberation movement. Large populations of
Bulgarians remained outside the new nation in Macedonia, Eastern
Rumelia, and Thrace, causing resentment that endured well into
the next century. (Bulgarians still celebrate the signing of the Treaty
of San Stefano rather than the Treaty of Berlin as their national
independence day.) In late 1878, a provisional Bulgarian government and armed uprisings had already surfaced in the Kresna and
Razlog regions of Macedonia. These uprisings were quelled swiftly
by the Turks with British support. During the next twenty-five
years, large numbers of Bulgarians fled Macedonia into the new
Bulgaria, and secret liberation societies appeared in Macedonia
and Thrace. One such group, the Internal Macedonian Revolutionary Organization (IMRO), continued terrorist activities in the
Balkans into the 1930s.

The Decades of National Consolidation

Despite strong dissatisfaction with the frontiers imposed by the
European powers, a new Bulgarian state was born in 1878. And
despite early political uncertainty, the first thirty-four years of
modern Bulgaria were in many ways its most prosperous and
productive.

Forming the New State

In 1879 a constituent assembly was duly convened in Tŭrnovo.
Partly elected and partly appointed, the assembly of 230 split into
conservative and liberal factions similar to those that had existed
before independence. The liberals advocated continuing the alliance of peasants and intelligentsia that had formed the independence movement, to be symbolized in a single parliamentary
chamber; the conservatives argued that the Bulgarian peasant class
was not ready for political responsibility, and therefore it should
be represented in a second chamber with limited powers. The framework for the Tŭrnovo constitution was a draft submitted by the
Russian occupation authorities, based on the constitutions of Serbia and Romania. As the assembly revised that document, the liberal view prevailed; a one-chamber parliament or *sŭbranie* would
be elected by universal male suffrage. Between the annual fall sessions of the *sŭbranie,* the country would be run jointly by the
monarch and a council of ministers responsible to parliament. The
liberals who dominated the assembly incorporated many of their
revolutionary ideals into what became one of the most liberal constitutions of its time. The final act of the Tŭrnovo assembly was
the election of Alexander of Battenburg, a young German nobleman

who had joined the Russians in the war of 1877, to be the first prince of modern Bulgaria.

From the beginning of his reign, Alexander opposed the liberal wing in Bulgaria and the Tŭrnovo constitution. After two years of conflict with the liberal council of ministers headed by Dragan Tsankov, Alexander received Russian backing to replace Tsankov. When the Russian Tsar Alexander II was assassinated, Russian policy changed to allow a grand national assembly to consider the constitutional changes desired by Prince Alexander. The assassination had spurred conservatism in Russia, and the Bulgarian liberals had alarmed the Russians by refusing foreign economic aid in the early 1880s. To the dismay of the liberals, Russia intervened in the election of the constitutional *sŭbranie,* frightening voters into electing a group that passed the entire package of amendments. Liberal influence was sharply reduced by amendments limiting the power of the *sŭbranie.* But, because the conservative approach to governing Bulgaria had little popular support, Alexander made a series of compromises with liberal positions between 1881 and 1885. The Tŭrnovo constitution was essentially restored by agreement between Tsankov and the conservatives in 1883, and the constitutional issue was resolved. In only the first two years of Bulgaria's existence, two parliaments and seven cabinets had been dissolved, but more stable times lay ahead.

By 1884 the conservative faction had left the government, but the liberals split over the high price of purchasing the Ruse-Varna Railway from the British, as required by the Treaty of Berlin. As on earlier issues, the more radical faction sought to reduce the influence of the European powers who had imposed the Treaty of Berlin. This group was led by Petko Karavelov, brother of revolutionary leader Liuben Karavelov and prime minister in the mid-1880s.

The most important issue of that period was Bulgaria's changing relationship with Russia. Bulgarian hostility towards the Russian army, refusal to build a strategic railway for the Russians through Bulgaria, and poor relations between Prince Alexander and Tsar Alexander III of Russia all contributed to increasing alienation. Because conservative Russia now feared unrest in the Balkans, Karavelov tried to appease the tsar by quelling the uprisings that continued in Macedonia. Radical factions in Bulgaria were persuaded to lower their goals from annexation of Macedonia and Thrace to a union between Bulgaria and Eastern Rumelia. When a bloodless coup achieved this union in 1885, however, Russia demanded the ouster of Prince Alexander and withdrew all Russian

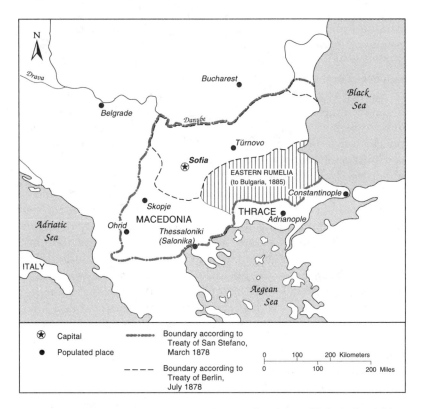

Source: Based on information from R.J. Crampton, *A Short History of Bulgaria*, Cambridge, 1987, frontispiece.

Figure 5. Territorial Changes in Bulgaria, 1878–85

officers from the Bulgarian army. Greece and Serbia saw their interests threatened, and the latter declared war on Bulgaria.

The Bulgarian army won a brilliant victory over Serbia, with no Russian aid, at the Battle of Slivnitsa. Although the victory was a source of great national pride for Bulgaria, Russia continued to withhold recognition of the union with Eastern Rumelia until Prince Alexander abdicated. Finally, Russian-trained Bulgarian army officers deposed the prince in August 1886.

The Stambolov Years

When Alexander left behind a three-man regency headed by Stefan Stambolov, the Bulgarian government was as unstable as it had been in its first year. A Russian-educated liberal, Stambolov became prime minister in 1887 and ceased tailoring Bulgarian policy to Russian requirements. The tsar's special representative in

Bulgaria returned to Russia after failing to block a *sŭbranie* called to nominate a new prince. Russo-Bulgarian relations remained chilly for the next ten years, and this break further destabilized Bulgarian politics and society. Stambolov brutally suppressed an army uprising in 1887 and began seven years of iron control that often bypassed the country's democratic institutions but brought unprecedented stability to Bulgaria. Meanwhile, Ferdinand of Saxe-Coburg-Gotha, a Catholic German prince, accepted the Bulgarian throne in August 1887.

Independence from the Ottoman Empire brought drastic economic and social changes to Bulgaria at the end of the nineteenth century. Industrialization proceeded rapidly (thirty-six major factories opened between 1878 and 1887), and a new class of industrial labor formed from displaced artisans and agricultural workers. Harsh working conditions led the urban poor to the cause of socialism, and in 1891 the Social Democratic Party was formed. (Later transformation of one of its factions into the Bulgarian Communist Party made that organization the oldest communist party in the world.) Town-centered trade and the guild structure were swept away by an influx of West European commerce to which Bulgaria had been opened by the terms of the Treaty of Berlin.

Despite industrialization, Bulgaria remained primarily an agricultural country. Liberation eliminated the Ottoman feudal landholding system. Bulgarian peasants were able to buy land cheaply or simply occupy it after Turkish landlords left, and a system of village-based small landholding began. Agricultural production rose in spite of heavy government land taxes. Many peasants were forced into the urban work force by taxes or high interest on borrowings for land purchase. Until the end of the nineteenth century, the vast majority of the Bulgarian population were small landholders or independent small tradesmen.

Russia and the other great powers did not recognize Ferdinand as rightful prince of Bulgaria until 1896. Supporters of Prince Alexander who remained in power used this failure as a weapon against the policies of Ferdinand and Stambolov. In 1890 a widespread plot against the government was discovered. As before, the basis of the plot was dissatisfaction with Stambolov's refusal to intercede with the Turks on behalf of Macedonian independence. In a masterful diplomatic stroke, Stambolov represented the insurrection to the Turks as an example of potential chaos that could be avoided by minor concessions. Fearing the Balkan instability that would follow an overthrow of Ferdinand, the Turks then ceded three major Macedonian dioceses to the Bulgarian exarchate. Stambolov thus gained solid church support and an overwhelming victory in the 1890 election, which legitimized his government among all Bulgarian factions and reduced the threat of radical plots.

In the next years, Stambolov and the People's Liberal Party he had founded in 1886 exerted virtually dictatorial power to suppress extreme nationalism and opposing parties and create conditions for economic growth. After the 1886 coup, the army was strictly controlled. Voters were intimidated to ensure the reelection of incumbent officials, and political patronage grew rampant. Using his own and Ferdinand's ties with Germany and Austria-Hungary, Stambolov built a capitalist Bulgarian economic system on foreign loans, protectionism, an expanded industrial and transport infrastructure, and a strict tax system for capital accumulation. Especially important to the Bulgarian economy was completion of the Vienna-to-Constantinople Railway through Bulgaria in 1888 and the Burgas-Yambol Railway in the early 1890s. Stambolov derived strong political support from the entrepreneurs who benefited from his industrial policy. The Stambolov era marked the victory of executive over legislative power in the Bulgarian political system.

Legitimacy of the Bulgarian throne remained an important symbolic issue in the early 1890s, and the threat of assassination or overthrow of the prince remained after Stambolov consolidated his power. Therefore, Stambolov found a Catholic wife for Ferdinand and maneuvered past Orthodox Church objections in 1893 to ensure Ferdinand an heir that would stabilize the throne. That heir, Boris, was born the next year. Meanwhile, Stambolov's autocratic maneuvering and tough policies won him many enemies, especially after the stabilization of the early 1890s appeared to make such tactics unnecessary. In 1894 Ferdinand dismissed his prime minister because the prince sought more power for himself and believed that Stambolov had become a political liability. The next year, Macedonian radicals assassinated Stambolov.

The Rule of Ferdinand

The new administration was mainly conservative, and Ferdinand became the dominant force in Bulgarian policy making. His position grew stronger when Russia finally recognized him in 1896. The price for recognition was the conversion of Prince Boris to Orthodoxy from Catholicism. The Russian attitude had changed for two reasons: Alexander III had died in 1894, and new Turkish massacres had signaled a collapse of the Ottoman Empire that would threaten Russian and Bulgarian interests alike. In the next twenty years, no strong politician like Stambolov emerged, and Ferdinand was able to accumulate power by manipulating factions. Several liberal and conservative parties, the descendants of the two preliberation groups, held power through 1912 in a parliamentary system that seldom functioned according to the constitution. The Bulgarian Social Democratic Party took its place in the new political order, advocating class struggle, recruiting members from the working class, and organizing strikes.

After relations with Russia had been repaired, Bulgaria's international position stabilized, allowing the economy to continue growing undisturbed until 1912. In this period, the government continued active intervention in agriculture and industry; it promoted new agricultural methods that improved the yield from fertile lands still being reclaimed from the Turks in 1900. Bulgarian economic growth continued because of a combination of factors: borrowing from West European industrial countries, a strong banking system, and a generally sound investment policy. Between 1887 and 1911, the number of industrial plants grew from 36 to 345. But the government's financial policy greatly increased the national debt, which by 1911 was three times the national budget and required 20 percent of the budget for interest payment. New land taxes and grain tithes were levied in the 1890s, leading to peasant revolts. In 1899 the Bulgarian Agrarian Union was founded, the result of a decade of growing rural discontent and resentment against the intellectual and governing class. Within two years, the union had evolved into an official party, the Bulgarian Agrarian National Union (BANU), which was accepted by most Bulgarian peasants as truly representing their interests. Soon, Bulgarian politicians viewed BANU as the most potent political group in the country.

The Macedonian Issue

Macedonian unrest continued into the twentieth century. Between 1894 and 1896, the government of Konstantin Stoilov reversed Stambolov's policy of controlling Macedonian extremists. When he sought to negotiate with the Turks for territorial concessions in Macedonia at the end of the century, Stoilov found that he could not control IMRO. By 1900 that group, which advocated Macedonian autonomy over the standard Bulgarian policy goal of annexation, had gained control of the Macedonian liberation movement inside Bulgaria. Russia and the Western powers now held Ferdinand responsible for all disruptions in Macedonia, causing suspicion of all Bulgarian activity in the Balkans. Greece and Serbia also laid claim to parts of Macedonia, giving them vital interests in the activities of IMRO as well. In 1902 Russia and Austria-Hungary forced Serbia and Bulgaria to cut all ties with IMRO.

In 1903 Macedonian liberation forces staged a widespread revolt, the Ilinden-Preobrazhensko Uprising. Despite strong public support for the Macedonian cause, Bulgaria sent no help, and the Turks again suppressed opposition with great violence. Large numbers of refugees now entered Bulgaria from Macedonia.

In the next four years, Austria-Hungary and Russia sought a formula by which to administer Macedonia in a way satisfactory to Bulgarian, Serbian, and Greek interests and approved by Constantinople. Although nominal agreement was reached in 1905, Serbian, Greek, and Bulgarian sympathizers clashed in Macedonia in 1906 and 1907. After the death of its leader Gotse Delchev in the 1903 uprising, IMRO's influence decreased. Bulgarian public sympathy for the Macedonian cause also diminished, and by 1905 the government's attention turned to internal matters.

Inspired by the 1905 uprisings in Russia, a series of riots and demonstrations between 1905 and 1908 were a reaction by workers, the poor, and some of the intelligentsia to several issues: domestic repression, government corruption, and the handling of the Macedonian issue. In 1906 anti-Greek riots and destruction of Greek property were ignited in some parts of Bulgaria by Greek claims to Macedonia. In spite of heavy fines and prohibitions against striking, a rail strike occurred in 1906, and in 1907 Prime Minister Nikola Petkov was assassinated.

Full Independence

The strikes and demonstrations remained isolated and had little practical effect, so Ferdinand remained in firm control. In 1908 the Young Turks, an energetic new generation of reformers, gained power in the Ottoman Empire. Their ascendancy temporarily restored the international self-confidence of the empire and threatened a renewed Turkish influence in the Balkans. To protect the territory it occupied in Bosnia and Hercegovina, Austria-Hungary annexed those regions. While the Turks were preoccupied with that situation, Ferdinand nationalized the Bulgarian section of his main international rail line and declared himself tsar of a fully independent Bulgaria. The Western powers, again seeing the threat of Ottoman collapse, were appeased by Russian-arranged financial compromises that saved face for the Turks. But tension between Bulgaria and Turkey increased dramatically after Ferdinand's declaration.

The arbitrary nature of Ferdinand's declaration also brought loud criticism from democratic-minded Bulgarian factions. Nonetheless, the grand national assembly held at Tŭrnovo in 1911 to incorporate the terms of independence into the constitution, ratified Ferdinand's title and expanded his power in conducting foreign affairs.

By 1911 the BANU, led by Aleksandŭr Stamboliĭski, had become the largest and most vocal opposition faction. Although the BANU never gained more than 15 percent of a national vote before World War I, the party had a large, unified following in the peasant class victimized by poor harvests, usurious interest rates, and high taxes. Stamboliĭski's political philosophy put the peasant and rural life ahead of all other classes and lifestyles. Hating bureaucrats and urban institutions, he proposed a government that would provide representation by profession rather than party, to ensure a permanent peasant majority. His goal was to establish a peasant republic that would replace the conventional parliamentary apparatus established at Tŭrnovo. The BANU was a controversial and powerful force in Bulgarian politics for the next two decades.

The Balkan Wars and World War I

Full independence made Bulgaria a more aggressive party in the complex of Balkan politics. The end of Ottoman occupation heightened territorial ambitions that involved Bulgaria and its neighbors in three wars within four years.

The First Balkan War

The period from 1908 to 1912 was one of colliding interests in the Balkans and collapse of the system created by the Treaty of Berlin. Beginning in 1908, the Young Turks attempted to consolidate Turkish influence in the Balkans while ensuring equality for all nationalities in their empire. Rivals Italy and Austria threatened to intervene on behalf of an Albanian revolt against the Turks in 1909. Russia then urged a Bulgarian-Serbian alliance to keep such foreign powers at bay and ensure continued Slavic control in the region. In 1912, after long negotiations, Serbia and Bulgaria reached temporary agreement on the disposition of Macedonia, the chief issue dividing them. Subsequent agreements by Greece with Serbia, Bulgaria, and Montenegro completed the Balkan League—an uneasy alliance designed by Russia to finally push the Turks out of Europe and curtail great-power meddling in the Balkans. The First Balkan War, which began in October 1912, coincided with Italy's campaign to liberate Tripoli from the Turks. Bulgarian forces moved quickly across Ottoman Europe, driving the Turks out of Thrace. However, the Bulgarians then overextended their position by a fruitless attack toward Constantinople. In the peace negotiations that followed, Bulgaria regained Thrace, but the fragile alliance against the Turks collapsed over the unresolved issue of Macedonia.

The Second Balkan War

The final removal of the Turks from Europe posed the problem of dividing Ottoman territory and heightened the worries of the European great powers about balancing influence in that strategic region. Disagreement about the disposition of Macedonia quickly rearranged the alliances of the First Balkan War and ignited a Second Balkan War in 1913. The Treaty of London that had ended the first war stipulated only that the Balkan powers resolve existing claims among themselves. The Bulgarians, having had the greatest military success, demanded compensation on that basis; the Serbs and Greeks demanded adjustment of the 1912 treaty of alliance to ensure a balance of Balkan powers; and the Romanians demanded territorial reward for their neutral position in the first war. Even before the First Balkan War ended, a strong faction in Bulgaria had demanded war against Serbia to preserve Bulgaria's claim to Macedonia. Ferdinand sided with that faction in 1913, and Bulgaria attacked Serbia. Turkey, Greece, and Romania then declared war on Bulgaria because they all feared Bulgarian domination of the Balkans if Macedonia were not partitioned. Because most Bulgarian forces were on the Serbian frontier, Turkish and Romanian troops easily occupied Bulgarian territory by mid-1913, and Bulgaria was defeated. The Treaty of Bucharest (1913) allowed Bulgaria to retain only very small parts of Macedonia and Thrace; Greece and Serbia divided the rest, humiliating Bulgarian territorial claims and canceling the gains of the First Balkan War (see fig. 6). This loss further inflamed Bulgarian nationalism, especially when Bulgarians in Serbian and Greek Macedonia were subjected to extreme hardship after the new partition. At this point, Russia, whose warnings Bulgaria had defied by attacking Serbia, shifted its support to the Serbs as its Balkan counterbalance against Austro-Hungarian claims.

World War I

The settlement of the Second Balkan War had also inflamed Bosnian nationalism. In 1914 that movement ignited an Austrian-Serbian conflict that escalated into world war when the European alliances of those countries went into effect.

Prewar Bulgarian Politics

Supported by Ferdinand, the government of Prime Minister Vasil Radoslavov declared neutrality to assess the possible outcome of the alliances and Bulgaria's position relative to the Entente (Russia, France, and Britain) and the Central Powers (Austria-Hungary and Germany). From the beginning, both sides exerted strong pressure and made territorial offers to lure Bulgaria into an alliance. Ferdinand and his diplomats hedged, waiting for a decisive military shift in one direction or the other. The Radoslavov government favored the German side, the major opposition parties favored the Entente, and the agrarians and socialists opposed all involvement. By mid-1915 the Central Powers gained control on the Russian and Turkish fronts and were thus able to improve their territorial offer to Bulgaria. Now victory would yield part of Turkish Thrace, substantial territory in Macedonia, and monetary compensation for war expenses. In October 1915, Bulgaria made a secret treaty with the Central Powers and invaded Serbia and Macedonia.

Early Successes

Catching the Entente by surprise, Bulgarian forces pushed the Serbs out of Macedonia and into Albania and occupied part of Greek Macedonia by mid-1916. British, French, and Serbian troops landed at Salonika and stopped the Bulgarian advance, but the Entente's holding operation in Greece turned into a war of attrition lasting from late 1916 well into 1917. This stalemate diverted 500,000 Entente troops from other fronts. Meanwhile, Romania had entered the war on the Entente side in 1916. Bulgarian and German forces pushed the poorly prepared Romanians northward and took Bucharest in December 1916. The Bulgarians then faced Russia on a new front in Moldavia (the part of Romania bordering Russia), but little action took place there.

Stalemate and Demoralization

Once the Bulgarian advance into Romania and Greece halted, conditions at the front deteriorated rapidly and political support for the war eroded. By 1916 poor allocation of supplies created shortages for both civilians and soldiers, and a series of government reorganizations provided no relief. By 1917 the military stalemate and poor living conditions combined with news of revolution in Russia to stir large-scale unrest in Bulgarian society. The agrarians and socialist workers intensified their antiwar campaigns, and soldiers' committees formed in army units. Bolshevik antiwar propaganda was widely distributed in Bulgaria, and Russian and Bulgarian soldiers began fraternizing along the Moldavian front. In December 1917, Dimitŭr Blagoev, founder and head of the Social Democratic Party, led a meeting of 10,000 in Sofia, demanding

31

Source: Based on information from Christ Atanasoff, *The Bulgarians,* Hicksville, New York, 1977, 214.

Figure 6. Division of Macedonia at the Treaty of Bucharest, 1913

an end to the war and overthrow of the Bulgarian government. A wave of unrest and riots, including a "women's revolt" against food and clothing shortages, swept through the country in 1918.

The government position weakened further when the Treaty of Bucharest, which divided the territory of defeated Romania among the central powers, left part of the disputed Romanian territory of Dobruja outside Bulgarian control. Having failed to secure even the least important territory promised by its war policy, the Radoslavov government resigned in June 1918. The new prime minister, Aleksandŭr Malinov, tried to unite the country by appointing the agrarian Aleksandŭr Stamboliĭski to his cabinet. But Malinov had vowed to fight, and the BANU leader refused the post as long as Bulgaria remained in the war. By September the Bulgarian army was thoroughly demoralized by antiwar propaganda and harsh conditions. A battle with the British and French at Dobro Pole brought total retreat, and in ten days Entente forces entered Bulgaria. On September 29, the Bulgarians signed an armistice and left the war.

Capitulation and Settlement

The retreat from Dobro Pole brought a soldier revolt that was crushed by German troops near Sofia. But the parties in power forced Ferdinand to abdicate at the end of September because they feared full-scale revolution and blamed the tsar for the country's chaotic state. Ferdinand's son Boris was named tsar, becoming Boris III. The immediate cause of social upheaval ended with the armistice, but shortages and discontent with the Bulgarian government continued. An ineffective coalition government ruled for the next year, then a general election was called. Meanwhile, Bulgaria was again left far short of the territorial goals for which it had declared war. In the Treaty of Neuilly-sur-Seine (November 1919), Thrace was awarded to Greece, depriving Bulgaria of access to the Aegean Sea. The newly formed Kingdom of the Serbs, Croats, and Slovenes took Macedonian territory adjoining its eastern border, and Southern Dobruja went to Romania (see fig. 7).

The treaty limited the postwar Bulgarian Army to a small volunteer force; Yugoslavia, Romania, and Greece were to receive reparations in industrial and agricultural goods; and the victorious Allies were to receive monetary reparations for the next thirty-seven years. On the other hand, the payment schedule was significantly improved in 1923, and Bulgaria's loss of 14,100 square kilometers was much less than the territorial losses of its wartime allies. Nationalist resentment and frustration grew even stronger because of this outcome, however, and Bulgaria remained close to Germany throughout the interwar period.

The Interwar Period

The period after World War I was one of uneasy political coalitions, slow economic growth, and continued appearance of the Macedonia problem. Although social unrest remained at a high level, Boris kept firm control of his government as World War II approached.

Stamboliĭski and Agrarian Reform

The 1919 election reflected massive public dissatisfaction with the war reparations, inflation, and rising taxes that prolonged the chaotic living conditions of the war. The socialist and agrarian parties tightened their organizations and increased membership. The left wing of the Bulgarian Workers' Socialist-Democratic Party (BWSDP) numbered only 25,000 in 1919, and the BANU emerged

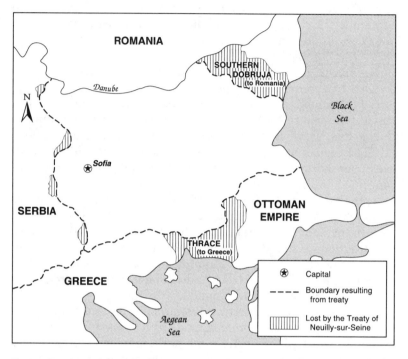

Source: Based on information from R.J. Crampton, *A Short History of Bulgaria,* Cambridge,
1987, frontispiece.

*Figure 7. Territorial Changes According to the Treaty of Neuilly-sur-Seine,
1919*

as the largest party in the country. The BANU received 28 percent
of the 1919 vote, giving it a plurality but not a majority in the new
sŭbranie. Stamboliĭski sought to include the Bulgarian Communist
Party (BCP)—which had finished second in the election—and the
BWSDP in a coalition government. (The BCP and the BWSDP
were the two factions of the Bulgarian communist movement that
had sprung from the Social Democratic Party founded in 1891; they
would remain separate until the former was disbanded after World
War II.) Stamboliĭski could not permit the two factions the control
they desired, however, so they refused participation.

The postwar governing coalition thus included only factions to
Stamboliĭski's right. The first major test for the Stamboliĭski government was a transport strike that lasted from December 1919 until
February 1920. Fomented by the communists and the social
democrats and joined by urban workers and middle-class Bulgarians, the striker protests were quelled harshly by the army and the

Orange Guard, a quasi-military force that Stamboliĭski formed to counter mass demonstrations by the parties of the left. Suppression of the strike, mobilization of the peasant vote, and intimidation at the polls gave the BANU enough support to win the parliamentary election of 1920 over the communists and form a non-coalition government. Tsar Boris and much of the Bulgarian middle class preferred the agrarians to the communists and social democrats, whom they feared much more. Stamboliĭski immediately began drastic economic reforms. He abolished the merchants' trade monopoly on grain, replacing it with a government consortium; broke up large urban and rural landholdings and sold the surplus to the poor; enacted an obligatory labor law to ease the postwar labor shortage; introduced a progressive income tax; and made secondary schooling compulsory. All aspects of the radical reform policy aimed at ridding society of "harmful" classes of society such as lawyers, usurers, and merchants, distributing capital and obligations more evenly through society, and raising the living standards of the landless and poor peasants.

In foreign policy, Stamboliĭski officially abandoned Bulgaria's territorial claims, which he associated with a standing army, monarchy, large government expenditures, and other prewar phenomena that the agrarians deemed anachronistic. After the war, no major power was available to protect Bulgarian interests in the Balkans. For this reason, the traditional approach to foreign policy was discarded in favor of rapprochement with all European powers and the new government of Kemal Atatürk in Turkey, membership in the League of Nations (see Glossary), and friendship with the new Kingdom of the Serbs, Croats, and Slovenes (later the Kingdom of Yugoslavia). Relations with Turkey were greatly improved by Bulgarian support of Atatürk's revolutionary Turkish Republic in 1920.

Reconciliation with Yugoslavia was a necessary step toward Stamboliĭski's ultimate goal of a multiethnic Balkan peasant federation. Improved Yugoslav relations required a crackdown on the powerful Macedonian extremist movement. Accordingly, Stamboliĭski began a two-year program of harsh suppression of IMRO in 1921; in 1923 Yugoslavia and Bulgaria agreed at the Niš Convention to cooperate in controlling extremists.

The Fall of Stamboliĭski

Led by a large Macedonian group in Sofia, the strong nationalist elements remaining in Bulgaria found the new pacifist policy alarming. The urban working class, unaided by agrarian reforms, gravitated to the communists or the socialist workers. Inflation and industrial exploitation continued. Many of Stamboliĭski's subordinates inflamed social tensions by taking very dogmatic positions in favor of peasant rights. The Bulgarian right, silent since the war, reorganized into a confederation called the National Alliance. Stamboliĭski's Orange Guard jailed the leaders of that group in 1922, temporarily stopping its momentum. Meanwhile, in late 1922 and early 1923, Macedonian nationalists occupied Kiustendil along the Yugoslav border and attacked government figures to protest rapprochement with Yugoslavia and Greece. Stamboliĭski responded with mass arrests, an accelerated campaign against IMRO terrorism, a purge of his own fragmented and notoriously corrupt party, and a new parliamentary election. These dictatorial measures united the agrarians' various opponents (IMRO, the National Alliance, army factions, and the social democrats) into a coalition led by Aleksandŭr Tsankov. The communists remained outside the group. Bulgaria's Western creditors would not protect a government that had rejected their reparations policy. In June 1923, Stamboliĭski was brutally assassinated by IMRO agents, and the conspirators shortly took control of the entire country with only scattered and ineffectual agrarian resistance.

The Tsankov and Liapchev Governments

Tsankov formed a new government, which Boris III quickly approved. An uprising by the communists, who had hoped the two major coalition factions would destroy each other, was easily suppressed in September 1923. Nonetheless, dominated by the Macedonian freedom factions and the National Alliance, Tsankov's government failed to restore order. When Tsankov outlawed the Bulgarian Communist Party in 1924, the militant communists led by exiles Georgi Dimitrov and Vasil Kolarov became dominant in that organization. The first response to this change was the bombing of Sveta Nedelia Cathedral in Sofia while the tsar was present in 1925, killing over 100. This attack brought a new government reign of terror against the communists and the agrarians. Disunited Macedonian factions also continued terrorist attacks from their virtually separate state at Petrich, causing alarm in Western Europe. In 1926 Tsankov was replaced by Andrei Liapchev, a Macedonian who remained prime minister for five years.

Liapchev generally was more lenient toward political opposition than Tsankov; the communists resurfaced in 1927 under cover of the labor-based Bulgarian Workers' Party, and an Independent Workers' Trade Union became the center of political activity by labor. IMRO also had much more latitude under the Macedonian prime minister; this meant that political assassinations and terrorism continued unabated. IMRO raids into Yugoslavia ended Bulgarian rapprochement with that country, and the Macedonians demanded preferential economic treatment under Liapchev. But compared with the years preceding, the late 1920s brought relative political stability to Bulgaria. Liapchev led a conservative majority in the *sŭbranie* and had the confidence of Boris. The press was relatively free, and educational and judicial institutions functioned independently. Industrial and agricultural output finally exceeded prewar levels, and foreign investment increased. But even after substantial reduction, Bulgaria's reparations payments were 20 percent of her budget in 1928, and the return to the gold standard that year weakened the economy one year before the onset of world depression.

In foreign policy, Liapchev tried unsuccessfully to improve British and French World War I reparation terms and bring Bulgaria out of its postwar diplomatic isolation. The country had already improved its international image by participating enthusiastically in the League of Nations, which reciprocated by forcing Greek invasion troops to leave southern Bulgaria in 1926. Boris made two European tours in the late 1920s to strengthen diplomatic ties.

In the late 1920s, the Macedonian independence movement split over the ultimate goal of its activity. The supremacist faction sought incorporation of all Macedonian territory into Bulgaria, while the federalist faction (including the IMRO terrorists) sought an autonomous Macedonia that could join Bulgaria or Yugoslavia in a protective alliance if necessary. Violence between the two groups reinforced a growing public impression that the Liapchev government was unstable.

The Crises of the 1930s

Political Disorder and Diplomatic Isolation

The world economic crisis that began in 1929 devastated the Bulgarian economy. The social tensions of the 1920s were exacerbated when 200,000 workers lost their jobs, prices fell by 50 percent, dozens of companies went bankrupt, and per capita income among peasants was halved between 1929 and 1933. A wave of strikes hit Bulgaria in 1930–31, and in 1931 the Liapchev government was defeated in what would be the last open election with proportional representation of parliamentary seats.

Liapchev's coalition fell apart, his defeat hastened by the rise of a supra-party organization, Zveno—a small coalition with connections to most of the major Bulgarian parties and to fascist Italy. The main goal of Zveno was to consolidate and reform existing political institutions so that state power could be exerted directly to promote economic growth. After 1931 Zveno used the economic crisis to instill this idea in the Bulgarian political system. In 1931 the new government coalition, the People's Bloc, readmitted the BANU in an attempt to reunite Bulgarian factions. But the BANU had become factionalized and isolated; its representatives in the coalition largely pursued political spoils rather than the interests of their peasant constituency.

Meanwhile, the Macedonian situation in the early 1930s blocked further attempts to heal Balkan disputes. Four Balkan conferences were held to address the Macedonian problem; but Bulgaria, fearing IMRO reprisals, steadfastly refused to drop territorial demands in Macedonia or quell Macedonian terrorist activities in the region. Such activities had continued under all Bulgaria's postwar governments, but the People's Bloc was especially inept in controlling them. The situation eventually led to the Balkan Entente of 1934, by which Yugoslavia, Greece, Turkey, and Romania pledged to honor existing borders in the Balkans. For Bulgaria the isolation inflicted by this pact was a serious diplomatic setback in southeastern Europe.

In 1932 Aleksandŭr Tsankov founded Bulgaria's first serious fascist party, the National Socialist Movement, which imitated the methods of Hitler's Nazi party. Although Tsankov's party never attracted a large following, its activities added to the chaotic fragmentation that forced the People's Bloc from power in May 1934.

Fragmentation of the People's Bloc coalition and the threat posed by the Balkan Entente led Zveno and various military factions to stage a right-wing coup. Under the leadership of Colonel Damian Velchev and Kimon Georgiev, the new prime minister, the new government began taking dictatorial measures. The government also took immediate steps to improve relations with Yugoslavia and made overtures to Britain and France. Diplomatic relations resumed with the Soviet Union in 1934, despite a marked increase in internal repression of communists and suspected communists. A concerted drive by the Bulgarian military against IMRO permanently reduced the power of that organization, which by 1934 had exhausted most of its support in Bulgarian society. The fact that sponsorship of Balkan terrorism finally ceased to hinder Bulgarian foreign policy was the single lasting contribution of the Velchev-Georgiev government.

The Zveno group abolished all political parties, citing the failure of such institutions to provide national leadership. The press was muzzled. Henceforward the state would be authoritarian and centralized; the *sŭbranie* would represent not political parties but the classes of society: peasants, workers, artisans, merchants, the intelligentsia, bureaucrats, and professionals. Velchev also proposed a wide-ranging program of social and technical modernization. In 1935, however, Tsar Boris III became an active political force in Bulgaria for the first time. Disillusioned by the results of the 1934 coup, Boris took action to regain his power, which the new regime had also curtailed. Boris used military and civilian factions alarmed by the new authoritarianism to maneuver the Zveno group out of power and declare a royal dictatorship.

The Royal Dictatorship

In the years following 1935, Boris relied on a series of uncharismatic politicians to run Bulgaria, weaken the political power of Zveno and the military, and keep other factions such as the BANU, the communists, and the national socialists from forming alliances against him. Boris chose not to restore the traditional political supremacy of the *sŭbranie* and ignored demands by many public figures to write a new Bulgarian constitution. In 1936 a broad coalition, the People's Constitutional Bloc, brought together nearly all leftist and centrist factions in a nominal opposition that had the blessing of the tsar. Boris delayed holding a national election until 1938. At that time, only individual candidates were allowed in a carefully controlled election procedure that excluded party candidate lists. Boris claimed that domination of the new *sŭbranie* by progovernment representatives justified his nonparty system, although the People's Constitutional Bloc seated over sixty delegates. Elections in the next two years were strictly limited in order to maintain Boris's control over his parliament.

The Interwar Economy

In the years between the world wars, Bulgarian efforts to raise agricultural and industrial standards closer to those of Western Europe yielded uneven results. Until the mid-1930s, political unrest, steep reparations payments, and the world financial crisis stymied growth. Reparations payments were finally canceled in 1932, however, and the stability of the royal dictatorship brought economic improvement in the late 1930s. Half the European average in 1930, per-capita agricultural production improved markedly when government control forced diversification, new methods, and new markets into the system. In the 1930s, a 75 percent increase in membership of agricultural cooperatives bolstered the financial stability of the agricultural sector, particularly benefiting small landholders. The most notable agricultural trend between the wars was the switch to industrial crops, especially tobacco, which replaced wheat as Bulgaria's top agricultural export. The predominance of small agricultural plots increased, however; in 1944 only 1 percent of holdings were over twenty hectares and the number of landless families had decreased (see Agriculture, ch. 3).

In the 1930s, Germany bought a huge percentage of Bulgaria's agricultural exports (67.8 percent in 1939), reinforcing economic dependency by selling finished industrial products for nonconvertible currency—a distinct advantage for the Bulgarian economy and a boon to the Bulgarian standard of living. Boris tried to balance German trade by expanding British and French markets, but he found little interest in either country. Although industry remained distinctly secondary to agriculture, contributing only 5.6 percent of the Bulgarian gross national product (GNP—see Glossary) in 1938, between 1929 and 1939 Bulgarian industry grew at an average rate of 4.8 percent, well ahead of the European average for the period. The role of state-owned enterprises dwindled steadily in the 1930s; by 1944, only coal mines, electrical power, railroads, and banks remained predominantly in that category. While large state-sponsored enterprise diminished, small private industries flourished in the 1930s. At the same time, Bulgarian commerce became largely state-controlled and centralized in Sofia, and the social and political dichotomy between rural and urban Bulgaria was even sharper as World War II began.

Foreign Policy in the Late 1930s

By 1939 Bulgaria had moved inexorably into the fascist sphere of Germany and Italy. The country was tied to the former for economic reasons and because Germany promised territorial revision for Bulgaria, and to the latter because Boris was married to the daughter of King Victor Emmanuel III of Italy. In the late 1930s, Bulgaria continued to seek rapprochement with Yugoslavia; a friendship treaty was signed in 1937 and a renunciation of armed intervention in 1938. Germany's takeover of the Sudetenland from Czechoslovakia in 1938 ended the anti-German Little Entente alliance of Yugoslavia, Czechoslovakia, and Romania and pushed Yugoslavia closer to Bulgaria. When World War II began in September 1939 with the German invasion of Poland, Bulgaria declared neutrality, but this position was inevitably altered by big-power relationships.

The Nazi-Soviet alliance of 1939 improved Bulgaria's relations with the Soviet Union, which had remained cool, and yielded a Bulgarian-Soviet commercial treaty in 1940. The pro-Western

Bulgarian Prime Minister Georgi Kioseivanov was deposed that year in favor of pro-German Bogdan Filov, who reduced cultural ties with the West and instituted a Nazi-type youth league. Meanwhile, Boris strove to maintain neutrality, rejecting Soviet treaty offers in 1939 and 1940. Boris also rejected membership in the Balkan Entente and in a proposed Turkish-Yugoslav-Bulgarian defense pact because such moves would anger Italy, Germany, the Soviet Union, or all three. Under pressure from Hitler, Romania ceded southern Dobruja to Bulgaria by the Treaty of Craiova in 1940. Needing Bulgaria to anchor its Balkan flank, Germany increased diplomatic and military pressure that year. The massing of German troops in Romania prior to Germany's invading Greece removed all remaining flexibility; aware that German troops would have to pass through Bulgaria to reach Greece, Bulgaria signed the Tripartite Pact with Germany and Italy in March 1941.

World War II

As in the case of World War I, Bulgaria fought on the losing German side of World War II but avoided open conflict with the Russian/Soviet state. Again the strains of war eroded public support and forced the wartime Bulgarian government out of office. But World War II heralded a drastic political change and a long era of totalitarian governance.

The Passive Alliance

Having failed to remain neutral, Boris entered a passive alliance with the Axis powers. The immediate result was Bulgarian occupation (but not accession) of Thrace and Macedonia, which Bulgarian troops took from Greece and Yugoslavia, respectively, in April 1941. Although the territorial gains were initially very popular in Bulgaria, complications soon arose in the occupied territories. Autocratic Bulgarian administration of Thrace and Macedonia was no improvement over the Greeks and the Serbs; expressions of Macedonian national feeling grew, and uprisings occurred in Thrace. Meanwhile, the Germans pressured Bulgaria to support the eastern front they had opened by invading the Soviet Union in June 1941. Boris resisted the pressure because he believed that Bulgarian society was still sufficiently Russophile to overthrow him if he declared war. After the Japanese attack on Pearl Harbor ended United States neutrality, Bulgaria declared war on Britain and the United States, but continued diplomatic relations with the Soviet Union throughout World War II. Acceleration of domestic war protests by the BCP in 1941 led to an internal crackdown on dissident activities of both the right and left. In the next three years, thousands of Bulgarians went to concentration and labor camps. The German eastern front received virtually no aid from Bulgaria, a policy justified by the argument that Bulgarian troops had to remain at home to defend the Balkans against Turkish or Allied attack. Hitler reluctantly accepted this logic. Boris's stubborn resistance to committing troops was very popular at home, where little war enthusiasm developed. Nazi pressure to enforce anti-Jewish policies also had little support in Bulgarian society. Early in the war, laws were passed for restriction and deportation of the 50,000 Bulgarian Jews, but enforcement was postponed using various rationales. No program of mass deportation or extermination was conducted in Bulgaria.

Wartime Crisis

In the summer of 1943, Boris died suddenly at age 49, leaving a three-man regency ruling for his six-year-old son, Simeon. Because two of the three regents were figureheads, Prime Minister Bogdan Filov, the third regent, became de facto head of state in this makeshift structure.

The events of 1943 also reversed the military fortunes of the Axis, causing the Bulgarian government to reassess its international position. Late in 1943, the Allies delivered the first of many disastrous air raids on Sofia. The heavy damage sent a clear message that Germany could not protect Bulgaria from Allied punishment. Once the war had finally intruded into Bulgarian territory, the winter of 1943-44 brought severe social and economic dislocation, hunger, and political instability. The antiwar factions, especially the communists, used urban guerrilla tactics and mass demonstrations to rebuild the organizational support lost during the government crackdown of 1941. Partisan activity, never as widespread as elsewhere in the Balkans during the war, increased in 1944 as the Red Army moved westward against the retreating Germans. To support antigovernment partisan groups, in 1942 the communists had established an umbrella Fatherland Front coalition backing complete neutrality, withdrawal from occupied territory, and full civil liberties.

Early in 1944, Bulgarian officials tried to achieve peace with the Allies and the Greek and Yugoslav governments-in-exile. Fearing the German forces that remained in Bulgaria, Filov could not simply surrender unconditionally; meanwhile, the Soviets threatened war if Bulgaria did not declare itself neutral and remove all German armaments from Bulgaria's Black Sea coast. Unable to gain the protection of the Allies, who had now bypassed Bulgaria in their strategic planning, Bulgaria was caught between onrushing Soviet forces and the last gambits of the retreating Nazis. At this point, the top priority of Bulgarian leaders was clearing the country of German occupiers while arranging a peace with the Allies that would deprive Soviet forces of an excuse to occupy Bulgaria. But in September 1944, the Soviet Union unexpectedly declared war on Bulgaria, just as the latter was about to withdraw from the Axis and declare war on Germany.

The Soviet Occupation

When Soviet troops arrived in Bulgaria, they were welcomed by the populace as liberators from German occupation. On September 9, 1944, five days after the Soviet declaration of war, a Fatherland Front coalition deposed the temporary government in a bloodless coup. Headed by Kimon Georgiev of Zveno, the new administration included four communists, five members of Zveno, two social democrats, and four agrarians. Although in the minority, the communists had been the driving force in forming the coalition as an underground resistance organization in 1942. The presence of the Red Army, which remained in Bulgaria until 1947, strengthened immeasurably the communist position in dealing with the Allies and rival factions in the coalition. At this point, many noncommunist Bulgarians placed their hopes on renewed relations with the Soviet Union; in their view, both Germany and the Allies had been discredited by the events of the previous fifteen years. In 1945 the Allies themselves expected that a benign Soviet Union would continue the wartime alliance through the period of postwar East European realignment.

The armistice signed by Bulgaria with the Soviet Union in October 1944 surrendered all wartime territorial gains except Southern Dobruja; this meant that Macedonia returned to Yugoslavia and Thrace to Greece. The peace agreement also established a Soviet-dominated Allied Control Commission to run Bulgaria until conclusion of a peace treaty. Overall war damage to Bulgaria was moderate compared to that in other European countries, and the Soviet Union demanded no reparations. On the other hand, Bulgaria held the earliest and most widespread war crimes trial in postwar Europe; almost 3,000 were executed as war criminals. Bulgaria emerged from the war with no identifiable political structure; the party system had dissolved in 1934, replaced by the pragmatic balancing of political factions in Boris's royal dictatorship. This condition and the duration of the war in Europe eight months after Bulgaria's surrender gave the communists ample opportunity to exploit their favorable strategic position in Bulgarian politics.

Communist Consolidation

Initial Maneuvering

In the months after the surrender, the communist element of the Fatherland Front gradually purged opposition figures, exiled Tsar Simeon II, and rigged elections to confirm its power. In December 1945, a conference of foreign ministers of the United States, Britain, and the Soviet Union theoretically allocated two seats to the newly consolidated opposition BANU in the Bulgarian Council of Ministers, but BANU leaders demanded an immediate national election and removal of communist ministers. Because the BANU was now a unified party with substantial political backing, these demands created a governmental stalemate with the Fatherland Front for one year. In a national referendum in September 1946, however, an overwhelming majority voted to abolish the monarchy and proclaim Bulgaria a people's republic.

The next month, a national election chose a *sŭbranie* to draft a new constitution. In a widely questioned process, Fatherland Front candidates won 70 percent of the votes. At this point, however, opposition to the front remained strong, as communist power grew steadily. In early 1947, opposition to aggressive communist tactics of confiscation and collectivization generated a loose anticommunist coalition within and outside the Fatherland Front, under BANU leader Nikola Petkov. The power struggle, which centered on the nature of the new constitution, reached its peak when the Paris peace treaty of February 1947 required that Soviet forces and the Allied Control Commission leave Bulgaria immediately. Once the United States ratified its peace treaty with Bulgaria in June 1947, the communist-dominated Fatherland Front arrested and executed Petkov and declared Bulgaria a communist state. Petkov's coalition was the last organized domestic opposition to communist rule in Bulgaria until 1989.

After 1946 Fatherland Front governments maintained nominal representation of noncommunist parties. But those parties increasingly bowed to the leadership of communist Prime Minister Georgi Dimitrov, who had been appointed in 1946. After two years of postwar turmoil, Bulgarian political and economic life settled into the patterns set out by the new communist constitution (referred to as the Dimitrov Constitution) ratified in December 1947. Dimitrov argued that previous Bulgarian attempts at parliamentary democracy were disastrous and that only massive social and economic restructuring could ensure stability. By the end of 1947, Bulgaria had followed the other East European states in refusing reconstruction aid from the Marshall Plan (see Glossary) and joining the

Graffiti-covered tomb of Georgi Dimitrov, first president of communist Bulgaria, Sofia, 1991
Courtesy Sam and Sarah Stulberg

Communist Information Bureau (Cominform—see Glossary). In 1948 the Fatherland Front was reorganized into an official worker-peasant alliance in accordance with Cominform policy. In December 1947, BANU leader Georgi Traikov had repudiated traditional agrarian programs; after a thorough purge that year, his party retained only nominal independence to preserve the illusion of a two-party system. All other opposition parties disbanded.

The Dimitrov Constitution

Dimitrov guided the framing of the 1947 constitution on the model of the 1936 constitution of the Soviet Union. The Bulgarian document guaranteed citizens equality before the law; freedom from discrimination; a universal welfare system; freedom of speech, the press, and assembly; and inviolability of person, domicile, and correspondence. But those rights were qualified by a clause prohibiting activity that would jeopardize the attainments of the national revolution of September 9, 1944. Citizens were guaranteed employment but required to work in a socially useful capacity. The constitution also prescribed a planned national economy. Private property was allowed, if its possession was not "to the detriment of the public good." By the end of 1947, all private industry had been confiscated and financial enterprises nationalized in the culmination of a gradual government takeover that began in 1944. The first two-year plan for economic rehabilitation began in 1947 (see Postwar Economic Policy, ch. 3).

Chervenkov and Stalinism in Bulgaria

In 1948 the newly formed Soviet empire in Eastern Europe was threatened by a split between Yugoslav President Josip Broz Tito and Soviet leader Joseph V. Stalin. After expelling Yugoslavia from the Cominform, Stalin began exerting greater pressure on the other East European states, including Bulgaria, to adhere rigidly to Soviet foreign and domestic policy. He demanded that the communist parties of those countries become virtual extensions of the Communist Party of the Soviet Union (CPSU) by purging all opposition figures. The Bulgarian government curtailed religious freedom by forcing Orthodox clergy into a Union of Bulgarian Priests in 1948, taking control of Muslim religious institutions, and dissolving Bulgarian branches of Roman Catholic and Protestant churches in 1949. The most visible political victim of the new policy was Traicho Kostov, who with Georgi Dimitrov and Vasil Kolarov had led the BCP to power in 1944. Accused by Dimitrov of treason, Kostov was shot in December 1949. Dimitrov died before Kostov's execution, Kolarov soon afterward. To fill the power vacuum left by those events, Stalin chose Vŭlko Chervenkov, a trusted protégé. Chervenkov would complete the conversion of the BCP into the type of one-man dictatorship that Stalin had created in the Soviet Union. Chervenkov assumed all top government and party positions and quickly developed a cult of personality like that of his Soviet mentor. At Stalin's command, Chervenkov continued purging party members from 1950 until 1953, to forestall in Bulgaria the sort of Titoist separatism that Stalin greatly feared. Rigid party hierarchy replaced the traditional informal structures of Bulgarian governance, and the purges eliminated the faction of the BCP that advocated putting Bulgarian national concerns ahead of blind subservience to the CPSU.

The Chervenkov period (1950–56) featured harsh repression of all deviation from the party line, arbitrary suppression of culture and the arts along the lines of Soviet-prescribed socialist realism, and an isolationist foreign policy. By early 1951, Chervenkov had expelled one in five party members, including many high officials, in his campaign for complete party discipline. In 1950 a new agricultural collectivization drive began. In spite of intense peasant resistance, the collectivization drive continued intermittently until the process was virtually complete in 1958.

Foreign and Economic Policies

The independent course taken by Tito's Yugoslavia in 1948 caused Bulgaria to seal the Yugoslav border; a 1953 Balkan Pact among Greece, Yugoslavia, and Turkey further isolated Bulgaria, which by that time had cut all relations with Western countries. The Soviet Union now was Bulgaria's only ally. It supplied military and economic advisers and provided the model for Bulgarian social services, economic planning, and education in the early 1950s. Over 90 percent of Bulgarian exports and imports involved Soviet partnership, although the Soviets often paid less than world prices for Bulgarian goods. Because the primitive, mainly agricultural Bulgarian economy closely resembled that of the Soviet Union, Soviet-style centralized planning in five-year blocks had more immediate benefits there than in the other European states, where it was first applied in the early 1950s.

After Stalin

The death of Joseph Stalin in March 1953 had strong repercussions in Bulgaria. By that time, Chervenkov had already moved slightly away from hard-line Stalinist domestic repression and international isolation, but the lack of clear ideological guidance from post-Stalin Moscow left him in an insecure position. Official approval in 1951 of Dimitŭr Dimov's mildly heretical novel *Tiutiun* (Tobacco) had loosened somewhat the official constraints on literature and other cultural activities. In 1953 Bulgaria resumed relations with Greece and Yugoslavia, some political amnesties were granted, and planners discussed increasing production of consumer goods and reducing the prices of necessities. At the Sixth Party Congress in 1954, Chervenkov gave up his party leadership but retained his position as prime minister. Todor Zhivkov, most prominent in the postwar generation of Bulgarian communist leaders, assumed the newly created position of first secretary of the party Central Committee. Several purged party leaders were released from labor camps, and some resumed visible roles in the party hierarchy.

In spite of the 1954 party shifts, Chervenkov remained the unchallenged leader of Bulgaria for two more years. The economic shift away from heavy industry toward consumer goods continued in the mid-1950s, and direct Soviet intervention in Bulgarian economic and political life diminished. By 1955, some 10,000 political prisoners had been released. In an attempt to win political support from the peasants, Chervenkov eased the pace of collectivization and increased national investment in agriculture. However, events in the Soviet Union ended this brief period of calm.

The Fall of Chervenkov

In 1955 the Belgrade Declaration restored Soviet-Yugoslav friendship and reinstated Tito to the fraternity of world communist leaders. Because Chervenkov had branded Tito and the Yugoslavs as arch-villains during his rise to power, this agreement eroded his position. Then, in February 1956, Nikita S. Khrushchev denounced Chervenkov's patron Stalin and Stalin's cult of personality at the twentieth congress of the CPSU. Unwilling to stray from the Soviet party line, the BCP also condemned the cult of personality (and, implicitly, Chervenkov's authoritarianism), advocating instead collective leadership and inner-party democracy. In his 1956 report to party leaders, Zhivkov expressed this condemnation and promised that the party would make amends for past injustices—a clear reference to the fate of Kostov and Chervenkov's other purge victims in the party. Having had his entire regime repudiated by the party leader, Chervenkov resigned. Zhivkov, who had thus far remained below Chervenkov in actual party power, now assumed the full powers of his party first secretary position. The 1956 April Plenum became the official date of Bulgarian de-Stalinization in party mythology; after that event, the atmosphere of BCP politics changed significantly.

Intellectual Life

The thaw in Bulgarian intellectual life had continued from 1951 until the middle of the decade. Chervenkov's resignation and the literary and cultural flowering in the Soviet Union encouraged the view that the process would continue, but the Hungarian revolution of fall 1956 frightened the Bulgarian leadership away from encouragement of dissident intellectual activity. In response to events in Hungary, Chervenkov was appointed minister of education and culture; in 1957 and 1958, he purged the leadership of the Bulgarian Writers' Union and dismissed liberal journalists and editors from their positions. His crackdowns effectively ended the "Bulgarian thaw" of independent writers and artists inspired by Khrushchev's 1956 speech against Stalinism. Again mimicking the Soviet party, which purged a group of high officials in 1957, the BCP dismissed three party leaders on vague charges the same year. Among those removed was deputy prime minister Georgi Chankov, an important rival of Zhivkov. The main motivation for this purge was to assure the Soviet Union that Bulgarian communists would not fall into the same heretical behavior as had the Hungarian party in 1956. Through the political maneuvers of the mid-1950s, Todor Zhivkov enhanced his position by identifying with the "Bulgarian" rather than "Soviet" branch of the BCP at the same time as he aligned himself with the new anti-Stalinist faction in the Soviet Union. He established especially close ties with Khrushchev at this time.

Domestic Policy and Its Results

Most aspects of life in Bulgaria continued to conform strongly to the Soviet model in the mid-1950s. In 1949 the Bulgarian educational system had begun a restructuring process to resemble the Soviet system, and the social welfare system followed suit. In the mid-1950s, Soviet-style centralized planning produced economic indicators showing that Bulgarians were returning to their prewar lifestyle in some respects: real wages increased 75 percent, consumption of meat, fruit, and vegetables increased markedly, medical facilities and doctors became available to more of the population, and in 1957 collective farm workers benefited from the first agricultural pension and welfare system in Eastern Europe.

In 1959 the BCP borrowed from the Chinese the phrase "Great Leap Forward" to symbolize a sudden burst of economic activity to be injected into the Third Five-Year Plan (1958–1962), whose original scope was quite conservative. According to the revised plan, industrial production would double and agricultural production would triple by 1962; a new agricultural collectivization and consolidation drive would achieve great economies of scale in that branch; investment in light industry would double, and foreign trade would expand (see The First Five-Year Plans, ch. 3). Following the Chinese model, all of Bulgarian society was to be propagandized and mobilized to meet the planning goals. Two purposes of the grandiose revised plan were to keep Bulgaria in step with the Soviet bloc, all of whose members were embarking on plans for accelerated growth, and to quell internal party conflicts. Zhivkov, whose "theses" had defined the goals of the plan, purged Politburo members and party rivals Boris Taskov (in 1959) and Anton Yugov (in 1962), citing their criticism of his policy as economically obstructionist. Already by 1960, however, Zhivkov had been forced to redefine the impossible goals of his theses. Lack of skilled labor and materials made completion of projects at the prescribed pace impossible. Harvests were disastrously poor in the early 1960s; peasant unrest forced the government to raise food prices; and the urban dissatisfaction that resulted from higher prices compounded a crisis that broke in the summer of 1962. Blame fell on Zhivkov's experiments with decentralized planning, which was totally abandoned by 1963.

The Zhivkov Era

Beginning in 1961, Todor Zhivkov skillfully retained control of the Bulgarian government and the BCP. His regime was a period of unprecedented stability, slavish imitation of Soviet policies, and modest economic experimentation.

Zhivkov Takes Control

Zhivkov was able to weather the social unrest of 1962 by finding scapegoats, juggling indicators of economic progress, and receiving help from abroad. In 1961 Khrushchev had once again denounced Stalin, requiring similar action in the loyal Soviet satellites. In October Chervenkov, who had retained considerable party power, was ousted from the Politburo as an unrepentant Stalinist and obstructor of Bulgarian economic progress (see The Chervenkov Era, ch. 4). When Khrushchev visited Bulgaria in 1962, the Soviet leader made clear his preference for Zhivkov over other Bulgarian party leaders. Within months Yugov had lost his party position, and Chervenkov was expelled from the party. Thus, in spite of disastrously unrealistic economic experimentation of the sort that contributed to Khrushchev's ouster in 1964, Zhivkov had greatly strengthened his position as party first secretary by the time his Soviet patron had fallen.

In the early 1960s, Zhivkov improved ties with the Bulgarian intelligentsia by liberalizing censorship and curbing the state security forces (see Zhivkov and the Intelligentsia, ch. 4). He also mended relations with the agrarians by granting amnesties to BANU members and appointing the leader of the party as head of state. These measures gave Zhivkov a political base broad enough to survive the fall of Khrushchev, but they did not prevent an army plot against him in 1965. Zhivkov used the plot as a reason to tighten control over the army and move security functions from the Ministry of the Interior to a new Committee of State Security, under his personal control. Several other plots were reported unofficially in the late 1960s, but after 1962 Zhivkov's position as sole leader of Bulgaria went without serious challenge.

Zhivkov's Political Methodology

In the 1960s, Zhivkov moved slowly and carefully to replace the deeply entrenched Old Guard in party positions. He believed that only an energetic, professional party cadre could lead Bulgaria effectively. Therefore, he gradually moved a younger group, including his daughter Liudmila Zhivkova and future party leader Aleksandŭr Lilov, into positions of power. At the same time, he juggled party positions enough to prevent any individual from becoming a serious rival. Unlike Chervenkov, with his Stalinist personality cult, Zhivkov cultivated an egalitarian persona that kept him in contact with the Bulgarian people. Unlike contemporaneous communist leaders in other countries, Zhivkov displayed a sense of humor even in formal state speeches. Because of the strong tradition of egalitarianism in Bulgarian political culture, the contrast of his approach with that of Chervenkov served Zhivkov very well.

The Constitution of 1971

In 1968 the Prague Spring outbreak of heretical socialism in Czechoslovakia caused the BCP to tighten control over all social organizations, calling for democratic centrism and elimination of unreliable elements from the party. This policy kept the BCP on a unified path in complete support of Soviet interests; it also led to a new Bulgarian constitution and BCP program in 1971. Approved by the Tenth Party Congress and a national referendum, the 1971 constitution detailed for the first time the structure of the BCP (highly centralized, in keeping with policy after 1968) and its role in leading society and the state. BANU was specified as the partner of the BCP in the cooperative governing of the country. A new State Council was created to oversee the Council of Ministers and exercise supreme executive authority (see The Constitution of 1971, ch. 4). In 1971 Zhivkov resigned as prime minister to become chairman of the State Council, a position equivalent to Bulgarian head of state. The new constitution also defined four forms of property: state, cooperative, public organization, and private. Private property was limited to that needed for individual and family upkeep.

Foreign Affairs in the 1960s and 1970s

In the first decade of the Zhivkov regime, Balkan affairs remained central to Bulgarian foreign policy, and relations with the Soviet Union remained without significant conflict. Because the Soviet Union showed relatively little interest in the Balkans in the 1950s and 1960s, Bulgaria was able to improve significantly its relations with its neighbors. In 1964 an agreement with Greece ended the long postwar freeze caused by Greek membership in the North Atlantic Treaty Organization (NATO—see Glossary). Bulgaria paid partial wartime reparations to Greece, and relations were normalized in culture, trade, and communications after the initial agreement. Turkish-Bulgarian relations were hindered by irritation over the Turkish minority issue: throughout the postwar period, wavering Bulgarian policy on internal treatment and emigration of Bulgarian Turks was the chief obstacle to rapprochement, although bilateral agreements on emigration and other issues were reached in the 1960s and 1970s (see The Turkish Problem, ch. 4; Foreign Policy, ch. 4).

Relations with Yugoslavia also were strained in the postwar years. The age-old Macedonian dispute was the principal reason that Yugoslavia remained untouched by Zhivkov's Balkan détente policy. In the mid-1960s, Tito and Zhivkov exchanged visits, but by 1967 official Bulgarian spokesmen were again stressing the Bulgarian majority in Yugoslav-ruled Macedonia, and a new decade of mutually harsh propaganda began. Although the polemic over Macedonia continued through the 1980s, it served both countries mainly as a rallying point for domestic political support, and Bulgaria avoided taking advantage of Yugoslav vulnerabilities such as the unrest in the province of Kosovo. In the early 1980s, much of Bulgaria's anti-Yugoslav propaganda aimed at discrediting heretical economic policy applications (feared by every orthodox communist neighbor of Yugoslavia) in Yugoslav Macedonia. In 1981 Zhivkov called for establishment of a Balkan nuclear-free zone that would include Romania, Greece, Turkey, and Yugoslavia. The concept was notable not because of its practical implications (Bulgaria was generally unsupportive of regional cooperation, and the potential participants had strongly differing international positions), but as a Soviet device to remove NATO nuclear weapons from Greece and Turkey at a time of superpower tension over European weapons installations.

In the 1970s, Zhivkov actively pursued better relations with the West, overcoming conservative opposition and the tentative, tourism-based approach to the West taken in the 1960s. Emulating Soviet détente policy of the 1970s, Bulgaria gained Western technology, expanded cultural contacts, and attracted Western investments with the most liberal foreign investment policy in Eastern Europe. Between 1966 and 1975, Zhivkov visited Charles de Gaulle and the pope and established full diplomatic relations with the Federal Republic of Germany (West Germany). As in 1956 and 1968, however, Soviet actions altered Bulgaria's position. The Soviet invasion of Afghanistan in late 1979, which Bulgaria supported vigorously, renewed tension between Bulgaria and the West. Bulgarian implication in the attempted assassination of Pope John Paul II in 1981 exacerbated the problem and kept relations cool through the early 1980s.

Bulgaria also followed the Soviet example in relations with Third-World countries, maintaining the image of brotherly willingness to aid struggling victims of Western imperialism. Student exchanges

already were common in the 1960s, and many Bulgarian techni-
cians and medical personnel went to African, Asian, and Latin
American countries in the 1970s and 1980s. Cultural exchange programs targeted mainly the young in those countries. Between 1978
and 1983, Zhivkov visited seventeen Third-World countries and
hosted leaders from at least that many.

Throughout the 1960s and 1970s, Bulgaria gave official military support to many national liberation causes, most notably in
the Democratic Republic of Vietnam (North Vietnam), Indone-
sia, Libya, Angola, Afghanistan, the Horn of Africa, and the Middle East. In 1984 the 9,000 Bulgarian advisers stationed in Libya
for military and nonmilitary aid put that country in first place
among Bulgaria's Third-World clients. Through its Kintex arms
export enterprise, Bulgaria also engaged in covert military support activities, many of which were subsequently disclosed (see Arms
Sales, ch. 5). In the 1970s, diplomatic crises with Sudan and Egypt
were triggered by Bulgarian involvement in coup plots. Repeated
discoveries of smuggled arms shipments from Bulgaria to Third-
World countries gave Bulgaria a reputation as a major player in
international arms supply to terrorists and revolutionaries. Arms
smuggling into Turkey periodically caused diplomatic problems
with that country in the 1970s.

Domestic Policy in the 1960s and 1970s

Zhivkov's domestic policy in the late 1960s and 1970s emphasized increased production by Bulgaria's newly completed base of
heavy industry, plus increased consumer production. The industrial base and collectivization of Bulgarian agriculture had been
achieved largely by emulating Khrushchev's approaches in the early
1960s; but after Khrushchev fell, Zhivkov experimented rather
freely in industrial and agricultural policy. A 1965 economic reform decentralized decision making and introduced the profit mo-
tive in some economic areas. The approach, a minor commitment
to "planning from below" in imitation of Yugoslavia's self-
management program, was abandoned in 1969. Taking its place,
a recentralization program gave government ministries full planning responsibility at the expense of individual enterprises (see The
Era of Experimentation and Reform, ch. 3).

Meanwhile, a new program for integration and centralization
of agriculture was born in 1969. The agricultural-industrial complex (agropromishlen kompleks—APK) merged cooperative and
state farms and introduced industrial technology to Bulgarian
agriculture. In the 1970s, the APK became the main supporting
structure of Bulgarian agriculture (see Agriculture, ch. 3). The social

and political goal of this program was to homogenize Bulgarian society, ending the sharp dichotomy that had always existed between rural and town populations and weakening the ideological force of the BANU. If the traditional gulf between Bulgarian agricultural and industrial workers were eliminated, the BCP could represent both groups. Despite this large-scale reorganization effort, the Bulgarian tradition of small peasant farming remained strong into the 1980s.

In keeping with the détente of the 1970s, Bulgaria sought independent trade agreements with the West throughout that decade, to furnish technology and credit not available within the Council for Mutual Economic Assistance (Comecon—see Glossary). Economic cooperation and license agreements were signed with several West European countries, most notably West Germany. Although the Western demand for Bulgarian goods remained generally low and Western commodities proved unexpectedly expensive in the late 1970s, Bulgaria's expansion of Western trade in that decade was unusually high for a Comecon member nation (see Foreign Trade, ch. 3).

The Political Atmosphere in the 1970s

Through the mid-1970s, Zhivkov continued balancing the older and younger generations and the reformist and conservative factions in his party, with only occasional purges of key officials. But in 1977, the purge of liberal Politburo member Boris Velchev introduced a massive reorganization of provincial party organizations that ousted 38,500 party members. This move was designed to limit the atmosphere of liberalization that had followed the 1975 Helsinki Accords (see Glossary). That mood and an economic crisis caused by oil shortages in the 1970s aroused discontent and demonstrations in Bulgaria in the late 1970s.

At the end of the decade, two more crises confronted Zhivkov: in 1978 the murder of exiled writer Georgi Markov was widely attributed to Bulgarian State Security, damaging the country's international image; and in 1980 the Polish Solidarity (see Glossary) movement alarmed the entire Soviet Bloc by attracting an active anticommunist following in a key Warsaw Pact (see Glossary) country. Although the magnitude of Bulgarian social discontent was much less than that in Poland, the BCP ordered production of more consumer goods, a reduction of party privileges, and limited media coverage of Poland in the early 1980s as an antidote to the "Polish infection."

Meanwhile, in 1980 Zhivkov had improved his domestic position by appointing his daughter Liudmila Zhivkova as chair of the commission on science, culture, and art. In this powerful position, Zhivkova became extremely popular by promoting Bulgaria's separate national cultural heritage. She spent large sums of money in a highly visible campaign to support scholars, collect Bulgarian art, and sponsor cultural institutions. Among her policies was closer cultural contact with the West; her most visible project was the spectacular national celebration of Bulgaria's 1,300th anniversary in 1981. When Zhivkova died in 1981, relations with the West had already been chilled by the Afghanistan issue, but her brief administration of Bulgaria's official cultural life was a successful phase of her father's appeal to Bulgarian national tradition to bind the country together.

Bulgaria in the 1980s

Despite the resumption of the Cold War, by 1981 several long-standing problems had eased in Bulgaria. Zhivkova had bolstered national pride and improved Bulgaria's international cultural image; Zhivkov had eased oppression of Roman Catholics and propaganda against the Bulgarian Orthodox Church in the 1970s, and used the 1,300th anniversary of the Bulgarian state for formal reconciliation with Orthodox church officials; the Bulgarian media covered an expanded range of permissible subject matter; Bulgaria contributed equipment to a Soviet space probe launched in 1981, heralding a new era of technological advancement; and the New Economic Model (NEM), instituted in 1981 as the latest economic reform program, seemingly improved the supply of consumer goods and generally upgraded the economy.

However, Zhivkova's death and East-West tensions dealt serious blows to cultural liberalization; by 1984 the Bulgarian Writers' Conference was calling for greater ideological content and optimism in literature. Once fully implemented in 1982, NEM was unable to improve the quality or quantity of Bulgarian goods and produce. In 1983 Zhivkov harshly criticized all of Bulgarian industry and agriculture in a major speech, but the reforms generated by his speech did nothing to improve the situation. A large percentage of high-quality domestic goods were shipped abroad in the early 1980s to shrink Bulgaria's hard-currency debt, and the purchase of Western technology was sacrificed for the same reason, crippling technical advancement and disillusioning consumers. By 1984 Bulgaria was suffering a serious energy shortage because its Soviet-made nuclear power plant was undependable and droughts reduced the productivity of hydroelectric plants (see Energy Generation, ch. 3). Like the cutback in technology imports, this shortage affected all of Bulgarian industry. Finally, Bulgarian implication in the plot to assassinate Pope John Paul II in 1981 and in international drugs and weapons trading impaired the country's international image and complicated economic relations with the West (see Security and Intelligence Services, ch. 5).

The problem of the Turkish minority in Bulgaria continued into the 1980s. Because birth rates among the Turks remained relatively high while Bulgarians approached a zero-growth birth rate in 1980, Bulgarian authorities sought to mitigate the impact of growing Turkish enclaves in certain regions. Hence, Bulgaria discontinued its liberal 1969 emigration agreement with Turkey (ostensibly to prevent a shortage of unskilled labor resulting from free movement of Turkish workers back to their homeland), and in 1984 began a massive campaign to erase the national identity of Turkish citizens by forcing them to take Bulgarian names. Official propaganda justified forced assimilation with the assertion that the only "Turks" in Bulgaria were descended from the Bulgarians who had adopted Islam after the Ottoman occupation in the fourteenth century. This campaign brought several negative results. Bulgaria's international image, already damaged by events in the early 1980s, now included official discrimination against the country's largest ethnic minority. The resumption of terrorist attacks on civilians, absent for many years, coincided with the new policy. And Bulgaria's relations with Turkey, which had improved somewhat after a visit by Turkish President Kenan Evren to Bulgaria in 1982, suffered another setback.

Bulgaria's close reliance on the Soviet Union continued into the 1980s, but differences began to appear. Much of Zhivkov's success had come from the secure support of Nikita Khrushchev's successor, Leonid Brezhnev, with whom Zhivkov had a close personal relationship. By contrast, relations between Zhivkov and Brezhnev's successor, Iuriĭ V. Andropov, were tense because Zhivkov had supported Andropov's rival Konstantin Chernenko as successor to Brezhnev. The advent of Mikhail S. Gorbachev as Soviet party leader in 1985 defined a new generational difference between Soviet and Bulgarian leadership. Gorbachev immediately declared that Bulgaria must follow his example in party reform if traditional relations were to continue.

By this time, the image of the BCP had suffered for several years from well-publicized careerism and corruption, and from the remoteness and advancing age of the party leadership (Zhivkov was seventy-four in 1985). The state bureaucracy, inordinately large in Bulgaria since the first post-liberation government of 1878, constituted 13.5 percent of the total national work force in 1977. Periodic anticorruption campaigns had only temporary effects. The ideological credibility of the party also suffered from the apparent failure of the NEM, whose goals were being restated by 1984. Although the BCP faced no serious political opposition or internal division in the early 1980s, the party launched campaigns to involve Bulgarian youth more fully in party activities. But these efforts had little impact on what party leaders perceived as serious and widespread political apathy (see The Bulgarian Communist (Socialist) Party, ch. 4). Thus, by 1985 many domestic and international signs indicated that the underpinning of the long, stable Zhivkov era was in precarious condition.

* * *

The most comprehensive English-language treatment of Bulgarian history is Richard J. Crampton's *A Short History of Modern Bulgaria*, which covers in detail the period from liberation (1878) to 1985. *The Bulgarian Communist Party from Blagoev to Zhivkov*, by John D. Bell, provides a political history from the viewpoint of the BCP, beginning with the pre-1900 origins of that party and concluding in 1984. *Modern Bulgaria: History, Policy, Economy, Culture*, edited by Georgi Bokov, contains a long historical section whose useful detail can be separated from its bias as a state publication of the Zhivkov era. Cyril Black's chapter "Bulgaria in Historical Perspective" in *Bulgaria* (edited by L.A.D. Dellin) is a balanced overview and perspective of all periods of Bulgarian history. And the "History and Political Traditions" chapter of Robert J. McIntyre's *Bulgaria: Politics, Economics, and Society* describes the evolution of political institutions from the First Bulgarian Empire to the late 1980s. (For further information and complete citations, see Bibliography.)

Chapter 2. The Society and Its Environment

Man in traditional costume, playing gaïda, a folk instrument

IN THE PAST 150 YEARS, vast changes have completely transformed the political and economic situation in Bulgaria, as well as the country's way of life. Poor peasants who served a foreign ruler first became land-owning peasants, then industrial workers who were mostly urbanized and disconnected from the land. Bulgarians who had traveled no farther than the next village began to migrate, often to gain a better education or to get a job in a growing industry. As villages and towns became less isolated, both internal migration and emigration became easier.

The decline in the agricultural way of life also made people susceptible to changes on a national level rather than on a village or regional level. People were less self-sufficient for their basic needs and therefore more vulnerable to fluctuations in the national economy. The traditional support systems of the extended family and cooperative work in the village were replaced by a vast network of national social welfare programs. Instead of receiving help from family and neighbors, the poor, elderly, and disabled grew dependent on governmental programs. The sick no longer relied solely on traditional village healers once villagers and city people alike fell under coverage of a national health system.

After 1944 much was written about the contrast between Bulgaria's traditional past and the modern way of life to which communism had accustomed Bulgarians. Indeed, during the postwar era, Bulgaria made great progress in establishing the structure of a modern, urbanized way of life. Mortality decreased markedly, life expectancy increased greatly, and the educational level of the population improved significantly. However, the modern way of life also generated much greater expectations for housing, education, health standards, work standards, and other aspects of life than the communist system could deliver. The centralization and bureaucracy of traditional communist social policy established a single, rather low standard for everyone, regardless of individual needs. Also, massive industrialization brought pollution and other environmental problems to a land that had been relatively unspoiled before World War II.

After democratization began in 1989, Bulgarians began looking westward and found that many aspects of their way of life were sadly lacking by the standards of Western Europe and the United States. The sense that Bulgaria needed to do fifty years' worth of catching up made the transition to democracy even harder.

Natural Features

The land area of Bulgaria is 110,550 square kilometers, slightly larger than that of the state of Tennessee. The country is situated on the west coast of the Black Sea, with Romania to the north, Greece and Turkey to the south, and Yugoslavia to the west. Considering its small size, Bulgaria has a great variety of topographical features. Even within small parts of the country, the land may be divided into plains, plateaus, hills, mountains, basins, gorges, and deep river valleys.

Boundaries

Although external historical events often changed Bulgaria's national boundaries in its first centuries of existence, natural terrain features defined most boundaries after 1944, and no significant group of people suffered serious economic hardship because of border delineation. Postwar Bulgaria contained a large percentage of the ethnic Bulgarian people, although numerous migrations into and out of Bulgaria occurred at various times. None of the country's borders was officially disputed in 1991, although nationalist Bulgarians continued to claim that Bulgaria's share of Macedonia—which it shared with both Yugoslavia and Greece—was less than just because of the ethnic connection between Macedonians and Bulgarians (see Macedonians, this ch.).

In 1991 Bulgaria had a total border of about 2,264 kilometers. Rivers accounted for about 680 kilometers and the Black Sea coast for 400 kilometers; the southern and western borders were mainly defined by ridges in high terrain. The western and northern boundaries were shared with Yugoslavia and Romania, respectively, and the Black Sea coastline constituted the entire eastern border. The Romanian border followed the Danube River for 464 kilometers from the northwestern corner of the country to the city of Silistra and then cut to the east-southeast for 136 kilometers across the northeastern province of Varna. The Danube, with steep bluffs on the Bulgarian side and a wide area of swamps and marshes on the Romanian side, was one of the most effective river boundaries in Europe. The line through Dobruja was arbitrary and was redrawn several times according to international treaties (see The Balkan Wars and World War I, ch. 1). In that process, most inhabitants with strong national preferences resettled in the country of their choice. Borders to the south were with Greece and Turkey. The border with Greece was 491 kilometers long, and the Turkish border was 240 kilometers long.

Topography

The main characteristic of Bulgaria's topography is alternating bands of high and low terrain that extend east to west across the country (see fig. 8). From north to south, those bands are the Danubian Plateau, the Balkan Mountains (called Stara Planina, meaning old mountains in Bulgarian), the central Thracian Plain, and the Rhodope Mountains. The easternmost sections near the Black Sea are hilly, but they gradually gain height to the west until the westernmost part of the country is entirely high ground.

More than two-thirds of the country is made up of plains, plateaus, or hilly land at an altitude less than 600 meters. Plains (below 200 meters) make up 31 percent of the land, plateaus and hills (200 to 600 meters) 41 percent, low mountains (600 to 1,000 meters) 10 percent, medium-sized mountains (1,000 to 1,500 meters) 10 percent, and high mountains (over 1,500 meters) 3 percent. The average altitude in Bulgaria is 470 meters.

The Danubian Plateau extends from the Yugoslav border to the Black Sea. It encompasses the area between the Danube River, which forms most of the country's northern border, and the Balkan Mountains to the south. The plateau slopes gently from cliffs along the river, then it abuts mountains of 750 to 950 meters. The plateau, a fertile area with undulating hills, is the granary of the country.

The southern edge of the Danubian Plateau blends into the foothills of the Balkan Mountains, the Bulgarian part of the Carpathian Mountains. The Carpathians resemble a reversed S as they run eastward from Czechoslovakia across the northern portion of Romania, swinging southward to the middle of Romania and then running westward, where they are known as the Transylvanian Alps. The mountains turn eastward again at the Iron Gate, a gorge of the Danube River at the Romanian-Yugoslav border. At that point, they become the Balkan Mountains of Bulgaria.

The Balkan Mountains originate at the Timok Valley in Yugoslavia and run southward towards the Sofia Basin in west central Bulgaria. From there they run east to the Black Sea. The Balkans are about 600 kilometers long and 30 to 50 kilometers wide. They retain their height well into central Bulgaria, where Botev Peak, the highest point in the Balkan Mountains, rises to about 2,376 meters. The range then continues at lower altitude to the cliffs of the Black Sea. Through most of Bulgaria, the Balkan Mountains form the watershed from which rivers drain north to the Danube River or south to the Aegean Sea. Some smaller rivers in the east drain directly to the Black Sea. The Sredna Gora (central hills) is a narrow ridge about 160 kilometers long and 1,600 meters high, running east to west parallel to the Balkans. Just to the south is the Valley of Roses, famous for rose oil used in perfume and liqueurs.

The southern slopes of the Balkan Mountains and the Sredna Gora give way to the Thracian Plain. Roughly triangular in shape, the plain originates at a point east of the mountains near Sofia and broadens eastward to the Black Sea. It includes the Maritsa River valley and the lowlands that extend from the river to the Black Sea. Like the Danubian Plateau, much of the Thracian Plain is somewhat hilly and not a true plain. Most of its terrain is moderate enough to cultivate.

The Rhodope Mountains occupy the area between the Thracian Plain and the Greek border to the south. The western Rhodopes consist of two ranges: the Rila Mountains south of Sofia and the Pirin Mountains in the southwestern corner of the country. They are the most outstanding topographic feature of Bulgaria and of the entire Balkan Peninsula. The Rila range includes Mount Musala, whose 2,975-meter peak is the highest in any Balkan country. About a dozen other peaks in the Rilas are over 2,600 meters. The highest peaks are characterized by sparse bare rocks and remote lakes above the tree line. The lower peaks, however, are covered with alpine meadows that give the range an overall impression of green beauty. The Pirin range is characterized by rocky peaks and stony slopes. Its highest peak is Mount Vikhren, at 2,915 meters the second-highest peak in Bulgaria.

The largest basin in Bulgaria is the Sofia Basin. About twenty-four kilometers wide and ninety-six kilometers long, the basin contains the capital city and the area immediately surrounding it. The route through basins and valleys from Belgrade to Istanbul (formerly Constantinople) via Sofia has been historically important since Roman times, determining the strategic significance of the Balkan Peninsula. Bulgaria's largest cities were founded on this route. Paradoxically, although the mountains made many Bulgarian villages and towns relatively inaccessible, Bulgaria has always been susceptible to invasion because no natural obstacle blocked the route through Sofia.

A significant part of Bulgaria's land is prone to earthquakes. Two especially sensitive areas are the borders of the North Bulgarian Swell (rounded elevation), the center of which is in the Gorna Oryakhovitsa area in north-central Bulgaria, and the West Rhodopes Vault, a wide area extending through the Rila and northern Pirin regions to Plovdiv in south-central Bulgaria. Especially strong tremors also occur along diagonal lines running between Skopje in the Republic of Macedonia and Razgrad in northeast Bulgaria, and from Albania eastward across the southern third of Bulgaria through Plovdiv. Sixteen major earthquakes struck Bulgaria between 1900 and 1986, the last two in Strazhitsa on the

N

Sea

ROMANIA

Danube

DANUBIAN
PLATEAU

Danube

Yantra

Razgrad

Varna

76

Tundzha

I

V

Tundzha

Burgas   *Black*

THRACIAN   PLAIN

div

Khaskovo

III

Maritsa

TURKEY

Aegean Sea

—·—·—	International bou
⊛	National capital
●	Populated place
▲	Spot elevation in
I	Balkan Mountain
II	Pirin Mountains
III	Rhodope Mounta
IV	Rila Mountains
V	Sredna Gora

0 10 20 30 40 50 Kilome

0   10   20   30   40

Figure 8. Topography and Drainage

Skopje-Razgrad fault line. Together the two quakes damaged over 16,000 buildings, half of them severely. One village was almost completely leveled, others badly damaged. Many inhabitants were still living in temporary housing four years later.

Drainage

The Balkan Mountains divide Bulgaria into two nearly equal drainage systems. The larger system drains northward to the Black Sea, mainly by way of the Danube River. This system includes the entire Danubian Plateau and a stretch of land running forty-eight to eighty kilometers inland from the coastline. The second system drains the Thracian Plain and most of the higher lands of the south and southwest to the Aegean Sea. Although only the Danube is navigable, many of the other rivers and streams in Bulgaria have a high potential for the production of hydroelectric power and are sources of irrigation water.

Of the Danube's Bulgarian tributaries, all but the Iskŭr rise in the Balkan Mountains. The Iskŭr flows northward to the Danube from its origin in the Rila Mountains, passing through Sofia's eastern suburbs and through a Balkan Mountain valley.

The Danube gets slightly more than 4 percent of its total volume from its Bulgarian tributaries. As it flows along the northern border, the Danube averages 1.6 to 2.4 kilometers in width. The river's highest water levels usually occur during June floods; it is frozen over an average of forty days per year.

Several major rivers flow directly to the Aegean Sea. Most of these streams fall swiftly from the mountains and have cut deep, scenic gorges. The Maritsa with its tributaries is by far the largest, draining all of the western Thracian Plain, all of the Sredna Gora, the southern slopes of the Balkan Mountains, and the northern slopes of the eastern Rhodopes. After it leaves Bulgaria, the Maritsa forms most of the Greek-Turkish border. The Struma and the Mesta (which separate the Pirin Mountains from the main Rhodopes ranges) are the next largest Bulgarian rivers flowing to the Aegean. The Struma and Mesta reach the sea through Greece.

Climate

Considering its small area, Bulgaria has an unusually variable and complex climate. The country lies between the strongly contrasting continental and Mediterranean climatic zones. Bulgarian mountains and valleys act as barriers or channels for air masses, causing sharp contrasts in weather over relatively short distances. The continental zone is slightly larger because continental air masses flow easily into the unobstructed Danubian Plain. The continental influence, stronger during the winter, produces abundant snowfall; the Mediterranean influence increases during the summer and produces hot, dry weather. The barrier effect of the Balkan Mountains is felt throughout the country: on the average, northern Bulgaria is about one degree cooler and receives about 192 more millimeters of rain than southern Bulgaria. Because the Black Sea is too small to be a primary influence over much of the country's weather, it only affects the immediate area along its coastline.

The Balkan Mountains are the southern boundary of the area in which continental air masses circulate freely. The Rhodope Mountains mark the northern limits of domination by Mediterranean weather systems. The area between, which includes the Thracian Plain, is influenced by a combination of the two systems, with the continental predominating. This combination produces a plains climate resembling that of the Corn Belt in the United States, with long summers and high humidity. The climate in this region is generally more severe than that of other parts of Europe in the same latitude. Because it is a transitional area, average temperatures and precipitation are erratic and may vary widely from year to year.

Average precipitation in Bulgaria is about 630 millimeters per year. Dobruja in the northeast, the Black Sea coastal area, and parts of the Thracian Plain usually receive less than 500 millimeters. The remainder of the Thracian Plain and the Danubian Plateau get less than the country average; the Thracian Plain is often subject to summer droughts. Higher elevations, which receive the most rainfall in the country, may average over 2,540 millimeters per year.

The many valley basins scattered through the uplands have temperature inversions resulting in stagnant air. Sofia is located in such a basin, but its elevation (about 530 meters) tends to moderate summer temperature and relieve oppressive high humidity. Sofia also is sheltered from the northern European winds by the mountains that surround its troughlike basin. Temperatures in Sofia average -2°C in January and about 21°C in August. The city's rainfall is near the country average, and the overall climate is pleasant.

The coastal climate is moderated by the Black Sea, but strong winds and violent local storms are frequent during the winter. Winters along the Danube River are bitterly cold; however, sheltered valleys that open to the south along the Greek and Turkish borders may be as mild as areas along the Mediterranean or Aegean coasts.

Environment

Like the other European members of the Council for Mutual Economic Assistance (Comecon—see Glossary), Bulgaria saw unimpeded industrial growth as a vital sign of social welfare and progress toward the socialist ideal. Because this approach made environmental issues a taboo subject in socialist Bulgaria, the degree of damage by postwar industrial policy went unassessed until the government of Todor Zhivkov (1962–89) was overthrown in late 1989. The Zhivkov government's commitment to heavy industry and lack of money to spend on protective measures forced it to conceal major environmental hazards, especially when relations with other countries were at stake. Factories that did not meet environmental standards paid symbolic fines and had no incentive to institute real environmental protection measures. Even as late as 1990, socialist officials downplayed the effects on Bulgaria of radiation from the 1986 nuclear power plant accident at Chernobyl'. Citizens were informed that they need not take iodine tablets or use any other protective measures.

In 1991 Bulgarian environmentalists estimated that 60 percent of the country's agricultural land had been damaged by excessive use of pesticides and fertilizers and by industrial fallout. By 1991 two-thirds of Bulgarian rivers were polluted, and the Yantra River was classified as the dirtiest river in Europe. Bulgaria's forests had also been damaged. By 1991, about two-thirds of the primary forests had been cut. However, despite its recognition of the need for greater environmental protection, Bulgaria budgeted only 10.4 billion leva (for value of the lev—see Glossary) to remedy ecological problems in 1991.

Perhaps the most serious environmental problem in Bulgaria was in the Danube port city of Ruse. From 1981 to 1989, the chemical pollution that spread from a chlorine and sodium plant across the Danube in Giurgiu, Romania, was a forbidden subject in Bulgaria because it posed a threat to good relations between two Warsaw Pact (see Glossary) countries. Chemical plants in Ruse also contributed to the pollution. Citizen environmentalists opposing the situation in Ruse organized the first demonstrations and the first independent political group to oppose the Zhivkov regime (see Other Political Organizations, ch. 4). During the Giurgiu plant's first year of operation, chlorine levels in Ruse almost doubled, reaching two times the permissible maximum in the summer of 1990. Over 3,000 families left the city in the 1980s despite government restrictions aimed at covering up the problem. Besides chlorine and its by-products, the plant produced chemical agents for the rubber industry, and in 1991 some sources reported that the plant was processing industrial waste from Western countries—both activities likely to further damage Ruse's environment. International experts claimed that half of Ruse's pollutants came from Giurgiu, and the others came from Bulgarian industries. In response to the formidable Bulgarian environmental movement, some Bulgarian plants have been closed or have added protective measures; the Giurgiu plant, however, was planning to expand in 1991.

Pollution of agricultural land from a copper plant near the town of Srednogorie provoked harsh public criticism. The plant emitted toxic clouds containing copper, lead, and arsenic. In 1988 it released toxic wastewater into nearby rivers used to irrigate land in the Plovdiv-Pazardzhik Plain, which includes some of Bulgaria's best agricultural land. The groundwater beneath the plain also was poisoned. Work has begun on a plan to drain toxic wastewater from the plant's reservoir into the Maritsa River. Environmental improvements for the copper plant and three other factories in the Plovdiv area (a lead and zinc factory, a chemical factory, and a uranium factory) also were planned, but they would take years to implement.

None of Bulgaria's large cities escaped serious environmental pollution. Statistics showed that 70 to 80 percent of Sofia's air pollution was caused by emissions from cars, trucks, and buses. Temperature inversions over the city aggravated the problem. Two other major polluters, the Kremikovtsi Metallurgy Works and the Bukhovo uranium mine (both in southwestern Bulgaria), contaminated the region with lead, sulfur dioxide, hydrogen sulfide, ethanol, and mercury. The city of Kŭrdzhali became heavily polluted with lead from its lead and zinc complex. In 1973 the petroleum and chemical plant near the Black Sea port of Burgas released large amounts of chlorine in an incident similar to the one in Srednogorie. Environmentalists estimated that the area within a thirty-kilometer radius of the plant was rendered uninhabitable by that release. The air in Burgas was also heavily polluted with carbon and sulfur dioxide in 1990.

In 1990 environmental scientists claimed that two-thirds of Bulgaria's population suffered from the polluted environment to some degree (see Health, this ch.). In 1991 Bulgaria began seeking international assistance in solving environmental problems. Besides joining Romania, Turkey, and the Soviet Union in joint scientific studies of the critically polluted Black Sea, Bulgaria actively sought environmental technology and expertise from Western Europe and the United States.

Population

Since ancient times, Bulgaria has been a crossroads for population movement. Early settlement occurred mainly in the most fertile agricultural lands. After World War II, however, Bulgarian cities grew rapidly at the expense of rural population in concert with state industrialization policy.

Administrative Subdivisions

In 1991 Bulgaria was divided into nine provinces (*oblasti*; sing. *oblast*). These administrative units included the city of Sofia (Grad Sofiya) and eight provincial districts: Burgas, Khaskovo, Lovech, Mikhaylovgrad, Plovdiv, Razgrad, Sofiya (the region outside the city), and Varna (see fig. 1). Each province was named for the city that was its administrative center. Excluding the city of Sofia, the provinces encompassed territories ranging from 9.5 percent of the country to 17.2 percent, and their population ranged from 7.5 percent to 14 percent of the national total (see table 2, Appendix). The eight provinces were divided into a total of 273 communities (*obshtini*; sing., *obshtina*); the city of Sofia was divided into districts (*raĭoni*; sing., *raĭon*). Because this system was established in 1987, references to another type of district, the *okrŭg* (pl. *okrŭzi*), remained common in the early 1990s. The new government that took office in 1991 announced that yet another change was needed in Bulgaria's political subdivisions because the 1987 system reflected the discredited policies of the Zhivkov regime.

Settlement Patterns

The first settlements sprang up in Bulgaria very early in the area's history (see Early Settlement and Empire, ch. 1). The biggest and most numerous villages appeared on fertile lands such as the Danubian Plateau, the Dobruja region, and the Maritsa and Tundzha river valleys. Settlements also took hold at very high altitudes (up to 1,500 meters in the Rhodope Mountains and up to 1,200 meters in the Balkans), but only in areas where it was warm enough to grow grain or other crops. During the rule of the Ottoman Empire, many Bulgarians were forced to move into villages at higher altitudes. After Bulgaria became independent in 1878, many people returned to the lower altitudes, but most of the upland villages remained. The process of urbanization began at that point, but it progressed slowly because of wars, lack of employment in population centers, and the emigration of the ethnic Turks who had supported the economies of some cities during the Ottoman era. The massive industrialization of the communist era again stimulated temporary settlement at high altitudes for mining or forestry. Generally, only the highest areas in the Rila, Pirin, and Rhodope mountains remained comparatively unsettled. These regions became known for their national parks and seasonal resort areas.

Cities

Bulgaria's cities grew much more rapidly after 1944. In 1946 only Sofia and Plovdiv had populations numbering over 100,000. By 1990, there were ten cities having populations exceeding 250,000: Burgas, Dobrich (formerly Tolbukhin), Pleven, Plodiv, Ruse, Shumen, Sliven, Sofia, Stara Zagora, and Varna (see fig. 9; table 3, Appendix). In 1990 nearly one-third of Bulgaria's population lived in the ten largest cities; two-thirds of the population was urban. Although the urban birth rate declined after the mid-1970s, large-scale migration from rural areas to cities continued through 1990 (see table 4, Appendix). At the same time, migration from cities to rural areas more than doubled from the 1960s to the 1980s, mainly because more mechanical and service jobs became available in agriculture during that period. In cities such as Sofia and Plovdiv, where industrialization started earliest, the population stabilized, and the repercussions of rapid population growth were less obvious in the 1980s.

The population of the average Bulgarian city grew by three to four times between 1950 and 1990. The rapidity of this growth caused some negative trends. The cities often lacked the resources to serve the needs of their growing populations: in particular, housing and social services could not grow fast enough. The cities' great need for social resources in turn diverted resources from smaller, more scattered population centers. The overall rural-to-urban migration pattern caused shortages of agricultural labor, especially in the villages surrounding large cities. The government discouraged new industries from locating in outlying areas because of the lack of workers.

Sofia was founded by the Thracians and has remained an important population center for 2,000 years. Its location in a basin sheltered by the Vitosha Mountains was strategically and esthetically desirable. Long-established communication routes pass though Sofia, most notably the route from Belgrade to Istanbul. Sofia's climate and location caused the Roman Emperor Constantine to consider the city when he selected an eastern capital for his empire in the early fourth century. Hot springs, which still exist today, were an added attraction. After it became the Bulgarian capital in 1879, Sofia became the administrative, educational, and cultural center of the country. Because of Sofia's rapid postwar growth (it grew by 36 percent between 1965 and 1986), in 1986 its city government closed the city to all internal immigrants except scholars and technical experts.

Plovdiv, the country's second most important city, was founded in the fourth century B.C. by Philip of Macedonia. Its exposed

Silistra

Danube

Ruse

Dobrich

Shumen

Varna

Yantra

Veliko Türnovo

Tundzha Sliven

Black
Sea

Burgas

Stara Zagora Yambol

Haskovo

TURKEY

N

International boundary

National capital

Population center (in thousands):
50-100

100-250

250-500

Over 1,000

0   25   50 Kilometers
0   25   50 Miles

Source: Based on information from Klaus-Detlev Grothusen (ed.), *Bulgarien*, Göttingen, Germany, 19

Figure 9. Population Centers, 1990

Population Trends

The 1985 census recorded Bulgaria's population at 8,948,649, an increase of 220,878 over the 1975 census figure. At the end of 1990, the Central Statistical Bureau had estimated an updated figure of 8,989,172, including about 100,000 more women than men. However, the estimates for 1989 and 1990 did not account for major emigrations in those years: first the massive emigration of Turks in 1989, then the emigration of ethnic Bulgarians in 1990. Adjusting for emigration figures, the population figure actually decreased between 1985 and 1990. Bulgaria's 1989 population density figure of eighty-one people per square kilometer made it one of the least densely populated countries in Europe.

Bulgaria's rate of population growth began a steady decrease in the mid-1920s, and the trend accelerated thereafter (see table 5, Appendix). Before World War II, a man's status in his community was determined by how many children (especially sons) he had. Women who did not marry, or who married but had no children, were seen as failures. As the country became more urbanized, however, such traditional views gradually disappeared. Large families were no longer the economic necessity they had been in agricultural society, and extra children became a burden rather than a boon. As women became more educated and less accepting of the traditional patriarchal family norms, their attitude toward childbearing changed. In 1990 the majority of Bulgarian women believed two children ideal for a family, but because of economic and social conditions, their personal preference was to raise only one. By the 1980s, this change in attitude had begun to prevail even in villages and with less-educated women. In 1985, 75 percent of Bulgarian women indicated that they would not like to have any more children. Families with three or more children became a rarity, and women who opted for more than two children had a lower standard of living and were generally less respected in society.

Although few social planners advocated a return to the large families of the past, Bulgarian policy makers were dismayed that the population did not increase. During the Zhivkov era, the mass media and scholarly journals expressed concern that the nine millionth Bulgarian had not yet been born, and that families were unwilling to have two children instead of one. By 1985 population experts were urging that 30 to 40 percent of families have three children to make up for those which had none or only one. Meanwhile, although the 1973 Politburo had affirmed a family's right to decide how many children to have and when they should be born, in the 1970s and 1980s contraceptives were not available in sufficient quantity for family planning. The Zhivkov regime had placed strict restrictions on abortions; these restrictions were not repealed until 1990. Partly because contraceptives were in short supply, abortions had surpassed births by 1985 despite the restrictions. Until 1990 bachelors and unmarried women had to pay a 5 to 15 percent "bachelors' tax" depending on their age. In a more positive step, laws provided family allowances for children under sixteen. The age limit for the family allowance was raised to eighteen in 1990 for children still in school.

In 1990 Bulgarian demographers recorded a negative growth rate (negative 35 births per 1,000 population) for the first time. At that point, the number of live births per woman was 1.8. Demographers reported that the figure must increase to 2.1 to maintain the country's natural rate of population replacement. Mortality figures in Bulgaria were also much higher than those of the developed European countries (see Health, this ch.).

The most alarming demographic trend of the late 1980s, however, was substantially greater emigration totals. The 1989 Turkish exodus caused by the Zhivkov assimilation campaigns had a severe impact on the Bulgarian labor force (see Turks, this ch.). Then, in 1990, economic reform brought harsh living conditions that stimulated a wave of emigration by ethnic Bulgarians (see Standard of Living, ch. 3.). As of March 1991, some 460,000 Bulgarians had emigrated, bringing the total number of Bulgarians living abroad to about 3 million. The majority of the émigré population remained in nearby countries (1.2 million in Yugoslavia, 800,000 in other Balkan countries, and 500,000 in the Soviet Union). Smaller numbers went as far as the United States (100,000 to 120,000), Canada (100,000), Argentina (18,000), and Australia (15,000).

Ethnographic Characteristics

Throughout its past, Bulgaria, like the rest of the Balkan Peninsula, had been home to many diverse ethnic groups that were able to preserve their national identities despite being shifted among the jurisdictions of powerful empires. In modern Bulgaria, the opposite has been true: the largest minority ethnic group, the Turks, remained in territory that their Ottoman ancestors had occupied. After the fall of the Zhivkov government, Bulgaria was forced to moderate its minority policy in order to improve its delicate relations with neighboring countries such as Turkey and Yugoslavia.

Government Minority Policy

The 1893 census listed the following nationalities and religious groups in order of prevalence: Eastern Rite Orthodox Bulgarians,

Gypsy with trained bear, Varna
Courtesy Sam and Sarah Stulberg

Turks, Romanians, Greeks, Gypsies, Jews, Muslim Bulgarians, Catholic Bulgarians, Tatars, Gagauz (a Turkish-speaking people of the Eastern Orthodox faith), Armenians, Protestant Bulgarians, Vlachs (a Romanian-speaking people in southwest Bulgaria), and foreigners of various nationalities, mainly Russians and Germans.

Migrations and boundary changes after the two world wars reduced the list somewhat; few Greeks and Romanians remained in Bulgaria by 1990 (see table 6, Appendix). However, Bulgaria's communist leaders often tried to deny the existence of minority groups by manipulating or suppressing census data or by forcibly assimilating "undesirable" groups. In 1985, at the height of the last anti-Turkish assimilation campaign, a leading Bulgarian Communist Party official declared Bulgaria "a one-nation state" and affirmed that "the Bulgarian nation has no parts of other peoples and nations."

After the fall of Todor Zhivkov in 1989, all the minorities in Bulgaria progressed somewhat toward self-determination and freedom of expression. New minority organizations and political parties sprang up, and minority groups began publishing their own newspapers and magazines. Non-Bulgarian nationalities regained the right—curtailed in the Zhivkov era—to use their original names, speak their language in public, and wear their national dress. In

1991 significant controversy remained, however, as to how far the rights of minorities should extend. Legislators making policy on such issues as approval of non-Bulgarian names and Turkish-language schools faced mass protests by nationalist Bulgarians, who successfully delayed liberalization of government policy on those issues (see The Turkish Problem, ch. 4).

Bulgarians

Bulgarians have been recognized as a separate ethnic group on the Balkan Peninsula since the time of Tsar Boris I (852-89), under whom the Bulgars were converted to Christianity. Early historians began mentioning them as a group then; however, it is not clear whether such references were to the earliest Bulgarians, who were Asiatic and migrated to the Balkan Peninsula from the Ural Mountains of present-day Russia, or to the Slavs that preceded them in what is now Bulgaria. By the end of the ninth century, the Slavs and the Bulgarians shared a common language and a common religion, and the two cultures essentially merged under the name "Bulgarian" (see The Slavs and the Bulgars, ch. 1).

Acceptance of the Eastern Orthodox church as the state religion of the First Bulgarian Empire in A.D. 864 shaped the Bulgarian national identity for many centuries thereafter. The Bulgarian language, which was the first written Slavic language, replaced Greek as the official language of both church and state once the Cyrillic alphabet (see Glossary) came into existence in the ninth century. National literature flourished under the First Bulgarian Empire, and the church remained the repository of language and national feeling during subsequent centuries of occupation by the Byzantine and Ottoman empires.

Ottoman rule was the most formidable test of Bulgarian ethnic identity. The Ottoman Turks forced many of their Christian subjects to convert to Islam, and the Turks differentiated their subjects only by religion, not by nationality. The latter policy meant that the empire usually considered the Bulgarians as Greeks because of their common Orthodox religion. Turkish recognition of the Greek Orthodox Church gave the Greeks the power to replace Bulgarian clergy and liturgy with Greek, further threatening Bulgarian national identity. Under the Ottomans, some Bulgarians who had converted to Islam lost their national consciousness and language entirely. Others (the Pomaks) converted but managed to retain their old language and customs.

During the Ottoman occupation, the monasteries played an important role in preserving national consciousness among educated Bulgarians. Later, during the National Revival period of the nineteenth century, primary schools and reading rooms (*chitalishta*) were established to foster Bulgarian culture and literacy in cities throughout Bulgaria. The vast majority of uneducated peasants, however, preserved their customs in the less accessible regions in the mountains. Traditional folk songs and legends flourished there and became richer and more widely known than the literature created by educated Bulgarians (see The Written Word, ch. 1).

Bulgarian is classified as a South Slavic language, together with Serbo-Croatian, Slovenian, and Macedonian. One of the oldest written languages in Europe, Bulgarian influenced all the other Slavic languages, especially Russian, in early medieval times. In turn, the Bulgarian language was enriched by borrowings from other civilizations with which it came into contact. Besides 2,000 words from the pre-Cyrillic Old Slavonic language, Bulgarians borrowed religious terms and words used in daily life from the Greeks; vocabulary relating to political, economic, and day-to-day life from Turkish; and many Russian words to replace their Turkish equivalents as Ottoman influence waned during the National Revival period. In the postwar era, many West European words began to appear in Bulgarian, especially in technological fields.

Turks

Because of their status as former occupiers, the Turks have had a stormy relationship with Bulgaria since the beginning of its independence. In 1878 Turks outnumbered Bulgarians in Bulgaria, but they began emigrating to Turkey immediately after independence was established. The movement continued, with some interruptions, through the late 1980s. Between 1923 and 1949, 219,700 Turks left Bulgaria. Then a wave of 155,000 emigrants either were "expelled" (according to Turkish sources) or were "allowed to leave" (according to Bulgarian sources) between 1949 and 1951. The number would have been far greater had Turkey not closed its borders twice during those years. In 1968 an agreement reopened the Bulgarian-Turkish border to close relatives of persons who had left from 1944 to 1951. The agreement remained in effect from 1968 to 1978.

The biggest wave of Turkish emigration occurred in 1989, however, when 310,000 Turks left Bulgaria as a result of the Zhivkov regime's assimilation campaign. That program, which began in 1984, forced all Turks and other Muslims in Bulgaria to adopt Bulgarian (Christian or traditional Slavic) names and renounce all Muslim customs. Bulgaria no longer recognized the Turks as a national minority, explaining that all the Muslims in Bulgaria were descended from Bulgarians who had been forced into the Islamic faith by the Ottoman Turks. The Muslims would therefore "voluntarily" take new names as part of the "rebirth process" by which they would reclaim their Bulgarian identities. During the height of the assimilation campaign, the Turkish government claimed that 1.5 million Turks resided in Bulgaria, while the Bulgarians claimed there were none. (In 1986 Amnesty International estimated that 900,000 ethnic Turks were living in Bulgaria.)

The motivation of the 1984 assimilation campaign was unclear; however, many experts believed that the disproportion between the birth rates of the Turks and the Bulgarians was a major factor. The birth rate for Turks was about 2 percent at the time of the campaign, while the Bulgarian rate was barely above zero. The upcoming 1985 census would have revealed this disparity, which could have been construed as a failure of Zhivkov government policy. On the other hand, although most Turks worked in low-prestige jobs such as agriculture and construction, they provided critical labor to many segments of the Bulgarian economy. The emigration affected the harvest season of 1989, when Bulgarians from all walks of life were recruited as agricultural laborers to replace the missing Turks. The shortage was especially acute in tobacco, one of Bulgaria's most profitable exports, and wheat.

During the name-changing phase of the campaign, which saw Turkish towns and villages surrounded by army units, citizens were issued new identity cards with Bulgarian names. Failure to present a new card meant forfeiture of salary, pension payments, and bank withdrawals. Birth or marriage certificates were issued only in Bulgarian names. Traditional Turkish costumes were banned; homes were searched and all signs of Turkish identity removed. Mosques were closed. According to estimates, 500 to 1,500 people were killed when they resisted assimilation measures, and thousands of others went to labor camps or were forcibly resettled.

Before Zhivkov's assimilation campaign, official policy toward use of the Turkish language had varied. Before 1958, instruction in Turkish was available at all educational levels, and university students were trained to teach courses in Turkish in the Turkish schools. After 1958, Turkish-language majors were taught in Bulgarian only, and the Turkish schools were merged with Bulgarian ones. By 1972, all Turkish-language courses were prohibited, even at the elementary level. Assimilation meant that Turks could no longer teach at all, and the Turkish language was forbidden, even at home. Fines were levied for speaking Turkish in public.

After the fall of Zhivkov in 1989, the National Assembly attempted to restore cultural rights to the Turkish population. In 1991 a new law gave anyone affected by the name-changing campaign

Woman in folk costume, Koprivshtitsa
Courtesy Sam and Sarah Stulberg

three years to officially restore original names and the names of children born after the name change. The Slavic endings -ov, -ova, -ev, or -eva could now be removed if they did not go with one's original name, reversing the effect of a 1950s campaign to add Slavic endings to all non-Slavic names. The law was important not only for Turks, but also for the minority Gypsies and Pomaks who had been forced to change their names in 1965 and 1972 respectively. In January 1991, Turkish-language lessons were reintroduced for four hours per week in parts of the country with a substantial Turkish population, such as the former Kŭrdzhali and Razgrad districts.

Pomaks

Pomaks—a term that loosely translates as *collaborators*—were the descendants of ethnic Bulgarians who accepted the Islamic faith during Ottoman rule, mostly between the sixteenth and eighteenth centuries. In 1990 about 150,000 Pomaks lived in mountain villages in southern and southwestern Bulgaria. They were chiefly employed in agriculture, forestry, and mining. Because of their relative isolation in the mountains, the Pomaks did not become ethnically mixed with their coreligionist Turks during the occupation, and they largely retained their Slavic physical features. Because the Ottoman Turks showed little interest in Pomak lands, and because the Pomaks were converted rather late, most of their traditional Bulgarian customs remained intact. Thus, for example, the Pomaks never learned to speak Turkish. The Bulgarian government always considered the Pomaks as Bulgarians rather than as a separate minority.

As a result of the 1972–73 assimilation campaign, about 550 Pomaks were arrested and imprisoned at Belene in north central Bulgaria and in Stara Zagora. Unrest flared in 1989 when Pomaks from the Gotse Delchev area in southwest Bulgaria were refused passports that would have enabled them to emigrate with the Turks. Some Pomaks in southwest Bulgaria were subjected to a second name change because the names they received the first time were not definitely Bulgarian. Riots, work stoppages, and hunger strikes ensued. According to reports from the Plovdiv region, local officials banned public gatherings of more than three Pomaks and forbade residents to leave their villages.

Macedonians

Beginning with the withdrawal of the Ottoman occupation, the region known as Macedonia was divided among two or more European states. The entire region was never included in a single political unit. In 1990 Macedonia included all of the Yugoslav republic of Macedonia, the Pirin region of southwest Bulgaria, the part of northern Greece bordering the Aegean Sea and including Thessaloniki, and a very small part of eastern Albania. The Macedonian language, in which no written documents are known to have existed before 1790, had three main dialects. One dialect was closest to Serbian, one most resembled Bulgarian, and a third, more distinctive group became the basis for the official language.

The region's location in the middle of the Balkans and its lack of defined ethnic character made the dispute over the existence and location of a separate Macedonian nationality and control over its territory one of the most intractable Balkan issues of the late nineteenth and twentieth centuries. In general, Bulgaria and Greece asserted that the Macedonians within their jurisdiction were ethnically indistinguishable from the majority population. Yugoslavia saw the Macedonians of all jurisdictions as a distinct ethnic group. But, beginning with independence in 1878, Bulgarians also claimed various segments of non-Bulgarian territory based on the ethnic Slavic commonality of the Bulgarians and the Macedonians. Residual claims on Macedonian territory were a primary reason for Bulgaria's decision to side with Germany during both world wars. In the division of territory after World War I, most of Macedonia became part of the Kingdom of the Serbs, Croats, and Slovenes (later the Kingdom of Yugoslavia), and was renamed "South Serbia." After World War II, Yugoslavia strengthened its hold by making Macedonia a separate republic and recognizing the Macedonians as a distinct nationality (see World War I and Foreign Policy in the Late 1930s, ch. 1).

The Bulgarian position maintained that leading patriots such as Gotse Delchev and Iane Sandanski (who had fought for Macedonian independence from the Turks) and cultural figures such as the Miladinov brothers (who promoted education and the Slavic vernacular during the National Revival period) were products of Bulgarian culture and considered themselves Bulgarians, not Macedonians. In 1990 many people in the Pirin region identified themselves as Bulgarian, but some opposition Macedonian organizations such as Ilinden (named after the 1903 Ilinden-Preobrazhensko uprising for Macedonian independence on St. Elijah's Day) sought recognition by the Bulgarian government as a minority separate from the Bulgarians. This position was based on the assertion that Macedonians were a separate nationality with a distinct language and history.

No reliable data showed how many people in Bulgaria, or in all of Macedonia, considered themselves Macedonian or spoke a Macedonian dialect in 1990. Those who considered the Slavs in Macedonia as Bulgarians cited statistics for the whole region at the time it was first divided after World War I. At that time, 1,239,903 Bulgarians, or 59 percent of the population, were listed. The Bulgarians were a majority in both Yugoslav (Vardar) Macedonia (759,468 people) and in Bulgarian (Pirin) Macedonia (226,700 people). Later Bulgarian censuses, however, showed sharply varying numbers of Macedonians according to what political agenda was to be supported by a given census. The 1946 census, for example, identified over 250,000 Macedonians, reportedly to back President Georgi Dimitrov's short-lived plan for federation with Yugoslavia. Then, between the censuses of 1956 and 1965, the number of Macedonians dropped from 187,789 to 9,632. After that time, the Bulgarian census ceased identifying citizens by nationality.

Gypsies

Although Gypsies are known to have lived in Bulgaria since the fourteenth century, most of the Gypsy population arrived in the past few centuries. The last known group was forced to settle in 1958, having remained nomadic until that time. The Gypsy population was divided into three groups. According to the 1965 census, the last that enumerated Bulgarians by nationality, 42.5 percent were Orthodox and spoke Bulgarian; 34.2 percent were Orthodox and spoke Romanian or Romany, the Gypsy language; and 22.8 percent were Muslim, spoke Turkish, and considered themselves ethnic Turks. Estimates in 1990 put the Gypsy population at about 450,000, some 10 percent of whom lived in the southeastern city of Sliven.

The Gypsies had a long history as one of Bulgaria's most disadvantaged and maligned nationalities. They were the focus of official name-changing campaigns in every postwar decade between 1950 and 1990. Despite their numbers, Gypsies did not contribute much to Bulgarian society because only about 40 percent of them attained the educational and cultural level of the average Bulgarian. The other 60 percent lived in extremely disadvantaged conditions, isolated from the mainstream of society by the Gypsy tradition of preserving ethnic customs and by Bulgarian government policy. Government programs to improve the lot of the Gypsies usually meant construction of new, separate Gypsy neighborhoods rather than integration into Bulgarian society. Housing in Gypsy neighborhoods was always poor and overcrowded. In 1959 when a new neighborhood was built in Sofia, 800 people moved into 252 apartments. Each apartment had one and one-half rooms and no kitchen or inside plumbing. By 1990 about 3,000 people lived in these same apartments.

The education of Gypsies who spoke Romany was inhibited because the language has no alphabet or written literature. Gypsy children were exposed to Bulgarian only in school, hampering completion of studies for many. The illiteracy rate among Gypsies was believed to be still quite high in 1990, although no statistics were available. According to the only known literacy figures for nationalities, given in the 1926 census, 8.2 percent of Gypsies were literate compared with 54.4 percent of Bulgarians overall (see Education, this ch.). The Gypsy community exerted little pressure on students to finish school; many dropped out before reaching legal working age, increasing the tendency to marry and begin having children early.

In 1990 about 70 percent of Gypsy workers were unskilled and worked as general laborers, custodians, street cleaners, dishwashers, or in other minimum-wage occupations. About 20 percent of Gypsies worked at skilled jobs. The small Gypsy intelligentsia, which included musicians, scholars, professionals in various fields, and political figures, tried to influence their countrymen to gain more education and job skills. Pressure also was exerted for elimination of separate Gypsy neighborhoods and official replacement of the derogatory Bulgarian word *tsiganin* with *rom*, the Romany word for Gypsy.

Other Minorities

Because of official suppression of nationality statistics, little information was available on less numerous minorities in Bulgaria between 1965 and 1990. Most of the Tatar population (6,430 in 1965) had migrated from the Crimea to the cities of the Dobruja area in the nineteenth century. The Greek minority (8,241 in 1965) comprised political émigrés from Greece and the remainder of a population in southern Bulgaria that had been largely forced out of Bulgaria by government oppression and violence between the world wars. The Armenian population (20,282 in 1965) was mostly added between 1896 and 1924 during the massive emigration of Armenians from the Ottoman Empire. The Armenians were concentrated in the cities, especially Sofia and Plovdiv. In 1946 some 44,209 Jews remained in Bulgaria, which had conducted no large-scale persecution despite its wartime alliance with Nazi Germany. But massive emigration of Jews to Israel in the 1950's substantially reduced that number.

Religion

The Bulgarian Orthodox Church, which played a crucial role in preserving Bulgarian culture during the Ottoman occupation, remained central to the sense of Bulgarian nationhood even under the postwar communist regimes. In spite of the official status of Orthodoxy, Bulgaria also had a tradition of tolerance toward other Christian religions. Tolerance of Islam, however, remained problematic under all forms of government because of that religion's historical identification with the occupation and subjugation of Bulgaria.

Eastern Orthodoxy

In 1991 most Bulgarians were at least nominally members of the Bulgarian Orthodox Church, an independent national church like the Russian Orthodox Church and the other national branches of Eastern Orthodoxy. Because of its national character and its status as the national church in every independent Bulgarian state until the advent of communism, the church was considered an inseparable element of Bulgarian national consciousness (see Bulgarians, this ch.). Baptism, before 1944 an indispensable rite establishing individual identity, retained this vital role for many even after the communists took power. The power of this tradition caused the communist state to introduce a naming ritual called "civil baptism."

Although communist regimes could not eliminate all influence, they did undermine church authority significantly. First, the communists ruled that the church only had authority on church matters and could not take part in political life. Second, although the constitution made the church separate from the state, the clergy's salaries and the fees needed to maintain the churches were paid by the state. This meant that the clergy had to prove its loyalty to the state. From 1949 until 1989, religion in Bulgaria was mainly controlled by the Law on Religious Organizations, which enumerated the limitations on the constitution's basic separation of church and state.

The number of Orthodox priests declined from 3,312 in 1947 to 1,700 in 1985. Priests associated with the prewar regime were accused of engaging in illegal or antisocialist activities, supporting the opposition, and propagandizing against the state. Upon taking control of all church property, the state had the choice of maintaining churches or closing them down. Thus, for example, Rila Monastery, the largest monastery in Bulgaria, became a national museum in 1961.

In 1987 the Orthodox Church in Bulgaria had 3,720 churches and chapels, 120 monasteries, 981 regular and 738 retired priests, 135 monks, and 170 nuns. The church was administered by a Holy Synod. Under communist rule, the synod had the authority to publish limited quantities of religious material such as magazines, newspapers, and church calendars. A new translation of the Bible was published in 1982, but in such small quantities that the size of the printing could not be determined. By 1988 the 1982 edition was being resold at ten times the original price.

Rila Monastery, for many centuries a cultural and religious center
Courtesy Sam and Sarah Stulberg

After the fall of Zhivkov, the Orthodox Church and other churches in Bulgaria experienced a revival. Church rituals such as baptisms and church weddings attracted renewed interest, and traditional church holidays were observed more widely. Christmas 1990, the first Christmas under the new regime, was widely celebrated and greatly promoted in the mass media. During the postwar years, Christmas had received little public attention. The government returned some church property, including the Rila Monastery, and religious education and Bible study increased in the early post-Zhivkov years. The Orthodox seminary in Sofia returned to its original home in 1990 and attracted over 100 male and female students in its first year of operation. The Konstantin Preslavski Higher Pedagogical Institute added a new theology department to train theology, art, and music teachers as well as priests. The Holy Synod planned to publish 300,000 Orthodox Bibles in 1992.

Islam

The Muslim population of Bulgaria, including Turks, Pomaks, Gypsies, and Tatars, lived mainly in northeastern Bulgaria and in the Rhodope Mountains. Most were Sunni Muslims (see Glossary) because Sunni Islam had been promoted by the Ottoman

Turks when they ruled Bulgaria. Shia sects (see Glossary) such as the Kuzulbashi and the Bektashi also were present, however. About 80,000 Shia Muslims lived in Bulgaria, mainly in the Razgrad, Sliven, and Tutrakan (northeast of Ruse) regions. They were mainly descendants of Bulgarians who had converted to Islam to avoid Ottoman persecution but chose a Shia sect because of its greater tolerance toward different national and religious customs. For example, Kuzulbashi Bulgarians could maintain the Orthodox customs of communion, confession, and honoring saints. This integration of Orthodox customs into Islam gave rise to a type of syncretism found only in Bulgaria.

As of 1987, Muslims in Bulgaria had 1,267 mosques served by 533 *khodzhai,* or religious community leaders. The Muslim hierarchy was headed by one chief mufti and eight regional muftis, interpreters of Muslim law, all of whom served five-year terms. The largest mosque in Bulgaria was the Tumbul Mosque in Shumen, built in 1744.

Bulgarian Muslims were subject to particular persecution in the later years of the Zhivkov regime, partly because the Orthodox Church traditionally considered them foreigners, even if they were ethnically Bulgarian. In addition, the Bulgarian communist regimes declared traditional Muslim beliefs to be diametrically opposed to communist and Bulgarian beliefs. This view justified repression of Muslim beliefs and integration of Muslims into the larger society as part of the class and ideological struggle.

Like the practitioners of the other faiths, Muslims in Bulgaria enjoyed greater religious freedom after the fall of the Zhivkov regime. New mosques were built in many cities and villages; one village built a new church and a new mosque side by side. Some villages organized Quran (also seen as Koran) study courses for young people (study of the Quran had been completely forbidden under Zhivkov). Muslims also began publishing their own newspaper, *Miusiulmani,* in both Bulgarian and Turkish.

Roman Catholicism

Roman Catholic missionaries first tried to convert the Bulgarians during the reign of Boris I. They were unsuccessful, and Boris I led the Bulgarians in their conversion to Orthodoxy. In 1204 the Bulgarian Tsar Kaloian (1197–1207) formed a short-lived union between the Roman Catholic Church and the Bulgarian Orthodox Church as a political tactic to balance the religious power of the Byzantine Empire. The union ended when Rome declared war on Bulgaria, and the Bulgarian patriarchate was reestablished in

1235. The Catholic Church had no influence in the Bulgarian Empire after that date.

Catholic missionaries renewed their interest in Bulgaria during the sixteenth century, when they were aided by merchants from Dubrovnik on the Adriatic. In the next century, Vatican missionaries converted most of the Paulicians, the remainder of a once-numerous heretical Christian sect, to Catholicism. Many believed that conversion would bring aid from Western Europe in liberating Bulgaria from the Ottoman Empire. By 1700, however, the Ottomans began persecuting Catholics and preventing their Orthodox subjects from converting.

After Bulgaria became independent, the Catholic Church again tried to increase its influence by opening schools, colleges, and hospitals throughout the country, and by offering scholarships to students who wished to study abroad. Prince Ferdinand of Saxe-Coburg-Gotha, first ruler of independent Bulgaria, was himself Catholic and supported the Vatican in these efforts. The papal nuncio Angelo Roncalli, who later became Pope John XXIII, played a leading role in establishing Catholic institutions in Bulgaria and in establishing diplomatic relations between Bulgaria and the Vatican in 1925.

The communist era was a time of great persecution for Catholics, nominally because Catholicism was considered the religion of fascism. Bulgarian communists also deemed Catholicism a foreign influence because, unlike Orthodoxy, it had no ties to Russia. The logic was that anything anti-Russian must also be anti-Bulgarian. Under the communist regimes, Catholic priests were charged with following Vatican orders to conduct antisocialist activities and help opposition parties. In 1949 foreign priests were forbidden to preach in Bulgaria, and the papal nuncio was forbidden to return to Bulgaria. Relations between the Vatican and Bulgaria were severed at that time. During the "Catholic trials" of 1951-52, sixty priests were convicted of working for Western intelligence agencies and collecting political, economic, and military intelligence for the West. Four priests were executed on the basis of these charges. In the early 1950s, the property of Catholic parishes was confiscated, all Catholic schools, colleges, and clubs were closed, and the Catholic Church was deprived of its legal status. Only nominal official toleration of Catholic worship remained.

In 1991 about 44,000 Roman Catholics remained in Bulgaria, mostly in Ruse, Sofia, and Plovdiv. Another 18,000 Uniate Catholics were concentrated in Sofia. (Uniate Catholics recognize the pope as their spiritual leader, but practice the Eastern Orthodox rite.) Bulgaria reestablished relations with the Vatican in 1990, and the Bulgarian government invited the pope to visit Bulgaria. Uniate Catholics began assisting Western-rite Catholics in conducting masses in Bulgarian, making the liturgy more accessible, and prompting predictions that the two branches would unite. Relations had not been established between the Bulgarian Orthodox Church and the Roman Catholic Church in 1991, however, and Catholics blamed official Orthodox intolerance for the continued rift.

Protestantism

Protestantism was introduced in Bulgaria by missionaries from the United States in 1857–58, amid the National Revival period. The two main denominations, the Methodists and Congregationalists, divided their areas of influence. The former predominated in northern Bulgaria and the latter in the south. In 1875 the Protestant denominations united in the Bulgarian Evangelical Philanthropic Society, which later became the Union of Evangelical Churches in Bulgaria. Besides setting up churches, the Protestants established schools, clinics, and youth clubs in Bulgaria, and distributed copies of the Bible and their own religious publications. The Union of Evangelical Churches produced the first translation of the entire Bible into Bulgarian in 1871 and founded the non-denominational Robert College in Constantinople, where many Bulgarian leaders of the post-independence era were educated. After independence in 1878, the Protestants gained influence because they used the vernacular in services and in religious literature.

The communist regimes subjected Protestants to even greater persecution than they did the Catholics. In 1946 church funding was cut off by a law curbing foreign currency transactions. Because many ministers had been educated in the West before World War II, they were automatically suspected of supporting the opposition parties. In 1949 thirty-one Protestant clergymen were charged with working for American intelligence and running a spy ring in Bulgaria. All church property was confiscated, and the churches' legal status was revoked. Most of the mainstream Protestant denominations maintained the nominal right to worship, as guaranteed by the constitution of 1947.

According to estimates in 1991, the 5,000 to 6,000 Pentecostals in Bulgaria made that sect the largest Protestant group (see table 7, Appendix). The Pentecostal movement was brought to Bulgaria in 1921 by Russian émigrés. The movement later spread to Varna, Sliven, Sofia, and Pleven. It gained popularity in Bulgaria after freedom of religion was declared in 1944, and the fall of Zhivkov brought another surge of interest. In 1991 the Pentecostal Church had thirty-six clergy in forty-three parishes, with sufficient concentration in Ruse to petition the government to establish a Bible institute there.

In 1991 the Adventist Church had 3,500 Bulgarian members, two-thirds of them young people. The Adventist movement began in the Dobruja region of Bulgaria at the turn of the century and then spread to Tutrakan, Ruse, Sofia, and Plovdiv. It gained momentum in Bulgaria after 1944. Under the communist regimes, mainstream Adventists maintained the right to worship. Some twenty parishes with forty pastors remained active through that era, although a breakaway reformed group was banned because of its pacifist beliefs. Some Adventists were imprisoned for refusal of military service.

Judaism

The Bulgarian communist regimes officially considered Jews a nationality rather than a religious group. For that reason, and because nearly 90 percent of the country's Jewish population emigrated to Israel after World War II, the Jewish society that remained in Bulgaria was mainly secular. Under the Zhivkov regime, synagogues rarely were open in Sofia, Samokov, and Vidin. In 1990 the Jewish population was estimated at about 71,000. At that time, only two rabbis were active, although several synagogues reportedly were reopened under the new regime. Most of the Jews in Bulgaria were Sephardic, descended from Spanish Jews who spoke Hebrew or Ladino (a Judeo-Spanish dialect). A much smaller number were Ashkenazi, with Yiddish-speaking ancestors. However, very few Jews in postcommunist Bulgaria remembered their ancestral languages, and frequent mixed marriages further diluted feelings of Jewish identity. The Jews of Bulgaria assimilated easily into Bulgarian society, partly because they traditionally lived in cities and worked as tradesmen or financiers.

The fate of Bulgarian Jews during World War II was a source of Bulgarian pride. The approximately 50,000 Jews then living in Bulgaria had long been well integrated into the fabric of Bulgarian city life. Because of this integration, neither society in general nor Tsar Boris III was inclined to follow the anti-Jewish policies of Bulgaria's Nazi ally. Boris tried to appease the Nazis by passing comparatively benign anti-Jewish laws, which nevertheless were protested widely, especially by the Bulgarian Orthodox Church. Twice in 1943, Boris personally blocked orders to deport Bulgarian Jews, sending them instead to so-called labor camps inside Bulgaria. Many Jews also received transit visas to Palestine at this time.

Social System

Most manifestations of traditional Bulgarian familial and societal relations disappeared in the initial postwar wave of modernization. Some traditions, however, proved surprisingly persistent and survived into the 1990s, especially in parts of western and southwestern Bulgaria. Although postwar communist regimes nominally emphasized emancipation of women, strong elements of paternalism and emphasis on traditional female roles remained in Bulgarian society. By 1990 economic forces had eliminated traditional extended families and limited the number of children, especially in urban areas. Some evidence of resurging traditional relationships was seen in the immediate post-Zhivkov years.

Traditional Society

Traditional Bulgarian society had three classes: the peasants (almost everyone in the villages), the *chorbadzhii* (a small wealthy class that owned large tracts of land and hired peasants to work them), and the *esnafi* (skilled tradespeople in towns, who later became the bourgeoisie). Most references to traditional Bulgarian society described village or peasant society because until the communist era the great majority of Bulgarians were peasants.

The most important institution of traditional Bulgarian society was the *zadruga,* an extended family composed of ten to twenty small families, related by blood, who lived and worked together, owned property jointly, and recognized the authority of a single patriarch. The extended family most often included four generations of men, the wives whom these men brought into the household through marriage, and the children produced through these marriages. Once a girl married, she would leave the *zadruga* of her parents for that of her husband. No member of the *zadruga* had any personal property other than clothes or the women's dowries.

Traditional Bulgarian society was strongly patriarchal. The *zadruga* leader, called the ''old man'' or the ''lord of the house,'' had absolute power over his family and was treated with the utmost respect. He was considered the wisest because he had lived the longest. His duties included managing the purchase and sale of all household property, division of labor among *zadruga* members, and settling personal disputes. Older men within the household could offer advice, but the ''old man'' had the final word. Obligatory signs of familial respect included rising whenever he appeared and eating only after he had begun and before he had finished his meal. The ''old man's'' wife (or the senior woman if he were widowed) had similar authority over traditional women's activities such as tending the garden, observing holiday rituals, and sewing. The senior woman commanded similar respect from *zadruga* members, but she was never allowed to interfere in functions designated for men.

When a *zadruga* broke up (normally because it became too large for easy management), property was divided equally among its members. Before the twentieth century, many villages were formed as outgrowths of an enlarged *zadruga*. The largest of the extended family organizations in Bulgaria began breaking up in the 1840s. At that time, the Ottoman Empire instituted new inheritance laws that did not take *zadruga* property patterns into account. A second stage of fragmentation occurred as the expectation of automatic integration into the extended family gradually weakened in younger generations: sons began leaving the *zadruga* at the death of the "old man," and newly arrived wives failed to adjust to the traditional system. As a result of such pressures, smaller households began to proliferate in the nineteenth century.

The *zadruga* breakup accelerated after Bulgaria gained its independence and began instituting Western-style laws that gave women equal inheritance rights, although in many parts of Bulgaria women did not begin demanding their legal inheritance until well into the twentieth century. The disintegration of large family holdings gradually led to the impoverishment of the peasants as land ownership became more fragmented and scattered with each generation. The durability of the extended family was reflected in the 1934 census, however, which still listed a category of household size as "thirty-one and over." Furthermore, even after extended families broke up, many peasants continued to work cooperatively.

The familial system sometimes extended to include godparents and adopted brothers and sisters—unrelated individuals enjoying the same status as close relatives. Godparenthood included another set of traditional relationships that knit village society together. Godparents kept close ties with their godchildren throughout their lives, and the godparent/godchild relationship could be transferred from generation to generation. Godparents were treated with the utmost respect and had an important role in all important events in a godchild's life, beginning with baptism. The familial relationship was so strong that a taboo developed against the marriage of children related to the same family only through godparenthood.

After the decline of the *zadruga,* the patriarchal system continued to flourish in the smaller families, where husbands gained ownership of family property and all the patriarchal status the old men once had. The status of wives remained distinctly secondary. Upon marriage a woman still severed all ties with her family if her husband's family lived in another village. Thus, couples always looked

Town of Melnik in Pirin Mountains
Courtesy Sam and Sarah Stulberg

forward to the birth of sons rather than daughters because sons would always remain family members. Men traditionally married between the ages of twenty and twenty-two; women, between eighteen and twenty. In areas where daughters were needed as laborers at home, marriage might be postponed until age twenty-five. Arranged marriages, common until the communist era, persisted in the most traditional villages until the 1960s.

Only in the twentieth century did men begin to consult their wives in family decisions. Until that time, wives were expected to give blind obedience to their husbands. A woman who dared question or interfere in a man's work was universally condemned. Women waited for a man to pass rather than crossing his path, and wives often walked with heavy loads while their husbands rode on horseback. The wife was responsible for all work inside the house and for helping her husband in the field as well.

Children typically began to share in household work at the age of five or six. At that age, girls began to do household work, and by age twelve they had usually mastered most of the traditional household skills. By age twelve or thirteen, boys were expected to do the same field work as adults. Alternatively, boys might begin learning a trade such as tailoring or blacksmithing at six or seven. As the size of farmland parcels diminished and field labor became less critical, more families sent children away from home to learn trades. Village boys apprenticed in cities sometimes became accustomed to city life and did not return to the village.

Family Life and Modern Society

Throughout the era of postwar communist modernization, family life remained one of the most important values in Bulgarian society. In a 1977 sociological survey, 95 percent of women responded that "one can live a full life only if one has a family." From the beginning of the twentieth century until the 1970s, the marriage rate in Bulgaria was stable at close to 10 percent per year. The rate was slightly higher just after the two world wars. The rate fell beginning in 1980, however, reaching 7 percent in 1989. Slightly more couples married in the cities than in the villages, a natural development considering the aging of the village population. Most women married between the ages of eighteen and twenty-five, most men between twenty and twenty-five. Village men and less educated city men typically married before they were twenty. The first men to marry often were those who had completed their military service, did not plan further education, and could support themselves financially (see Recruitment and Service Obligations, ch. 5; Education, this ch.). Those who continued their education often delayed marriage until their late twenties. In choosing their spouses, the less educated and those from more traditional regions of Bulgaria sought qualities most highly valued in traditional society: love of hard work, modesty, and good character. Among the educated classes, values such as personal respect, commonality of interests, and education were more often predominant in the choice of a spouse.

Until 1944 divorce was quite rare in Bulgaria, and great stigma was attached to all individuals who had divorced. After 1944 the divorce rate rose steadily until 1983, when it reached 16.3 percent. Between 1983 and 1986, however, the rate fell to 11.2 percent. In the 1980s, the divorce rate in the cities was more than twice that in the villages, in part because the village population was older. The divorce rate was especially high for couples married five years or less; that group accounted for 44 percent of all divorces. In 1991 the rate was increasing, however, for those married longer than five years.

Concerned about Bulgaria's low birth rate, the government issued new restrictions on divorce in its 1985 Family Code. The fee to apply for a divorce was more than three months' average salary, and every application for a divorce required an investigation. The grounds most often listed in a divorce application were infidelity, habitual drunkenness, and incompatibility.

In 1991 the average Bulgarian family included four people. Families of two to five people were common, whereas families of six or more were rare. In the larger families, moreover, the additional members usually included one or two of the couple's parents. In 1980 extended families spanning three or even four generations made up 17 percent of all households, indicating the persistence of the extended family tradition. Although the tradition was more prevalent in the villages of western and southern Bulgaria than in the cities, many urban newlyweds lived with their parents because they could not afford or obtain separate apartments.

Socialist Bulgaria greatly emphasized the emancipation of women. The 1971 constitution expressly stated that "all citizens of the People's Republic of Bulgaria are equal before the law, and no privileges or limitations of rights based on national, religious, sex, race, or educational differences are permitted" and that "women and men in the People's Republic of Bulgaria have the same rights." Bulgaria's Family Code also affirmed equal rights for men and women.

In 1988 Bulgaria's work force included an almost equal number of men (50.1 percent) and women (49.9 percent). By 1984 nearly 70 percent of working women surveyed said that they could not imagine life without their professional work, even if they did not need the pay. Only 9 percent of the women preferred being house-wives. However, most men surveyed in 1988 cited economics as the reason for their wives to work, asserting that the wives should give up their work if they were needed at home.

Household chores remained primarily the responsibility of women, including most working wives. In 1990 the average work-ing woman spent eight and one-half hours at her job and over four and one-half hours doing housework: cooking, washing dishes, washing clothes, ironing, mending, and tending the children. In many households, such tasks were still considered "women's work," to which husbands contributed little.

In their social planning, Bulgarian legislators usually viewed their country's women mainly as mothers, not as workers. Besides the laws passed in an effort to increase the country's birth rate, legis-lators passed laws giving certain privileges to women in the work-place, often keeping their reproductive capability in mind. Women were prohibited by law from doing heavy work or work that would adversely affect their health or their capacities as mothers. Women sought such jobs because they generally offered better pay and benefits. The list of prohibited jobs changed constantly. Depend-ing on the type of work, women could retire after fifteen or twenty years, or after reaching age forty-five, fifty, or fifty-five. Women who had raised five or more children could retire after fifteen years of work, regardless of their age or type of work. Men were gener-ally offered retirement after working twenty-five years or reach-ing age fifty, fifty-five, or sixty. Some jobs were restricted to women unless no women were available. Without exception these were low-skill, low-paying jobs such as archivist, elevator operator, ticket seller, coat checker, and bookkeeper. Other jobs, such as secre-tary, stenographer, librarian, cashier, and cleaning person were considered "appropriate for women." Men in the workplace often expressed resentment of women in positions of authority.

Social Groups and Their Work

Postwar Bulgarian society was divided into three social groups, according to type of work: *Workers,* who held jobs in the "produc-tive" manufacturing sector of the economy; *Employees,* who worked in "non-productive" service and education jobs; and *Agricultural workers.* The intelligentsia, usually considered a subsector of the employee category, held professional or creative positions requir-ing specific qualifications. In 1987 nonagricultural workers made up 63 percent of the population, employees made up 18 percent, and agricultural workers made up 19 percent. The intelligentsia

Male dance ensemble at folk festival held every five years at Koprivshtitsa
Courtesy Sam and Sarah Stulberg

made up 13.5 percent of the total population in 1985. Both the nonagricultural worker and the employee category grew about 15 percent between the censuses of 1975 and 1985, but the number of agricultural workers dropped steadily through the 1970s and 1980s (see table 8, Appendix). Of all people in the work force in 1990, only 21.7 percent were rated as highly qualified. According to sociologists, that figure would have to more than double if Bulgaria were to become economically competitive with the West.

Most of those registered as workers had jobs in industry. Between 1975 and 1985, the number of workers in the machine-building, spare-parts and metal-processing industries increased. Other industries, such as the food industry, the lumber industry, and the fuel industry, lost workers. Most workers were comparatively young, with little education and few work qualifications (see table 9, Appendix). In 1990 some 66.8 percent of industrial workers had a basic education or less. However, young workers were valued because they were considered most capable of adapting to new technology—a critical requirement for upgrading Bulgaria's outdated industrial infrastructure (see Labor Force, ch. 3).

In the 1980s, employment grew in the trade, supply, construction, and transportation sectors. Growing the fastest, however, were the sectors requiring primarily intellectual work: research and

101

research services, education, and administration. After growing by 90 percent between 1965 and 1985, administration included 26 percent of all employees and was the largest division of this category. The housing sector was the only component of the employee category that lost jobs between 1975 and 1990.

The number of agricultural workers decreased markedly from 50 percent of all workers in 1965 to 20 percent in 1985. As agricultural production intensified, many agricultural workers were transferred to nonagricultural jobs. In the late 1980s, however, a shortage of agricultural workers occurred because so many people had left the villages. For this reason, labor-intensive farm activities such as harvesting required recruitment of brigades from schools and nonagricultural enterprises. Many of the remaining farm workers could not adapt to new technology. This lack of adaptation inhibited the modernization and mechanization of agricultural processes.

The democratization that followed the Zhivkov regime raised the problem of unemployment, unknown in Bulgaria after 1944 (see Labor and Economic Reform, ch. 3). As of April 1991, some 124,000 Bulgarians were unemployed. With the country in the midst of economic restructuring, enterprise shutdowns, and scarcity of raw materials, employment figures showed no sign of improvement. The highest unemployment rates occurred in Plovdiv and Sofia. Most unemployed persons were under age thirty, and over 60 percent were women. Job vacancies continued to decline in 1991; most remaining opportunities were in low-skilled jobs or jobs requiring hard physical labor. Persons with the highest level of education, such as engineers, economists, and teachers, were least likely to find suitable positions. In 1990 the lack of skilled professional positions spurred a "brain drain" emigration that further threatened Bulgaria's ability to compete on technologically oriented world markets. In the meantime, the country's economy had lost its protected position as a member of the defunct Comecon, putting more pressure on the domestic labor force (see Bulgaria in Comecon, ch. 3).

Because the national welfare system could only accommodate those who lost their jobs because of enterprise shutdown, in 1990 the Bulgarian government began seeking ways to create more jobs. It considered rewarding businesses that added shifts or offered part-time or seasonal work, and it encouraged development of small business. One proposed solution, replacing working pensioners with young unemployed workers, was unworkable because enterprises found it less expensive to continue hiring pensioners.

Social Services

Between independence and the communist era, the Bulgarian government had used its social welfare funds mainly for government

St. Paraskeva Orthodox Church, Nesebŭr
Courtesy Sam and Sarah Stulberg

workers, army officers, white-collar workers, craftsmen, and trades-men. The 1949 social welfare law founded a new social welfare sys-tem that endured into the 1990s. The new system greatly expanded the categories of people eligible and the amounts they could receive. The social welfare system in 1991 was largely based on the 1951 section of the Labor Code that regulated monetary compensation and supplements, and the 1957 Law on Pensions. Both laws were revised countless times and no longer agree with each other. The National Assembly delayed creation of a new law until the new constitution was ratified in the summer of 1991.

In 1991 two-thirds of Bulgaria's social welfare budget was spent on pensions; the rest went for monthly child-care allowances and other programs. As of late 1990, the Bulgarian government provided over 4 billion leva per year to 2,300,000 pensioners—about one fourth of the entire population. To keep pace with the rising cost of living in the transition to a Western economic system, the govern-ment had to index pensions several times in 1990. By the begin-ning of 1991, some 165 leva were being added monthly to every pension, casting doubt on the long-term possibility of maintain-ing the program. The ratio of Bulgaria's pensioners to its total popu-lation was the largest in the world, almost twice that of most Western countries. Because the society was aging, some experts declared that workers should be encouraged to remain in the work force and participate actively in society much longer than had been the practice under the communist regimes.

In early 1991, in a further effort to keep pace with the rising cost of living, the Council of Ministers established a new minimum wage and new subsidy levels for all social welfare programs. Anyone who had received the old monthly minimum wage of 165 leva would now be compensated 270 leva to provide for a new minimum wage of 435 leva. This minimum wage was subsequently changed three times in 1991, peaking at 518 leva. The 1991 program also gave 242 leva to pregnant or nursing women and to those on temporary workers' disability. Child-care compensation for households with children under three years of age was raised to 90 leva, with a monthly supplement of 100 leva per child. In 1991 several cost-of-living increases were added to those categories as well. In 1991 unemployment compensation was set at 270 leva per month; students over eighteen received 130 leva per month; graduate students, 230 leva. Those payments were funded from the state budget and from enterprise salary budgets, neither of which seemed adequate to keep pace with rapidly changing prices in 1991.

Under socialism all citizens who had been awarded the title "active fighter against fascism and capitalism" for military or civilian contributions in World War II received a large pension and special privileges such as free public transportation, free medical prescriptions, and free vacations at special resorts. After much controversy, those privileges were abolished in 1990.

Health

Until the 1920s, peasants relied on traditional medicine and went to a doctor or hospital only as a last resort. Traditional healers believed that many illnesses were caused by evil spirits (*baĭane*) and could therefore be treated with magic, with chants against the spirits, with prayers, or by using medicinal herbs. The knowledge of healing herbs was highly valued in village society. For healing one could also drink, wash, or bathe in water from mineral springs, some of which were considered holy. Even in postcommunist Bulgaria, some resorted to herbal medicine or to persons with reputed extrasensory healing powers. Herbalists and "extrasenses" regained popularity in Bulgaria after the overthrow of Zhivkov. Because of the skepticism of conventional doctors, little research was done on the validity of traditional herbal medicine, but in 1991 doctors began to consider rating skilled herbalists as qualified specialists.

Beginning in 1944, Bulgaria made significant progress in increasing life expectancy and decreasing infant mortality rates. In 1986

Bulgaria's life expectancy was 68.1 years for men and 74.4 years for women. In 1939 the mortality rate for children under one year had been 138.9 per 1,000; by 1986 it was 18.2 per 1,000, and in 1990 it was 14 per 1,000, the lowest rate in Eastern Europe. The proportion of long-lived people in Bulgaria was quite large; a 1988 study cited a figure of 52 centenarians per 1 million inhabitants, most of whom lived in the Smolyan, Kŭrdzhali, and Blagoevgrad regions.

The steady demographic aging of the Bulgarian population was a concern, however. In the 1980s, the number of children in the population decreased by over 100,000. The prenatal mortality rate for 1989 was 11 per 1,000, twice that in West European countries. In 1989 the mortality rate for children of ages one to fourteen was twice as great as in Western Europe. The mortality rate for village children was more than twice the rate for city children. However, in 1990 some Bulgarian cities had mortality rates as low as 8.9 per 1,000, which compared favorably with the rates in Western Europe.

Poor conditions in maternity wards and shortages of baby needs worried new and prospective mothers. Hospital staff shortages meant that doctors and nurses were overworked and babies received scant attention. Expensive neonatal equipment was not available in every hospital, and transferral to better-equipped facilities was rare. In 1990 the standard minimum weight to ensure survival at birth was 1,000 grams, compared with the World Health Organization standard of 500 grams.

The number of medical doctors, nurses, and dentists in Bulgaria increased during the 1980s. Bulgaria had 27,750 doctors in 1988, almost 6,000 more than in 1980. This meant one doctor for every 323 Bulgarians. Some 257 hospitals were operating in 1990, with 105 beds per 1,000 people.

Like other aspects of society, health services underwent significant reform after 1989. In 1990 health officials declared that the socialist system of polyclinics in sectors serving 3,000 to 4,000 people did not satisfy the public's need for more complex diagnostic services. They claimed the system was too centralized and bureaucratic, provided too few incentives for health personnel, and lacked sufficient modern equipment and supplies. Thereafter, new emphasis was placed on allowing free choice of a family doctor and providing more general practitioners to treat families on an ongoing basis. Beginning in 1990, Bulgaria began accepting donations of money and medicine from Western countries. During the reform period, even common medicines such as aspirin were sometimes in short supply. Prices for medicines skyrocketed. Shortages of antibiotics, analgesics, dressings, sutures, and disinfectants were chronic.

In November 1989, the Council of Ministers decreed that doctors could be self-employed during their time off from their assigned clinics. Doctors could work for pay either in health facilities or in patients' homes, but with significant restrictions. When acting privately, they could not certify a patient's health or disability, issue prescriptions for free medicine, perform outpatient surgery or abortions, conduct intensive diagnostic tests, use anesthetics, or serve patients with infectious or venereal diseases. In 1990 the National Assembly extended the right of private practice to all qualified medical specialists, and private health establishments and pharmacies were legalized. Church-sponsored facilities were included in this provision. The 1990 law did not provide for a health insurance system, however, and establishment of such a system was not a high legislative priority for the early 1990s.

In 1991 the government created a National Health Council to be financed by 2.5 billion leva from the state budget plus funds from donors and payments for medical services. The goal of the new council was to create a more autonomous health system. Also in 1991, the Ministry of Health set up a Supreme Medical Council and a Pharmaceuticals Council to advise on proposed private health centers, pharmacies, and laboratories and to regulate the supply and distribution of medicine.

In 1988 the top three causes of death in Bulgaria were cardiovascular illnesses, cancer, and respiratory illnesses. An expert estimated that 88 percent of all deaths were caused by "socially significant diseases" that resulted from an unhealthy lifestyle and were thus preventable. Strokes, the most prevalent cause of death, killed a higher percentage of the population in Bulgaria than anywhere else in the world. In 1985 nearly 58,000 Bulgarians suffered strokes, and nearly 24,000 of them died. The mortality rate for strokes was especially high in northern Bulgaria, where it sometimes exceeded 300 fatalities per 100,000 persons. In villages the rate was three times as high as in the cities. Doctors cited unhealthy eating habits, smoking, alcohol abuse, and stress as lifestyle causes of the high stroke rate.

In 1990 about 35 percent of Bulgarian women and 25 percent of men were overweight. Sugar provided an average of 22 percent of the calories in Bulgarian diets, twice as much as the standard for balanced nutrition. Another 35 percent of average calories came from animal fat, also twice as much as the recommended amount. That percentage was likely much higher in the villages, where many animal products were made at home. Modernization of the food supply generally led to increased consumption of carbohydrates and fats. In contrast, the traditional Bulgarian diet emphasized dairy products, beans, vegetables, and fruits. Large quantities of bread were always a key element of the Bulgarian diet. Average salt consumption was also very high. In 1990 the average Bulgarian consumed 14.5 kilograms of bread, 4.4 kilograms of meat, 12.6 kilograms of milk and milk products, 15 eggs, and 15 kilograms of fruits and vegetables per month.

In the 1980s, Bulgaria ranked tenth in the world in per capita tobacco consumption. Tobacco consumption was growing, especially among young people. Each Bulgarian consumed 7.34 liters of alcohol per month, not including huge amounts of homemade alcoholic beverages. Between 1962 and 1982, recorded alcohol consumption increased 1.6 times.

In 1990 an estimated 35 percent of the population risked serious health problems because of environmental pollution (see Environment, this ch.). In the most polluted areas, the sickness rate increased by as much as twenty times in the 1980s. By 1990, pollution was rated the fastest-growing cause of "socially significant diseases," particularly for respiratory and digestive disorders. Doctors in the smelting center of Srednogorie found that the incidence of cancer, high blood pressure, and dental disorders had increased significantly in the 1980s.

Pollution had an especially adverse effect on the immune systems of children. In the first few years of the Giurgiu plant's operation, the number of deformed children born across the Danube in Ruse increased 144 percent. From 1985 to 1990, this number increased from 27.5 to 39.7 per 1,000. Miscarriages, stillbirths, and premature, low-weight births doubled during that period. The infant mortality rate in Srednogorie was three times the national average in 1990. Excessive lead in the soil and water at Kŭrdzhali had caused a great increase in skin and infectious diseases in children there. In 1990 environmental authorities named the village of Dolno Ezerovo, near Burgas, the "sickest village in Bulgaria" because over 60 percent of its children suffered from severe respiratory illnesses and allergies.

In 1987 Bulgarian health authorities instituted limited mandatory testing for human immunodeficiency virus (HIV), which causes acquired immune deficiency syndrome (AIDS). All prospective marriage partners, all pregnant women, and all transportation workers arriving from outside Bulgaria were required to be tested. Hemophiliacs, Bulgarian navy sailors who had traveled abroad after 1982, and students and workers visiting vacation resorts also fell under this rule. As of October 1989, some 2.5 million people in

Bulgaria, including about 66,000 foreigners, had been tested for HIV, and 81 Bulgarians were diagnosed as HIV-positive. According to government figures, six of that number had contracted AIDS. Foreigners diagnosed as HIV-positive were ordered to leave the country. Bulgaria estimated it would spend over US$4 million to treat AIDS and HIV-positive patients in 1991.

Housing

In the postwar era, housing in Bulgaria improved significantly as more and better-quality homes were built. Expectations for housing availability also increased significantly in that time, however. According to a 1990 survey, 51 percent of all Bulgarians were dissatisfied with their current housing, and 73 percent (especially young families) did not believe that their current housing would be adequate for their future needs.

In 1990 the average home in Bulgaria had three rooms and an area of 65 square meters. This small average size reflected the policy of the command economy, which was to build many small one- or two-room apartments in large prefabricated housing complexes in order to maximize the number of available housing units and meet growing demand. In 1985 some 15.6 percent of all homes had one room, 31.5 percent had two rooms, 29.6 percent had three rooms, 14.4 percent had four rooms, and only 8.9 percent had five or more rooms. As a result, 65 percent of the population averaged only half a room per family member. Only 36 percent of families with children under eighteen had a separate children's room; 65 percent used the living room as a bedroom; and 57 percent used the kitchen as a bedroom. By 1990 communal apartments were becoming rarer, however; at that time, 12 percent of families shared a kitchen with another family.

The predominance of small housing units put larger families at a disadvantage. The situation was also difficult for young couples, 60 percent of whom were forced to stay in their parents' homes after marriage. In 1990 over 40 percent of homes included two or more families or other relatives of one family. Members of three or even four generations often lived together. Traditional acceptance of the extended family contributed to this situation, but long waits for separate housing also played a critical role. In 1979 the government established a special Young Newlywed Families Fund that ensured that new families would receive at least 25 percent of new government housing. This program delivered more housing to young families in the 1980s, but waiting lists also grew longer during that period.

Living space was much more available in villages than in cities. One-room homes were unusual in villages, and villagers were much more likely to live in separate homes than in apartment complexes. Village houses usually had more rooms, but they lacked many of the modern conveniences available in city apartments.

In 1985 hot running water, a shower or bathtub, and an indoor toilet were available in only 42.4 percent of homes. Between the 1975 and 1985 censuses, the number of households with bathtubs or showers almost doubled, from 34.0 percent to 63.7 percent. Still, only 39.3 percent of villagers had a bathtub or shower, and only 7.3 percent of them had an indoor toilet. In 1990 many villages lacked a sewage system and relied on wells for water. At that time, about 30 percent of Bulgarian homes had electric heating, and 34 percent were connected to a steam central heating system.

Housing planners often overlooked the need for convenient schools, stores, and recreational facilities. (For Bulgarians, proximity generally meant fifteen minutes' walk.) On the average, 70 to 80 percent of construction funds went to constructing the housing complexes themselves, and only 20 to 30 percent went to building facilities to serve the residents of the complexes. This was especially true in Sofia, where some of the newest neighborhoods were isolated from the rest of the city.

Housing was affected by the drastic reform-period price hikes in Bulgaria. At the end of 1990, apartment owners in Sofia were offering to sell two-room apartments at between 100,000 and 200,000 leva, or to rent them for 600 leva per month. Moreover, the new economic system gave landlords the right to evict tenants for nonpayment of rent. In 1990 prospective homebuyers frustrated by the steeper housing prices established a tent city in Sofia to dramatize the threat of homelessness (see The Ferment of 1988–90, ch. 4).

Also at risk for homelessness were many Bulgarian Turks who had emigrated in 1989 but returned after the overthrow of Zhivkov. By 1991 the state had bought many of the Turks' homes and resold them; other homes were occupied illegally. In 1991 many who lost their homes in this way went through the bureaucratic process of reclaiming their property. In 1990 Sofia created a new foundation to help the homeless, especially elderly and single people, and to aid in the building and financing of homes.

Education

Before the National Revival of the mid-nineteenth century, education usually took the form of memorization of the liturgy and other religious material. Supporters of the National Revival movement were instrumental in establishing and supporting Bulgarian schools in the cities—first for boys, and later for girls as well. These activists also introduced the *chitalishta*. Often located next to a school, the *chitalishta* served as community cultural centers as well as reading rooms. The first schools, which began opening in the early nineteenth century, often did not go beyond a basic education; students wishing to continue their education had to go abroad.

The educational system established after Bulgaria gained its independence retained the same basic structure through 1989. The 1878 Temporary Law on National Schools established free compulsory education in primary school for both sexes. The schools were designed to teach reading, writing, and basic arithmetic. In practice, not everyone received that education, but the law gave the villages an incentive to open new schools. By the turn of the century, one-third of all Bulgarian villages had primary schools. In the early days, the immediate demand for a large number of teachers meant that many new teachers had little more education than their students. Later reforms specified a seven-year standard education with a curriculum based on a West European model. Some peasants, especially uneducated ones, withdrew their children from school because they believed the classes were unrelated to peasant life. This situation led to the offering of textbooks and prizes as an incentive for students from poorer families to remain in school.

Communist rule in Bulgaria brought forth a new approach to education as a means of indoctrinating Marxist theory and communist values. Literacy was promoted so that the communist-controlled press could be disseminated throughout society. New classes for both adults and children aimed at providing as many as possible with a high-school education and abolishing illiteracy. Schools switched their focus from liberal arts to technical training and introduced a curriculum modeled on that of the Soviet Union. Russian language study was introduced for all, from kindergartners to adults who had already completed their education. Copies of *Pravda*, the primary newspaper of the Communist Party of the Soviet Union, were distributed even in isolated villages. After the overthrow of Zhivkov, however, English became the most studied foreign language in Bulgaria, and the study of Russian declined dramatically.

In 1979 Zhivkov introduced a sweeping educational reform, claiming that Marxist teachings on educating youth were still not being applied completely. Zhivkov therefore created Unified Secondary Polytechnical Schools (*Edinna sredna politekhnicheska uchilishta,* ESPU), in which all students would receive the same general education. The system united previously separate specialized middle schools in a single, twelve-grade program heavily emphasizing technical subjects. In 1981 a national program introduced computers to most of the ESPUs. The change produced a chaotic situation in which teaching plans and programs had to be completely overhauled and new textbooks issued to reflect the new educational emphasis. This project proved unworkable, and by 1985 new specialized schools again were being established (see table 10, Appendix).

The fall of Zhivkov resulted in a complete restructuring of the country's educational system. In retrospect Bulgarian educators recognized that the socialist way of educating was not only bureaucratic, boring, and impersonal, but also led to disregard for the rights of the individual, intolerance of the opinions of others, and aggressive behavior. The centralized system with its regional hierarchies was therefore scrapped in favor of a system of educational councils in which every 400 teachers could elect a delegate to the National Council of Teachers. The first goal of the new organization was to depoliticize the schools in cooperation with the Ministry of Public Education.

In 1991 the Bulgarian educational system consisted of three types of schools: state, municipal, and private (including religious). The grade levels were primary (first to fourth grade), basic (fifth to seventh grade), and secondary (eighth to twelfth grade). Children began first grade at age six or seven and were required to attended school until age sixteen. Parents also had the option of enrolling their children in kindergarten at age five. Secondary school students had the choice of studying for three years at professional-vocational schools or for four years at technical schools or general high schools. Religious schools operated only on the high-school level. Specialized high schools taught foreign languages, mathematics, and music; admittance to them was by special entrance exams. Special programs for gifted and talented children began as early as the fifth grade. Special schools also operated for handicapped children. Children suffering from chronic illnesses could receive their schooling in a hospital or sanatorium.

Prior to the postcommunist reform era, about 25,000 students dropped out every year before reaching their sixteenth birthday; another 25,000 failed to advance to the next grade. Under the new system, parents could be fined 500 to 1,000 leva if their children failed to attend school; fines also were levied for pupils retained in grade for an extra year.

Public opinion on the educational reform focused mainly on depolitization. By the 1990–91 school year, new textbooks had been introduced in many subjects, but many of them were not completely free of socialist rhetoric. A first-grade mathematics textbook published in 1990 contained the following exercise: "Count how many words there are in this sentence: 'I am grateful to the Party, for it leads my country to beautiful, radiant life and vigilantly protects us from war.'" A newly published music book contained songs about the party, a communist youth organization, and Lenin. Many teachers likewise continued to espouse the communist rhetoric in which their profession had been long and firmly indoctrinated. In late 1990, about 50,000 Sofia University students demonstrated against poor education and against continued requirements to attend courses in Marxism. Their protest caused the university to eliminate compulsory political indoctrination courses. The 1991 Law on Public Education declared that "no political activity is allowed in the system of public education."

Depolitization was expected to be a slow process because of the extent to which the schools had been politicized before 1990. At the end of 1990, over 90 percent of all teachers were still members of the Bulgarian Socialist (formerly Communist) Party. For this reason, the Law on Public Education prohibited teachers from becoming members of political parties for a period of three years, beginning in 1991. Because the Zhivkov regime had tinkered often with Bulgaria's educational system, longtime teachers had developed a cynicism toward reform of any type. This attitude hampered the removal of the old socialist structures from the educational system.

Some students married and began families while they were still in school, and two-student families were not uncommon. Such families often depended on help from parents because of their low income and because of a shortage of student family housing. By 1990 most Bulgarian students worked in their free time, unlike their predecessors in the 1970s and early 1980s.

Reform also reached higher education. In 1990 a new law on academic freedom emphasized the concept of an intellectual market in which universities, teachers, and students must maintain high performance levels to stay competitive. The law gave every institution of higher learning the right to manage its teaching and research activities without government interference. This right included control over curriculum, number of students, standards for student admissions and teacher hirings, training and organization of faculty, and the level of contact with other institutions of higher learning in Bulgaria and abroad. Students received the right to choose their own professors. The higher education law was criticized for withholding students' rights and because the legislature had failed to consult students in the law's formulation.

In 1991 experts evaluated the state university system as weak in critically needed technical fields of study. The availability of interested students was also questioned. In the 1990–91 school year, no graduate students with enterprise scholarships majored in subjects such as computer systems, artificial intelligence systems, or ecology and environmental protection. Graduate programs in critical nontechnical fields such as management economics, marketing, production management, and finance also had no students.

After the overthrow of Zhivkov, France and Germany made early commitments to help Bulgaria carry out educational reforms. In 1991 the United States began planning a new American college in Blagoevgrad, where students would be taught in English using American educational methods. The first 200 students were to include 160 Bulgarians, 20 students from neighboring European countries, and 20 Americans majoring in Balkan studies. The University of Maine was to supply the teachers. Plans called for business and economics to be the major areas of concentration. Affordability was a potential barrier to participation in this plan by Bulgarian students; the cost was low by American standards, but far above the average Bulgarian's price range. And the tuition-free Bulgarian university system was expected to lure many qualified students from the new university. Nevertheless, Western education assistance was an important symbolic step in moving the social institutions of Bulgaria into the European mainstream, from which they had been isolated for forty-five years.

* * *

Because the societal change stimulated in Bulgaria by the process of democratization is likely to continue through the 1990s, translations of the Bulgarian press are an invaluable source of current information. A wide variety of articles and broadcasts on social topics, as well as government documents and laws, is translated in the Foreign Broadcast Information Service's *Daily Report: East Europe* and the Joint Publication Research Service's *JPRS Report: East Europe*. Amnesty International's *Bulgaria: Imprisonment of Ethnic Turks* is an impartial source of information on the Turks and other minorities during the assimilation campaign of the 1980s. Hugh Poulton's *The Balkans: Minorities and States in Conflict* includes material on ethnic policy and regional issues after the overthrow of Zhivkov. *Kak Zhiveem* (How We Live) is a new Bulgarian-language sociological magazine that includes Western-style surveys on topics such as housing and the standard of living. *Bulgarien,* volume six in the German series of southeast European handbooks, offers chapter-length treatment of most aspects of society, including education, minorities, population, and religion; some articles are in English, most are in German. (For further information and complete citations, see Bibliography.)

Chapter 3. The Economy

A potter, one of many artisans practicing their trade in modern Bulgaria

FROM THE END OF WORLD WAR II until widespread revolution in Eastern Europe swept aside most communist governments in 1989, the Bulgarian Communist Party (BCP) exerted complete economic control in Bulgaria. The party's ascent to power in 1944 had marked the beginning of radical economic change for Bulgaria. After World War II, Bulgaria followed the Soviet model of economic development more closely than any other East Bloc country. The new regime shifted much of the labor force from the countryside to the city to provide workers for new large-scale industrial complexes. At the same time, the focus of Bulgarian international trade shifted from Central Europe to Eastern Europe.

These new policies resulted in impressive initial rates of growth. But this was partly because the country was starting from a low level of economic development. Throughout the postwar period, economic progress also was assisted substantially by a level of internal and external political stability unseen in other East European countries during the same period and unprecedented in modern Bulgarian history.

Nonetheless, beginning in the early 1960s low capital and labor productivity and expensive material inputs plagued the Bulgarian economy. With disappointing rates of growth came a high degree of economic experimentation. This experimentation took place within the socialist economic framework, however, and it never approached a market-based economy.

In the late 1980s, continuing poor economic performance brought new economic hardship. By that time, the misdirection and irrationality of BCP economic policies had become quite clear. Finally, on November 10, 1989, a popular movement toppled Todor Zhivkov, long-time party leader and head of state, and orthodox communist dictatorship ended. But unlike the communist parties in most other East European states, the BCP retained majority power after the transition in Bulgaria by winning the first free national elections in June 1990. By that time, however, changes in party leadership and reduction of the BCP's power base permitted economic reorientation toward a market system. This difficult transition combined with political instability to seriously worsen economic conditions during 1990.

Bulgaria's success in transforming its economy from central planning to a market-based system remained unmeasured in 1991. Undoubtedly, any form of Bulgarian government faced a daunting

117

task at that point. Because its financial and productive resources had been allocated ineffectively for many years, the economy urgently needed major reforms. The manufacturing sector was uncompetitive in world markets, was technologically outmoded, and consumed energy and materials at enormously wasteful rates. The agricultural sector, once the most productive sector of the Bulgarian economy, had degenerated to the point that the country could scarcely feed its own people. A new trade regime with traditional partners would strain already low hard currency reserves, restricting access to raw materials and sophisticated technology. External and internal debt was enormous when Zhivkov fell. Inflation was high, environmental problems were severe, and skilled labor was insufficient.

Several factors complicate the quantification of socialist economies from a capitalist perspective. Prices in socialist economies serve primarily an accounting function; they do not reflect relative scarcities and demand for a product as they do in capitalist economies. Hence, comparisons of value indicators are difficult. In addition, some socialist statistics simply are calculated differently. For example, the socialist equivalent of national income, referred to as net material product (NMP—see Glossary), excludes the value of most services, including government, that are unrelated to physical production.

Accurate assessment of Bulgarian economic policies and performance under communist regimes also is complicated by incomplete, inaccurate, or misleading statistics. Some Western economists have attempted, however, to extrapolate data based on a combination of Bulgarian statistics, various economic assumptions, and statistical techniques.

Resource Base

Bulgaria is relatively poor in both quantity and quality of natural resources. This situation has been an important factor in planning the national economy and foreign trade. The primary indigenous mineral resources are coal, copper, lead, zinc, and iron ore.

Coal and Minerals

Lignite, by far the most prevalent form of coal, is mined chiefly in the Maritsa-zapad (West Maritsa) and Maritsa-iztok (East Maritsa) sections of the Maritsa Basin (see fig. 10). The main source of other grades of brown coal is the Bobov Dol deposit in the Rila Mountains of southwest Bulgaria. There is little bituminous coal in the country. Copper is mined chiefly in the Sredna Gora (central hills) in the western Balkans, and at Chelopets in south-central Bulgaria. There are also large deposits of lead, zinc, and iron ore,

the largest of which are at Kremikovtsi. Bulgaria became self-sufficient in the production of pig iron in 1987. Manganese, uranium, gold, salt, and chromium also are mined. Small amounts of oil are extracted offshore in the Black Sea and inland near Pleven.

Agricultural Resources

In 1987 approximately 56 percent of Bulgaria's total land mass of 11,055,000 hectares was used for agriculture. Of that total, 3,825,000 hectares, or 35 percent of the total land mass, was arable. Although natural conditions are very good for some crops, not all of the land is ideal for agricultural purposes. Large portions of the western uplands are suitable only for tobacco and vegetable cultivation. Grain fields on the rolling plain to the north of the Balkan Mountains receive limited rainfall and experience periodic droughts.

Environmental Problems

Although Bulgaria has had serious environmental problems for some time, they were not openly discussed until the overthrow of Zhivkov. Ecological groups were at the forefront of anti-Zhivkov demonstrations in 1989, when an all-European ecology conference focused world attention on Sofia. After acknowledging the problem, post-Zhivkov policy makers rated degradation of the air, water, and soil as one of the most serious problems facing Bulgaria. In April 1990, the Ministry of Public Health declared the cities of Asenovgrad, Dimitrovgrad, Kŭrdzhali, Panagyurishte, Plovdiv, Ruse, and Vratsa ecologically endangered regions and announced that residents of these regions would be given medical examinations. But after forty years of touting heavy industry as the pathway to national advancement, Bulgaria could not easily remedy the intense pollution emitted by chemical plants in Ruse and Dimitrovgrad or the copper smelters at Srednogorie without further damaging its already shaky economy. Likewise, the Kozloduy Nuclear Power Plant on the Maritsa River, provider of over 20 percent of the country's electric power but a persistent emitter of radiation, could not be closed without severe impact on the economy. Radiation from the 1986 Chernobyl' accident in the Soviet Union also remained an environmental hazard in 1991 (See Environment, ch. 2).

Labor Force

Because of a low birth rate, labor shortages began to appear in Bulgaria in the 1980s. Then in 1989, deportation of 310,000 ethnic Turks created critical shortages in certain economic sectors. The dislocation caused by the large-scale economic reform that began in 1990 introduced high rates of unemployment and social insecurity to a system that nominally had no unemployment under the central planning regime. A period of protracted readjustment of labor to enterprise needs was expected to begin in 1991.

Factors of Availability

The total labor force in Bulgaria was 4.078 million in 1988. Of that total, 35.9 percent were classified as industrial workers, 19 percent as agricultural workers, and 18.9 percent as service workers. In 1985 some 56 percent of the population was of working age (16 to 59 years old for men and 16 to 54 for women); 22.9 percent were under working age, and 21.1 percent were over working age. These figures indicate that the population had aged demographically since 1946, when 30 percent of the population was under the working age and only 12 percent was over. Small growth rates and occasional declines of the Bulgarian labor force increasingly inhibited economic growth in the 1980s. The meager growth in the labor force was caused primarily by a birthrate that began declining before World War II.

Declining population growth did not affect Bulgarian economic planning and performance for a number of years. In the 1950s and 1960s, the expanding labor requirements of industrial growth were accommodated by a steady influx of peasant labor from the countryside and by the nationalization of artisan shops in 1951. This migration slowed, however, and complaints of an industrial labor shortage were common by the late 1960s. The situation was exacerbated in 1974 when the government reduced the work week from 48 to 42.5 hours (see Agriculture, this ch.). By the early 1980s, Bulgaria's urban working-age population had begun to decline in absolute terms. Then in May 1989, ethnic strife caused thousands of ethnic Turks to leave Bulgaria for Turkey. In August Turkish authorities finally closed the border, but only after 310,000 ethnic Turks had left the country, taking with them a substantial chunk of the Bulgarian work force. In addition, a significant "brain drain" threatened in 1990 when large numbers of young, highly educated Bulgarians applied to leave the country. In the first four months of 1990, at a time when the country desperately needed its professional class to restructure society and the economy, 550,000 such applications were received.

Labor statistics reflect a distinct change of economic priorities from agriculture to industry under communist regimes. From 1948 to 1988, the shares of labor in industry and agriculture shifted dramatically. Industry's share rose from 7.9 to 38 percent, while agriculture's share fell from 82.1 to 19.3 percent. Among other sectors, in 1988 construction, transportation and communications, and trade respectively accounted for 8.3, 6.7, and 8.7 percent of employment.

Labor and Economic Reform

Under communist rule, unemployment officially was nonexistent. Like many other Soviet-style economies, however, the Bulgarian system included much underemployment and hoarding of surplus workers, particularly in industry. While in power, the BCP set wage and work norms. Average annual earnings rose from 2,185 leva (for value of the lev, see Glossary) in 1980 to 2,953 leva in 1988. Earnings were highest in the research, state administration, construction, transport, and finance sectors, in that order. Agriculture and forestry were among the lowest paid sectors.

After the overthrow of Zhivkov, reasonable use of industrial capacity was expected to maintain a tight labor market for the foreseeable future because the labor force had ceased to grow. Women already accounted for approximately 50 percent of the labor force in 1988; therefore, little additional growth was expected from that part of the population. Similarly, little growth was expected from among voluntarily employed pensioners and invalids. However, the tight labor supply was not the most pressing concern of the first post-Zhivkov economic planners. The economic transformation from centralized planning to a market economy meant increased influence by market factors on wage and unemployment rates in the future. This transformation also made high unemployment likely as state enterprises closed and generation of goods and services shifted to an expanded private sector. But this intermediate dislocation was thought necessary to achieve correlation between wages and productivity.

Unemployment, which stood at 72,000 at the beginning of 1991, was expected to jump to at least 250,000 by the end of that year because of the planned transition to a market structure. In 1990 the interim government of Petŭr Mladenov created a national labor exchange to assist in placing unemployed workers. Unemployment assistance remained a state responsibility, but the state had very little money for this purpose in 1991. Plans called for eventual contribution by private employers to a designated unemployment fund.

Economic Structure and Control Mechanisms

Until late 1989, Bulgaria had a command economy based on centralized planning rather than on market forces. In such a system, crucial economic decisions such as allocation of output, rates of expansion of various sectors, values of goods and services, and the exchange rate of the national currency were made administratively, not by the market. Bulgaria's faithful adherence to the Soviet model of economic planning included rapid industrialization, large-scale investments, and other resource allocation to heavy industry at the expense of light industry and agriculture, higher rates of spending for capital investment than for consumption purchases, and forced nationalization of industry and collectivization of agriculture.

The Centrally Planned Economy

Proponents of centrally planned economies (CPEs) maintained that the advantages of such systems far outweighed the disadvantages. They believed that in many respects economic competition wasted society's resources. In other words, what Marx called the "anarchy of the market" led producers and consumers to expend resources in activities that became unnecessary when they worked in harmony rather than in competition. Planning could give priority to social goals over economic ones. Should the government decide that the development of health professionals was important to society, for example, it could earmark funds for that purpose. Proponents of CPEs also claimed that they could insulate their economies from the ups and downs of the business cycle, a phenomenon that Western economies never have been able to avoid. Theoretically, CPEs were designed to be immune to economic (and social) losses such as reduced output and unemployment associated with economic downturns. (As their national economies became more interrelated with international markets, however, CPE proponents admitted the difficulty of isolating themselves from swings in world economic conditions.) Another theoretical advantage was that economic decisions could be based on long-range goals because the financial losses of any individual enterprise or industry could be offset by profits in other areas of the economy. And, since the organization of the entire industrial and agricultural base was determined administratively, economies of scale could easily be incorporated into the planning process.

Western economists were generally critical of the CPE, however. Their criticisms had two essential components. First, central economic planners often were unable to plan an economy efficiently; and second, even when they could plan well, they were unable to achieve the goals they planned. These general assertions proved true regarding specific aspects of Bulgaria's command economy, and they had ramifications for efforts to reorganize that economy in the 1990s.

The CPE induced enterprises to seek low production targets, concealing productive capacity and never overfulfilling the plan by too much, lest higher targets be set in the next plan. The result was underutilized resources. Plans tended to stress quantity over quality. Simply requiring a particular level of output was insufficient if that output were of such poor quality that no one bought it, or if there were no need for such a product in the beginning. The consumer had no effective control over the producer when quality was low, and the artificial price structure prevented price signals from alerting producers to consumer preferences. Also, because enterprises were judged on their fulfillment of the plan, producers geared production levels for satisfying the plan, not consumers.

The CPE could induce technical progress from above, but it could not stimulate it from below. The plan discouraged enterprise innovation, because innovation meant interrupting current production, hence jeopardizing plan fulfillment. The system also encouraged waste and hoarding of fixed and working capital, and the wage system failed to encourage workers to work harder or managers to economize on labor. Under Zhivkov, Bulgaria attempted to deal with these problems by a series of reforms in both industry and agriculture. These reforms included alternately centralizing and decentralizing economic management; adding and deleting economic ministries and committees; revising the economic indicators for plan fulfillment; and encouraging or discouraging elements of private enterprise. Despite such experimentation, however, Bulgaria remained faithful to the general Soviet model for over four decades. In the years after the end of communist rule, the CPE remained the predominant structural element in the Bulgarian economy, especially in large enterprise management.

The Planning System

Prior to 1990, the planning hierarchy in Bulgaria included several levels. The ultimate economic authority was the BCP. The party determined general economic policies, identified economic reforms and their structure, and monitored economic activity. Planning and control were the responsibility of the Council of Ministers, which was roughly equivalent to a Western cabinet. The most important planning committee within the Council of Ministers was the State Planning Committee (SPC). Within the Council of Ministers were specialized economic ministries, such as the Ministry of Finance and the Ministry of Foreign Trade, and various governmental committees and commissions. The composition and authority of the ministries underwent frequent change. In 1986, for example, six ministries with economic powers were eliminated and five cabinet-level "voluntary associations" were formed. The aftermath of these changes, however, showed few new power relationships. In the later Zhivkov years, the prime responsibilities of ministry-level agencies included forecasting development of their industries, assessing development bottlenecks, and generally overseeing state development policy. However, the ministries were not to participate actively in planning. That was a function of the associations.

The associations, also known as trusts, were an intermediary organization between the ministries and the lowest level of the planning hierarchy, the enterprise. The association integrated production, research and development, design, construction, and foreign trade functions. Unlike associations in the Soviet Union, which were merely an intermediary link in the chain of economic command, Bulgarian associations retained several essential decision-making prerogatives and were in direct contact with centers of economic power such as the SPC, the Ministry of Finance, and the Bulgarian National Bank (BNB). At the bottom of the economic hierarchy, enterprises were distinct economic entities that operated under an independent accounting system. They were expected to earn a planned amount of profit, a portion of which went to the state as a profits tax.

In the Bulgarian command economy, almost all economic activity was directed toward plan fulfillment. Economic directives were outlined extensively in the plans, which were not merely guidelines but binding, legal documents. The best known of these was the Five-Year Plan, although planning was done for longer and shorter periods as well. Most important for the day-to-day operations of enterprises were the annual and monthly plans.

One of the most important tasks of central planning was what was referred to as *material balances*—planning for correspondence between supply and demand of goods. At the draft plan stage, this required that supply (planned output, available stocks, and planned imports) equal demand (domestic demand and exports) for every industry. When demand exceeded supply, planners could increase planned output, increase imports, or reduce domestic demand. The SPC usually favored the last alternative. This manipulation limited the flow of inputs to low-priority industrial branches, which most often made consumer items, resulting in shortages of those goods.

The party began the planning process by providing priorities and output targets for critical commodities to the SPC, which reconciled them with required inputs. A draft plan then was created by a process of negotiation and information exchange up and down the planning hierarchy. After negotiating with the SPC on targets and resources and formulating specific guidelines, the associations then negotiated with their individual enterprises to establish final figures. The output targets then went back to the SPC for a final negotiation with the associations.

The final version of the plan was submitted to the Council of Ministers for approval or modification, after which the approved targets were sent down the hierarchy to the individual firms. Thus enterprises were informed of their binding norms for a planning period, including volume and mix of output, procurement limits, level of state investment, foreign currency earnings, foreign currency limits for imports, and wage rates. An important element of the plan fulfillment stage was manipulation of resources by ministries and the SPC to ensure fulfillment of priority targets and minimize bottlenecks. Occasionally, reforms allowed enterprises rather than higher echelons to make many of these decisions. For most of the communist era, however, this was not the case.

Economic Policy and Performance

Bulgarian postwar economic development can be divided into four phases: the revolutionary period (1944 through 1948); the development of socialism (1949 through 1960); the age of intermittent reform (1961 through 1989); and the transformation to a market economy (beginning in 1990).

Postwar Economic Policy

After the BCP came to power in 1944, the transition to socialism began slowly. Before World War II, the Bulgarian economy had been agrarian and decentralized; as a result, the industrial base was relatively undeveloped (see The Interwar Economy, ch. 1). Following the Soviet model, the BCP first sought control over as many facets of the economy as possible. Thus, restructuring included collectivizing agriculture, confiscating private enterprises, nationalizing industry, and enacting various fiscal and monetary measures.

In the 1940s, the BCP viewed the agricultural sector as a major obstacle to the transformation of the economy. Although collectivization proceeded slowly at first, state power in the agricultural markets was quickly established by nationalizing internal and foreign commodity trade. To accomplish this, the BCP used the wartime organizations that had overseen distribution of major crops.

Industry continued to decentralize from 1944 until 1947. In those years, the majority of labor leaving the military and the farms entered small factories and unmechanized artisan shops. These small enterprises were quite the opposite of the modern, large-scale industry that the BCP was committed to creating. Small enterprises also competed with state enterprises for scarce raw materials and skilled labor. Labor discipline also was a major problem during this phase; unexcused absences, sporadic strikes, and high labor turnover plagued the new state enterprises. In September 1947, a decision to accelerate the nationalization of industry was taken at a meeting of the Communist Information Bureau (Cominform— see Glossary). As a result, in December 1947 trained groups of party members entered all the approximately 6,100 remaining private

127

enterprises, seized their capital, and announced their immediate nationalization. This act effectively erased Bulgaria's small class of private industrial entrepreneurs. Also in 1947, government monopolies were established over all items of retail trade. By the end of 1948, 85 percent of the means of production were run by the state.

Although Bulgaria had few private banks when the BCP came to power, by December 1947 those few were merged with the BNB. The BCP also enacted a series of fiscal and monetary measures to gain control over Bulgaria's financial resources by the end of 1947. Monetary reform froze all bank accounts over 20,000 leva, and a tax was imposed on the remaining accounts. These actions reduced the money supply by two-thirds. The new policy also levied high taxes on private income and high profits to absorb any potential new deposits.

This first phase of postwar economic development included a tentative Two-Year Plan (1947–48) that foreshadowed later policies. Aimed principally at speedy recovery from wartime stress, the program began large-scale industrialization and electrification; it sought to raise industrial production by 67 percent and agricultural production by 34 percent over prewar levels. The first plan disproportionately allocated funds away from agriculture and encountered severe organizational and technical problems, mistakes by inexperienced management, and shortages of energy and production equipment—problems that would continue in ensuing development phases.

The First Five-Year Plans

The next phase of Bulgarian postwar economic development included the First Five-Year Plan. This plan made an important contribution to the pattern of Bulgaria's socialist economic development by creating the institutional apparatus for long-term industrial planning. Already in 1945, the wartime Directorate for Civilian Mobilization had been replaced by a Supreme Economic Council that extended the previous organization's authority over resource allocation. Now the state's existing economic ministries were subdivided into one ministry for each branch of production. By January 1948, a separate and politically powerful State Production Committee (SPC) was established. By October 1948, representatives of the new SPC and the existing Main Directorate for Statistics had set out the criteria for calculating plan fulfillment.

The announced targets for the First Five-Year Plan (1949–53) confirmed the economic priorities indicated by the previous Two-Year Plan. Agriculture was to receive 17 percent of new investment and industry 47 percent. Gross industrial output was to grow by 119 percent, primarily because of a 220 percent increase in heavy industry. Light industry and agriculture were to raise output by 75 and 59 percent, respectively. The rapid collectivization and mechanization of agriculture were expected to achieve the last target while freeing labor for industry, construction, and transportation. Because about 25 percent of the country's national income was invested in the economic infrastructure, the standard of living remained low.

In 1952 the plan was declared fulfilled a year ahead of schedule, but statistics on the period were too incomplete and contradictory to evaluate its actual results. Substantial bottlenecks existed in material inputs and outputs. Agriculture received less investment than planned (only 13 percent) and showed no growth through the period (see table 12, Appendix). The effect of low agricultural output rippled through other sectors of the economy, hindering production in related industries. Substantial material and technical aid came from the Soviet Union, but with a steep price: Bulgaria was expected to sell products to the Soviet market at below-market prices, and the arrogance of Soviet economic advisers caused serious resentment.

Continuing problems with excessive labor turnover forced the regime to cut back the targets for heavy industry in the Second Five-Year Plan (1953–57), and average annual industrial growth fell from 20.7 to 12.7 percent during that period. This was the first of several dramatic swings that characterized Bulgarian economic development throughout the postwar period. The average annual growth rate of agriculture increased from negative 0.9 percent to 4.9 percent in the Second Five-Year Plan, but the same indicator for the overall NMP dropped from 8.4 to 7.8 percent. The industrial share of the NMP exceeded that of agriculture for the first time in this period.

Two important economic events occurred at the Seventh Party Congress of the BCP, which met in mid-1958. The party declared that Bulgaria was the first country besides the Soviet Union to achieve full collectivization of agriculture (estimates put the figure at 92 percent at this time), and it announced the goals for the Third Five-Year Plan. That plan, which began in 1958, set relatively moderate initial quotas that included substantially more production of consumer goods. In 1959, however, a BCP decision to make a "Great Leap Forward" (borrowed by the press from Mao Zedong's concurrent program for the Chinese economy) drastically raised quotas: by 1965 industrial output was to be three to four times the 1957 level, and by 1961 agriculture was to produce three times as much as it had in 1957. To achieve the latter goal, agriculture was again reorganized. Amalgamation of collective farms cut their number by 70 percent, after which average farm acreage was second only to the Soviet Union among countries in Eastern Europe. The grandiose Zhivkov Theses, as the quota program came to be known, were tempered noticeably by 1961, when the economy's inability to achieve such growth was obvious to all.

Meanwhile, throughout the late 1950s urban unemployment had been a major problem. The new collectivization drive brought another wave of peasant migration to urban centers. Compounding this problem was a cutback in Soviet imports of industrial inputs, which created some excess capacity in heavy industry. Thus, the intensified industrialization of the Third Five-Year Plan also aimed at absorbing surplus labor.

Trade relations with the Soviet Union and Eastern Europe also played a large role in the investment priorities of the Third Five-Year Plan. Food processing and agriculture were earmarked for greatest growth because these sectors, together with chemical fertilizers and small electric equipment, were now areas of Bulgarian responsibility in the plans of the Council for Mutual Economic Assistance (Comecon—see Glossary) for greater East European trade. After a reduction in 1955, Bulgaria faced greatly increased export obligations to the USSR, Czechoslovakia, and the German Democratic Republic (East Germany) in the late 1950s. The latter two could provide badly needed industrial machinery in return, and the USSR provided vital raw materials and energy.

The party leadership initially resolved to fulfill the third plan, like the first, within three or four years; although none of its goals were reached, the party declared fulfillment in 1960, and Zhivkov survived the popular disillusionment and economic upheaval caused by his totally unrealistic theses. At that point, the twelve years of the second phase of Bulgarian postwar economic development had wrought major structural changes in the Bulgarian economy. Industry's share of the NMP increased from 23 percent to 48 percent as agriculture's share fell from 59 percent to 27 percent. By 1960 the value produced by heavy industry matched that of light industry, although food processing for export also grew rapidly. Throughout the second phase, budget expenditures consisted primarily of reinvestment in sectors given initial priority. Meanwhile, the completion of collectivization had shifted 678,000 peasants, about 20 percent of the active labor force, into industrial jobs. The average annual increase in industrial employment peaked at 11.5 percent between 1955 and 1960.

The Era of Experimentation and Reform

The first full five-year plans proved the Bulgarian system's capacity for extensive growth in selected branches of industry, based on massive infusions of labor and capital. In the first postwar decades, that system was much more successful in reaching goals than were the command economies in the other East European countries, largely because Bulgaria had started with a much more primitive industrial infrastructure. By the early 1960s, however, changes to the system were obviously needed to achieve sustained growth in all branches of production, including agriculture. Specific incentives to reform were shortages of labor and energy and the growing importance of foreign trade in the "thaw" years of the mid-1960s. Consequently, in 1962 the Fourth Five-Year Plan began an era of economic reform that brought a series of new approaches to the old goal of intensive growth.

Industrial Decentralization

In industry the "New System of Management" was introduced in 1964 and lasted until 1968. This approach intended to streamline economic units and make enterprise managers more responsible for performance. In June 1964, about fifty industrial enterprises, mostly producers of textiles and other consumer goods, were placed under the new system. Wages, bonuses, and investment funds were tied to enterprise profits, up to 70 percent of which could be retained. Outside investment funds were to come primarily from bank credit rather than the state budget. In 1965 state subsidies still accounted for 63 percent of enterprise investment funds, however, while 30 percent came from retained enterprise earnings and only 7 percent from bank credits. By 1970 budget subsidies accounted for only 27 percent of investment funds, while bank credits jumped to 39 percent, and retained enterprise earnings reached 34 percent. The number of compulsory targets for the Fourth Five-Year Plan was cut to four: physical output, investment funds, input utilization, and foreign trade targets. The pilot enterprises did very well, earning profits that were double the norm. By 1967 two-thirds of industrial production came from firms under the new system, which by that time had embraced areas outside consumer production.

Another distinctive feature of the Bulgarian economy during the 1960s was the high level of net capital investment (total investment minus depreciation). The average of 12 percent from 1960 to 1970 was the highest in all of Eastern Europe. As in the past, investment in heavy industry received the lion's share—over 80 percent of total industrial investment. Capital accumulation (net investment plus net inventories) averaged 29 percent from 1960 to 1970, also a very high level.

Industrial Recentralization

Before the end of the 1960s, however, Bulgarian economic planning moved back toward the conventional CPE approach. Many Western analysts attributed the Bulgarian retreat from the reforms of the 1960s to tension caused by the Soviet invasion of Czechoslovakia in 1968. International events may well have played a role, but the timing of the retreat and the invasion suggest another component: dissatisfaction among the BCP elite with the results and ideological implications of the reform. For example, in July 1968, one month before the invasion of Czechoslovakia, Bulgaria's unorthodox, three-tiered pricing system was eliminated. The party leadership had never accepted the concept of free and flexible pricing for some products, which was an important Bulgarian departure from centralized planning in the 1960s. Resistance to reform was further encouraged by a series of cases in which major enterprise directors used newly decentralized financial resources to line their own pockets.

Despite the general retreat from reform, two important measures remained intact, one each in agriculture and industry. The first involved new operating procedures introduced on the larger collective farms in the early 1960s. To better exploit the new equipment introduced during the consolidation of the late 1950s, farms were assigned more agronomists and labor was specialized by establishing fixed brigades. Production target negotiations between the Ministry of State Planning and the agricultural collectives also were simplified.

The industrial reform that survived retrenchment in 1968 gave associations, not ministries, responsibility to supervise the new system of supply contracts between enterprises. This system continued to grow, with prices determined on the basis of enterprise bargaining rather than ministerial fiat. Interenterprise allocations clearly functioned more efficiently with this arrangement.

Larger Economic Units

Just as most reforms were being rescinded, the BCP began the last phase of postwar agricultural restructuring. Prompted by the labor shortage, the new streamlining of collective farms that began in 1969 introduced the so-called agricultural-industrial complex (*agrompromishlen kompleks*—APK). The new structure was to industrialize agricultural production, boost the value-added component in Bulgarian exports by processing more agricultural goods, and raise the food supply to cities without diverting labor back from industry. In the late 1960s, relatively poor agricultural performance

*Craftsman working at lathe,
Plovdiv
Courtesy Sam and Sarah Stulberg*

*Spice vendor, Bachkovski Manastir
Courtesy Sam and Sarah Stulberg*

under the existing structure had prevented those goals from being reached.

The idea of combining existing enterprises into a smaller, presumably more manageable number of units spread quickly from agriculture to industry. By the end of the 1970s, the number of associations into which industrial enterprises were grouped was reduced by half. The sixty-four new, larger associations were granted the authority to make decisions for their enterprises about new investments, bank credits, and budget subsidies. Within an association, the larger enterprises (called subsidiaries) still could sign their own supply contracts and maintain their own bank accounts, but they ceased to be legal entities. Smaller enterprises (called subdivisions) became fully dependent on their association.

The main advantage of this streamlined organization was seen as economy of scale through increased specialization and a simplified flow of information. Associations also were assumed to be better able to make investment decisions and oversee material and labor distribution than either a small number of ministries or a large number of enterprises. The new structure would link specific industrial enterprises with scientific institutes in the same way as the agricultural complexes had linked them.

These reforms proved disappointing. Reformed planning techniques continued to leave unused industrial capacity, and quality control failed to improve. Both Western and domestic customers remained dissatisfied with the quality of many Bulgarian manufactures. New planning indicators that set norms for cost reduction actually reduced quality in a number of cases. Individual members of institutes could not convey their ideas to associations or ministries, where decisions to import or to invest in new technology were made. Thus the new framework only accentuated the dangers of socialist monopoly. Party meetings and the press criticized monopolistic abuses resulting from irrational decisions at the top and poor implementation of rational policies at the enterprise level. By the end of the 1970s, a new set of reforms was prescribed.

The New Economic Model

Initiated in 1981, the next program of reforms was designated the New Economic Model (NEM). This program involved both agricultural complexes and industrial enterprises. Goals of the NEM included updating the technical infrastructure of Bulgarian industry and improving the quality of Bulgarian exports to raise hard-currency income. Centralized planning now was relegated to setting gross profits and overseeing the national scientific program. In

1982–83 the NEM's principal instruments were financial incentives and accounting regulations aimed at all levels of management, but especially at the smallest unit of labor, the brigade. Brigades, each containing thirty to fifty workers, now would set labor and material input levels and dispose of finished products. In an effort to remedy the chronic distribution problems of the central economy, higher economic institutions became financially accountable for damage inflicted by their decisions on subordinate levels.

Several important initiatives were launched in 1978. The long-standing limits on enterprise investment were lifted. In their place, a new investment plan was based on the enterprises' contractual obligations and credits with the BNB. The bank monitored the cash balance of enterprise contracts with customers and suppliers, granting credits only when required. Three separate reinvestment funds received first claim on the net income of the enterprise. Although budgetary subsidies were not eliminated, the NEM directives assigned responsibility for financial losses to all levels of enterprises. Self-financing became the watchword for all economic organizations.

Another major change eliminated the automatic first claim of salaries and wages on gross enterprise income. This meant that wages could rise only after an increase in labor productivity, and then only by 50 percent of that increase. Moreover, management salaries could be cut by as much as 20 percent if the complex or enterprise failed to meet its norms for production and productivity. The formula for sanctions against management salaries changed several times. Finally, binding performance criteria were limited to five financial indicators for agricultural complexes and industrial associations, and to four for individual enterprises. Profit criteria were set only for the complexes or associations. Complexes and associations were given explicit freedom to sign their own contracts with suppliers and customers at home and abroad.

The BNB was granted some flexibility in restricting its terms of lending and in charging interest rates above the nominal 2 percent. These measures were designed to bestow greater rewards for efficiency and to reduce the number of unfinished or unprofitable new projects. The latter accounted for 57 percent of all Bulgarian investment as late as 1976. A provision for joint ventures with foreign firms met little enthusiasm from abroad.

The Last Round of Zhivkov Reforms

By 1982 economists and the party leadership admitted that the NEM had not led to the anticipated upturn in overall productivity and efficiency. Even upwardly skewed official statistics indicated that aggregate economic growth had dropped to its lowest postwar level. Under the NEM, enterprises could still get approval from state pricing authorities for price increases with marginal or non-existent quality improvement—an important factor in evaluating official figures.

The differences between the Western concept of gross national product (GNP—see Glossary) and NMP make performance comparisons problematic. However, a Western economist who calculated growth rates for the Bulgarian economy according to the conventional GNP standard used in market economies determined the official Bulgarian growth rates between 1961 and 1980. The calculated rate for 1981–2 was 2.9 percent.

The Bulgarian response to declining growth rates under NEM was to initiate a second set of NEM reforms. Measures in 1982 and 1983 concentrated almost exclusively on financial incentives and prices. Net income was identified as the major basis for judging plan fulfillment. The only other targets were tax payments, domestic and imported input limits, and minimum export levels. The emphasis on self-supporting net income was extended downward to the brigade and upward to the associations. Guarantees of a minimum wage were removed for workers and all levels of management. Ministers themselves now were subject to salary reductions if their industrial association failed to meet the streamlined list of targets. Ministry access to budgetary subsidies for new investment was drastically cut and limited to a fixed term. Most investment capital outside net income had to be procured from the BNB. The bank's increasingly independent guidelines included the authorization to hold regional competitions for investment funds. Interest rates remained low however, ranging between 2.5 and 8 percent.

All these reforms did little to invigorate economic growth. In the Eighth Five-Year Plan (1981–5), the NMP growth rate dropped to 3.7 percent, its lowest postwar level. Officially, industry grew at a rate of 7 percent and construction at 5.4 percent, but agriculture declined by 3.9 percent per year.

In 1985 Mikhail S. Gorbachev visited Bulgaria and reportedly pressured Zhivkov to make the country more competitive economically. This pressure led to a Bulgarian version of the Soviet *perestroika* program (see Glossary). New Regulations on Economic Activity took effect in January 1987. These directives, intended to stimulate "socialist competition," allowed enterprises to retain a much greater share of their profits and also required them to compete for investment capital from newly formed commercial banks. In June 1987, in response to widespread dissatisfaction and confusion over the measures, a decree on collective and individual labor activities made it possible for state economic organizations to lease small trading and catering facilities to private individuals by offering contracts at public auctions. The auctions were an abject failure, however, because of high taxes, high rents, restricted access to capital, uncertain supplies, the short duration of the contracts, and legal insecurity. The idea was quietly abandoned.

Finally, in January 1989, the party issued Decree Number 56. This decree established "firms" as the primary unit of economic management. Theoretically, four types of firm could be created: joint-stock firms, firms with limited responsibility, firms with unlimited responsibility, and citizens' firms. The differences among the first three types of firms were small. But citizens' firms offered the potential of individual, collective, and associative ownership arrangements. In a fundamental departure from the socialist prohibition of private citizens hiring labor, as many as ten people could now be hired permanently, and an unlimited number could be hired on temporary contracts. A wave of reorganizations produced new, larger firms, depriving numerous enterprises of their self-management status. Nonetheless, hundreds of private and cooperative firms were authorized by Decree Number 56.

Other elements of the decree allowed firms to issue shares and bonds and pay dividends, with a number of restrictions. Some clauses sought to encourage foreign investment in the country. State-owned enterprises that were transformed into joint-stock firms now could have foreign shareholders. Although tax incentives and legal guarantees were provided for joint ventures, little foreign investment was stimulated. In 1989 and 1990, only 117 joint ventures were consummated, totaling US$10 million in Western capital. In all probability, low labor costs were not enough to attract foreign investment given remaining organizational disadvantages, poor infrastructure, low political credibility, the nonconvertability of the lev, and close economic ties to the Soviet Union.

This last round of reforms by the Zhivkov regime confused rather than improved economic performance. Statistics on growth for 1986–88 indicated a 5.5 percent annual rate, up from the 3.7 percent rate achieved during the previous five-year plan. However, these statistics were internally inconsistent and widely disputed in the press. Expert observers speculated that they were the minimum growth the regime could tolerate given the 6 percent target rate in the five-year plan.

Ultimately, the reforms failed to radically change the economic conditions in the country. Public discontent increased, and, finally, emboldened by revolutions throughout Eastern Europe, the public

137

erupted in a popular revolt that ousted Todor Zhivkov in November 1989. By early 1990, the first attempts were being made to establish a market-based economy.

Economic Sectors

Bulgaria's consistent emphasis on developing heavy industry at any cost created raw material demands well beyond the country's domestic resources. This problem was compounded by the inefficient industrial use of energy and raw materials: Bulgaria used more energy per unit of NMP than any Western economy. For this reason, one of the most salient aspects of the Bulgarian postwar economy was reliance on imported Soviet natural resources.

Fuels

In 1989 Soviet imports supplied Bulgaria with 95 percent of its coal, 90 percent of its crude oil, and 100 percent of its natural gas (see fig. 10). Although Bulgaria imported the majority of its raw materials for energy and industrial requirements, some domestic fuels and minerals were available. A small supply of hard coal was depleted rapidly in the 1980s; in 1987 only 198,000 tons were mined. More ample deposits of low-quality lignite yielded 31,400,000 tons in 1987, but those fuels were relatively inefficient energy producers and high polluters. In 1990 the Maritsa Basin in south-central Bulgaria was expected to remain the prime source of lignite for the foreseeable future; yearly production at its Maritsa-iztok open-pit mines was projected to reach forty million tons after the year 2000.

Energy Generation

In 1988 Bulgaria produced approximately 43 billion kilowatt hours of electricity (in contrast to 384 billion for France and 83.5 billion for Yugoslavia). At that point, planners expected power consumption to increase by about 3.5 percent per year through the year 2000. The 1988 Program for Energy Development through 1995 and in Perspective until 2005 set general long-term goals for the Bulgarian power industry, including more effective integration of machine building and construction industries into power projects, improved balance between supply and demand of energy, and more effective use of low-quality coal and local hydroelectric plants. In 1988 Bulgaria and the Soviet Union signed a bilateral agreement for scientific and technical cooperation in thermoelectric, hydroelectric, and nuclear power generation. That year 59 percent of Bulgaria's electricity came from thermoelectric plants (primarily coal-powered); 35 percent came from nuclear reactors, the remainder from hydroelectric stations. Total generating capacity in

1988 was 11,300 megawatts (in contrast to 103,400 for France, 20,000 for Yugoslavia).

Conventional Power Generation

About 1,500 megawatts of Bulgaria's thermoelectric generation capacity were idle in the late 1980s because of inefficient fuel delivery or equipment breakdown. About half the capacity of local heat and power plants, relied upon to supplement major electrical plants and provide heat for industries and homes, was unavailable for the same reasons.

In the early 1990s, Bulgarian energy planners faced serious dilemmas. At the Maritsa-iztok-1, Maritsa-iztok-2 and Dimo Dichev thermoelectric plants, located in the Maritsa-iztok coal fields, long-term plans called for gradual replacement of old generating equipment in existing stations. But most such projects were far behind schedule in 1990. The 1990 decision not to complete the Belene Nuclear Power Plant meant increased reliance on Maritsa-iztok coal for heat and power generation. In 1990 that source provided 70 percent of the country's coal, and its three power stations contributed about 25 percent of total power generation.

The Maritsa-iztok Industrial-Power Complex (with its machine building and repair enterprises one of the largest industrial centers in Bulgaria, employing 22,000 people in 1991) had been in operation since 1951; by 1991 the quality of its coal and the reliability of its infrastructure were steadily declining. But at that crisis point in the national economy, funds were unavailable for capital investment, especially to buy expensive foreign technology (see Market Reform, this ch.). At the same time, industry authorities acknowledged burning high-sulfur coal and strip mining at Maritsa-iztok as a severe environmental problem whose amelioration would cost at least a billion leva, mostly hard currency.

Hydroelectric power generation was concentrated in southwestern Bulgaria, but few Bulgarian rivers offered large-scale hydroelectric potential. The major hydroelectric project in the Ninth Five-Year Plan (1986–90) was completion of the Chaira station, which would add 864 megawatts of generating capacity. Development of local hydroelectric stations on small streams was a planning priority for the 1990s.

Nuclear Power

Nuclear power provided Bulgaria a way of easing its dependence on imported fuels, although the Soviet Union and Czechoslovakia provided the expertise and equipment on which Bulgaria built its nuclear power industry. Lacking hard currency to buy enough oil,

139

and reaching the toleration limit for pollution by coal-burning plants, Bulgaria increasingly made nuclear power the center of its energy policy in the 1980s. In 1974 the first nuclear power plant was opened at Kozloduy north of Sofia on the Danube River. After completing the original four-reactor complex in 1982, Kozloduy added a fifth unit in late 1987. This was the first 1,000-megawatt reactor in Eastern Europe outside the Soviet Union. A sixth unit was installed in 1989. At that point, Bulgaria ranked third in the world in per capita nuclear power generation, and the extent of its reliance on a sole nuclear power plant was unsurpassed in the world.

The Bulgarian nuclear power industry was beset with major problems from the beginning. The Kozloduy station had a history of technical difficulties and accidents, many of which were related to the low quality or poor design of Soviet and Czechoslovak equipment. The fifth reactor, a constant source of trouble, was out of commission for several months in 1991 because of extensive turbine damage. This setback put the entire country on a brownout schedule that shut off electricity two out of every four hours.

The Chernobyl' disaster in 1986 made nuclear safety a sensitive political issue in Bulgaria, and by the late 1980s public opinion, now a much more significant factor for policy makers, had turned strongly against the nuclear industry. A second nuclear power complex was started at Belene, to add six 1,000-megawatt reactors by the end of the Tenth Five-Year Plan. But construction was halted in 1989 by public opposition and disclosure that both Kozloduy and Belene were located in earthquake-prone regions. Long-term plans for nuclear heat generation also were shelved at that time. In 1991 the government's Commission on Nuclear Power Supply reported that the supply system was poorly organized and managed, and that managers relied on expensive foreign technical help instead of available domestic engineers. The commission also reported that, once Soviet specialists left, a shortage of qualified personnel delayed activation of the sixth reactor at Kozloduy (considered a top priority once Belene was rejected), and that most monitoring instruments in the first four Kozloduy reactors were out of operation.

In mid-1991 the International Atomic Energy Agency (IAEA) declared the Kozloduy reactors unsafe. Two reactors were shut down. Meanwhile, also in 1991, the planned activation of the two newest reactors at Kozloduy raised the problem of nuclear waste disposal because the Soviet Union had begun charging hard currency to reprocess waste from East European reactors, formerly one of its functions under Comecon. In 1991 Bulgaria requested

European Economic Community (EEC—see Glossary) aid to build its first permanent domestic repository for nuclear waste. The Bulgarian power transmission network was supplemented in 1988 when a high-capacity transmission line from the South Ukraine Nuclear Power Station in the Soviet Union reached the northeastern port city of Varna. But like Soviet fuels, imported Soviet electricity required hard currency in 1991, mitigating the advantages of the old Comecon agreement.

Industry

From 1956 through 1988, industrial production rose an average of 8.9 percent per year according to official figures, but the actual rates declined steadily during the thirty-three-year period. The annual average rate of industrial growth for the periods 1956-60, 1961-70, 1971-80, and 1981-88 was 15.5, 11.6, 7.5, and 4.4 percent, respectively. By the late 1980s, Bulgarian industry had completely exhausted the advantages it had used in earlier decades to post impressive growth statistics (see table 12, Appendix).

Industrial Policy

The cost of Bulgaria's industrial growth was substantial. Besides environmental problems, the commitment to heavy industry came at the expense of light industry—especially food processing and textiles—and agriculture. These were sectors in which prewar Bulgaria had relatively high production potential. But de-emphasis held the official annual NMP growth figures for light industry and agriculture to 7.5 and 2.8 percent, respectively, between 1956 and 1988.

In the postwar command economy, the chief beneficiaries of this emphasis were the chemical, electronics, and machinery industries. Their respective share of total industrial production rose from 1.9, 0, and 2.4 percent in 1939 to 8.8, 14.4, and 15 percent in 1988. Similar statistics indicate big drops in production shares for the food processing and textiles industries—from 51.2 to 23.3 percent, and from 19.8 to 5.1 percent, respectively, in the same period.

Besides the unchanging commitment to heavy industry, two other major trends appeared in postwar industrial policy. The first was steady and substantial support for a basic ferrous metals industry, regardless of cost, in order to reduce dependence on imports. The second was an effort to produce machinery competitive in international markets, with special emphasis on electrical equipment.

A result of the first policy was the Kremikovtsi Metallurgical Complex. In 1954 Soviet-supported geological surveys indicated major new deposits of higher quality iron ore that would support a second complex to supplement the existing V.I. Lenin Ferrous Metals Combine at Pernik. Although the deposits were actually found to be inadequate, the extremely expensive Kremikovtsi plant finally opened in 1963 and used Soviet iron ore to produce over half of the national production of steel and iron through 1978.

The Kremikovtsi complex brought numerous problems. By the mid-1970s, over 75 percent of its ore and coking coal was imported. Costs were inflated by premium wages paid to maintain the labor force and by delays in construction and delivery. Production at Kremikovtsi consistently failed to meet planned targets, and less than three-quarters of plant capacity was used. The enterprise never showed a profit; in 1989 it lost 99.5 million leva despite receiving 600 million leva in state subsidies. Using 15 percent of the country's total energy output, Kremikovtsi generated only 1 percent of national income in the late 1980s.

The strategy of heavy equipment production for export fared better than did metallurgy in the 1970s and 1980s. In fact, the most competitive Bulgarian industries were those most committed to export markets. The machine building and electronics industries averaged 16 percent growth between 1960 and 1980 while their combined share of export value jumped from 13 to 55 percent from 1960 to 1982. The primary exports in these sectors were forklift trucks and electrical hoisting gear produced by the Balkancar enterprise. Computer equipment and chemicals also showed improved export performance.

Bulgaria's postwar industrialization was clearly positive in some sectors. Two notable examples were the construction of electric power plants in the 1950s, which made possible the nationwide spread of industry and the development of an electrical equipment industry that produced exportable products. Nonetheless, as the 1980s drew to a close, it became increasingly clear that even the most competitive sectors had serious problems that the BCP's halfway reforms could not solve. After the initial postwar climb, four decades of socialist central planning had left the industrial sector in a very poor state.

Industrial Centers

Bulgarian heavy industries, mostly machine building, chemicals, and electronics, were concentrated in relatively few production centers. Important machine tool plants were the Bolshevik Tool Plant at Gabrovo, the Nikola Vaptsarov Combine at Pleven, and the Radomir Heavy Equipment Plant in southwest Bulgaria. The Electronic Materials Processing and Equipment Scientific-Production Combine was a combined scientific and industrial center at Sofia. Electronic instrument production centers were located at the Plovdiv Power Electronics Plant, the Shabla Electromechanical Plant on the northeast coast, the Stara Zagora Industrial Robot Plant, the Pravets Instrument Plant in the southwest, and the Petkov Instrument Plant at Tŭrgovishte. Major chemical and petrochemical producers were the Industrial Petrochemical Plant at Pleven (specializing in vehicle lubricants and oils), the Burgas Petrochemical Combine (plastics), the Vratsa Industrial Chemical Combine (chemical fertilizers), and four chemical plants at Dimitrovgrad (see fig. 10). Bulgaria also built large numbers of ships, many for Soviet customers, at its Ruse and Varna shipyards on the Black Sea. The Shumen Vehicle Plant assembled LIAZ-Madara heavy trucks in a three-way arrangement with the Liberac Auto Plant of Czechoslovakia and the Soviet Union.

Obstacles to Industrial Growth

In 1989 the domestic market still featured little or no competition. Over 80 percent of exports went to Comecon countries, and 75 percent of that total went to the Soviet Union. This situation insulated the computers, industrial robots, microprocessors, and other high-technology exports of Bulgarian industry from the market competition that would require backing by substantial investment in research and development. Bulgaria thus developed a practice of expending a small proportion of its national income on applied science, even compared with other East European states.

Falling productivity was a major problem in a number of key industries. Many of these industries were inherently uncompetitive, and attempts to raise productivity through large-scale production concentrated industrial and research facilities into enormous enterprises that further reduced industrial flexibility. Unprofitability made Bulgarian industry dependent on a system of widespread state subsidies. It was reported at the BCP Central Committee plenum in December 1989 that a quarter of all state companies had received state support during the year, totaling 7 billion leva— almost a quarter of the national income. Machine building, one of Bulgaria's key export industries, became a problem area for the economy in the 1980s. Because it was the chief consumer of the overpriced, low-quality output of the metallurgical industry, the machine industry eventually became unprofitable as well. In 1990 Balkancar, the country's biggest company, one of its most successful exporters, and another major customer of the metallurgy enterprises, lost money for the first time.

A critical economic policy decision in the late 1980s was Zhivkov's special emphasis on several energy-intensive industries, despite the inadequacy of domestic energy supply. In the early 1990s, the new regime faced a choice of dismantling many of those enterprises, finding less expensive energy sources to keep them running, or acquiring enough hard currency to upgrade their technological level and make them less energy-intensive. To further complicate industrial policy, beginning in 1991 the Soviet Union began charging market prices in hard currency for its oil and gas.

Finally, emergence of a significant, fast-growing environmental movement cast the tradeoff of environmental quality for economic growth in starkly negative terms. Barring substantial technical aid (most likely from the West) to reduce industrial waste, public demand for environmentally sound economic policy stood as a formidable obstacle to industrial expansion.

Agriculture

Prior to World War II, agriculture was the leading sector in the Bulgarian economy. In 1939 agriculture contributed 65 percent of NMP, and four out of every five Bulgarians were employed in agriculture (see fig. 11). The importance and organization of Bulgarian agriculture changed drastically after the war, however. By 1958 the BCP had collectivized a high percentage of Bulgarian farms; in the next three decades, the state used various forms of organization to improve productivity, but none succeeded. Meanwhile, private plots remained productive and often alleviated agricultural shortages during the Zhivkov era.

Early Collectivization Campaigns

When the BCP came to power, Bulgarian agriculture consisted primarily of 1.1 million peasant smallholdings. The party saw consolidation of these holdings as its most immediate agricultural objective. It dismantled the agricultural bank that had been a primary source of investment for the agriculture and food processing sectors before World War II.

The first attempts at voluntary collectivization yielded modest results, partly because open coercion was impossible until a peace treaty was signed with the Allies. The labor-cooperative farm (*trudovo-kooperativno zemedelsko stopanstvo*—TKZS) received official approval in 1945. It closely resembled Soviet cooperatives in organization, although members were guaranteed a share of profits and membership was (nominally) completely voluntary. By 1947 only 3.8 percent of arable land had been collectivized. After the communists won the first postwar election and the peace was concluded in 1947, pressure on private landholders increased. Although most small farmers had joined collectives, by 1949 only

Figure 11. Principal Crops, 1990

Source: Based on information from Sophie Gherardi, "Bulgaria No Longer Able to Feed Itself," *Guardian*.

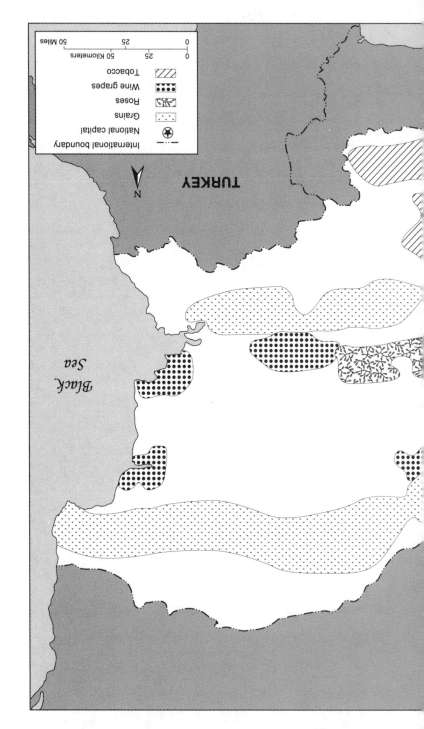

Black Sea

TURKEY

N

International boundary
National capital
Grains
Roses
Wine grapes
Tobacco

0   25   50 Kilometers
0   25   50 Miles

12 percent of arable land was under state control—mainly because the collectivization program alienated many peasants. But between 1950 and 1953, the Stalinist regime of Vŭlko Chervenkov used threats, violence, and supply discrimination to produce the fastest pace of collectivization in Eastern Europe. Sixty-one percent of arable land had been collectivized by 1952. The process was declared complete in 1958 when 92 percent of arable land belonged to the collective farms. This ended the first phase of Bulgarian postwar agricultural restructuring.

Farm Consolidation in the 1960s

At this stage, Bulgarian collectives were much smaller than the Soviet organizations on which they were modeled. To fulfill the ambitious goals contained in the Zhivkov Theses (January 1959) for the Third Five-Year Plan (1958–60), further consolidation was deemed necessary. This process reduced the number of collectives from 3,450 to 932, and the average size of a collective grew from 1,000 to 4,500 hectares.

In the late 1960s, an agricultural labor shortage combined with fascination for China's agrarian amalgamation to prompt further consolidation of collective farms into APKs. By the end of 1971, all of Bulgaria's 744 collectives and 56 state farms had been merged into 161 complexes, most of which were designated APKs. These units averaged 24,000 hectares and 6,500 members. The consolidation continued until there were only 143 complexes in 1977. Several complexes were larger than 100,000 hectares, and twenty-five were between 36,000 and 100,000 hectares. In the short term, they were to achieve horizontal integration by specializing in three or fewer crops and one type of livestock. In the longer term, they would be the basis for linking agriculture with manufacturing and commerce. On the political level, this consolidation was to be a symbolic merger of the agricultural and urban workers, who had remained quite distinct parts of the Bulgarian population since the nineteenth century in defiance of the theory of the unified socialist society.

The new organizations never met the higher agricultural quotas of the late 1970s, however. For some products, yield did not keep pace with investment. Overall growth in agriculture continued to fall after the creation of the APKs. And the goal of freeing farm workers to take industrial jobs was not reached. On the contrary, the annual reduction in agricultural employment dropped from 4 to 2 percent while farm labor productivity declined. As a result, agriculture's share of gross investment in fixed capital fell to 18 percent by 1976, a level last seen in the mid-1950s. In 1978 this failure triggered a new policy emphasizing smaller complexes. Reduced agricultural quotas in the Eighth Five-Year Plan (1981–85) were an admission that too much had been expected from the constant tinkering process.

Reform in the 1980s

By 1982 the total of old and new APKs reached 296, the average size was halved to 16,000 hectares, and the management hierarchy was simplified. Most importantly, the number of annual indicators of plan fulfillment was reduced from fourteen to four. The new, simpler approach also allowed greater freedom for APKs to negotiate prices on surplus production and to purchase their own supplies.

In the last Zhivkov years, the communist regime attempted other agricultural reforms, including autonomy for the collectives. At that point, the only funds the state received from agriculture were 60 percent of foreign currency from exports. Even then, government delivery prices remained so low that state foodstuff monopolies received only the absolute minimum supply. In 1989 the exodus of 310,000 ethnic Turks, many of whom had cultivated personal plots, also hurt agricultural output.

Despite these handicaps, the United States Department of Agriculture estimated that within Eastern Europe Bulgaria was second only to Hungary in agricultural trade surpluses through 1987. After that time, however, agricultural output dropped so far that the country could no longer feed its own people. In 1990 the first rationing and shortages since World War II were the most obvious indications of this situation. Because of domestic shortages, export of several agricultural products was banned in 1990.

Agricultural Products

Two long-term policies strongly determined priorities in Bulgarian agricultural production after 1960. First, livestock was promoted at the expense of crop cultivation, mainly to meet export demand. Between 1970 and 1988, the share of livestock in agricultural production rose from 35.3 to 55.6 percent. As a result, less land was available for crops in that period. Pig and poultry production increased the most, but large numbers of sheep also were raised. The second policy was a shift away from industrial crops (primarily tobacco and cotton), toward production of fruit (most notably apples), vegetables (most notably tomatoes), and grapes. Bulgaria remained an important exporter of tobacco, however, averaging 65 percent of East European exports of that crop in the 1980s. Grain production concentrated on wheat, corn,

Maize combine at work in Vratsa District
Courtesy Sofia Press Agency
Coal dredger, used in opencast mining, receives final adjustments
at the Radomir plant.

and barley, crops that are vulnerable to weather conditions. Poor harvests in 1985 and 1986 led to grain imports of 1.8 and 1.5 million tons, respectively. Sugar beets, potatoes, sunflower seeds, and soybeans also were important crops at the end of the 1980s. In 1990 Bulgaria was the world's largest exporter of attar of roses, used in making perfume (see fig. 11).

The Role of Private Plots

After 1970 the only consistent contribution to agricultural production growth was family farming on private plots leased from the agricultural complexes. These plots could not be bought or sold or worked by hired labor, but their yield belonged to the tenant. In 1971 special measures were instituted to increase the number and the availability of personal plots. Beginning in 1974, peasant households were permitted to lease additional plots and given free access to fertilizer, fodder seed, and equipment belonging to their agricultural complexes. To encourage this practice, the government extended loans and waived income taxes. More importantly, delivery prices increased for agricultural products. In the mid-1970s, a reduced work week for urban workers and relaxed requirements for plot leasing encouraged weekend cultivation of personal plots by the nonagricultural population. Plot size limits were removed in 1977.

By 1982 personal plots accounted for 25 percent of Bulgaria's agricultural output and farm worker income. In 1988 personal plots accounted for large shares of basic agricultural goods: corn, 43.5 percent; tomatoes, 36.8 percent; potatoes, 61.5 percent; apples, 24.8 percent; grapes, 43.2 percent; meat, 40.8 percent; milk, 25.2 percent; eggs, 49.4 percent; and honey, 86 percent. The sales from plots to town markets meant that despite low overall agricultural growth rates in the 1980s, the urban food supply actually improved in many areas during the early and mid-1980s.

Post-Zhivkov Agricultural Reform

In 1991 privatization of agriculture was a top priority of the government of Prime Minister Dimitŭr Popov. That spring the National Assembly passed a new Arable Land Law, revising the conditions for ownership and use of agricultural land. The law allowed every Bulgarian citizen to own as much as thirty hectares of land, or twenty in areas of intensive cultivation. Use of this land was at the complete discretion of the owner. Conditions were stated for voluntary formation of cooperatives by private landowners and resale of their land. With some limitations, landowners whose property had been incorporated into state farms were to receive "comparable" plots elsewhere or other appropriate compensation. The state or municipality retained title to land not in private hands. Another provision described redistribution of land seized by the state from cooperatives and individuals during Zhivkov's several agricultural consolidations. A National Land Council under the Council of Ministers was to oversee land distribution and arbitrate disputes, aided by a system of municipal land commissions.

As was true for reform elsewhere in the Bulgarian economy, agricultural reform encountered stout resistance from entrenched local Zhivkovite officials. Pre-collectivization land ownership records were destroyed, and farmers were threatened or bribed to remain in collectives rather than seeking private farms. Although the Arable Land Law was widely hailed as an equitable and useful economic reform, its association with the Bulgarian Socialist Party (BSP, formerly the BCP) majority brought criticism from the opposition Union of Democratic Forces (UDF). Some farmers circumvented the law simply by seizing land. The government, meanwhile, announced that no state land would be redistributed before the 1991 harvest.

In early 1991, staples such as sugar and olive oil were unavailable in many areas; livestock feed rations had been cut by more than half; a grain shortfall of 1.7 million tons was expected; meat, withheld from markets until new government prices were announced, was very scarce and expensive in cities; and fertilizers for the year's crops were in very short supply. Western firms expressed interest in joint agricultural ventures in Bulgaria, but hesitated because of uncertainty about political and legal conditions for such projects. A new round of government price-fixing in February 1991 substantially raised food prices but did restore supplies of some items.

Transportation

The Bulgarian transportation system in 1987 was poorly developed compared with systems elsewhere in Europe. The rail system totaled 4,300 kilometers of track, of which 4,055 were standard gauge, 2,510 were electrified, and 917 were double track. In the 1980s, Bulgaria moved away from diesel engines toward electrical rail haulage. By 1988 some 83 percent of freight was moved by this method, compared with 60 percent in 1980. In 1987 the rails carried 83 million tons of freight and 110,000,000 passengers. In 1987 Bulgaria had 36,908 kilometers of roads, 33,535 of which were hard surfaced and 242 of which were classified as motorways (highways). In 1987 some 940 million passengers and 917 million tons of freight traveled by road. No major extension of the rail or the road system was built in the late 1980s.

In 1988 the freight system moved 103 billion ton kilometers (see Glossary) of freight, the majority (62.9 percent) by seagoing transport (see fig. 12). Of the dozen Bulgarian ports on the Danube, the most important was Ruse. The remaining freight was moved by rail (17.1 percent), road (16.9 percent), inland waterway (2.1 percent), and pipeline (1 percent). In 1988 the national airline, Balkan Airline, totalled 32 billion passenger kilometers (see Glossary). Rail provided 25.5 percent of passenger transport, roads 62.2 percent, and air 12.2 percent.

The Bulgarian transportation system suffered financial neglect through most of the communist era. Investment in this sector was never extremely high, but in 1988 overall investment fell almost 25 percent. The largest drops were in sea transport (96 percent), river transport (63 percent), pipeline transport (62 percent), and rail transport (18 percent). The Bulgarian State Railroad typified the neglect and overuse of the transportation system. In 1990 authorities estimated that 27 million leva would be needed to restore the railroads to satisfactory operating condition. Meanwhile, rail revenues fell by 10 million leva during the first five months of 1990 as a result of lower industrial production and equipment breakdowns. At that point, about one-third of Bulgaria's passenger railcars and two-thirds of railroad equipment were completely depreciated, and 78 locomotives and 3,500 freight cars were idle due to breakdowns. Some 300 kilometers of track were classified as urgently needing repair.

Communications

Throughout the communist period, the state controlled all media. In 1987 Bulgaria had eighty radio and forty-three television transmitters. Two television networks broadcast over nineteen stations in 1991, with 250 low-power repeaters extending coverage to rural areas. The radio system featured three networks with twenty long- and medium-wave stations. Foreign-language programming in Albanian, Arabic, English, French, German, Greek, Italian, Portuguese, Serbo-Croatian, Spanish, and Turkish was broadcast from short- and medium-wave stations in Vidin, Stolnik, Kostinbrod, and Plovdiv. Bulgaria was a member of the Intervision East European television network, but in 1991 it had not joined the International Telecommunications Satellite Organization (Intelsat). In 1990 approximately 2 million radio receivers and 2.1 million television sets were in use. Some 2.23 million telephones were in operation in 1987 (see table 14, Appendix).

In 1991 Bulgaria began privatizing its communications sector. The Commission on Communications and Information Science, with the help of West European communications experts, developed a plan for formation of ten independent companies to operate in communications services, the equipment industry, construction, and other related areas. The companies would operate under authority of a state regulatory organization similar to those in Western Europe. This plan would mean gradually dismantling the national communications monopoly while retaining the unified national telegraph, postal, telephone, radio, and television services. Meanwhile, private companies outside the existing networks were to be encouraged to compete for new customers, and prices were to rise accordingly from the artificially low levels of the command economy period.

Banking and Finance

Under the Zhivkov regime, Bulgaria followed the customary communist pattern of a single state-run bank performing all banking and investment functions. Investment policy was the province of state planning agencies, with substantial input from the BCP and the national bank. Post-Zhivkov reform aimed at privatizing and compartmentalizing the banking system, a goal that would likely require years of gradual reform.

Currency and Exchange

The national currency of Bulgaria is the lev (plural, leva—see Glossary), which is divided into 100 stotinki (sing., stotinka). Throughout the communist era, the lev could be used only in domestic transactions because it was not convertible into foreign currency. Bulgarian nationals were prohibited from owning foreign currency, and the law prohibited citizens and foreigners from entering or leaving the country with leva. As was true for domestic prices, the value of the lev was administratively determined. This fact led to frequent overvaluing of the lev in terms of hard currencies and black market rates well below official exchange rates. Besides official rates, which were based on a gold parity developed after World War II, a commercial rate was used for business transactions and statistical purposes, and a tourist rate determined the amount received by foreigners in Bulgaria for their domestic currencies. None of these arbitrary rates reflected the relationship of domestic and foreign prices. Trade with Western countries was conducted in hard currency, while the transferable ruble, an accounting device with no convertible value, was primarily used to clear commercial accounts within Comecon. In 1990 the lev was devalued several times, finally settling at rates of about 0.76 lev to the United States dollar (official), 3 leva to the dollar (commercial), and 7 leva to the dollar (tourist). The black market rate fluctuated considerably, but ended 1990 at approximately 11 leva to the dollar. In mid-1991 the Bulgarian National Bank (BNB) issued conversion tables for the lev into major world currencies (see table 15, Appendix). The official value at that time was 18 leva to the United States dollar.

Banking System

As the chief financial instrument of economic policy making, the BNB assumed virtually all of the financial functions in the country under the centrally planned economy. Only the granting of foreign trade and consumer credits were separate functions, performed respectively by the Bulgarian Foreign Trade Bank and the State Savings Bank—both of which were subordinate to the BNB. The BNB worked with the Ministry of Finance to finance capital investments in the economy. The BNB also monitored the economic organizations that received investment funds to ensure their use for accomplishing plan targets. As enterprises became more self-financing in the 1970s, a greater share of their investment capital was composed of bank credits granted by the BNB. Between 1965 and 1975, the BNB share of investment funds jumped from 7 percent to 54 percent; the trend then moderated as enterprises began to rely more on retained earnings to finance investments.

Like industry and agriculture, banking under the BCP experimented occasionally with decentralization but remained quite centralized until shortly before the overthrow of Zhivkov. A 1987 reform nominally split Bulgarian banking into a two-tiered system. The function of the BNB was restricted to money supply, although it also retained significant supervisory power. The reform also created several specialized banks including the Agricultural and Cooperative Bank, the Biochemical Bank, the Construction Bank, the Electronics Bank, the Transportation Bank, and the Transport, Agricultural, and Building Equipment Bank—each responsible for an industrial sector.

Post-Zhivkov banking reform began hesitantly but grew more comprehensive in 1991. In a controversial policy decision, the government first increased interest rates from 4.5 to 8 percent in 1990, then let them float freely beginning in 1991. Although the first private commercial bank was established in May 1990, a new National Bank Bill was not passed until June 1991. That law provided for a two-tier bank system independent of direct government control but accountable to the National Assembly. The first tier

of the new system was to be the Central Bank, the second a separate system of commercial banks and lending institutions serving private citizens and enterprises. Three-month bank credits would be available to cabinet ministries. The BNB was to issue monthly balance statements and report semiannually to the National Assembly.

Investment Policy

In choosing among alternative investment projects, Bulgarian planners in the Zhivkov era faced greater difficulties than investment decision makers in Western economies. True relative costs of labor and materials were masked by state assignment of prices, meaning that funding allocations among projects often were arbitrary. In most cases, investments were not based on efficiency criteria, but rather on plan goals. Artificially low interest rates also discouraged enterprises from efficient investment fund allocation.

The state budget also guided party economic policy under the old regime. Until the reforms of the 1970s, the budget was the primary source of funds for enterprise investment. Budget revenues were originally derived mainly from the turnover tax, a retail sales tax that was also used to regulate demand for various products. Beginning in the mid-1960s, budget revenues were derived progressively less from the turnover tax and more from taxes on net enterprise income.

Prices

Investments in inefficient operations and subsidies on consumer items often led to budget deficits. Often the state simply printed more money to cover its obligations. Eventually this practice led to circulation of excess currency compared with consumer goods and services available at prevailing prices. Because prices were administratively set, shortages and long lines occurred more often than inflation under the CPE. But party-directed general price increases such as the average 15 percent rise in 1979 usually were quite steep.

In the post-Zhivkov era, economic planners saw market-determined prices for most goods and services as their long-term goal. In 1990 the prices of 40 percent of goods and 60 percent of services were freed from administrative control. In the second half of 1990, price liberalization raised consumer prices an average of over 50 percent. In February 1991, price controls were removed from all goods and services except fuels, heat, and electricity. Immediately after this step, average food prices were nearly six times their 1989 level; housing was up 3.7 times, clothing three times more expensive. These levels, established by an independent trade union study, were above the level triggering new talks on compensation payments. (For the second consecutive year, a government indexation program was established to reimburse a share (estimated at an average 65 percent) of the higher cost of living caused by the new price policy in the first half of 1991.) In a two-month period of early 1991, consumption dropped by over 50 percent, but total consumer spending still increased by 11.5 percent.

Foreign Trade

Membership in Comecon tied Bulgarian trade policy closely to the Soviet economic sphere following World War II. By 1991, however, trade policy was on the verge of significant diversification. With the trade protection of Comecon no longer available, Bulgaria aggressively sought new markets in the West while seeking to retain the most advantageous commercial relations with its former Comecon partners.

Postwar Trade Policy

The adoption of the Soviet economic model had direct and indirect impact on Bulgarian international trade after World War II. Among direct results was the decision to reduce dependency

*Roses cultivated in Valley of Roses
to produce attar of roses for
perfume industry
Courtesy Sam and Sarah Stulberg*

*Drying tobacco, one of Bulgaria's
major export crops, Melnik
Courtesy Sam and Sarah Stulberg*

159

on prewar Western trade partners. This decision meant strong promotion of import substitution policies to bolster domestic production of goods previously imported. In 1960 Bulgaria's total foreign trade (exports plus imports) was 31 percent of NMP, quite low for a country with a small internal market and few natural resources. By the 1980s, however, this figure had risen to over 90 percent. Before World War II, Germany was well-established as Bulgaria's top trading partner. Postwar economic policy diverted trade from Central Europe to Eastern Europe, and primarily to the Soviet Union. The new domestic economic priorities dictated a revised foreign trade structure (see table 16; table 17, Appendix). The policy of promoting heavy industry, for example, required huge imports of machinery and raw materials (see table 18; table 19, Appendix). Beginning in the mid-1950s, imports of machinery accounted for approximately half the value of total imports, while fuels, metals, and minerals made up more than a quarter of this value. Lower postwar investment in agriculture eventually lessened the share of foodstuffs in total exports.

The state monopoly of foreign trade also changed the way decisions were reached on international allocation of goods. Trade decisions were reached administratively by planning authorities or negotiated with other members of Comecon. Overall control of foreign trade was shared among the Ministry of Foreign Trade, the Ministry of Finance, and the Bulgarian Foreign Trade Bank.

Import and export operations were conducted by foreign trade enterprises, most of which were affiliated with one or more associations but retained a legal identity outside the associations. Although reform measures by the Zhivkov regime gave associations some profit incentives in international trade, the producing enterprises themselves were completely isolated from the foreign customer. This situation meant that world quality standards had no influence on Bulgarian producers.

Bulgaria in Comecon

The most important event in postwar Bulgarian international economic relations occurred in 1949 when it became a founding member of Comecon. Comecon was an attempt by the socialist economies to simplify the planning process by synchronizing the five-year plans of member countries and, more importantly, by achieving what Marxists called an international division of labor. Countries within Comecon would specialize in the products they made most efficiently and export the surplus. Products that a country could not produce efficiently would be available from one or more of its Comecon partners. This design was intended to eliminate some redundancies inherent in the Soviet economic model where each country produced goods of all categories. Although the concept achieved isolated successes such as Bulgarian forklift trucks, broad growth was blocked by the uniform socialist preoccupation with heavy industry and the lack of a single convertible currency. The currency issue in particular made intra-Comecon trade a cumbersome process requiring negotiation of annual bilateral trade agreements for all member nations.

In the 1980s, exports to the Soviet Union consisted primarily of machinery, electronic components, and agricultural goods. These included forklift trucks, electric engines, telephones, tobacco, fresh fruits and vegetables, and wine. Imports from the Soviet Union were mainly energy and raw materials, including oil, natural gas, iron ore, ferrous metals, and cotton. In 1988 Bulgaria still relied almost entirely on Soviet oil and natural gas. East Germany and Czechoslovakia were the next most important Comecon trading partners, accounting for 5.2 and 4.6 percent of exports, respectively, and 5.9 and 5.4 percent of imports, respectively. Exchanges of goods between Bulgaria and these countries emphasized both exports and imports of machinery and the export of agricultural products.

In the initial years of Bulgaria's Comecon membership, the country benefited from energy prices below world levels, especially for oil, in two ways. The cost of developing otherwise inefficient industries was lower, and reexport of crude and refined oil for hard currency bought Western technology to upgrade the industrial infrastructure. Comecon members paid for their imports through bilateral clearing agreements, with no exchange of hard currency. In the initial stages of Comecon, Bulgaria exported mainly food, the price of which was lower in Comecon than on the world market. Later, however, Bulgaria paid for imported Soviet raw materials largely with machinery that was priced higher than on the world market.

Beginning in 1974, Soviet energy exports were based on a floating five-year average of world prices that rarely matched market prices at a given time. Even when Comecon prices were above the world level, Bulgaria benefited from the lack of currency exchange in the Comecon system. But dependence on Comecon trade, especially Soviet energy exports, damaged Bulgaria tremendously when economic reform swept through the Soviet sphere in 1989 and 1990. Of Bulgarian exports, 62.5 percent still went to the Soviet Union in 1988, and 53.5 percent of imports came from that country. The new trade system, established after reforms, required trade accounts to be cleared in hard currency at current world prices as of January 1, 1991. (Bilateral protocols for this procedure had not been signed by that time, however; Bulgaria still owed Hungary 87 million transferable rubles in 1991.)

After the political reforms in Eastern Europe, the Soviet Union announced cutbacks in energy exports to Eastern Europe. The cutbacks caused energy and raw materials shortages. In 1990 Bulgarian industry was forced to curtail production sharply; meanwhile, consumers endured severe shortages of gasoline as fuel prices doubled. A new set of export and import regulations adopted in mid-1991 removed import taxes from 200 types of raw materials and consumer goods in critically short supply. The same regulations set export price minimums to eliminate pricing below world market levels; export of crude oil, metals, grains, and textile raw materials was banned.

Trade with the West and the Third World

After 1960 Bulgaria's trade with the West increased, partly because Bulgaria needed Western machinery to supplement the outdated, overpriced manufacturing equipment supplied by Comecon. Between 1960 and 1975, the Western share of Bulgarian imports went from 13.6 percent to 23.6 percent. In the same period, however, exports dropped from 12.4 to 9.3 percent, creating an external debt problem with the West. Increased exports to Third World nations did little to help Bulgaria reduce this trade deficit because most Third World trade was not in convertible currencies.

Throughout the 1970s, Bulgarian trade balances alternated between solvency and high deficits. Although the trade deficit was eliminated in 1975, many short-term debts to West European banks remained. By 1976 Bulgarian debt was 13 percent of estimated GNP—the highest ratio in Eastern Europe at the time. Bulgaria greatly diminished this debt by reexporting Soviet oil to Western buyers in the late 1970s.

From that point, Bulgaria maintained trade surpluses in hard currency until 1985, when emergency imports of grain and coal created a deficit of US$200 million. A series of poor harvests, high machinery imports in the investment push of the Ninth Five-Year Plan (1986–90), and sharply dropping oil prices deprived Bulgaria of hard currency and created a major new trade deficit. Libya and Iraq, the main Third World customers with which a surplus had been accumulated, also reduced their purchase of Bulgarian goods at this time.

The resulting trade deficits were financed by credits from Western banks. After the overthrow of Zhivkov, the government announced that the gross hard currency debt had reached US$10.6 billion by

The shipyards at Varna
Courtesy Sofia Press Agency

the end of 1989. Net indebtedness was somewhat lower at US$7.7 billion, but much of the hard currency export credits that Bulgaria granted were to Libya and Iraq, who were likely to default on many of their deals. Bulgaria had arranged for Iraq to repay these loans with oil, but in 1991 the trade embargo and ensuing Persian Gulf War negated that agreement. In March 1990, the incoming Bulgarian government announced unilateral suspension of principal payments on outstanding debt, and later interest payments were suspended as well. Western lines of credit immediately were frozen, and Bulgarian hard currency holdings dropped to the minimal level of US$200 million in May 1990.

Bulgaria's main Western trading partners were the Federal Republic of Germany (West Germany) before German unification in 1990, Switzerland, and Italy. Exports to these countries were relatively minor, accounting for between 1 and 0.7 percent of total exports. Imports from West Germany were 4.9 percent of the total, while Switzerland accounted for 1.4 percent of imports, and Italy 1.1 percent. Trade with the developed, Western economies resembled trade between an undeveloped country and an industrialized one. Bulgaria imported mostly machinery from those countries and sold them raw and semifinished materials and agricultural products.

163

The most important Third World trading partners, Iraq and Libya, purchased 2.8 and 2.3 percent of Bulgarian exports, respectively. These exports consisted mainly of major construction projects and agricultural goods. The overthrow of the Zhivkov regime revived talk of establishing a Black Sea Trading Zone that also would include Turkey and Greece and perhaps Romania. In establishing its new trade policy in 1991, Bulgaria faced a choice of expanding its traditional commercial ties with Germany and Germany's partners in the EEC or cultivating new ties with closer markets such as Turkey. In 1991 Turkey offered to invest US$13 billion in Bulgaria's economy. An independent Union for Cooperation between Bulgaria and Turkey was founded to foster direct cooperation between enterprises of the two countries, and transportation links were solidified by ministerial agreements in 1991. Talks with the EEC early in 1991 yielded assurance of short-term EEC financial support through the PHARE (Polish and Hungarian Assistance for the Reconstruction of Europe) program and closer future ties, assuming that Bulgaria continued to make progress in its political and economic reform programs.

New Trade Conditions, 1990

The end of central planning opened the Bulgarian economy to world competition and began a wrenching transition for which it was ill-equipped in finance, industrial diversity, agricultural infrastructure, and available natural resources. The transition was made doubly difficult because the long years of privileged access to energy had fostered inefficient energy use in the Bulgarian economy.

Under the new economic conditions, imports would be purchased only in hard currency. Although Western firms and governments offered some credits and aid in 1991, Western investors preferred Poland, Hungary, and Czechoslovakia to Bulgaria. Those countries were more familiar to Westerners, and they had had relatively advanced market economies before World War II. For these reasons, in the early 1990s they received the lion's share of a rather meager Western investment in Eastern Europe.

Standard of Living

From the end of World War II until the 1960s, the Bulgarian standard of living experienced no significant improvements. A net decline may have occurred during some of the collectivization drives. The first improvements came when the government instituted a minimum agricultural wage as part of its reconciliation with the peasants after the Zhivkov Theses failed in 1960. Increases in real incomes in agriculture rose by 6.7 percent per year during the 1960s. During this same period, industrial wages increased by 4.9 percent annually. Early in the 1960s, higher prices offset those wage increases; but by 1970, increased urban food supplies made improved urban incomes meaningful. According to official data, from the Fourth through the Eighth Five-Year Plans (1961–85), growth in real wages ranged from 5.3 percent (1966–70) to 0.5 percent (1976–80). The latter figure is low because a major price revision in 1979 raised prices of foodstuffs by 25 percent and consumer goods by 15 percent. Real growth in Bulgaria at that point was the lowest in Europe. Bulgarian statistics indicating real income growth often were inaccurate, however. A major distortion resulted from the failure of official figures to account for variations in availability of commodities or services or for government subsidies for food, housing, education, and health care—vital factors in evaluating standard of living and purchasing power.

In 1990 a Bulgarian economist made an independent attempt to construct a consumer price index for the period 1979 through 1989. Based on those findings, inflation during that period was 131 percent, or 8.7 percent per year. Official data showed a 9.0 percent increase in consumer prices between 1980 through 1988, or 1.1 percent annually. The same study compared the quantity of various food items that could be purchased with the average monthly salary in nine different countries, including four in the West (Austria, France, West Germany, and Britain). Of ten basic food categories, the lowest amount that average monthly earnings could purchase in the Western economies was 3.3 times the amount obtainable from average monthly earnings in Bulgaria. Even in comparison with the other socialist countries in the study, Bulgarian purchasing power was the lowest by at least 25 percent. A mitigating factor in the latter set of comparisons is that official encouragement of private plots spurred substantially greater availability (albeit at greater cost) than in most other East European economies.

Some improvement was achieved in the Bulgarian diet in the 1970s and 1980s. Wary of popular discontent, Zhivkov made a major speech in December 1972 in which he promised a ten-year program to raise living standards in general and to raise food consumption to the "scientific norms" set by the United Nations (UN). Zhivkov never was entirely successful in this effort, however. Bread and sugar were the only foods for which Bulgarian consumption rates reached or exceeded UN norms in the later Zhivkov years.

Availability of consumer durables significantly improved in the 1970s. According to official statistics, between 1965 and 1988 the number of televisions per 100 households increased from 8 to 100;

radios increased from 59 to 95; refrigerators from 5 to 96; washing machines from 23 to 96; and automobiles from 2 to 40. Available automobiles were primarily Soviet Fiats, some of which were manufactured in Bulgaria. Assembly of the Soviet Moskvich began at the Lovech Vehicle Assembly Plant in 1988.

Housing was one of the most serious shortcomings in the Bulgarian standard of living. Residential construction targets in the Five-Year Plans were regularly underfulfilled. Consequently, families often waited several years for apartments; in Sofia, where overcrowding was at its worst, the wait was as long as ten years (see Housing, ch. 2).

Market Reform

The first year of post-Zhivkov governance brought substantial political confusion and paralysis, despite the country's desperate need to concentrate on economic reform. The interim cabinet and parliament of 1990 provided only stopgap measures, not the long-term planning that all factions believed necessary. The coalition government of Dimitŭr Popov came to power at the beginning of 1991 with broad support but under the worst economic conditions since World War II (see Governance after Zhivkov, ch. 4). The Popov program planned first to use support from the International Monetary Fund (IMF—see Glossary), the European Bank for Reconstruction and Development (EBRD—see Glossary), and the EEC to achieve financial stability. The second phase of the plan was privatization of the Bulgarian enterprise system. The hard winter of 1990–91 began to break the policy stalemate between the ruling BSP and its increasingly powerful opposition, the UDF (see Nongovernmental Political Institutions, ch. 4).

Reform Mechanisms

Although both the BSP and the UDF agreed on the need for market-oriented reforms, disagreements on methods and timing continued in 1991. The BSP advocated slow transformation, to minimize economic dislocations and hardship (and also to preserve privileged positions for party members whenever possible). The UDF believed that a market economy could not be installed piecemeal, but could be effective only as a form of "shock therapy." The UDF saw free market features such as market prices and privatization as incompatible with socialist institutions such as large state-owned enterprises. The huge operating losses of such enterprises were largely responsible for a severe 1990 decline in NMP. The model advocated by the UDF was the renaissance of the Polish economy through private enterprise. This model justified severe, short-term social costs because only by inflicting them

*Bulgarian Orthodox Church of St. George enclosed by courtyard of
Balkan Sheraton Hotel, Sofia
Courtesy Sam and Sarah Stulberg*

could the economy be disentangled from the moribund apparatus
that remained from the central planning era.

Progress was made on some fronts even before formation of the
first coalition government in early 1991. In September 1990, Bulgaria's admission to the IMF promised access to hard currency loans
and help in restructuring the economy. New agricultural banks
began providing credit to private farmers tilling the land provided
in the 1991 Arable Land Law; the first private bank was opened;
and Bulgaria applied for membership to the General Agreements
on Tariffs and Trade (GATT—see Glossary) and the World Bank
(see Glossary) (see Agriculture, this ch.).

The Economic Policy Commission

By 1991 the Economic Policy Commission was the most important advisory body on economic reform for its parent body, the
National Assembly. A number of economic proposals made in 1990
by the government of Prime Minister Andreĭ Lukanov were found
inadequate and redrawn in 1991. A particularly difficult obstacle
in establishing truly private enterprises was Decree Number 56,
the 1989 formula that established semi-decentralized operating principles for firms and commercial organizations (see The Era of

167

Experimentation and Reform, this ch.). In 1991 the National Assembly considered new laws addressing aspects of the transition to a market economy: the Commercial Law was to replace Decree Number 56 as the basic description of commercial enterprise operation; a complex of auditing and statistical laws were to put Bulgarian commerce on the same standards as potential Western investors. The Privatization Law was the last and most problematic item because, unlike the recipients of agricultural land under the Arable Land Law, private recipients of former state commercial enterprises had not been identified. The first goal of the Economic Policy Commission was to use tight monetary policy to eliminate unprofitable enterprises inherited from the CPE era; this would finally stabilize productivity after the precipitous fall that began in 1990 and accelerated in 1991. Once stability was reached, a full-scale privatization process would begin; the 1991 timetable called for the latter process to be well under way by early 1992.

Domestic and International Economic Policies in the 1990s

Whatever the pace of the Bulgarian economic transition, 1991 promised substantial dislocation before an upturn could be expected. In 1990 industrial production had fallen by 10.7 percent. Prime Minister Popov warned that as much as 25 percent of the population would require social assistance in 1991, an increase from the 20 percent of 1990. Although the Popov government launched a consensus economic reform plan, pending national elections in mid-1991 it remained only a caretaker government. Popov's commitment to tough financial measures and the political calm that prevailed during the crisis period encouraged foreign financial assistance. IMF loan requirements included liberalizing foreign trade policy, lifting price and currency controls, compensating for social dislocation that resulted from reforms, maintaining a low national budget deficit, eliminating centralized production and resource allocation, initiating privatization of small firms, and de-emphasizing trade with Comecon countries.

In January 1991, the United States extended most-favored-nation status to Bulgaria; the United States Congress approved the move in April. The recently chartered EBRD committed between 100 and 120 million European currency units (ECUs—see Glossary) to Bulgaria in 1991 and 1992. Most of the money was to go through the PHARE program. Of that amount, 40 percent was earmarked for restructuring the economy, 25 percent for agriculture, 20 percent for health care, and 10 percent for the environment. In March 1991, the IMF approved US$500 million in loans, and the EEC added a loan of US$377 million. A request to reschedule part of

Bulgaria's international debt was denied in early 1991, however. Western aid was conditioned on visible evidence that the government remained in control of its reform program. The immediate goal of the reform program was to reduce inflationary pressure by removing the surplus money supply that had been caused by shortages. Prices would remain subject to the Regulations on the Control of Prices issued in February 1991, to limit price fluctuations and prevent monopolies from gaining huge profits. Meanwhile, privatization remained a potential political quagmire because, unlike many of the measures in the first phase, differences in approach and timing remained substantial among major political factions. The National Assembly still included many politicians from the Zhivkov years who would lose their power base if reform went too far. For that reason, the National Assembly delayed deliberation on several vital economic bills in 1991. For the same reason, many remaining Zhivkovite industrial managers opposed application of reforms to their enterprises. Advocates of reform hoped that the 1991 parliamentary elections would redistribute legislative power, enabling reform to continue and shortening the traumatic transitional period.

* * *

Several English-language monographs provide useful information on the Bulgarian economy. Unquestionably, the most comprehensive is John R. Lampe's *The Bulgarian Economy in the Twentieth Century,* which covers economic structure, development, and performance and provides abundant statistics. Although somewhat dated and less inclusive, *Growth and Reforms in Centrally Planned Economies* by George R. Feiwel covers the same general field. Robert J. McIntyre's *Bulgaria: Politics, Economics, and Society* devotes a chapter to postwar economic development through the 1980s, and John D. Bell's *The Bulgarian Communist Party from Blagoev to Zhivkov* analyzes the theory and practice of Bulgarian economic planning from 1947 through 1985. The *Statistical Yearbook of the People's Republic of Bulgaria* (the English-language version of which is an abridgement of the Bulgarian state publication) provides comprehensive economic data. Periodicals such as the Radio Free Europe/Radio Liberty *Report on Eastern Europe* and *Business Eastern Europe* cover current economic issues. (For further information and complete citations, see Bibliography.)

Chapter 4. Government and Politics

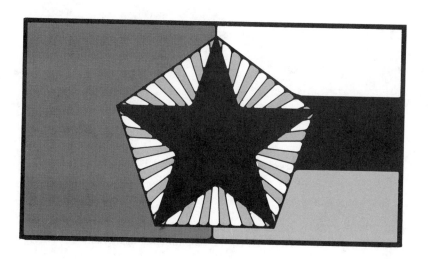

Official party banner combining Soviet and Bulgarian flags, hanging above national party congress of Bulgarian Communist Party, Sofia, 1970

ON NOVEMBER 10, 1989, after thirty-five years as undisputed leader, Todor Zhivkov resigned his positions as head of the Bulgarian Communist Party (BCP) and head of state of Bulgaria. This act, forced by political opposition and turmoil, was the symbolic watershed between two very different eras in Bulgarian governance. One year after Zhivkov's resignation, Bulgaria had at least some of the primary building blocks for a democratic state: a freely elected parliament, a coalition cabinet, independent newspapers, and vigorous, independent trade unions.

Beginning with Soviet occupation of Nazi-allied Bulgaria in September 1944, the political culture of that country had been totally dominated by a monolithic communist party. In the following three years, that party took advantage of the presence of Soviet troops, decades-long disorder in the Bulgarian political system, and its own high visibility as an anti-Nazi resistance force to complete a rapid communization process.

Postwar communist rule in Bulgaria can be divided into three periods with varying political characteristics. The first period, 1944 through 1947, saw the consolidation of communist power. The Fatherland Front, which began in 1942 as a small illegal antifascist coalition, led a coup that coincided with the 1944 Soviet invasion and installed communists for the first time in crucial government positions. In the next three years, the BCP gradually eliminated disorganized blocks of political opposition, cut Bulgaria off from foreign influences except that of the Soviet Bloc, and confiscated most private economic resources. By the end of 1947, the last effective political opposition had been eliminated and Soviet troops had left Bulgaria. Longtime communist leader Georgi Dimitrov was prime minister of a Bulgarian government that ruled according to a new constitution modeled after that of the Soviet Union. Although that constitution left the political institutions of prewar Bulgaria nominally intact, the consolidation period set the pattern for a very different set of political relationships. Actual political power was concentrated entirely in the national BCP. From 1947 until 1989, nominations and elections to judicial, legislative, and executive posts required party approval. During that time, a nominal second party existed, but party nominees were elected without opposition at all levels of government. The National Assembly (Narodno Sŭbranie) met only to rubber-stamp proposals from the party or the executive branch.

The second phase of the communist period, from 1948 through 1953, strengthened Bulgaria's traditionally close ties with the Soviet Union and established a pattern of imitating the Soviet Union in all major aspects of foreign and domestic policy. The first Bulgarian Five-Year Plan began in 1949, by which time most means of production were in state hands. In 1949 Dimitrov was succeeded by Vŭlko Chervenkov, a protégé of Soviet leader Joseph V. Stalin. Chervenkov imitated his patron's cult of personality by assuming total control of the BCP and the government and enforcing complete conformity to party policy through 1954. Chervenkov intensified the sovietization that began under Dimitrov; the only vestiges of political diversity at this point were a few national party leaders who survived Chervenkov's purges.

In 1953 the death of Stalin brought a strong reaction in Soviet politics against the cult of personality and in favor of collective leadership. Accordingly, in 1954 Todor Zhivkov replaced Chervenkov as first secretary of the BCP. In the next eight years, Zhivkov gradually consolidated his position as supreme leader. In doing so, he maintained the totalitarian state machinery of his predecessors but showed flexibility and resiliency—especially in maintaining power at home while following the winding path of Soviet policy to which Bulgaria remained scrupulously loyal. In spite of dramatic international changes and crises between 1954 and 1989, the Zhivkov era was the longest period of stable rule by a single administration in the history of the modern Bulgarian state.

In the 1980s, however, the Zhivkov regime was overtaken by the wave of political liberation that swept all of Eastern Europe, and by the lethargy and corruption of an administration totally without opposition for nearly thirty years. Immediately after Zhivkov's fall, Bulgaria returned to its precommunist political culture, a shifting mosaic of major and minor parties and coalitions. The National Assembly was resurrected as the vehicle for democratic representation, and the first free parliamentary election was held in 1990. Unlike the communist parties of other East European nations, the BCP (which changed its name in 1990 to the Bulgarian Socialist Party, BSP) was based on a domestic political movement that predated the 1917 Russian Revolution. Partly for this reason, the BSP was able to win the first free elections that followed overthrow of the old regime. But internal fragmentation, economic crisis, and the party's connection with the wrongs of the Zhivkov era diminished the BSP's popular support as the 1990s began.

Meanwhile, based on very brief experimentation with true parliamentary democracy before World War II, and imitating its

East European neighbors, Bulgaria had decisively rejected repressive one-party rule and professed allegiance to democracy. But formation of democratic institutions on the ruins of the early 1900s proved a formidable task in the early years of the postcommunist era. Coalition government, the main device of political stability in the precommunist era, functioned unevenly in solving the massive problems of the early 1990s, and the remaining power centers of the old regime hindered reform.

The Prewar Political Context

From its separation from the Ottoman Empire in 1878 until 1947, Bulgaria was ruled as a constitutional monarchy, with a parliamentary system based on the Tŭrnovo Constitution of 1879. Although that document was one of the most progressive national constitutions in the world when it was written, actual governance of Bulgaria under it was a constant struggle for power among the tsar, the unicameral parliament, and the Council of Ministers. The many political factions that proliferated in the twentieth century added another dimension to this struggle. Parliaments were elected and dissolved for purely political reasons; strong prime ministers such as Stefan Stambolov (1886–94) and Aleksandŭr Stamboliĭski (1918–23) ignored parliament to advance their own programs (the constitution had no provision for consultation among government branches, although the Council of Ministers was nominally subordinate to parliament); a succession of weak prime ministers were controlled by the tsar or by political factions such as the pro-fascist Zveno coalition of the 1930s; the need to placate the forces of Macedonian irredentism distorted both domestic and foreign politics throughout the post-independence period; and no prime minister survived without stitching together tenuous coalitions of parties, many of which had only narrow political agendas. Frequent appeals were made to amend the Tŭrnovo Constitution; in other cases, the constitution simply was ignored.

The last arrangement of Bulgarian political forces before World War II was the royal dictatorship of Boris III. Boris devised a system of "controlled democracy" after the short totalitarian regime of Zveno had virtually abolished conventional political parties in 1934 (see The Crises of the 1930s, ch. 1). Boris's system was based on judicious appointments and the balancing of civilian politicians against the army. His purpose was not authoritarian rule but to achieve a temporary centralization of power that would allow Bulgaria to return to stable constitutionality after the chaotic post-World War I period. Boris believed that independent parties would hinder this process, so such parties did not reemerge in Bulgaria under his rule. National elections were not held between 1931 and 1938, and subsequent prewar elections were held under strong government control. In spite of that control, an opposition bloc including the communists gained sixty parliament seats in the 1938 election, compared with ninety-five for Boris's nonpartisan government candidates. In the late 1930s, Boris struggled in vain to form a lasting coalition that could provide solid middle ground between the communist and pro-Nazi factions, both of which rapidly gained support between 1935 and 1940. But when Bulgaria entered the war in 1940, the same "temporary" balance remained in place.

The Early Communist Era

During World War II, the BCP actively opposed Bulgaria's Axis alliance by forming partisan terrorist and sabotage groups. In 1942 the broad Fatherland Front coalition was formed as the communists attempted to involve legal opposition groups in exerting antiwar pressure on the government. The coalition's activities brought severe government reprisals. By 1944 partisan units also were being formed in the Bulgarian army.

The Red Army invasion of September 1944 found a temporary Bulgarian government desperately trying to avoid accommodation with the communist left or the pro-German right, but under intense diplomatic and military pressure from both Germany and the Soviet Union. Boris had died in 1943, and by 1944 severe wartime shortages (partly caused by peasants hoarding food supplies) had eroded support for the government.

When Soviet troops entered Bulgaria, the Fatherland Front engineered a bloodless coup displacing the government of Prime Minister Konstantin Muraviev. In 1946 the first Fatherland Front government divided ministries among the BCP, Zveno, the Bulgarian Agrarian National Union (BANU), and the Bulgarian Social Democratic Party (BSDP). Within a year, the BCP had used that power base to purge the government of all key opposition figures and dominate the Fatherland Front. In 1946 a national referendum rejected the monarchy in favor of a people's republic, leading to the immediate exile of Simeon II, nine-year-old son of Boris III. The following month, the communists easily won a national election for representatives to a *sŭbranie* to write a new constitution over the objections of BANU, which sought a return to the Tŭrnovo Constitution. In early 1947, the conclusion of peace between Bulgaria and the Allies eliminated the Allied Control Commission, through which Britain had maintained some influence on domestic Bulgarian politics. By that time, the only remaining obstacle to total BCP domination was Nikola Petkov's BANU, in a

176

coalition with other noncommunist parties. The power struggle ended abruptly in mid-1947, when the Fatherland Front arrested and executed Petkov as a Western agent. This event paved the way for unanimous adoption of a new constitution in December 1947. The new document was closely modeled on the 1936 Soviet constitution.

The parliamentary election of fall 1946 gave the BCP 275 of 465 seats and made Georgi Dimitrov prime minister. The communists gained control of all significant ministries, beginning the last stage of consolidating communist dictatorship. The ensuing regimes of Dimitrov and Chervenkov defined Bulgaria as a highly conventional communist state and isolated it from nearly all noncommunist commercial and cultural influences.

The State under Dimitrov

In the 1946 elections, noncommunist parties in the Fatherland Front lost influence far out of proportion to the numerical election results. The most salient new feature of the Dimitrov Constitution was that it rejected the separation of powers among government branches in favor of a "unity of state power," lodged in a presidium wielding legislative, judicial, and executive powers and chosen by the National Assembly with party approval. As before, the National Assembly was a unicameral legislature; elections were to be held every four years, and members could be recalled at any time. The assembly would meet in regular sessions twice a year, or by special order of the Presidium—making the full assembly little more than a rubber-stamp body. The Presidium met continuously and exercised all constitutional powers of the National Assembly when the assembly was not in session. The Presidium's powers included controlling the selection of the Council of Ministers, amending the constitution, approving the national economic plan, declaring war, and making peace. The president of the nineteen-member Presidium thus became one of the two most powerful men in Bulgaria.

The Council of Ministers retained a nominal executive authority as a cabinet, but it was overshadowed by the designation of the National Assembly as "supreme organ of state power." In practice, the council chairman, who by office was prime minister of the country, was always the first secretary of the BCP. This gave the prime minister power equal to that of the Presidium president. The judiciary, now also chosen by the legislative branch at all levels of government, lost all independence. Independent local political power was eliminated when province and district jurisdictions were restructured into people's councils. The councils elected executive committees analogous to the national Presidium and overseen by that body. As at the national level, local government bodies were filled primarily with party officials. Thus, the Dimitrov Constitution achieved unprecedented centralization of political power in Bulgaria.

Like its Soviet model, the 1947 constitution guaranteed broad freedoms to all citizens (religion, conscience, assembly, speech, the press, emancipation of women, and inviolability of person, domicile, and correspondence). The Bulgarian document differed from the Soviet by allowing private property, but only if the privilege were not used "to the detriment of the public good." All means of production shifted to state ownership. Universal suffrage was guaranteed, as were welfare and employment. Guaranteed employment was restricted to socially useful occupations, however.

Government practice soon eroded the constitutional guarantee of religious freedom. Between 1948 and 1952, several official acts repressed the Bulgarian religious community. In 1948 the exarch of the Bulgarian Orthodox Church was forced into retirement for his refusal to defend the communist state and the Soviet Union. In 1949 the Law on Religious Organizations put all churches under state control; over the next four years, Catholic and Protestant clergy were harrassed and imprisoned as part of an overall policy of preventing contact with the West. During this period, the Dimitrov government continued purging party and nonparty officials, imitating the contemporaneous Stalinist practice of eliminating all possible political rivals. The most notable victim was the hardline Stalinist and long-time party leader Traĭcho Kostov, convicted and executed in 1949 as a collaborator with the fascists and Josip Broz Tito, the heretical Yugoslav communist leader.

The Chervenkov Era

The Fifth Party Congress, held in December 1948, rightfully celebrated the complete political dominance of socialism in Bulgaria. When Dimitrov died in 1949, his successor, Stalin protégé Vŭlko Chervenkov, began four years of intense party purges (disqualifying nearly 100,000 of 460,000 Bulgarian communists). Chervenkov's cultivation of a cult of personality earned him the nickname "Little Stalin." The breakaway of Tito's Yugoslavia from the Cominform (Communist Information Bureau—see Glossary) in 1948 caused Stalin and Chervenkov to put additional pressure on the BCP to conform with the Soviet line. Stalin's death in 1953 introduced new Soviet leaders who disapproved of Chervenkov's methodology, but the Bulgarian leader remained prime minister and dominated politics until 1956. Chervenkov announced a "new course'' in 1953, police terror abated, and some political prisoners were released. Meanwhile, the Bulgarian government under the communists followed a postwar East European pattern by creating large numbers of bureaucratic posts that were filled by party-approved functionaries, the *nomenklatura*. A swollen bureaucracy had been traditional in Bulgaria since the modern state was founded in 1878; but previously appointments had depended on membership in the civil service elite, not on membership in a particular party.

The Zhivkov Era

Todor Zhivkov was the dominant figure in Bulgarian government for about thirty-five years, during which time the political scene remained remarkably stable. In the context of post-Stalinist communist statecraft, Zhivkov was a masterful politician. In the context of popular demands for meaningful reform, he was an anachronism whose removal symbolized the beginning of a new approach to governance.

The Rise of Zhivkov

The Chervenkov era firmly established Bulgarian reliance on the Communist Party of the Soviet Union (CPSU) for policy leadership and resolution of domestic party rivalries. Just as Stalin's condemnation had doomed Kostov, so condemnation of the cult of personality by Stalin's successors doomed Chervenkov and prepared the way for his successor, Todor Zhivkov. Zhivkov, who began his political career in the party youth organization and worked his way to the party Central Committee in 1948, became party chief when Chervenkov resigned that position in 1954. Both the Moscow authorities who ultimately chose new Bulgarian leaders and the BCP leaders in Sofia approved Zhivkov's flexibility, youth (he was forty-two when selected), and lack of powerful friends and enemies.

In 1956 Bulgarian politics again felt the influence of the Soviet Union. When Nikita S. Khrushchev became leader of the CPSU, he began a new phase of de-Stalinization and party reform that echoed strongly in Bulgaria. This action left Chervenkov without support outside Bulgaria. Then, in 1956 the April Plenum of the BCP Central Committee began a broad party liberalization policy that caused Chervenkov to resign as prime minister. Rather than break completely with the past, however, the party retained Chervenkov as a member of a de facto ruling triumvirate that included Zhivkov and longtime party leader and purge participant Anton Yugov, who became prime minister. Although party liberalization was stalled by 1956 uprisings in Hungary and Poland, the April Plenum identified Zhivkov as the leader of the Politburo. In doing so, it also shifted power conclusively to the "home" branch of the BCP, more attuned to Bulgarian issues and less to total obedience to the Soviet line.

Zhivkov Takes Control

By the end of 1961, a new wave of Soviet anti-Stalinism gave Zhivkov the support he needed to oust Chervenkov and Yugov. Zhivkov's political position had deteriorated because his grandiose, failed plans for industrialization and agricultural collectivization had evoked strong social protests between 1959 and 1961, but he succeeded Yugov as prime minister in 1962 (see The First Five-Year Plans, ch. 3). Khrushchev formally endorsed Zhivkov with a state visit to Bulgaria in 1962. Although no additional changes occurred in the party or the government until 1971, Zhivkov began introducing a new generation of leaders in the mid-1960s, and political repression eased noticeably. The old guard of officials remaining from the 1944 revolution remained a powerful party element with important Soviet connections; therefore, Zhivkov provided that group enough Politburo positions to ensure its support. Meanwhile, Zhivkov selectively purged officials throughout the early period to prevent development of alternative power centers in the party. In 1964 Zhivkov earned peasant support by appointing Georgi Traikov, chief of the nominally independent BANU, head of state and by pardoning comrades of the executed BANU leader Petkov.

In 1966 a strong resurgence of the conservative wing of the BCP at the Ninth Party Congress curtailed Bulgarian diplomatic and economic overtures to the West and to its Balkan neighbors. The new conservatism also tightened government control over the media and the arts, and the government resumed anti-Western propaganda to protect Bulgarian society from bourgeois influences. As was the case in the 1956 invasion of Hungary, Bulgarian support for the 1968 Soviet invasion of Czechoslovakia brought tighter party control of all social organizations and reaffirmation of "democratic centralism" within the party—all with the goal of reassuring the Soviet Union that Bulgaria would not follow in the heretical footsteps of Czechoslovakia.

The Constitution of 1971

A later echo of the events of 1968 was the drafting of a new constitution at the Tenth Party Congress in 1971. Unlike the Dimitrov Constitution, the new document specified the role of the BCP as

Todor Zhivkov one year after his ouster, in confinement at his villa, November 1990
Courtesy Charles Sudetic

"the leading force in society and the state," and the role of the BANU as its collaborator within the Fatherland Front. The 1971 constitution also defined Bulgaria as a socialist state with membership in the international socialist community. As before, broad citizen rights were guaranteed but limited by the requirement that they be exercised only in the interest of the state. Citizen obligations included working according to one's ability to build the foundation of the socialist state and defend the state, compulsory military service, and paying taxes. Most of the governmental structure specified in the Dimitrov Constitution remained, but a new body, the State Council, replaced the Presidium as supreme organ of state power. This council consisted of twenty-two members and a chairman who was de facto head of state. The State Council was more powerful than the Presidium because it could initiate as well as approve legislation, and because it exercised some of the nongovernmental supervision normally delegated to ruling parties in East European communist states of that period. Council members, nominally elected by the National Assembly, were members of the BCP or other mass organizations (see Nongovernmental Political Institutions, this ch.).

In 1971 Zhivkov resigned as prime minister to become chairman of the State Council. The National Assembly, traditional center of political power in Bulgaria until the 1947 constitution stripped it of power, received some new responsibilities. Permanent commissions were to supervise the work of ministries, and legislation could now be submitted by labor and youth groups (all of which were party-controlled). In practice, however, the National Assembly still rubber-stamped legislation and nominations for the State Council, Supreme Court, and Council of Ministers. As a follow-up to the constitution's prescription of private property rights, the 1973 Law on Citizens' Property virtually abolished private ownership of means of production, confining such ownership to "items for personal use."

The Tenth Party Congress also devised a new BCP program to coincide with the new constitutional description of party power. The program specified an orthodox hierarchical party structure of democratic centralism, each level responsible to the level above. The lowest-level party organizations were to be based in workplaces; all other levels would be determined by territorial divisions. Loyalty to the CPSU was reiterated. The BCP goal was described as building an advanced socialist society lacking differentiation by property and social standing—at that point, all of society was to be a single working class. Science and technology were to receive special attention by the party, to improve production that would make possible the next jump from advanced socialism to the first stage of communism (see The Bulgarian Communist (Socialist) Party, this ch.).

After a decade of political calm and only occasional purges of party officials by Zhivkov, social unrest stirred in the mid-1970s and alarmed the Zhivkov government. International events such as the Helsinki Accords (see Glossary) of 1975, the growth of Eurocommunism in the 1970s, and the 1973 oil crisis stimulated hope for liberalization and discontent with the domestic economy. Zhivkov responded in 1977 by purging Politburo member Boris Velchev and 38,500 party members—the largest such change since the early 1960s. Provincial party organizations also were substantially reorganized. In May 1978, the Bulgarian government acknowledged for the first time that an antigovernment demonstration had occurred—indicating that the 1977 measures had not quelled domestic discontent.

The Last Zhivkov Decade

The period between 1978 and 1988 was one of political calm. With minor exceptions, the structure and operations of the government and the BCP remained unchanged. But the avoidance of meaningful change, despite cosmetic adjustments in the Zhivkov government, assumed that Bulgarian governance was the same uncomplicated procedure it had been in the 1970s and early 1980s—a major miscalculation.

Celebration of the 1,300th anniversary of the Bulgarian state in 1981 brought official liberalization and rehabilitation for some segments of Bulgarian society. Bourgeois political factions that had opposed the BCP before World War II were exonerated and described as comrades in the fight for Bulgarian democracy. Zhivkov also raised the official status of the Orthodox Church to codefender of the Bulgarian nationality, and restrictions on religious observances were eased.

By the second half of the 1980s, substantial maneuvering and speculation centered on identifying the successor to the seventy-four-year-old Zhivkov, who was increasingly isolated from everyday governance. Four younger politicians divided most of the key responsibilities of government and party in 1986. Although speculation grew that Zhivkov had become a figurehead or was preparing to resign, in the late 1980s he was still able to divide the power of his rivals and avoid naming a single successor.

The BCP maintained complete control over all major programs and policies in the Bulgarian government, although the role of the party in specific instances was not clear. In 1987, facing a budding opposition movement and pressure from the Soviet Union, the BCP began planning for multiple-candidate (not multiparty) regional elections to end citizen apathy toward both government and the party. Although some reforms were made in the nomination process, local electoral commissions retained control over final lists of nominees.

By February 1989, at least nine independent political groups had emerged. Spurred by the liberalized domestic policies of Mikhail S. Gorbachev in the Soviet Union, such groups demanded similar concessions from the Bulgarian government. Given Bulgaria's long record of mimicking Soviet policy changes, this was a natural expectation. In fact, the 1987 BCP Central Committee plenum had officially endorsed *perestroika* (see Glossary) and *glasnost* (see Glossary), the cornerstones of the Gorbachev reform program. The plenum also substantially reduced official state ceremonies, rituals, personal awards, and propaganda, explaining that such formalities alienated the people.

In the three years following the 1987 plenum, however, the Bulgarian government and the BCP gave lip service to Soviet reforms, while quietly taking a more hard-line approach to many issues. During this period, reform in the BCP and the government apparatus was confined to reshuffling ministries, departments, and personnel as a gesture of solidarity with *perestroika*. At the same time, dissident groups were harrassed, put under surveillance, and accused of unpatriotic activities.

Issues of Dissent

In the late 1980s, official repression of the Turkish minority was the most visible domestic issue in Bulgaria. By 1989 this policy had brought harsh international condemnation and provided a human rights issue for the domestic opposition. A total of 310,000 ethnic Turks were expelled or emigrated voluntarily in 1989, and the Bulgarian economy suffered greatly from this depletion of its work force (see Labor Force, ch. 3, and The Turkish Problem, this ch.).

In July 1989, more than a hundred well-known Bulgarian intellectuals petitioned the National Assembly to restore rights to the ethnic Turks suffering forced emigration. Bulgarian Turks formed the Movement for Rights and Freedoms, advocating a wide range of government reforms besides the Turkish issue. The regime responded by accusing Turkish agents of fomenting ethnic strife, denying the existence of a Turkish minority in Bulgaria, and fanning the racial animosity of Bulgarians toward Turks.

In addition to ethnic and political problems, in the late 1980s Bulgaria faced the need for strenuous economic reforms to improve efficiency, technology, and product quality. Between 1987 and 1989, the Zhivkov regime promised expansion of trade and joint ventures with the West, banking reform, currency convertability, and decentralized planning. In actuality, however, the thirty-five-year-old regime lacked the political will and energy to press drastic economic reform (see Era of Experimentation and Reform, ch. 3). The economic stagnation that began in the early 1980s, with which Zhivkov had become identified, continued unchallenged and became another major cause of political discontent.

The Removal of Zhivkov

Despite the appearance of numerous opposition groups in the preceding year, the Zhivkov regime was unprepared for the successive fall of communist regimes across Eastern Europe in late 1989. In October an all-European environmental conference, Ecoforum, was held in Sofia under the auspices of the Conference on Security and Cooperation in Europe (CSCE—see Glossary). This event focused world attention on Bulgaria's history of repressing environmental activism and stimulated open demonstrations by human rights advocates and the Bulgarian Ekoglasnost environmental group (see Other Political Organizations, this ch.). Although some demonstrators were beaten and detained, direct communication with the West inspired them to greater self-expression. This activity culminated in a mass demonstration in Sofia on November 3. Meanwhile, in a speech to a plenum of the BCP in late October, Zhivkov admitted that his latest restructuring program, begun in 1987 to achieve "fundamental renewal" of society, politics, and the economy, had been a failure. He unveiled a new, detailed program to counteract "alienation of the people from the government and the production process." Other party spokesmen increasingly noted recent drastic reforms in other socialist states and pointed to Bulgaria's failure to keep pace. Then, at the regular plenary meeting of the BCP Central Committee in November, Prime Minister Georgi Atanasov announced Zhivkov's resignation.

Although the resignation appeared voluntary, Western observers agreed that top party figures, increasingly dissatisfied with Zhivkov's refusal to recognize problems and deal with public protests, had exerted substantial pressure on him. The leaders of the movement to remove Zhivkov—Atanasov, Foreign Minister Petŭr Mladenov (who became head of state), and Defense Minister Dobri Dzhurov— had received the advance blessing of Moscow and the majority of the Bulgarian Politburo. Soviet leader Gorbachev apparently approved the change because Zhivkov had not heeded warnings that cosmetic reform was insufficient given the drastic restructuring sought by Gorbachev. Within a month of his resignation, Zhivkov was expelled from the BCP, accused of abuse of power, and arrested. Mladenov became chairman of the State Council and chief of the BCP.

Governance after Zhivkov

The Zhivkov ouster brought rapid change in some political institutions, little or no change in others. The official name of the country, dropping the term "People's," became simply the Republic of Bulgaria. For two years, the BCP remained entrenched as the most powerful party, slowing reform and clinging tenaciously to economic and political positions gained under Zhivkov. But a new constitution was ratified in mid-1991, laying the basis for accelerated reform on all fronts.

The Mladenov Government

The first few months of the Mladenov regime brought few of the dramatic changes seen in Czechoslovakia or the German Democratic Republic (East Germany) in the same period. Mladenov, who came to power without a personal following, left much of the old government in power and failed to separate state from party functions. Although initial reforms came from the Politburo, Mladenov achieved popularity by immediately legalizing political protest,

185

giving the media unprecedented freedom, abolishing privileges of party officials, and scheduling free elections within six months. Article 1 of the 1971 constitution, which established the leading role of the BCP in Bulgarian government and society, was abolished in January 1990. Public repudiation of Zhivkov allowed his subordinates to treat him as a scapegoat, thus protecting themselves from blame by the proliferating opposition groups.

The Bulgarian communists avoided the immediate political rejection suffered by their East European comrades for several reasons. Because the BCP had begun as an indigenous Bulgarian movement in 1891, Bulgarians did not resent it as an artificially imposed foreign organization. In 1989 nearly one in nine Bulgarians belonged to the party, a very high ratio that included a large part of the intelligentsia. Early opposition groups were concentrated in Sofia and did not have the means to reach the more conservative hinterlands, reflecting a political dichotomy between town and country that had existed since pre-Ottoman times (see Electoral Procedures, this ch.). Visible reorganization and reform occurred in the BCP shortly after Zhivkov left power; the Politburo was abolished and some old-guard communists were purged. The BCP invited opposition representation in the government and conducted a series of round-table discussions with opposition leaders. In February 1990, Mladenov resigned as party chief, removing the stigma of party interference in government; in April, the State Council was abolished and Mladenov was named president.

The 1990 Stalemate

The first free election of the postwar era, the national election of June 1990, was anticipated as an indicator of Bulgaria's post-Zhivkov political mood and as an end to the extreme uncertainty that followed the Zhivkov era. But the election results provided no decisive answers or conclusions. During the political maneuvering that preceded the election, the contest for control of the National Assembly narrowed to the BCP and the Union of Democratic Forces (UDF), a coalition of several major and many minor parties and groups with diverse interests (see The Union of Democratic Forces, this ch.). The BCP presented a reformist image, liberally blaming Zhivkov for national problems and changing its name to the Bulgarian Socialist Party (BSP) to stress that a new era had begun. In March an agreement with opposition groups had made approval of legislative proposals by the round table necessary before the BCP-dominated National Assembly could consider passage (see The Role of Unofficial Organizations, this ch.). The round table also signed accords defining future legal changes in the political system, including multiple parties, separation of powers, constitutional protection of media freedom, and legalization of private property.

The parliamentary election was followed by three months of inactivity and drift in the summer of 1990. Although the Council of Ministers had resigned immediately after the election, a new government was not formed until late August. BSP party official Andreĭ Lukanov finally became prime minister in an all-socialist cabinet because UDF and other opposition parties refused to form a coalition. At the same time, the National Assembly required several weeks to agree on compromise candidate Zheliu Zhelev to replace Mladenov as president. The most significant political situation was outside government institutions. The two major parties became deadlocked over UDF demands that the BSP acknowledge its responsibility for the economic ruin of Bulgaria, and that the government adopt the UDF plan for radical economic reform similar to that in Poland (see Market Reform, ch. 3). Although much of the Zhivkov old guard had been forced out in favor of middle-of-the road socialists in 1990, the UDF demands activated strong pockets of reaction. Zhelev, a dissident philosopher and UDF leader, spent the rest of 1990 seeking compromises among the factions.

The Lukanov government, tied to an aging, largely conservative constituency and full of little-known BSP figures, met few of the reform demands. In October Lukanov presented a 100-day economic reform plan to serve as a transition to longer-term planning in 1991. The plan borrowed major parts of the program advocated by the UDF. The National Assembly remained too divided on the reform issue to give Lukanov the legislative support he needed. Meanwhile, polls showed a definite drop in popular support for the BSP; under these circumstances, the UDF intensified efforts to turn out the government by refusing to support any of Lukanov's proposals.

In November Bulgaria was paralyzed by student demonstrations and general strikes called to topple Lukanov (see Trade Unions, this ch.). Lukanov's resignation ended the opposition's refusal to form a coalition government. Zhelev, who then commanded more political power than any other figure, proposed a compromise candidate, Dimitŭr Popov, as prime minister. Popov, a judge with no party allegiance, received a mandate to form a new cabinet and proceed with reforms as soon as possible. After considerable deliberation, cabinet posts were distributed among major factions, and reform legislation began slowly moving into the National Assembly in the first half of 1991.

Government Structure

In the years immediately following the Zhivkov regime, the nominal structure of the Bulgarian government remained essentially unchanged. Actual decision making, however, moved from the elite level of the communist leadership to a variety of political figures and institutions.

The Role of Unofficial Organizations

An important quasigovernmental institution in the early stages of this process was the national round table. Conceived by opposition groups shortly after Zhivkov's fall, the round table format was accepted by the Atanasov government under threat of general strikes. In March 1990, a declaration on the role and status of the national round table, formulated by all major political groups, gave the round table approval rights to all major legislation proposed by the government, prior to formal consideration by the National Assembly. In 1990 round table discussions included key government figures and representatives of all constituent groups of the UDS and other opposition parties and trade unions. This forum was an effective bridge across the chaotic months preceding the first free election. It reached key compromises on election law, major provisions of the new constitution, and economic reforms. Compromise measures were then forwarded to the parliament for ratification. By mid-1990 round table proposals were dominated by the platform of the UDF, for which that forum had become the chief input to government policy. The national round table thus replaced the BCP as the de facto source of legislative initiatives, in the absence of a coalition government representing the major Bulgarian political factions.

In late 1990, President Zhelev convened a Political Consultative Council that was able to unite all major factions behind formation of a coalition government in December 1990. This step ended the threat that chaos would follow the resignation of the Lukanov government (see The Council of Ministers, this ch.). In January 1991, the parties represented in the National Assembly signed a detailed agreement describing political rights, the legislative agenda for 1991, BCP (BSP) responsibility for the mistakes of the Zhivkov regime, property rights, resolution of social conflicts, and ethnic questions. The stated purpose of this agreement was to ease national tensions and provide a proper working atmosphere for the immense reform program envisioned for 1991.

The National Assembly

In the post-Zhivkov reforms, the National Assembly returned

to its prewar status as a forum for debate of legislation among representatives of true political factions. This status had been lost completely from 1947 to 1989, when the assembly rubber-stamped legislation originating in the BCP hierarchy.

The Assembly under Zhivkov

According to the 1971 constitution, the unicameral National Assembly was the supreme organ of state power, acting as the national legislature and electing all the other bodies of the national government. In practice under the Zhivkov regime, the National Assembly met for three short sessions each year, long enough to approve policies and legislation formulated by the Council of Ministers and the State Council. The National Assembly had a chairman (until 1990 elected by the entire body at the recommendation of the BCP Central Committee) and four deputy chairs. In the intervals between sessions, the functions of the assembly were conducted by permanent commissions whose number and designation varied through the years. Not designated in the 1971 constitution, the duties of the commissions often overlapped those of the ministerial departments. The National Assembly had the power to dissolve itself or extend its term in emergency session.

During the Zhivkov years, new assemblies were elected every five years to coincide with party congresses; the Central Committee of the BCP met immediately before the first session of each new assembly to approve candidates who were then rubber-stamped by the National Assembly for the leadership positions of the assembly, State Council, and Council of Ministers. The ninth National Assembly (1986–90) was rarely even notified of policy decisions of the Zhivkov-led State Council. Nevertheless, election of the National Assembly remained the most important political ritual in Bulgaria throughout the communist period, and the return to free assembly elections in 1990 recalled the direct popular representation prescribed in the Tŭrnovo Constitution of 1879, still revered as a model for Bulgarian governance.

The First Freely Elected Assembly, 1990

The first significant post-Zhivkov act of the holdover (ninth) National Assembly was passage of twenty-one measures of constitutional reform. These measures included abolition of the article of the 1971 constitution giving the BCP sole right to govern. In April 1990, that National Assembly dissolved itself to make way for national election of a Grand National Assembly, charged with writing and ratifying a new constitution; this was the first voluntary adjournment of that body since World War II.

In accordance with the provisions under which the 1990 parliamentary elections were held, after passing the new constitution in July 1991 the Grand National Assembly voted to dissolve itself and continue working as a normal parliament until election of the new body. Thus, in the second half of 1991 work would continue on critical legislation covering issues such as privatization, election procedures, and local government reform.

After the 1990 national elections, the National Assembly remained a weak legislative body, but for a new reason. No longer required to follow party orders precisely, representatives often were split quite evenly on reform issues. The majority BSP included reform and reactionary factions, and the 144 UDF members were a formidable opposition group. Unlike the brief assemblies of the Zhivkov era, the new body remained in session several days a week throughout the remainder of 1990 and through mid-1991, struggling for compromise on reform legislation.

The State Council and the Presidency

The State Council, technically an executive committee within the National Assembly, was created by the 1971 constitution as the primary executive agency of the national government. Because of that role, the chairman of the council was automatically president of the country and thus one of the two most powerful figures in Bulgaria in the Zhivkov years. The State Council included representatives from trade unions, the Communist Youth League of Bulgaria (Komsomol), and other mass organizations. The council supervised the Council of Ministers and had the right to repeal ministry decisions—a function that clearly reduced the Council of Ministers to secondary executive status. In addition to its executive functions, the State Council could issue direct decrees with full legal authority when the National Assembly was not in session, with no provision for later approval by the full legislative body. Under Zhivkov most members of the State Council were high officials of the BCP. When Petŭr Mladenov replaced Zhivkov as chairman of the State Council, he did not automatically become head of state. When the State Council was abolished in April 1990, the round table named Mladenov president of the republic, a new title for the Bulgarian head of state. The appointment was made with the understanding that the new constitution would set guidelines for this office. Meanwhile, Mladenov and his successor Zheliu Zhelev retained the power to form cabinets with the consent of the National Assembly, to represent the country abroad, and to act as commander in chief of the armed forces.

*President Zheliu Zhelev meets with United States president George
H.W. Bush, Washington, fall 1990
Courtesy White House Photo Office*

The Council of Ministers

The constitution of 1971 substantially diminished the power of
the Council of Ministers, or cabinet, which had been an intermittent center of executive authority in Bulgarian governments since
1878. In the last two decades of the Zhivkov regime, the council
acted as an advisory board to the State Council and directed everyday operations of the government bureaucracies. All members of
the Council of Ministers belonged to the BCP or the BANU, and
many held top party posts and ministries simultaneously. Longtime Politburo member Stanko Todorov headed the executive committee of the council from its creation in 1971 until 1989. Within
their areas of responsibility, the ministries had authority to form
administrative organs and to overturn acts by local government
agencies. The exact makeup of the council was not prescribed in
the constitution; the National Assembly had authority to make
changes as necessary, and the council's shape and size changed
often in the last Zhivkov years.

After the elections of 1986, the Council of Ministers was reorganized and reduced in size. In the last years of the Zhivkov regime, it included eleven ministers, a chairman (the prime minister),

a deputy prime minister, and the chairman of the Committee on State and People's Control (see Security and Intelligence Services, ch. 5). In early 1990, the new provisional council had fourteen ministries: agriculture and forests; construction, architecture, and public works; economy and planning; finance; foreign affairs; foreign economic relations; industry and technology; internal affairs; internal trade; justice; national defense; national education; public health and social welfare; and transport. The ambassador to the Soviet Union also had full cabinet status, as did the heads of the committees for protection of the environment and state and people's control. Five deputy prime ministers also sat in that cabinet, which was headed by Zhivkov-era holdover Georgi Atanasov. The second provisional cabinet, under Andreĭ Lukanov, included ministers of the environment, culture, and science and higher education in its seventeen departments. The ambassador to the Soviet Union was dropped, and a minister for economic reform added.

The new status of the Council of Ministers as the power center of Bulgarian government was signaled by the targeting of Prime Minister Lukanov for opposition pressure in the fall of 1990. A second signal was intense bargaining between the BSP and opposition parties for positions in the Popov cabinet. That bargaining produced a compromise agreement that gave the key ministries of foreign economic relations and finance to the BSP, with national defense going to the UDF. The Ministry of the Interior, very sensitive because of its role under Zhivkov as the enforcer of state security, was largely reorganized and headed by a nonpolitical figure whose two deputies represented the major parties. The splitting of the deputy minister positions was a key compromise to gain approval of the Popov cabinet. In all, five of the seventeen ministers in the new cabinet were politically unaffiliated; seven remained from the last Lukanov cabinet to soften the transition; and the UDF filled only three posts. The multiparty conference that reached this agreement also allowed for further adjustments in the cabinet structure for the Popov government. As an interim head of government, Popov's main goal was to establish minimal political and economic conditions favorable to long-term reforms.

The Judiciary

Members of the highest national judicial body, the Supreme Court, were elected to five-year terms by the National Assembly. Until 1990, however, National Assembly approval really meant control by the State Council, hence by the BCP. The national court system was divided into criminal, civil, and military courts; the Supreme Court had jurisdiction in both original and appellate cases, and it controlled the activities of all lower courts. The 1971 constitution called the court system and state prosecutor's office "weapons of the dictatorship of the proletariat." The chief prosecutor, chief legal official of Bulgaria, was responsible for compliance with the law by ordinary citizens, local and national political entities and officials, and other public organizations. The powers of this office were extended by law in 1980 in an effort to forestall public dissatisfaction with the crime prevention system. Like the justices of the Supreme Court, the chief prosecutor served at the approval of the State Council. Together with the chief justice of the Supreme Court, the chief prosecutor provided absolute BCP control of the Bulgarian judicial system until 1990. The election of all judicial officials further guaranteed this control.

Lower courts functioned at the provincial and municipal levels; election was by people's councils at the provincial level and directly by citizens at the municipal level, using party-approved lists. In 1990 each of Bulgaria's provinces (including Sofia) had a province court. The 105 provincal courts tried minor offenses. Both professional judges and lay assessors sat in the lower courts. Specialized disputes were heard outside the regular court system. For example, international trade cases went to the Foreign Trade Court of Arbitration of the Bulgarian Chamber of Commerce and Industry, civil disputes among enterprises and public organizations were heard by the State Court of Arbitration, and labor disputes were settled by the conciliation committees of enterprises.

Criticized before and after the fall of Zhivkov, the Bulgarian justice system changed little with the reform programs of 1990 and 1991. The round table resolutions of early 1990 alluded only to separation of the judicial, legislative, and executive branches to avoid concentration of power in any single branch. However, establishment of an independent, authoritative judiciary would be complicated by the universal view, instilled by forty-five years of complete control by the BCP, that the Bulgarian court system was only an extension of the state's executive power. In a 1991 poll, only 1.7 percent of Bulgarians expressed trust in the courts and the prosecutor's office. In 1990 the youngest judges were over forty years old, and the most talented had left for other careers because of the short term of office, poor pay, low professional status, and party control. In late 1990, Judge Dimitŭr Lozanchev became the first politically neutral chairman of the Supreme Court since World War II.

Local Government

In 1987 Bulgaria consolidated its local government structure by combining its twenty-eight districts (*okrŭzi*; sing., *okrŭg*), into nine provinces (*oblasti*; sing., *oblast*), including the city of Sofia (see fig. 1). A tangible part of the Zhivkov regime's massive (and largely theoretical) plan for economic and political restructuring, the reorganization imitated restructuring plans in the Soviet Union. Local government consolidation was to eliminate the complex and inefficient *okrŭg* bureaucracies and improve the operation of "people's self-management," the system by which people's councils nominally managed area enterprises. The latter improvement was to result from narrowing the primary function of the new *oblast* government to the assistance of local workers' collectives. At the same time, municipalities and townships became somewhat more autonomous because the restructuring gave them some of the administrative power removed from the higher level.

Although the number of districts had remained stable from 1959 until the 1987 reform, the number and allocation of smaller urban and rural political entities changed rapidly during that period as the population shifted (see Population, ch. 2). In 1990 there were 299 political divisions smaller than the *oblast* and twenty-nine separate urban areas. Both *oblasti* and smaller constituencies were ruled by people's councils, elected for thirty-month terms. The local multiple-candidate elections of February 1988 were another aspect of the restructuring program. Although local election commissions retained considerable influence over nominations, about 26 percent of successful candidates were nonparty in 1988. At that time, 51,161 councillors and 3,953 mayors were elected.

The people's councils at all levels were run by elected executive committees that met continuously. These committees had full executive power to act between sessions of the people's councils, in the same way as the State Council acted for the National Assembly in the Zhivkov-era national government. Each council was responsible to the council at the next higher level; financial planning was to conform to the goals of national economic programs. Local councils had authority over the People's Militia, or police, as well as over local services and administration. The Popov government scheduled new local elections for February 1991, after which time reforms were expected in the local government system. Meanwhile, most provincial governments remained under the control of Zhivkovite officials, intensifying the schism between the urban and provincial political climates.

Electoral Procedures

The round table reforms of 1990 included a new election law ratified by the National Assembly. As in other aspects of governance,

A Bulgarian Orthodox priest participating in the election demonstrations of 1990, Sofia
Courtesy Charles Sudetic

prescribed election procedures did not change greatly under the new regime, but the intent and practice of the law did. The right to vote by direct secret ballot remained universal for all Bulgarians over eighteen, and the officials they elected remained theoretically responsible only to the voters. Prescriptions for eligibility for nomination and the nomination process changed little with the new law. The main difference was that in practice the BCP (BSP) no longer could indiscriminately remove elected representatives or members of people's councils, nor did it control the nomination function nominally given to public organizations, trade unions, youth groups, and cooperatives.

Under the election law of 1953, all candidate lists were approved by the communist-controlled Fatherland Front. Under the 1990 law, all parties and registered nonparty organizations could submit candidates; individuals could be nominated for the assembly with 500 signatures of voters from their district, and an unlimited number of candidates might run from each district. The State Council formerly had the power to call elections; for the 1990 Grand National Assembly election, the date was fixed by agreement of the UDF and the BCP. The Central Election Commission, formerly a creature of the State Council, was to supervise the equitable implementation of election laws, overseeing the operation of equivalent commissions at local levels. Election commissions at all levels included members from various parties; the Central Election

Commission was headed by a professor of law with no political connection.

The new law also revised the representational system of the National Assembly. The new assembly continued to have 400 seats, but it would sit for four instead of five years. A new electoral structure also was introduced. Half the National Assembly members were elected in multiple-seat districts, in proportion to total votes cast for each party in the district. A 4 percent minimum was required for a party to achieve representation. The law designated twenty-eight multiple-seat voting districts, based on the pre-1987 *okrŭzi*. The other 200 members were elected from 200 single-seat voting districts. A runoff election was held in each district where no candidate received 50 percent of the initial vote (this occurred in 81 of the 200 districts). All voters in the 1990 election had one vote in each type of district (see The National Assembly, this ch.).

The election was supervised by the CSCE. According to impartial observers and the parties themselves, the election was reasonably free of interference and coercion, considering that most of the electorate had never faced a true political choice and the registration and voting systems were quite complex. Party strategies were dictated by timing and geography. The UDF, lacking time and resources to campaign in the provinces, confined its efforts to the more congenial constituency in Sofia and other large cities. The BSP campaigned as a reform party in progressive Sofia, but it took advantage of the substantial residue of Zhivkovite local officials in the provinces (many of whom were accused of exerting pressure on their constituents to vote BSP) to gain 211 assembly seats to the UDF's 144. The UDF outpolled the BSP in Sofia, Plovdiv, Varna, and most other Bulgarian cities.

The timing of the next national election was the topic of heated debate in the first half of 1991 as political factions maneuvered for advantage. After the new constitution was ratified in July 1991 and a new election law was scheduled for August, elections were tentatively set for October 1991. The new election law was to free the system of the cumbersome procedure used in 1990. Controversial elements of the law were a BSP-backed clause disallowing absentee ballots from émigrés and the restriction of all campaign activities to the Bulgarian language. The 1991 law prescribed a Central Electoral Commission of twenty-five, to be appointed by the president in consultation with major political factions. The central commission would then appoint and oversee like commissions at lower jurisdictions and set policy for election administration. National elections were to be held by the proportional system, eliminating the two-part system of 1990. Recognized parties, coalitions of parties, individual nominees, and combinations of individuals and parties would be eligible to run. The country was divided into thirty-one electoral constituencies, three of which were in Sofia.

Nongovernmental Political Institutions

Until 1989 the BCP exerted firm control over such nongovernmental political institutions as trade unions, youth groups, women's groups, and the nominally oppositionist BANU. The ouster of Zhivkov, however, brought a torrent of new and revived groups into the political arena. In the new open political climate, the groups' fragmented constituencies often spoke loudly for their own special interests, greatly complicating the process of coalition-building and compromise needed to accomplish national reform.

The Bulgarian Communist (Socialist) Party

The Bulgarian Communist Party (BCP), which renamed itself the Bulgarian Socialist Party (BSP) several months after the fall of Zhivkov, boasted one of the highest membership-to-population ratios (one in nine Bulgarians) in any communist country in the late 1980s. Between 1958 and 1987, membership grew by 442,000, mainly by adding bureaucrats and blue-collar workers in younger age groups. In 1986 women made up 32.7 percent of party membership, but few women held high positions. The proportion of worker members had grown to 44.4 percent by 1986, and the proportion of farm members had dropped to 16.3 percent, reflecting an even sharper drop in the overall farming population of Bulgaria (see table 20, Appendix). Party recruitment in the 1980s targeted individuals already successful in public or economic life, and the proportion of white-collar members increased in that decade.

In 1987 the BCP was organized into 2,900 local units. Until 1990 primary party organizations were based primarily in workplaces. The next level in the hierarchy was municipal organizations, which were overseen by city or province and ultimately national bodies. At every level, party and government personnel were closely interwoven, and the principle of democratic centralism kept the lower levels strictly subordinate to the national party. The primary organizations were charged with recruitment and mobilization. A major concession by the post-Zhivkov party was removal of party cells from all state offices, the judiciary, educational and health agencies, as well as all nongovernmental workplaces—a concession forced by the UDF's threat to boycott the round table negotiations that would set a national agenda for political reform early in 1990. That change significantly altered the primary level of party organization.

Until 1990 the top level of party leadership was the Politburo, of which Zhivkov was general secretary. That position had been abolished in the 1950s in the BCP as part of de-Stalinization. It was restored in 1981, however, to recognize Zhivkov's long service and conform to Soviet restoration under Leonid Brezhnev. Politburo members usually were selected from the central committee and nominally elected by party congresses, which normally met every five years. In 1986 the Thirteenth Party Congress elected an eleven-member Politburo dominated by party loyalists of Zhivkov's generation but supplemented by a few younger specialists in politics and economics. Following tradition, the 1986 congress made few changes in the previous Politburo. The party congresses were nominally the top policy-making body of the party, but, like the National Assembly, they rubber-stamped decisions handed them by the party elite.

The BCP hierarchy also included the Central Committee, whose members the congress unanimously approved from candidates supplied by the party leadership. Through a number of specialized departments, the Central Committee performed administrative party work between sessions of congress. After considerable size variation, the last Central Committee included 190 members and 131 candidate members in early 1990. The third elite group was the BCP Secretariat, a group somewhat smaller than the Politburo (its number also varied during the Zhivkov years), entrusted with implementing party policy.

Membership in the BCP required recommendation by three established members; if accepted at the primary and next-highest level, a candidate received full membership with no probationary period. Criminal or unethical behavior caused withdrawal of membership. Without benefit of explanation, a varying number of members also failed to receive the new party cards issued before each party congress. Abrupt purging of cadre and membership elements deemed potentially hostile to current programs was a procedure that Zhivkov used with great skill to balance and weaken opposition forces throughout his tenure in office.

The fall of Zhivkov brought immediate and dramatic changes in the BCP, including removal of the word "communist" from its name. The Extraordinary Fourteenth Party Congress of the BCP was held in the winter of 1990, over a year sooner than scheduled. That congress abolished the Central Committee and the Politburo in favor of a Supreme Party Council headed by a presidency. To streamline party activity, the new council had only 131 members, 59 fewer than the last Central Committee. The Secretariat was abolished. The party emerged from the congress with significant splits between reform and conservative factions and a new temporary program. Only about 10 percent of previous Central Committee members became members of the new Supreme Party Council; several party stalwarts who had survived the Zhivkov overthrow, including Prime Minister Atanasov, were not elected. The BCP's constitutional guarantee of the leading role in Bulgarian society already had been abolished. In a compromise with the UDF shortly after the congress, party organizations were banned from workplaces and the armed forces. The BSP had full control of the government (the UDF refused to form a coalition both before and after the 1990 elections), but BSP popularity and power ebbed rapidly during 1990 and 1991. By the first anniversary of Zhivkov's resignation, party membership had decreased to an estimated 250,000. (Membership had been reported as 984,000 at the time of the Fourteenth Party Congress.)

The Union of Democratic Forces

The Union of Democratic Forces (UDF; Bulgarian Sayuz na Demokratichnite Sili—SDS), which emerged as the chief opposition faction to the BCP after 1989, was a motley coalition of several major and many minor parties and groups. Some of the parties, such as the BANU, predated the communist era by several decades. Others, such as the Green Party, were organized after the overthrow of Zhivkov. When the UDF was founded in December 1989, it included ten organizations; by the following spring, six more parties and movements had joined.

The basis of the UDF was the dissident groups that formed under the faltering Zhivkov regime in the late 1980s. The all-European Ecoforum of October 1989 allowed many such groups to meet and exchange ideas for the first time; once Zhivkov fell, the initial contacts spawned an organizational declaration that envisioned a loose confederation. Within the confederation, constituent groups would continue to work for their own specific interests. The coordinating council was to include three members from each organization. Longtime dissident philosopher Zheliu Zhelev was elected chairman and Petŭr Beron, a well-known environmental scientist, was chosen secretary.

The diversity of membership required substantial compromise in the UDF program. At least one issue central to each member group was included in the program, however. The general goals of the program were a civil society, market economy, multiparty system, and constitutional government. Sixteen specific steps were outlined to achieve those goals. The main criterion for acceptance

199

of new member organizations was compatibility of their goals with those in the UDF program.

Shortly after the UDF was founded, a vital policy decision confronted its leaders: the BCP-dominated government revoked the Zhivkov program of Bulgarizing the names of all Turkish citizens. Alienating the extreme nationalist factions that opposed compromise with the ethnic minority, the UDF supported the government decision in its first major policy statement.

In the first half of 1990, the stature of the UDF was enhanced by its participation as an equal in round table discussions with the BCP (BSP) on a range of policy issues that would set future economic and political policy. By March 1990, the coalition's main goal was clearly stated: to push the interim National Assembly to draft a democratic constitution and urgent reform legislation as quickly as possible, over the opposition of remaining BSP hardliners and noncommunist splinter groups. All factions recognized that once this was completely accomplished, the coalition would dissolve and members would act as independent political parties with varying agendas.

In the parliamentary elections of June 1990, the UDF platform advocated a wide range of drastic reforms in government structure, the media, foreign policy, and the economy. Detailed proposals were offered for education, the environment, and a two-phase "shock therapy" reform leading to a free market economy. Finally, the UDF blamed the previous communist regime for Bulgaria's current crises. The UDF failed to gain a majority in the National Assembly because many rural areas remained in control of Zhivkovite BSP politicians. Many peasants had felt relatively secure under the old collective system, and the timing of the election had forced opposition parties to concentrate campaigns in the cities, their strongest regions. The BSP won 211 of the 400 seats.

In the year following parliamentary elections, BSP obstructionism stymied legalization of the UDF's reform goals. On the other hand, the UDF's refusal to participate in the Lukanov cabinet proved its popular strength by stalemating Lukanov's economic reform program. In the crisis-driven formation of the Popov government in December 1990, the UDF gained strategic cabinet posts. In January 1991, the UDF and the BSP agreed on a timetable for passage of the new constitution and other urgent legislation, but early in 1991 parliamentary disagreements set back the schedule. In March 1991, the UDF sponsored a protest rally attended by more than 50,000 people in Sofia. In May legislators from several smaller parties walked out of the National Assembly to protest its inaction; the BANU contingent promised to do the same if the parliament

A group of demonstrators for the Union of Democratic Forces (identified by SDS on their banner) prior to the election of June 1990
Courtesy Charles Sudetic

had not passed a new constitution by the end of June. Meanwhile, however, official UDF policy continued seeking to break the long stalemate by convincing the socialists in the National Assembly to abandon their go-slow approach to reform.

By mid-1991 a split developed between the largest member groups (the reconstituted BSDP, the BANU, Ekoglasnost, and the Green Party) and the smaller ones over using quotas and preferential lists in the next election—a practice that would contradict the UDF's role as a single national movement and give larger parties substantially more influence in policy making. Easily the largest member organizations with about 100,000 members each, the BANU and the BSDP would benefit most from such a shift. In July 1991, voting in the National Assembly on the new constitution clarified the split between factions viewing the UDF as a single national movement and those seeking individual identity within a loose confederation. The main issue was the constitutional prescription for legislative representation by party. By summer 1991, disagreements on ratification of the constitution had led splinter groups to form a new Political Consultative Council to rival the UDF's existing National Coordinating Council as a controlling agency of the UDF. This action threatened to split the UDF into two or three slates of candidates for the 1991 national elections. Thus, by mid-1991 the relative harmony of the UDF's first year had evolved into persistent divisiveness affecting tactics, organizational structure, and the pace of reform. In spite of conciliatory efforts by the coordinating council, the effective united front that had forced major concessions from the BSP in 1990 seemed less potent in 1991.

Trade Unions

The Bulgarian trade union movement was rejuvenated in the pluralist post-Zhivkov political atmosphere after being forced to adhere totally to BCP policy throughout the postwar period. By 1990 unions were a powerful policy-making force, using well-organized strikes and walkouts to emphasize their positions.

Unions under Communist Regimes

In the decade before World War II, the benign dictatorship of Tsar Boris III abolished independent trade unions in favor of a single government-sponsored Bulgarian Workers' Union. As Bulgaria emerged from the war under Soviet occupation, communists abolished that union and replaced it with a General Workers' Professional Union that included both white- and blue-collar workers. Gradually, independent union organizations were forced to

disband or join the communist organization. By 1947 union leaders were an important instrument in consolidation of the party's
power. When capitalism was declared illegal in 1948, the Dimitrov
government united thirteen unions under the Central Council of
Trade Unions, which endured until 1989 as the single umbrella
organization representing Bulgarian workers.

During that entire period, all workers' and professional organizations followed faithfully the economic policies of the BCP. The
official goals of the Bulgarian trade unions were first to help management to fulfill state economic plans, then to defend workers' interests
when they did not conflict with such fulfillment. As institutions
the unions had no policy input. In individual enterprises, union
leaders and managers developed informal advisory relationships.
The only official role of the unions was as transmitters of party
policies to the working masses. Although union and BCP membership were theoretically separate, officials at the national and local
levels often overlapped to give the party direct control of workers.
For example, members of the district-level people's councils often
were also union executives (see Local Government, this ch.).

General congresses of trade unions were held explicitly to carry
out BCP policy; congress delegate structure (2,997 attended the
ninth congress in 1982) and the holding of preliminary district congresses mimicked BCP procedures. The many industrial reorganization plans of the Zhivkov regime meant periodic restructuring,
if not new roles, for the unions. In the early 1980s, for example,
the decentralizing reforms of the New Economic Model (NEM)
changed the labor union structure from one divided by region to
one divided by brigade, collective, and enterprise, matching the
NEM industrial structure of the time. Although this change was
controversial, it did little to improve the influence of the Bulgarian working class on enterprise policy.

In the 1980s, union membership approached 4 million, encom-
passing an estimated 98 percent of Bulgarian workers. Almost a
year before the fall of Zhivkov, the Independent Labor Federation, Podkrepa, organized as a white-collar opposition group inspired by the Polish Solidarity (see Glossary) movement. In 1989
Podkrepa consistently was persecuted for its outspoken criticism
of Zhivkov's policies.

Independent Union Organizations

When the communist regime was overthrown, the central council began restructuring the trade union system, declaring the organization independent of the BCP and renaming its umbrella

organization the Confederation of Independent Trade Unions (CITU). In 1990 BCP organizations were banned from work places, although the continuing overlap of party and union officials maintained substantial communist influence in the CITU at local levels. In the early reform years, the CITU and Podkrepa were the two major trade union federations, although many independent unions also emerged in this revival period for the movement. Early in 1990, Podkrepa established its credibility by exacting an agreement with CITU guaranteeing its members all the rights (and the substantial privileges) accorded official trade unions under the previous system. From the beginning, Podkrepa sought maximum influence on government policy, repeatedly demanding radical economic reform.

Podkrepa grew rapidly in 1990 because of its roles as a charter member of the UDF, as a participant in the policy round tables with the BCP, and as the organizer of strikes and demonstrations against the communist-dominated Lukanov government. In early 1990, an estimated 300 strikes helped convince the government that talks with opposition groups were necessary. Although Podkrepa ran no candidates in the national elections of 1990, it vigorously supported candidates who espoused labor views. In late 1990, another wave of strikes pushed the Lukanov government out and led to the coalition Popov government. Although CITU and other unions participitated, Podkrepa usually was the prime organizer in such actions.

CITU, whose membership of 3 million dwarfed the 400,000 of Podkrepa, remained politically passive in the early post-Zhivkov period. In mid-1990 CITU began issuing statements critical of government inactivity, and it mobilized 500,000 workers to participate in the November 1990 strikes initiated by Podkrepa against the Lukanov government.

The strikes that forced Lukanov's resignation also raised criticism of the political role of both labor organizations late in 1990 (see Governance after Zhivkov, this ch.). CITU received criticism for both its continued ties with the BSP and its aggressive reformist stance. The Supreme Party Council of the BSP declared a policy of noninterference in CITU affairs. Meanwhile, Podkrepa, led by controversial, outspokenly anticommunist Konstantin Trenchev, responded to internal and external criticism by changing from active membership to observor status in the UDF.

The unions continued active participation in political decision making in 1991, however. Because economic reforms brought substantial unemployment and workplace disruption, representing worker interests was synonymous with such involvement in this period. In January 1991, CITU and Podkrepa signed a "social peace agreement" with the Popov government to refrain from striking during the first phase of economic reform in exchange for limitations on work-force cutbacks (see Market Reform, ch. 3). However, jurisdictional and policy disputes threatened to undermine the agreement. Although both organizations continued to support the Popov government, in March 1991 Podkrepa proposed that UDF representatives boycott the National Assembly because it failed to pass reform measures.

As opposition to the communists declined as a uniting factor, Bulgaria's trade unions maneuvered to shape new roles for themselves in 1991. Representing 40 percent of the population in a wide-open political culture, they exerted tremendous influence on policy even in the first post-Zhivkov year. The radical economic reform envisioned by Bulgarian leaders would include entirely new relationships among the government, enterprise management, and unions. Movement to a Western-style free-market economy would mean conceding some worker rights taken for granted under the command economy, but compromise with the Podkrepa-led union movement promised to be a severe test for other political institutions.

Youth Organizations

Following the model of the Soviet Union, the BCP put massive resources into its party youth organization when it came to power. Officially called the Communist Youth League of Bulgaria (later the Dimitrov Communist Youth League of Bulgaria) and abbreviated to Komsomol, the league sought to ensure that proper socialist values would pass to the next generation and to supply new members for the party. With a peak membership of 1.5 million in 1987, the Komsomol had the same organizational structure as the BCP, with a secretariat and executive bureau analogous to the Politburo at the top and a pyramid of local and regional sub-organizations. Besides instilling party dogma in Bulgarian youth, the organization was a vehicle for enforcing party directives, a source of reserve personnel, an organizer of social and recreational activities, and, in the 1980s, an instrument for encouraging computer training in the schools. Beginning in the mid-1970s, the Komsomol's lack of self-confidence was revealed in a series of party meetings, speeches, and programs aimed at explaining and combatting apathy and materialism in Bulgarian youth. By the late 1980s, the Komsomol was widely seen as a hollow facade; between 1987 and 1989, membership dropped by 30 percent after compulsory registration ended in secondary schools.

Immediately after the overthrow of Zhivkov, alternative youth groups began to form. One such group, the Federation of Independent Students' Unions (FISU), gained support by advocating complete separation of student groups from the BCP/BSP and its ideological constraints and by proclaiming itself a student voice on questions of national policy. FISU gained stature by being a charter member of the UDF.

Meanwhile, the Komsomol acknowledged past failures, changed its name to the Bulgarian Democratic Youth (BDY), and began issuing policy statements on student rights and broader social issues. The organization was decentralized by giving local affiliates substantial autonomy, and democratized by limiting the terms of officials. Election of a political unknown, Rosen Karadimov, as first secretary was another signal that the youth organization had broken with conventional communist party practices.

The BDY was overwhelmed by a wave of student activism in alternative groups. Student strikes in support of the anti-Lukanov labor strikes in late 1990 shut down major universities. And, like the BSP, the BDY faced reminders and accusations of its misdeeds in the prereform era. In late 1990, the BDY returned to the state much of the property the Komsomol had accumulated during decades of BCP funding. It also renounced socialism and recast itself as an apolitical social organization.

The Movement for Rights and Freedoms

With 120,000 members, the Movement for Rights and Freedoms (MRF) was the fourth largest political organization in Bulgaria in 1991, but it occupied a special place in the political process. The leader of the movement, Ahmed Dogan, was imprisoned in 1986 for opposition to the Zhivkov policy of assimilating ethnic Turks (see Bulgaria in the 1980s, ch. 1). Founded in 1990 to represent the interests of the Turkish ethnic minority, the MRF gained twenty-three seats in the first parliamentary election that year, giving it the fourth-largest parliamentary voting bloc. Its agenda precluded mass media coverage or building coalitions with other parties, because of the strong anti-Turkish element in Bulgaria's political culture. By mid-1991, the UDF had held only one joint demonstration with the MRF; their failure to reconcile differences was considered a major weakness in the opposition to the majority BSP. In early 1990, the MRF protested vigorously but unsuccessfully its exclusion from national round table discussions among the major Bulgarian parties.

In 1991 the MRF broadened its platform to embrace all issues of civil rights in Bulgaria, aiming ''to contribute to the unity of the Bulgarian people and to the full and unequivocal compliance with the rights and freedoms of mankind and of all ethnic, religious, and cultural communities in Bulgaria.'' The MRF took this step partly to avoid the constitutional prohibition of political parties based on ethnic or religious groups. The group's specific goals were ensuring that the new constitution protect ethnic minorities adequately; introducing Turkish as an optional school subject; and bringing to trial the leaders of the assimilation campaign in the 1980s. To calm Bulgarian nationalist resentment, the MRF categorically renounced Islamic fundamentalism, terrorism, and ambitions for autonomy within Bulgaria. Political overtures were made regularly to the UDF, and some local cooperation occurred in 1991. Although the MRF remained the fastest growing party in Bulgaria, however, the sensitivity of the Turkish issue caused official UDF policy to keep the MRF in isolation.

Other Political Organizations

Besides the BSP and the BANU, parties officially sanctioned under Zhivkov, an unofficial list of political organizations in early 1990 contained fourteen political parties, seven unions and labor federations, and sixteen forums, clubs, movements, committees, and associations—diverging widely in scope, special interests, and size.

Ecological Organizations

Two ecological organizations, the Green Party in Bulgaria and Ekoglasnost, were founding members of the UDF. The Greens, which separated from Ekoglasnost shortly after Zhivkov's fall, included mostly scientists and academics. Their platform stressed decentralized government and a strong role for the individual in determining quality of life and preservation of the environment. The government was to play a leading role, however, in providing social security, health care, and support for scientific reasearch. Ekoglasnost, which described itself as nonpolitical despite its role in the UDF, was founded in early 1989 as an open association of environmentally concerned citizens. Its purpose was to collect and publicize ecological information about proposed projects, and to assist decision makers in following environmentally sound policy. Ekoglasnost had a membership of 35,000 at the end of 1990.

Revived Prewar Parties

The Bulgarian Social Democratic Party (BSDP) was an offshoot of the movement that produced the BCP. The main socialist party in Bulgaria between the world wars, the BSDP was disbanded by the communists in 1948. It resurfaced in 1990, resuming its advocacy of government reform and elimination of social privilege. The BSDP saw a freely elected National Assembly as the chief instrument of popular democracy. The BSDP party platform also called for close economic ties with Europe, disarmament, and respect for private property. The BSDP was a founding member of the UDF and, under the controversial leadership of Petŭr Dertliev, one of its most active participants.

The history of the BSDP followed closely that of the communists, except that the latter had a larger following. The BSDP recovered official status in 1990 after being disbanded in 1948. Representing the middle class, the party stood for private property rights, a multiparty parliamentary system of government, radical reduction of the military budget, and active participation in the European Community. Membership in 1991 was 25,000 to 30,000.

The Petkov branch of the Bulgarian Agrarian National Union (BANU), the third of the prewar parties to emerge as an independent entity after Zhivkov, was the part of the agrarian movement that had actively opposed the communists between 1944 and 1947 and thus did not survive the postwar communist consolidation. The "official" BANU, showpiece opposition party to the BCP from 1947 until 1989, also was revitalized in 1990. In 1990 and 1991, efforts were made to reunite the two factions. (Petkov himself was officially rehabilitated by the National Assembly in 1990.) In its new incarnation, the Petkov branch advocated complete government decentralization, extensive support for agricultural privatization and investment, punishment of the communists and "official" agrarians for crimes against the Petkov branch, and a general return to the populist ideas of Stamboliĭski (see Stamboliĭski and Agrarian Reform, ch. 1). Together with the BSDP, the Petkov BANU was the largest (110,000 members in 1991) and most active constituent of the UDF.

The Monarchist Movement

Simeon II, exiled son of Tsar Boris III, was 54 years old in 1991, healthy, and popular with many Bulgarians. In the difficult reform years, he was the center of a small but significant movement that saw restoration of the monarchy as a solution to the dilemmas of governing society. Simeon encouraged the movement by agreeing to return if his people wished a restoration. Newly available publications on the history of the Bulgarian monarchy, especially Boris III, had evoked considerable public interest by 1991. A referendum on monarchy-versus-republic was scheduled for July 1991, then cancelled by the National Assembly because of its potentially divisive impact and because of strong opposition from the BSP and most UDF factions. The new constitution's description of Bulgaria as a republic ended official consideration of restoration in 1991, but Simeon's personal popularity preserved monarchism as a political option for many disillusioned Bulgarians in the early 1990s.

The Public and Political Decision Making

In the post-Zhivkov era, extreme diversification of political organizations and activities paralleled a similar liberation in the media and the arts. Under Zhivkov, Bulgaria had followed the totalitarian formula for media control, allowing only official radio and television stations and newspapers that were conduits for the official party line on all subjects. Limited artistic freedom came in several "thaw" periods (notably in the mid-1960s and the late 1970s) that closely followed similar relaxation in the Soviet Union. The charisma of Liudmila Zhivkova, appointed by her father to oversee cultural affairs in 1975, notably lightened the Bulgarian cultural scene from the late 1970s through 1981. The early 1980s was a time of unprecedented freedom for media discussion of controversial topics; the Law on Plebiscites (1983) was to have promoted discussion of preselected issues of public interest, but by 1984 party reactionaries had reasserted control. The 1984 Bulgarian Writers' Conference called for more ideological content in literature, signaling a change that lasted through the end of the Zhivkov regime.

The Intelligentsia

Intellectual groups developed no formal organizations comparable to groups in other East European countries because the small intellectual community centered in one city (Sofia) required no such measures. Furthermore, the Bulgarian Writers' Union already contained a large percentage of the intelligentsia. Especially during the "thaw" periods, factions in the union showed substantial diversity in their approach to the role of art versus that of the state. A much smaller Bulgarian Artist's Union and Bulgarian Journalists' Union had similar status. A *samizdat* (underground publication) network did circulate dissident writings from the Soviet Union and elsewhere. Among official publications, *Narodna kultura* (People's Culture) gained a singular reputation between 1984 and 1988 by publishing provocative articles on politics, economics, education, and the environment. In 1988 Zhivkov fired its editor Stefan Prodev for helping found a dissident organization.

Zhivkov and the Intelligentsia

Until the late 1980s, Zhivkov successfully prevented unrest in the Bulgarian intellectual community. Membership in the writers' union brought enormous privilege and social stature, and that drew many dissident writers such as Georgi Dzhagarov and Liubomir Levchev into the circle of the officially approved intelligentsia. On the other hand, entry required intellectual compromise, and refusal to compromise led to dismissal from the union and loss of all privileges. The punishment of dissident writers sometimes went far beyond loss of privileges. In 1978 émigré writer Georgi Markov was murdered in London for his anticommunist broadcasts for the British Broadcasting Corporation, and Blaga Dimitrova was harshly denounced for her critical portrayal of party officials in her 1982 novel *Litse*.

Zhivkov also softened organized opposition by restoring symbols of the Bulgarian cultural past that had been cast aside in the postwar campaign to consolidate Soviet-style party control. Beginning in 1967, he appealed loudly to the people to remember "our motherland Bulgaria." In the late 1970s, Zhivkov mended relations with the Bulgarian Orthodox Church, and in 1981 Liudmila Zhivkova's national celebration of Bulgaria's 1,300th anniversary raised patriotic feeling. Zhivkov's extensive campaign of cultural restoration provided at least some common ground between him and the Bulgarian intelligentsia.

The Ferment of 1988–90

In late 1987, dissatisfaction with government corruption, pollution, the Turkish issue, and repeated failure of economic reform programs began to stimulate open political dissent. By that time, a younger generation had matured, unimpressed by communist doctrine and disinclined to blind obedience. In November 1987, the Federation of Clubs for Glasnost and Democracy (originally the Discussion Club for Support of Glasnost and Perestroika) was founded by communist intellectuals to promote openness in Bulgarian society. In early 1988, the appearance of the Independent Association for Defense of Human Rights in Bulgaria publicized the repression of the regime. Meanwhile, the fragmented intellectual community had been galvanized by a single issue: environmental degradation. In the winter of 1987–88, an ecological exhibition in Ruse, one of the most seriously polluted industrial centers in Bulgaria, received national media attention. The communist regime's failure to protect its people from such dangers became a symbol for the general aura of incompetence that surrounded Zhivkov in the late 1980s.

In mid-1988 Zhivkov responded to the new opposition by purging two high pro-*glasnost* party officials, signaling that the party would permit *glasnost* only on its own terms. The BCP also tried to preempt environmental opposition by forming the Movement for Environmental Protection and Restoration amid promises for stiffer environmental regulation.

In late 1988 and early 1989, many leaders of independent Bulgarian groups were deported or harrassed. Nevertheless, by mid-1989 at least thirteen independent associations and committees had been founded for the defense of human rights and the environment. Then in 1989, communism was discredited by successful freedom movements in Hungary, Poland, East Germany, and Czechoslovakia. By that time, *glasnost* had stimulated political dialog in the Soviet Union, which was still the model for Bulgarian political behavior. Under these new conditions, government intimidation failed. Although Zhivkov sought reconciliation with the intelligentsia by proclaiming a ''new cultural revolution'' in early 1989, the unions of writers, journalists, and artists leveled strong criticism on the environment and other issues. When Ekoglasnost was formed that year, it made a formidable public appeal for an accounting of economic policies that harmed the environment (see Other Political Organizations, this ch.).

In 1989 the Federation of Clubs backed the National Assembly petition against Turkish assimilation by characterizing the policy as against the best traditions of the Bulgarian nation. According to one theory, the Zhivkov policy toward the Turks was calculated to alienate the intelligentsia from the ethnocentric Bulgarian majority by forcing the former to take sides with the Turks; whatever its purpose, the policy failed amid the massive Turkish exodus of 1989. Leaders of the Movement for Rights and Freedoms, deported for defending the Turks, were welcomed at a session of the CSCE, severely damaging Zhivkov's image in Europe. In the fall of 1989, dissident groups received further validation at the CSCE Conference on the Environment in Sofia, where they held public meetings and were received by Western delegates. The mass demonstrations that followed convinced the BCP that the Zhivkov regime could not survive.

Dramatic expression of public discontent continued after the Zhivkov ouster. In mid-1990 tent-city demonstrations in Sofia continued for several weeks, encountering no effective official resistance. Patterned after peaceful antigovernment protests of the 1960s in the West, the Sofia campsite of over 100 tents near the BSP headquarters building began as a protest against communist retention of power in the national elections of June 1990. The protest eventually included demonstrators of many political viewpoints. Besides election fraud by the BSP, issues targeted were the Chernobyl' coverup, corruption among former and present BCP/BSP officials, Bulgaria's role in the invasion of Czechoslovakia, and past actions of present government officials such as Lukanov and Interior Minister Atanas Semerdzhiev. The tent city played an important role in publicizing reform issues as a new national government was being formed.

The Media and Public Issues

In the wake of Zhivkov's overthrow, fast-spreading pluralism in the media and intellectual circles brought a din of conflicting opinion to the public. In 1987 Bulgaria had seventeen daily newspapers, most of which were local. By 1991 eight national newspapers were publishing, and an expanding variety of local and weekly papers was available. Until 1990 the chief daily newspaper was *Rabotnichesko delo,* the official organ of the BCP. After the fall of Zhivkov, the daily was renamed *Duma;* in its new format, it began to feature more balanced accounts of national problems, reflecting the moderate image now cultivated by its sponsoring organization. The fragmentation of politics in 1990 brought a newspaper boom that included a full spectrum of political views. In 1991 the leading papers by circulation were *Duma, Demokratsiya* (an independent), the trade union daily *Trud,* and *Zemia,* aimed primarily at rural readers. The most popular weeklies were *Stŭrshel,* featuring folk humor, and the long-running *Pogled.* The weekly *168 Chasa* went furthest in rejecting traditional Bulgarian journalism in favor of sophisticated parody and Western-style in-depth features.

Universities dropped their required study of Marxist-Leninist ideology, and student organizations emerged immediately to assert positions on a wide variety of issues (see Youth Organizations, this ch.). In numerous national polls, the public expressed dissatisfaction with government leaders, economic policies (as both too radical and too conservative), and the BSP. Vestiges of the traditional gap between city and village remained, however: on the average, rural Bulgarians expressed less support for market reform and noncommunist leaders, placed less blame on the communists for current problems, and opposed complete rights for the Turkish minority more strongly.

In 1990–91 the media featured major exposés on malfeasance by the Zhivkov regime (acknowledged by the present BSP under public pressure), coverups of radiation exposure from the Kozloduy Nuclear Power Plant and the Chernobyl' disaster in the Soviet

Demonstrators outside parliament building in Sofia demand resignation of the Bulgarian Socialist Party government, November 1990.
Courtesy Charles Sudetic

Union, and the murder of Georgi Markov (a full-scale investigation of which opened in 1990). In mid-1991 Bulgaria opened its archives to an international commission investigating the 1981 assassination attempt on Pope John Paul II. In spite of those developments, in 1991 government agencies and individuals still threatened independent publications with court action for ''treasonous'' statements. In a 1991 poll by the independent *168 Chasa*, 46 percent of respondents expressed the belief that a campaign had been organized to control the Bulgarian media (the BSP and party officials were most often named responsible), and 37 percent said that freedom of the press was not in danger in Bulgaria.

The Permanent Commission for Human Rights and the National Problem was created in 1990 as an advisory and investigatory agency of the National Assembly. Composed of thirty-nine members of parliament, the commission received the nominal assignment of investigating past and present human rights violations in Bulgaria, recommending appropriate compensation, and drafting new human rights legislation. Among the issues addressed in the commission's first year were restoration of government-confiscated property to churches and Turkish citizens; verifying complaints of unfair sentencing and inhumane prison conditions; proposing laws to replace restrictive legislation such as the Law on Religious Beliefs and the Law on Passports; and erecting legal barriers against state persecution for political reasons (see Religion, ch. 2). In January 1991, commission chairman Svetoslav Shivarov reported that all political prisoners in Bulgaria had been freed.

The Turkish Problem

As in other parts of Eastern Europe, the repeal of single-party rule in Bulgaria exposed the long-standing grievances of an ethnic minority. Especially in the 1980s, the Zhivkov regime had systematically persecuted the Turkish population, which at one time numbered 1.5 million and was estimated at 1.25 million in 1991. Mosques were closed, Turks were forced to Slavicize their names, education in the native language was denied, and police brutality was used to discourage resistance (see Turks, ch. 2). The urban intelligentsia that partcipated in the 1990 reform movement pushed the post-Zhivkov governments toward restoring constitutionally guaranteed human rights to the Turks. But abrogation of Zhivkov's assimilation program soon after his fall brought massive protests by ethnic Bulgarians, even in Sofia.

In January 1990, the Social Council of Citizens, a national body representing all political and ethnic groups, reached a compromise that guaranteed the Turks freedom of religion, choice of names, and unimpeded practice of cultural traditions and use of Turkish within the community. In turn, the Bulgarian nationalists were promised that Bulgarian would remain the official language and that no movement for autonomy or separatism would be tolerated. Especially in areas where Turks outnumbered Bulgarians, the latter feared progressive ''Islamification'' or even invasion and annexation by Turkey—a fear that had been fed consciously by the Zhivkov assimilation campaign and was revived by the BSP in 1991. Because radical elements of the Turkish population did advocate separatism, however, the nonannexation provision of the compromise was vital.

The Bulgarian governments that followed Zhivkov tried to realize the conditions of the compromise as quickly as possible. In the multiparty election of 1990, the Turks won representation in the National Assembly by twenty-three candidates of the predominantly Turkish MRF (see The Movement for Rights and Freedoms, this ch.). At that point, ethnic Bulgarians, many remaining from the Zhivkov regime, still held nearly all top jobs in government and industry, even in predominantly Turkish Kŭrdzhali Province. Nevertheless, parts of Bulgarian society felt threatened by the rise of the MRF. In 1990 that faction collided with a hard-line Bulgarian group, the National Committee for Defense of National Interests—an organization containing many former communists instrumental in the Zhivkov assimilation program. In November 1990, Bulgarian nationalists established the Razgrad Bulgarian Republic in a heavily Turkish region to protest the government's program of restoring rights to the Turks. In the first half of 1991, intermittent violence and demonstrations were directed at both Turks and Bulgarians in Razgrad.

These conditions forced the government to find a balance between Turkish demands and demonstrations for full recognition of their culture and language, and Bulgarian nationalist complaints against preferential treatment for the ethnic minority. In 1991 the most important issue of the controversy was restoring Turkish-language teaching in the schools of Turkish ethnic districts (see Education, ch. 2). In 1991 the Popov government took initial steps in this direction, but long delays brought massive Turkish protests, especially in Kŭrdzhali. In mid-1991 continuing strikes and protests on both sides of the issue had brought no new discussions of compromise. Frustration with unmet promises encouraged Turkish separatists in both Bulgaria and Turkey, which in turn fueled the ethnocentric fears of the Bulgarian majority—and the entire issue diverted valuable energy from the national reform effort. Although most political parties supported full minority rights, in 1991 the strength of Bulgarian nationalist sentiment, deeply rooted in centuries of conflict with the Ottoman Empire and not inclined to compromise, promised to make the Turkish question the most pressing human rights issue in Bulgaria for the foreseeable future.

Foreign Policy

From World War II until 1989, Bulgarian foreign policy revolved around the Soviet Union. Without exception Sofia imitated or supported Soviet twists and turns such as Khrushchev's denunciation of Stalin in 1956 and the invasion of Czechoslovakia in 1968. Substantial historical and economic ties supplemented the ideological foundation of the relationship. In the 1970s and 1980s, Bulgaria improved its diplomatic relations with nations outside the Soviet sphere. But in 1989, domestic and international events jolted Bulgaria from forty years of uniformity and forced it to consider for the first time major diversification of its foreign policy, abandoning its paramount reliance on the Soviet Union. This meant a lengthy period of reevaluation, during which general goals were agreed upon but specific policy was hotly debated.

In 1991 Foreign Affairs Minister Viktor Vŭlkov listed several general goals of his ministry: the integration of Bulgaria as fully as possible into the unified European Community to facilitate development of a market economy and Western political institutions; improving relations with all Bulgaria's Balkan neighbors and the countries of the Black Sea region, with emphasis on mutual territorial integrity and sovereignty; active participation in the United Nations and other international organizations able to guarantee the security of small states; and maintaining as much as possible of Bulgaria's unique relationship with the Soviet Union while drawing much closer to the United States. Once the economic advantages of membership in the Council for Mutual Economic Assistance (Comecon—see Glossary) disappeared in 1990 and instability became chronic in the Soviet Union, other sources of economic and geopolitical security became the primary quest in Bulgaria's pragmatic search for foreign partners (see Bulgaria in Comecon, ch. 3). In 1990 indications of the new pragmatism were recognition of the Republic of Korea (South Korea) and Israel and an official invitation for the pope to visit Bulgaria.

The Foreign Policy Establishment

Major changes were made in the organizations conducting Bulgarian foreign affairs after the ouster of Zhivkov. Post-Zhivkov governments ended the practice of selecting members of the Ministry of Internal Affairs for diplomatic positions in which they gathered intelligence and carried out subversive activities abroad (see Security and Intelligence Services, ch. 5). Admitting that the Bulgarian intelligence presence abroad had been extensive under Zhivkov, the Ministry of Foreign Affairs declared in mid-1991 that henceforth only a single, identified intelligence officer would remain in each Western embassy. In a sharp streamlining of the diplomatic corps, 200 of Bulgaria's 544 foreign diplomats were called home in 1990 and 1991, and 20 of its 79 foreign missions were closed, mostly in Third World countries (relations with those countries continued, however).

Under the communist Lukanov government of 1990, President Zheliu Zhelev assumed major responsibilities as head of state in talks with foreign leaders; his nonpartisan political position at home and his direct approach to foreign and economic issues gained Zhelev respect as a spokesman in Bulgaria and abroad, as well as large-scale commitments of aid from several Western sources (see Domestic and International Economic Policies in the 1990s, ch. 3). When Popov formed his government in 1991, Vŭlkov (leader of the BANU) replaced a former Zhivkovite intelligence official as minister of foreign affairs, supplementing Zhelev's efforts and improving the world image of Bulgaria's official foreign policy agency.

Relations with Balkan Neighbors

Although the Zhivkov regime often advocated closer relations and multilateral cooperation with Yugoslavia, Turkey, Greece, Albania, and Romania, a number of traditional issues barred significant improvement until the late 1980s. Bulgarian proposals to make the Balkans a zone free of chemical and nuclear weapons, or a "zone of peace and understanding" (advanced by Zhivkov at the behest of the Soviet Union, to eliminate weapons of the North Atlantic Treaty Organization (NATO—see Glossary) from the region) was vetoed on several occasions. But in 1990, Zhelev was able to remove some of the suspicion that had barred rapprochement by the Zhivkov regime. Post-Zhivkov regimes sought closer relations with both Greece and Turkey, partly in the hope that NATO would grant Bulgaria membership to form a bridge between its two mutually hostile members.

Yugoslavia

Bulgarian relations with Yugoslavia were conditioned by old issues of Balkan politics and by strong domestic political forces at work in both countries. Throughout the 1980s, the Yugoslav media complained loudly that Bulgaria mistreated its Macedonian citizens by insisting that Macedonians were ethnically Bulgarians, making separate ethnic recognition inappropriate. The Zhivkov regime (and its successors), fearing that inflamed nationalism in Yugoslavia would intensify demands for Macedonian autonomy across the border in Bulgaria, largely ignored the Yugoslav propaganda campaign on the Macedonian issue. The dispute over Macedonia survived and prospered after communism lost its grip on both countries. Bulgarian nationalists, stronger after Zhivkov, held that the Slavic population of the Republic of Macedonia was ethnically Bulgarian, a claim leading naturally to assertion of a Greater Bulgaria. To defuse nationalist fervor on both sides, and in keeping with the policy of improved relations with all neighbors, Zhelev officially advocated nonintervention in the ethnic affairs of other nations.

The nonintervention strategy assumed greater importance when the Republic of Macedonia sought independence from the Yugoslav federation in 1991 in an effort to escape the increasing dominance of the Republic of Serbia in the federation. That effort reinforced the protective attitude of Macedonian nationalists in Bulgaria toward Yugoslav Macedonia, which had been part of Serbia in the interwar period. Serbia's use of force to prevent the breakup of the Yugoslav federation in 1991 triggered Bulgarian fears of wider destabilization in the Balkans if Serbian expansionism were fully revived.

In 1991 Bulgarian policy toward Yugoslavia was complicated by the rejuvenation of Macedonian national groups in Bulgaria. The largest of these was the Union of Macedonian Societies, a long-standing cultural and educational society that in 1990 took the prefix IMRO (Internal Macedonian Revolutionary Organization), which was the name of the terrorist organization active in Bulgaria, Greece, and Serbia between 1893 and 1935 (see The Macedonian Issue, ch. 1). But the threat posed by such groups remained small because the focus of Bulgarian nationalism was the Turkish issue in 1991, and because economic reform was the major concern of all factions. In spite of claims by the Serbian press that Bulgaria was aiding Croatia in the civil war of 1991 and that Bulgaria owed Serbia reparations from World War II, Bulgaria followed Zhelev's policy of nonintervention as the Yugoslav civil war continued.

Romania

In the early 1980s, Bulgarian relations with Romania featured regular official visits by Zhivkov and Romanian President Nicolae Ceauşescu and diplomatic avoidance of differing approaches to internal control (Romania being the more totalitarian) and the Warsaw Pact (see Glossary) (Bulgaria being the more loyal member). At that point, both countries concentrated on more pressing foreign issues, and both advocated creating a Balkan nuclear-free zone. But during the 1980s, relations were strained by the independent foreign policy of Romania, its opposition to *perestroika* in the late 1980s, and mutual accusations of environmental pollution affecting the other country. Deteriorating personal relations between Zhivkov and the maverick Ceauşescu also may have contributed to the decline. But, in the name of Warsaw Pact solidarity, the Zhivkov regime subdued criticism of chemical pollution from Romanian plants across the Danube, and it remained neutral in the Hungarian-Romanian dispute over Romanian treatment of ethnic Hungarians in that country in the late 1980s. After the emergence of the environment as a political issue in 1989, however, accusations became more harsh on both sides. In 1991 joint commissions attempted to reach a compromise on the environmental issue and restore the pragmatic, relatively amicable relationship of the postwar years.

Greece

Bulgarian relations with Greece, a traditional enemy, were stable throughout the 1970s and 1980s, in spite of major government changes in both countries. Zhivkov made this stability a model for the overall Balkan cooperation that was a centerpiece of his foreign policy in the 1980s. In 1986 the two countries signed a declaration of good-neighborliness, friendship, and cooperation that was based on mutual enmity toward Turkey and toward Yugoslav demands for recognition of Macedonian minorities in Bulgaria and Greece. An important motivation for friendship with Greece was to exploit NATO's Greek-Turkish split, which was based on the claims of the two countries in Cyprus. In early 1989, Bulgaria signed a ten-year bilateral economic agreement with Greece.

The main historical issue between Bulgaria and Greece, disposition of their Macedonian minorities, was settled during the 1970s; after that time, the parties adopted mutual policies of strict noninterference in internal affairs. In mid-1991 the possibility of independence for Yugoslav Macedonia threatened to renew tension in that area. Post-Zhivkov Bulgarian policy toward Greece remained very conciliatory, however; in 1991 Zhelev stressed cooperation with Greece as a foundation for Balkan stability and reassured the Greeks that Bulgarian rapprochement with Turkey did not threaten this relationship.

Turkey

In spite of intermittent rapprochement, Turkey was hostile to Bulgaria through most of the 1980s because of Zhivkov's mistreatment of Bulgarian Turks and the economic hardship caused in Turkey by mass immigration of Turks from Bulgaria in 1989. The last rapprochement, a protocol of friendship in early 1988, was signed by Bulgaria to defuse international criticism of its ethnic policy. That agreement dissolved rapidly in 1988, when Turkey saw no change in Bulgarian ethnic assimilation; by 1989 Turkey was vowing to defend the Turkish minority, while Bulgaria claimed that its ''Turks'' were all Bulgarians converted to Islam under the Ottoman Empire (see The Turkish Problem, this ch.).

The ouster of Zhivkov and subsequent Bulgarian commitment to repatriate deported Turks and grant them full human rights brought a marked change in Turkish policy. Despite delays and complaints from the Bulgarian Turks, Turkey remained patient and positive toward all signs of progress. The former dissident Zhelev, long a vocal critic of assimilation, became president and met with Turkish President Turgut Özal in September 1990. That meeting began a series of high-level economic talks in 1990-91 that yielded Turkish loans and technical assistance to Bulgaria and promised to bolster bilateral trade, which had shrunk by 80 to 90 percent in the mid-1980s. A new treaty of friendship and cooperation was prepared in the summer of 1991.

Despite the thaw, obstacles remained in Bulgarian-Turkish rapprochement. The ill will caused by Zhivkov's shrill anti-Turkish propaganda remained fresh in the early 1990s. Strident anti-Muslim and anti-Turkish statements in the media by Bulgarian nationalist factions kept tension high, and minor border incidents continued in 1991. And Bulgarian friendship with Greece created a precarious balancing act that required caution toward such moves as the Bulgarian-Turkish nonagression pact proposed by Turkey in late 1990.

The Soviet Union

In the post-Zhivkov era, the most controversial foreign policy problem was defining Bulgaria's new relationship with its traditional protector and best trading partner, the Soviet Union. Although Zhivkov's relations with Gorbachev had not been as warm as those with earlier Soviet leaders, Bulgaria remained strongly dependent on the Soviet Union economically even in the years immediately following Zhivkov's ouster (permission for which Bulgarian Politburo members duly sought and received from Moscow). In mid-1992 the 1967 Treaty for Cooperation, Security, and Friendship with the Soviet Union was to expire.

Because the treaty called for notice of abrogation to be given a year in advance, by mid-1991 Bulgarian national opinion was divided over what terms should be included in the National Assembly's draft of a new treaty. Led by the BSP, one body of Bulgarian opinion advocated essentially renewing the existing treaty, giving the Soviet Union top priority in the new foreign policy to ensure continued supply of fuels and other vital materials. A second body of opinion, led by the UDF and Podkrepa, conceded the pragmatic necessity of continued economic relations but urged that a new treaty eliminate all subordination of Bulgarian to Soviet interests and provide complete flexibility for Bulgaria to establish commercial and diplomatic ties with the West. Amid heated public debate, the Popov government reached agreement with the Soviet Union on a short-term abrogation followed by accelerated joint development of a new treaty reflecting the changed positions of both sides. The Bulgarian National Assembly was expected to pass a bill to that effect in August 1991 (see Foreign Trade, ch. 3; see Foreign Military Relations, ch. 5).

Because the two countries had no disputed territory and were on roughly parallel paths of political reform in 1991, major issues between them were mostly economic. The primary Bulgarian concern was to protect its newborn geopolitical independence from any recurrence of the Warsaw Pact mentality in Moscow. Other critical goals in 1991 were stabilizing the unpredictable supply of Soviet oil, protecting large numbers of Bulgarian guest workers threatened with layoff in the Komi Autonomous Soviet Socialist Republic (Komi ASSR), and reestablishing Soviet markets for Bulgarian goods that had shrunk drastically in 1990. A new bilateral defense agreement also was a priority in the wake of Warsaw Pact disestablishment. In July 1991, Bulgaria set a precedent by signing a trade agreement with the Byelorussian Republic, the first intergovernmental pact made directly with one of the Soviet republics.

Western Europe and the United States

Under Zhivkov, Bulgaria's policy toward Western Europe and the United States was determined largely by the position of the Soviet Union. Events such as the invasions of Czechoslovakia and Afghanistan automatically distanced Bulgaria from the West; then, in the early 1980s Soviet efforts to split NATO by cultivating Western Europe brought Bulgaria closer to France and the Federal Republic of Germany (West Germany)—a position that continued through the 1980s. A 1988 application for membership in the General Agreement on Tariffs and Trade (GATT—see Glossary) was refused because of the Turkish assimilation program, after widespread expectations of success.

Decades of complete isolation from the West left traces on Bulgarian policy even in the 1980s. In early 1989, President François Mitterrand of France was the first Western head of state to visit Bulgaria since before World War II. Between 1945 and 1989, the highest visiting United States official was an assistant secretary of state. And in 1985 Sir Jeffrey Howe became the first British foreign secretary to visit Bulgaria since the nineteenth century—an indication that isolation began before the onset of communism.

The first post-Zhivkov regime recognized quite early, however, that Cold War politics no longer could limit Bulgaria's choice of economic or diplomatic partners. Within a few months of the Zhivkov ouster, the National Assembly Committee on Foreign Policy had received the head of the Council of Europe and received a pledge of closer ties, and Bulgarian diplomats and businessmen had described reform goals, priorities, and investment opportunities to a CSCE Conference on Economic Cooperation. Shortly thereafter Prime Minister Lukanov visited the headquarters of the European Economic Community (EEC—see Glossary) in Brussels. Lukanov signed a treaty on trade and economic cooperation to remove all trade barriers by 1995 and guarantee Bulgarian access to EEC markets. Lukanov also gained substantial support for Bulgarian membership in the International Monetary Fund (IMF—see Glossary), the International Bank for Reconstruction and Development, and GATT.

A critical stage in the new policy was Zhelev's meeting with Western leaders in Europe and the United States in the fall of 1990. Zhelev explained Bulgaria's nonaligned position and its needs to United States President George H.W. Bush and to Mitterrand, receiving substantial pledges of aid from both leaders. Traditional trading partner Austria also pledged substantial new investment in the Bulgarian economy during Zhelev's tour of the West.

Bulgaria's new policy toward the West was reflected in a series of decisions taken in 1990. Diplomatic relations were restored with South Korea and Israel, Western allies in sensitive areas of Cold War confrontation. An official invitation for Pope John Paul II to visit Bulgaria constituted a new level of recognition of that religious leader's authority. And in early 1991, Bulgaria sent token noncombat forces in support of the United States-led Persian Gulf War effort. In 1991 Zhelev's cooperation with an international investigation of the Markov murder was another significant gesture to the Western world.

From the beginning, the success of Bulgaria's intense campaign for closer relations with the West depended on continued progress in economic and human rights reform and was measured in economic terms. As the stature of the Soviet Union dwindled steadily in 1991, the hope of gaining full status in the European community was a powerful weapon for reformers within Bulgaria. Given Bulgaria's strategic position and chronic instability elsewhere in the Balkans, Western nations monitored Bulgaria carefully and rewarded its progressive steps. Nonetheless, in 1991 Bulgaria remained far behind Hungary, Czechoslovakia, and Poland in receiving Western aid.

* * *

Few monographs have been written on the Bulgarian government and politics of the late 1980s. Background to that period is provided by the politics sections of Robert J. McIntyre's *Bulgaria: Politics, Economics and Society* and John D. Bell's *The Bulgarian Communist Party from Blagoev to Zhivkov*. More recent political events are reported authoritatively in numerous journal articles, including "Long Memories and Short Fuses," by F. Stephen Larrabee; "Bulgaria: An Eastern European Revolution in Suspension," by Steven Chiodini; "Bulgaria's Time Bind: The Search for Democracy and a Viable Heritage" by Joel Martin Halpern and Barbara Kerewsky-Halpern; and "'Post-Communist' Bulgaria," by John D. Bell. Also extremely valuable are the Radio Free Europe/Radio Liberty *Report on Eastern Europe,* each covering a particular aspect of the current political situation. (For further information and complete citations, see Bibliography.)

Chapter 5. National Security

Thracian warrior in Roman mural, Serditsa

IN 1991 BULGARIA GRAPPLED with political changes and economic difficulties that threatened its national security. The country's most intractable problems were internal crises rather than external threats. The Warsaw Pact (see Glossary), which had guided national security policy since 1955, became defunct as a military organization on April 1, 1991. A concurrent shift from one-party communist rule to multiparty politics made the future political character and role of the Bulgarian People's Army (BPA) uncertain. Grave economic problems also portended that a smaller proportion of national resources would be devoted to defense in the future. The European strategic environment seemed less tense and threatening than at any time in the recent past, largely because of the waning of the Cold War; however, the more immediate situation in the Balkans appeared less secure in 1991. Neighboring countries Yugoslavia and Greece were apprehensive that Bulgarians might renew their interest in the Greater Bulgaria established briefly under the Treaty of San Stefano in 1878.

The Bulgarian military establishment was substantial and well equipped considering the small size and population of the country. One expert observer described it aptly as a regional force of significance. The data exchanged at the signing of the Treaty on Conventional Armed Forces in Europe (CFE—see Glossary) on November 19, 1990, revealed previously unknown details on the command organization, structure, strength, and disposition of Bulgaria's ground and air forces. The BPA appeared to be a relatively cohesive force without serious ethnic or other internal fragmentation. Despite the end of the Warsaw Pact, a continued military relationship with the Soviet Union was expected, based on genuine affinity and mutual interest between the two countries. In the late 1980s, Bulgaria imitated several major military reforms then being introduced in the Soviet Armed Forces, which long had served as the model for developing Bulgaria's armed forces. The BPA instituted unilateral force reductions, restructuring, defense industry conversion, and a new openness in military affairs that imitated Soviet *glasnost* (see Glossary).

In 1991 Bulgaria's uncertain internal security situation reflected the unsettled state of politics and the economy. Increased political freedom, economic hardship, and the inability or reluctance of the governments that followed the regime of Todor Zhivkov (1962–89) to use force or coercion against the population created the potential for domestic unrest. These factors made possible increased reliance on the internal security apparatus, and ultimately the BPA, to maintain order and even to carry out basic government functions. In the immediate post-Zhivkov years, the army was the pivotal institution protecting legitimate national security interests and territorial integrity during the transition to democracy and the rule of law.

Development of the Armed Forces

The ancestors of the modern Bulgarians established a respectable martial tradition during centuries of combat with the Byzantine and Ottoman empires. After Russian armies freed it from Ottoman control in the late nineteenth century, Bulgaria became an independent military force in the Balkans. Bulgaria's neighbors viewed it as the major regional power with outstanding territorial ambitions; for that reason, they joined forces to offset Bulgarian military power before 1914. Bulgaria participated actively in combat operations as a German ally in World War I. Although again allied with Germany in World War II, Bulgaria did not join in German offensive operations. After World War II, Bulgaria came under Soviet military influence and in 1955 joined the Soviet-led Warsaw Pact (see World War II, ch. 1). In that capacity, Bulgaria became an integral part of Soviet military and political policy toward the southern flank of the North Atlantic Treaty Organization (NATO—see Glossary). Although the end of superpower confrontation in Europe had loosened the bilateral military connection to the Soviet Union by 1991, extensive military ties remained.

Early Development

For several centuries after they migrated to the Balkans in the middle of the seventh century A.D., the Bulgars were the primary rivals of the Byzantine Empire for control of the eastern Balkans. In the seventh and eighth centuries, Bulgar kings established an independent empire that inflicted several defeats on the Byzantines in Macedonia and Thrace. King Terbelis defeated the Byzantine army at the Battle of Anchialus in 708, drove through Thrace to the walls of Constantinople, and besieged the Byzantine capital in 712. In 717, however, Terbelis allied with the Byzantine Emperor Leo III against the Arabs. Terbelis led the Bulgar army into Thrace, won the Battle of Adrianople in 718, and defended Constantinople against a Muslim siege from across the Bosporus. Emperor Constantine V reasserted Byzantine control over the Bulgars in the mid- to late eighth century. King Kardan regained the initiative by the end of the century and forced Byzantium to pay tribute to the Bulgars.

The power of the First Bulgarian Empire waxed during the ninth and early tenth centuries. The Bulgars continued their struggle with Byzantium and encountered new foes as well. They fought the Magyars and Pechenegs, who raided them from north of the Danube River (see fig. 2). Beginning in 808, Tsar Krum fought a successful war against the Byzantines, winning the Battle of Versinikia in 813, capturing Adrianople, and advancing to the walls of Constantinople. However, Krum's son was defeated at the Battle of Mesembria in 817. Tsar Simeon fought successful wars against the Byzantines in the late ninth and early tenth centuries, capturing Thessaly, Macedonia, and Albania from the Byzantines, conquering Serbia, and threatening Constantinople itself.

Between 967 and 969, the Byzantines and Russians invaded and annexed Bulgaria. Samuil, an expatriate noble, then regained control of eastern Bulgaria and Serbia by defeating the Byzantines near Sofia in 981. Throughout the late tenth and early eleventh centuries, he fought the Byzantines in Macedonia and Thrace. In 1014, however, the Byzantines crushed the Bulgarian army and reoccupied Bulgaria.

Bulgaria became a vassal state of the Byzantine Empire as well as a march route and battleground for advancing Mongols, Turks, Serbs, Magyars, and European crusaders beginning in the twelfth century. The Bulgarians fought alongside the Serbs in the unsuccessful Battle of Kosovo Polje in 1389—a defeat that began nearly five centuries of Ottoman domination during which tsarist Russia represented the only hope for liberation.

From the Struggle for National Independence to World War I

Uprisings against Ottoman control in 1875 and 1876 began military action that finally brought Bulgaria conditional independence in 1878. Bulgaria was a major battleground in the Russo-Turkish War of 1877–78. Russia fought the war as the champion of Slavs living under the Ottoman Empire in the Balkans. Under the Treaty of San Stefano, signed March 3, 1878, Bulgaria became an autonomous state under Russian protection. The same year, the European powers forced Bulgaria to sign the Treaty of Berlin, returning substantial territory to the Ottoman Empire in the name of regional balance. Bulgaria retained its autonomy, however.

Conflict with Balkan neighbors began when the new nation sparked a brief war with Serbia in 1885 over control of the province of Eastern Rumelia. Seeking compensation for Bulgaria's annexation, Serbia invaded the province and was defeated by Prince

Alexander, modern Bulgaria's first ruler. After inconclusive fighting, Bulgaria and Serbia agreed to the Treaty of Bucharest, which restored prewar borders in 1886.

During the twentieth century, persistent territorial disputes and dissatisfaction with borders determined Bulgaria's position in four wars. In 1912 Bulgaria entered the Balkan League, a military alliance with Serbia and Greece, to eliminate the last vestiges of Turkish rule in the Balkans and to expand its own territory in the process. Fielding approximately 180,000 troops, Bulgaria provided the bulk of the military personnel for operations against Turkish forces in the First Balkan War. Bulgarian armies besieged Constantinople in November 1912, but they were driven back temporarily by the Turks. When the key city of Adrianople fell to Bulgarian and Serbian forces in March 1913, Turkey capitulated. It surrendered its European possessions under the Treaty of London in May 1913.

A dispute over the spoils of the First Balkan War led directly to the Second Balkan War. Bulgaria asserted that Serbia occupied more of Macedonia and Thessaloniki than it was allowed by the prewar agreement. In June 1913, Bulgarian armies attacked Serbian forces in Macedonia and another army advanced into Thessaloniki. After checking this offensive, Serbian and Greek forces pushed the Bulgarians back into Bulgaria in July. Romania then declared war on Bulgaria and advanced unopposed toward Sofia, while Turkey capitalized on the situation to retake Andrianople. Bulgaria sued for peace and lost territory in Macedonia, Thrace, and Southern Dobruja to Greece, Serbia, and Romania, respectively, in the Treaty of Bucharest (August 1913).

Bulgaria's rivalry with Serbia and Greece defined its participation in World War I. Bulgaria avoided involvement in the war until 1915 when it mobilized 1.2 million soldiers and joined the Central Powers in attacking Serbia. Bulgaria took this action in the expectation that a victory by the Central Powers would restore Greater Bulgaria. In October 1915, two of Bulgaria's armies drove west into Serbia while allied Austro-Hungarian and German armies drove south. Bulgarian forces blocked British and French troops in Thessaloniki from linking with Serbian forces.

In mid-1916 over 250,000 British, French, and Serbian troops prepared for an offensive from Thessaloniki northwest along the Vardar River. Although the Germans and Bulgarians preempted the offensive and drove this force beyond the Struma River by late August, the war then settled into a long, costly stalemate along the Vardar. Seriously weakened by a poor military supply system and widespread unrest among the soldiers, Bulgaria collapsed and surrendered in 1918. The country suffered greatly during the war. Mobilization disrupted food production, and German requisitioning of grain and other foodstuffs taxed stored food supplies. About 100,000 Bulgarian soldiers were killed in combat, and 275,000 noncombatants died as a direct result of the war (see World War I, ch. 1).

The Interwar Years and World War II

The harsh terms of the Treaty of Neuilly-sur-Seine (November 1919) limited the postwar Bulgarian army to 20,000, and conscription was forbidden. Many embittered former officers became politically active in the Military League, a formidable and well-organized opposition faction in the 1920s and 1930s. Irredentism made Bulgaria a natural ally of Germany during the interwar years. After border skirmishes with Bulgaria in 1925 and 1931, Greece joined Romania, Yugoslavia, and Turkey in forming the Balkan Entente in 1934 to contain perceived Bulgarian expansionism. Bulgaria began to rearm in 1936 with German, British, and French assistance. Meanwhile, the Military League had been influential in staging coups in the early 1930s. In 1936, however, Tsar Boris III (1918–43) dismantled the organization, stripping the military of the political influence it had accumulated after World War I.

After several years of hesitating between alignment with Germany or the Soviet Union, Bulgaria finally sought to satisfy territorial claims to the south and west by signing the Tripartite Pact with the Axis powers in March 1941. But Bulgaria minimized its involvement in the war, managing to satisfy the terms of alliance with Germany without a declaration of war on the Soviet Union.

In spite of its passive policy, Bulgaria was a vital pivot for German operations in the Balkans, North Africa, and on the eastern front against the Soviet Union. Germany launched invasions of Greece and Yugoslavia from Bulgaria in April 1941, and Bulgaria occupied parts of the territory it expected to retain after the war. German forces used the country as a rear area for transporting troops and supplies and providing training, and as a rest and recreation point. Its railroads and ports were critical to the German war effort. More than fifty German ships and submarines were berthed in the harbor at Varna as late as the summer of 1944.

The Bulgarian Communist Party (BCP) dominated the anti-German partisan movement that arose in 1941. Although the movement had a central military commission to direct armed activities, the partisans generally were poorly organized and armed. Their total number never exceeded 18,000 and, unlike partisans elsewhere, they were more active in the cities than in the countryside.

The partisans received arms and supplies from the Soviet Union and Britain. The most successful aspect of partisan activity was pro-Soviet propaganda, demonstrations, terrorism, and sabotage against installations in Bulgaria critical to the German war effort. Among assassination attempts against German officials and Bulgarian fascists, the assassination of Minister of War Khristo Lukov in 1943 had the greatest impact. Harsh recriminations discouraged such activities, however. In 1943 the partisans formed the first fighting units of the People's Revolutionary Army of Liberation (PRAL), which eventually included brigade-sized units. Still, their armed attacks on German forces generally ended in failure. As late as 1944, entire units were captured or killed in action.

The Soviet Union declared war on Bulgaria on September 5, 1944, as the Red Army forces of the Third Ukrainian Front under General Fedor Tolbukhin crossed its northern border from Romania. Bulgaria changed sides on September 8 and declared war on Germany. Tolbukhin took command of the Bulgarian forces and reorganized them. By September 17, a Bulgarian army of 200,000 troops was mobilized and attached to the Third Ukrainian Front fighting German forces in Macedonia and Serbia. At the end of World War II, Bulgaria again returned the Greek and Yugoslav territory that it had occupied in 1941.

Postwar Development

The Red Army met little hostility during its occupation of Bulgaria from 1944 to 1947. At the time of invasion, the Soviet Union did not regard Bulgaria as an enemy state, because Bulgaria had not declared war or participated actively in the German eastern front. According to the Yalta agreements of 1945, the Allied Control Commission for Bulgaria, assigned to administer the country until a peace treaty was signed, was essentially an extension of the Red Army military administration. Under pressure from Britain, the preponderant interest of the Soviet Union in Bulgaria was recognized by giving it 75 percent control of the commission.

The Soviet Union immediately reorganized the Bulgarian Army to ensure that the BCP would have a leading role. More than 40 generals and 800 officers discredited by their association with the German Army were purged or resigned when Bulgaria switched sides in the war. Although former Minister of War Damian Velchev returned to his post in the Fatherland Front coalition government, the BCP used the presence of Soviet occupation forces to push the old officer corps out of domestic politics. In July 1946, control of the army shifted from the Ministry of War to the full cabinet, 2,000 allegedly reactionary officers were purged, and

Velchev resigned in protest. The combination of events provided an opening for the BCP to establish full control over the military. It conducted a decisive purge in October 1947. Accusing the remaining noncommunist senior officers of plotting to overthrow the Fatherland Front, the BCP dismissed one-third of the officer corps. After 1949 the BCP dominated the army, and party membership was obligatory for officers on active duty.

In the first postwar years, Bulgaria closely followed the example of Soviet military development and served Soviet interests in the Balkans. BCP leader Georgi Dimitrov exhorted Bulgarian officers to learn from the experience, strategy, and military art of the Soviet Union. He wanted the BPA to be exactly like the Soviet armed forces, with common missions, organization, weapons and equipment, and military science.

In 1946 Bulgaria participated in the initial conflict of the Cold War by aiding communist forces in the Greek civil war. Bulgarian support, including operating bases on Bulgarian territory, made possible communist victories near the border. As a result, Greece charged Bulgaria with numerous violations of its northern border. In 1947 the United Nations (UN) confirmed the Greek charges and later officially condemned Bulgaria for aiding communist guerrilla forces.

In the late 1940s, the Bulgarian armed forces were composed almost entirely of former partisans, peasants, and workers. Approximately 75 percent were members of the BCP or the Communist Youth League of Bulgaria (Komsomol). Many peasants and workers were attracted to the military by upward mobility and pay that was higher than in factories or farms. The armed forces were officially named the Bulgarian People's Army (BPA) in 1952. Bulgaria joined the Warsaw Pact on May 14, 1955, and contributed a token battalion to the Soviet-led invasion of Czechoslovakia on August 20, 1968. Bulgaria initiated a major military modernization program in the 1980s, adding its first T–72 tanks, MiG-23 fighters, Su-25 fighter-bombers, Mi-24 attack helicopters, and 130 surface-to-surface missiles to its inventory. During that period, the education level and technical competence of the officer corps rose; by 1985 nearly 85 percent had received at least a secondary education (see Education, ch. 2).

National Defense Posture

In 1991 the Warsaw Pact disbanded as a military alliance. Bulgarian commitment to the Soviet-led alliance accordingly ceased to be the main direction of its national defense. The disintegration of the Warsaw Pact presaged a major shift in threat perception, military doctrine, and strategy. Historical, geographic, and economic factors promised to assume greater importance in shaping Bulgaria's approach to national defense. Traditional allies and adversaries such as Germany and Turkey now exerted critical influence on decisions about military requirements, doctrine, and strategy. The country's geopolitical position in the volatile Balkans at the crossroads of Europe and Asia was another important determinant. Economic considerations limited the development and retention of military capabilities. In the early 1990s, Bulgarian officials began to stress guaranteeing national security through political agreements with neighboring countries rather than military force.

Threat Perception

Bulgaria was the only Warsaw Pact country without a frontier with the Soviet Union. Of the nearly 1,900 kilometers of land borders, 520 were with Romania, 500 with Yugoslavia, 480 with Greece, and 380 with Turkey. With the general exception of Romania, Bulgaria had had serious past conflicts with each of these countries. Bulgaria and neighboring NATO members Greece and Turkey had historical disputes that long predated the establishment of their respective rival alliances after World War II. However, unlike its former Warsaw Pact allies in Europe, Bulgaria's traditional enemies were NATO members or nonaligned nations. Relations with Greece had been friendly since 1980, based primarily on a shared antipathy toward Turkey. In 1986 Bulgaria and Greece signed a joint declaration of friendship and cooperation.

The issue of Macedonia was a source of potential conflict between Bulgaria and its neighbors. In 1991 the prospect of civil war in Yugoslavia raised concern that Bulgaria could reclaim Macedonia as a step toward reestablishing the Greater Bulgaria prescribed in the Treaty of San Stefano (see San Stefano, Berlin, and Independence, ch. 1). Bulgaria's Macedonian border had been tense since the Second Balkan War; in 1989 the ouster of Zhivkov escalated the risk that Macedonia would set off political or military conflict with all of Yugoslavia or with its neighboring Republic of Serbia. Bulgarian spokesmen denied having territorial ambitions against Yugoslav Macedonia, but they added ambiguity by referring to it as an open issue. Unlike the Yugoslavs, the Bulgarians did not recognize Macedonians as an ethnic group distinct from Bulgarians.

Proximity to NATO members Greece and Turkey, both with strong armed forces and significant military potential, was Bulgaria's primary strategic concern in the post-Warsaw Pact era. The plan for the development of the BPA was measured against the military programs of those two neighbors. The BPA leadership openly rated both their armies as superior to its own forces, stressing that Turkey boasted military manpower second only to the United States among NATO countries and a population of over 100 million. In the view of the Bulgarian military establishment, the size of the Turkish armed forces was the primary standard for determining appropriate reductions in BPA forces, as well as in strategic defense planning. Despite the relative lack of tension in bilateral relations with Turkey and an apparent absence of hostile intentions on its part in 1990, the treatment of ethnic Turks in Bulgaria remained an irritating and potentially explosive issue in bilateral relations. In 1987 veiled threats by Turkey to resolve the issue by force had caused alarm in Bulgaria. The outburst of pro-Turkish and Bulgarian nationalist rhetoric that followed the fall of the BCP regime, which had been willing to suppress ethnic unrest by force, raised ethnic tensions in a period when central government control over society had substantially decreased (see The Turkish Problem, ch. 4).

Even in decline, the Warsaw Pact alliance remained a major factor in Bulgarian threat perception and military planning. Bulgaria continued to count on an ongoing close military relationship and practical cooperation with the Soviet Union to balance perceived security threats. In 1991 the Bulgarian government conducted negotiations for a new bilateral treaty with the Soviet Union to guarantee it against external aggression. In return Bulgaria would pledge not to join any organization, such as NATO, perceived hostile to the Soviet Union. Whatever its relation to the Soviet Union, by 1991 Bulgaria was entering a new, shifting local balance of power similar to the balance that existed in the Balkans before World War II.

Doctrine and Strategy

The assigned mission of the BPA under the Warsaw Pact was to defend the southwestern border of the alliance. In practice, this mission was considerably more oriented to offensive operations than official pronouncements implied. Located within what the Soviet General Staff called the Southwest Theater of Military Operations, Bulgaria would have confronted Turkey in case of a Warsaw Pact conflict with NATO. As indicated by several joint amphibious landing exercises undertaken with the Soviet Union, Bulgaria's principal objectives would have been to control Thrace and to help Soviet forces seize and hold the critical straits at the Bosporus and the Dardanelles.

In the new geopolitical climate of 1991, military spokespersons emphasized different sources of military doctrine, including the constitution, resolutions passed by the National Assembly (Sŭbranie), the United Nations Charter, international law, and declarations of the Conference on Security and Cooperation in Europe (CSCE—see Glossary). Military spokespersons cited active efforts to pursue mutual security and trust with Turkey and Greece as well as good relations with Yugoslavia, Romania, and other European nations. The military denied all territorial claims against neighboring countries and stressed that participation in the CSCE process indicated its respect for the inviolability of European borders. It publicly rejected the threat or use of force against any country except in legitimate self-defense of territorial integrity, national independence, and sovereignty. Arms control was an important element of military doctrine before and after the overthrow of Zhivkov. Bulgaria had long advocated, without success, the establishment of a nuclear-free zone in the Balkans. In the mid-1980s, the Zhivkov government arranged several unproductive meetings of the Balkan countries on nuclear disarmament. The primary aim of this effort was elimination of NATO nuclear weapons in Turkey. A signatory to the Nuclear Nonproliferation Treaty of 1968, Bulgaria regularly pledged not to possess or produce nuclear weapons or other weapons of mass destruction. In 1990 the country was embarrassed, however, by the revelation that it possessed eight Soviet-made SS–23 missile launchers eliminated from the Soviet inventory under the terms of the Treaty on the Elimination of Intermediate- and Shorter-Range Nuclear Missiles in 1987. Although acknowledging receipt of SS–23 missiles and launchers in 1986, Bulgaria categorically denied having any nuclear capability associated with them. It offered to dismantle the systems in accordance with the treaty. Similar allegations about the presence of intermediate-range Soviet SS–20 missile launchers in Bulgaria had appeared in the foreign press in 1984 but were never substantiated. Zhivkov called for a ban on chemical weapons in the Balkans in 1985 at the same time as the United States accused Bulgaria of storing chemical weapons on its territory.

The Treaty on Conventional Armed Forces in Europe (CFE) was a contentious issue within the Warsaw Pact in 1990. The treaty committed Bulgaria to limiting its ground and air forces to a percentage of the Warsaw Pact's combined ceiling of 20,000 tanks, 30,000 armored combat vehicles, 20,000 artillery pieces, 6,800 combat aircraft, and 4,000 attack helicopters. However, the Warsaw Pact divided its overall ceilings so that the Soviet Union received most of the apportionment and the other former Warsaw Pact countries were limited to smaller quotas. Bulgaria's quotas were 1,475 tanks, 2,000 armored combat vehicles, 1,750 artillery pieces, 235 combat aircraft, and 67 attack helicopters. In 1990 the minister of national defense disclosed that the Warsaw Pact debate over weapons allocation had been acrimonious because each member had tried to maximize its quota, hence its security, before the alliance's military organization dissolved.

In 1991 Bulgaria did not have a formal law on national defense, and its military doctrine was still largely defined by Warsaw Pact declarations and documents. The Warsaw Pact's Political Consultative Committee had formally adopted a defense doctrine and the principle of reasonable sufficiency during its May 1987 meeting in Berlin. Closely following this doctrine and the Soviet example, Bulgaria then implemented a new national defensive doctrine calling for reasonable sufficiency. In the inexact and halting process of quantifying this term, military leaders basically agreed on the need to ensure national security at the lowest possible level of armaments. But the levels required to deter potential enemies or defend the country against them proved to be more debatable. By 1990 some clear steps had been taken toward reducing offensive weapons systems in favor of defensive ones (see Armed Services, this ch.).

Like professional military officers in other countries, the Bulgarian general staff viewed doctrine less from its political and diplomatic aspect than from its strictly technical military aspect. The technical side of doctrine focused on planning for a number of likely military contingencies and scenarios threatening national security. Although Bulgaria's political stance was based on a lack of enemies, the technical or worst-case military planning aspect of doctrine was dictated by the country's geopolitical position, the decline of the Warsaw Pact, and the possibility of instability in the Balkans.

Defense Organization

Like most other national institutions, the defense establishment was in the midst of a major transition in 1991. The new political course brought changes to a military system long based on the Soviet model. Democratic, multiparty politics brought the issue of depoliticization in the armed forces to the forefront. The state organization for national security and defense decision making, including the high command, retained its former structure. Major changes, including unilateral reductions and restructuring in accordance with defensive doctrine, were carried out in the ground, air and air defense, and naval forces.

The Military in the Political System

In 1991 Bulgaria was in the midst of shifting from a highly politicized army to a depoliticized one. The military had always been involved in domestic political struggles. The Military League exerted strong political influence through its support for the Zveno coalition after World War I (see The Crises of the 1930s, ch. 1). In 1934 the Military League took a leading role in overthrowing the government, and as recently as 1965 military officers were involved in political intrigue. The reported 1965 coup attempt led by General Ivan Todorov-Gorunia was allegedly aimed at replacing Zhivkov and establishing a more nationalist, less pro-Soviet leadership in the country. By 1990 communist Bulgaria had apparently made more progress in separating the military from politics than the Soviet Union, but perhaps less than other communist countries of Eastern Europe.

After World War II, the BCP quickly established control over the army. It purged old officers and made political loyalty to the new regime a more important criterion than professional competence for the selection of new officers (see Postwar Development, this ch.). Political officers in the ranks of the BPA ensured loyalty by extending the party apparatus throughout the military establishment. As in the Soviet Union and other Soviet-allied countries, party membership in the officer corps exceeded 80 percent.

Despite more than forty years of efforts to ensure communist control of the armed forces, the BPA took no action when BCP General Secretary Todor Zhivkov was ousted by party officials in November 1989. According to many reports, the conspicuous lack of military support for Zhivkov dissuaded his security forces from intervening to prevent the overthrow. In the immediate post-Zhivkov era, the BPA and its leadership declared an intention to be an apolitical, stabilizing factor in the peaceful transition to democracy.

The shift to multiparty politics brought opposition pressure to depoliticize the armed forces, in part because all parties feared the BPA could split into partisan armed factions or become the instrument of one party as it had been for the BCP. In the new climate of open political discourse, national security and defense became frequent topics of debate among political parties. The military leadership, however, complained that some parties failed to show a sufficiently responsible attitude toward these issues.

In January 1990, at the direction of the reform wing of the BCP, the State Council repealed the section of Article 1 of the constitution that had institutionalized the exclusive political role of the party in the armed forces. The decree replaced BCP political organs in the army with educational work organs. The State Council followed that action with a more specific decree ordering complete depoliticization of the armed forces. The Military Administration Department of the BCP Central Committee and the Main Political Administration of the BPA were removed from the Ministry of National Defense and their functions curtailed. The decree effectively eliminated control by the BCP (which in early 1990 renamed itself the Bulgarian Socialist Party, BSP) over the army by removing cells of the party and the Komsomol from the army. In September 1990, the National Assembly approved a new law on political parties. The law depoliticized several government institutions, including the army, and required them to respond to the state rather than the ruling party. By the end of the year, 98 percent of all soldiers reportedly had relinquished their membership in political parties in accordance with the law. If they refused to do so, they were discharged from the service. In 1991 the Ministry of National Defense campaigned for exclusion of active-duty military personnel from voting in elections.

Besides changing the legal framework for the relationship between the military and the political system, the new political course in Bulgaria brought practical changes in everyday army life. The content of military education shifted dramatically from emphasizing the defense of the communist system to the defense of the homeland without regard to political considerations. Bulgarian sources indicated that the adjective *People's* in Bulgarian People's Army now was interpreted to mean ''national'' and not ''proletarian.'' Defense of national independence, sovereignty, and territorial integrity replaced the defense of socialism as the primary mission of the military. Professional competence replaced political allegiance and reliability as the most important measure of officer qualifications. The military post of political officer was eliminated officially, although plans called for retraining some political officers for new educational duties within the armed forces. The remainder would have to qualify as regular line officers or leave the service. Nevertheless, the Union of Democratic Forces (UDF) opposition coalition accused the BSP of continued party recruitment among cadets and newly enlisted personnel after the State Council decree on depoliticization.

Government Organization for Defense

Prior to November 1989, the chairman of the State Defense Committee was the commander in chief of the BPA, and as such made every important decision about internal and external security. The secretary general of the BCP and president of the State Council automatically held the position of chairman of the State Defense Committee as well. The consolidation of these three positions had enabled a single person, Todor Zhivkov, to make political decisions on security issues and supervise their implementation within the government apparatus, especially as they concerned the economy and defense industries.

In the post-Zhivkov order, the commander in chief of the armed forces was the president of the republic, a position independent of party affiliation. In 1990 the National Security Council was formed as a consultative organ under the president after the State Defense Committee was abolished. The National Security Council advised the president in making decisions on a range of domestic and foreign policy issues related to national security, including defense preparedness, organization, training, and deployment of the armed forces, public order, and use of the internal security forces. The National Security Council included the vice president; the chairman of the Council of Ministers; the ministers of foreign affairs, national defense, internal affairs, and economy and planning; and the chief of the General Staff. Decisions were implemented through the Council of Ministers, the Ministry of National Defense, and the General Staff.

The democratization of 1990 allowed the National Assembly to participate in making decisions on security issues rather than merely rubber-stamping decisions made elsewhere. In 1990 the National Assembly established a new legislative body, the Commission on National Security, to provide oversight for government activities in internal and external security. The commission's role remained largely undefined in 1991, but its nominal function was to enforce government compliance with the rule of law in security matters and to protect the rights of citizens.

Despite these organizational changes, the constitutional provisions, most laws and statutes, and instructions and regulations pertaining to national security and defense adopted by the government under the former BCP remained in effect. A complex of laws, drafted for inclusion in the new constitution ratified by the National Assembly in 1991, were designed to codify the many individual changes made in military practice and institutions after 1989.

During and after the ouster of Zhivkov, the prestige of the military among the people appeared to remain quite high. Despite its association with the former BCP regime, the military was credited for remaining in the barracks during the political transition. Although some long-serving, high-ranking officers were removed later, others remained and even advanced as a result of the ouster.

Longtime Minister of National Defense and BCP Politburo member Army General Dobri Dzhurov was dismissed in 1990 in the aftermath of the democratic opening. However, Colonel General Atanas Semerdzhiev, first deputy minister of defense and chief of the General Staff under Zhivkov, rose to the post of minister of the interior in 1990. The retention and promotion of an officer like Semerdzhiev, formerly decorated and favored by Zhivkov himself, indicated the value placed on the stabilizing role of the military during this turbulent period.

High Command

The high command consisted of the Ministry of National Defense and the General Staff. The minister of national defense was always a professional officer bearing the rank of army general or colonel general. In 1990, however, reformers called for a civilian defense minister to ensure civilian control over the armed forces. The military flatly rejected such demands, insisting that the minister of national defense must be a professional officer because civilians lacked the required expertise—despite evidence of able civilian administration of defense ministries in other countries.

The Ministry of National Defense was responsible for implementing the decisions of the National Security Council and the National Assembly within the armed forces. The ministry recruited, equipped, and administered the armed forces according to directives of the executive and legislative branches of government. The ministry linked the armed forces to the national economy for the purpose of procuring weapons and military equipment. The Ministry of National Defense was organized according to a Soviet model. The first deputy minister of national defense was also the chief of the General Staff, responsible for planning and directing the operational deployment of the armed forces and coordinating the actions of the three armed services in peacetime and wartime. The deputy minister's staff included a first deputy, several deputy chiefs, and a disarmament inspectorate. All military commands reported to the General Staff. The country was divided into three military districts. Daily military administration, however, was performed at the level of military regions corresponding to the eight provinces and the city of Sofia (see Local Government, ch. 4). Besides two communications brigades and the usual service and support battalions, the General Staff controlled several other organizations, including a military scientific research institute, military history institute, military mapping and topography institutes, the Georgi Rakovski Military Academy, the Military Medical Academy, and the military medical infrastructure throughout the country.

The commanders of the ground, air, and naval forces were deputy ministers of national defense controlling separate service commands within the Ministry of National Defense. The service commands were concerned primarily with training and maintaining combat readiness in their units. Other deputy ministers of national defense included the chief of weapons and military equipment, the chief of the Material-Technical and Rear Support Command, and the chief of civil defense. Other elements reporting to the minister of national defense included the office of the inspector general; the departments of personnel, military education, medical services, international relations, military counterintelligence, military justice and procuracy, cultural institutions, and public information; and the radiation and chemical detection command post. The International Relations Department maintained contacts with foreign military establishments and their attachés in Bulgaria. The Cultural Institutions Department was responsible for several military museums, officers' clubs, theaters, cinema and art studios, and the BPA performing ensemble. The Public Information Department managed the press center, military publishing house, nine military newspapers and journals, and television and radio programs for the Ministry of National Defense.

In late 1990, the minister of national defense announced that reductions in the armed services would affect the command elements and administrative organizations within the Ministry of National Defense in proportion to reductions in operational forces. Some directorates with related functions reportedly were merged, but the full extent of reductions in the Ministry of National Defense was not yet evident in 1991.

Armed Services

In 1991 the three armed services of the BPA were the ground, air and air defense, and naval forces. The ground forces, or army, clearly was the most important service. In addition, each service had several combat arms and support branches. Some support services, such as the construction or civil defense troops, were not subordinate to a particular armed service. In 1991 the BPA was reducing, restructuring, and modernizing its forces. The Ministry of National Defense announced that, while the air and air defense and naval forces would retain their basic structure, substantial changes in the ground forces were expected.

In 1991 the military had 107,000 personnel, a reduction of more than 45,000 since 1988 (see Military Personnel, this ch.). More than 80 percent were conscripts. In late 1990, the minister of national defense had announced plans for further reductions in 1991,

Observation post in military exercises in Khaskovo District, 1985
Courtesy Sofia Press Agency

including elimination of one motorized rifle division, one tank brigade, and one air force regiment—a total of 10,000 personnel, 200 T-62 tanks, 200 artillery pieces, and 20 MiG-21 aircraft. The minister also announced that over 500 T-34 tanks held in storage were to be destroyed. The navy planned to decommission five older combat ships in 1991.

At the same time, the minister of national defense stressed a need to restructure the BPA into a more modern, professional, and better trained force. Such a force could be smaller because the new defensive doctrine required fewer forces. Tank and mechanized infantry units were reduced in favor of more antitank, air defense, and other defensive systems. The major problem for the BPA's future development was improving the quality of armaments while reducing their quantity. However, the minister of national defense publicly expressed concern that domestic industries could not produce many types of modern weapons that used new technologies. In the area of personnel, the minister announced plans to modernize military training programs by updating curricula at military educational establishments and making field training and exercises more realistic.

Ground Forces

Ground forces combat units included motorized rifle, tank,

243

artillery and missile, and antiaircraft troops, as well as several combat support branches. The ground forces numbered over 70,000 soldiers, the majority of whom were conscripts. As recently as 1990, they had consisted mainly of eight motorized rifle divisions and five tank brigades. In 1991 the active ground forces deployed four motorized rifle divisions and two tank brigades, with four divisions and one brigade in reserve status. In implementing the new defensive doctrine, the ground forces further reduced tanks in the remaining motorized rifle divisions by 30 percent, converting their tank regiments into motorized rifle regiments. Defensive weapons in divisions were increased by adding more antitank, combat engineering, reconnaissance, and electronic warfare units. The attachment of several antiaircraft elements to the ground forces command indicated that the command operated its own air defense network to protect deployed ground units. The antiaircraft attachments included one air defense command post, one air defense brigade, several antiaircraft maintenance brigades, one radiotechnical or radar battalion, and one antiaircraft artillery test range.

In all, the ground forces had over 2,400 tanks, including more than 300 T-72, 1,300 T-55, and 600 older T-34 vehicles. The more than 2,000 armored combat vehicles included nearly 150 modern BMP armored fighting vehicles and over 600 BTR-60 and 1,100 MT-LB armored personnel carriers. The ground forces operated 2,500 large-caliber artillery systems. These included 450 85mm D-44 and 100mm SU-100 and T-12 antitank guns; 200 122mm BM-21 multiple rocket launchers; over 1,600 122mm and 152mm howitzers and guns, including nearly 700 self-propelled 2S1, 500 M-30, and smaller numbers of D-20, M-1937, and M-46 towed guns; and 350 mortars, including the self-propelled 120mm Tundzha produced in Bulgaria. The ground forces had 64 launchers for surface-to-surface missiles. That number included modern SS-1 missiles and older, less accurate FROG-7 missiles with respective ranges of 300 and 75 kilometers. Besides these battlefield missiles, eight longer-range SS-23 launchers were available (see *Doctrine and Strategy,* this ch.). The Soviet-made AT-3 was the main antitank guided missile in the inventory. Air defense for the ground forces consisted of 50 mobile SA-4, SA-6, and man-portable SA-13 tactical surface-to-air missiles and nearly 400 self-propelled and towed 100mm, 85mm, 57mm, and 23mm air defense guns.

The bulk of the ground forces were deployed along two primary operational directions: the west-southwest, opposite Yugoslavia and Greece, and the southeast, opposite Turkey. Stationed in Sofia, Plovdiv, and southern Khaskovo provinces, the First Army faced Yugoslavia and Greece with more than 600 tanks, 700 armored combat vehicles, and 800 large-caliber artillery weapons. The Third Army was located primarily in Burgas and northern Khaskovo provinces facing Turkey and had over 800 tanks, 900 armored combat vehicles, and 700 heavy artillery pieces. The active units of the Second Army, a low-strength formation to be staffed by reserves in wartime, were based in central Bulgaria, in Plovdiv, and northern Khaskovo provinces. The Second Army was positioned to support either the First Army in the west or the Third Army in the east when fully mobilized during wartime. Relatively few ground forces were deployed in the north opposite Romania or in the east along the Black Sea coast.

At nearly full strength, the First and Third Armies had two motorized rifle divisions each. Strategic reserves consisted of one independent tank brigade and one artillery, antitank, and antiaircraft regiment each. In 1991 the Third Army opposite Turkey had a second independent tank brigade reinforced with two artillery battalions. The tank brigades each had four to six battalions and as many as 200 tanks. Support units included supply, maintenance, and artillery-technical brigades; communications and combat engineering regiments; and radio relay cable, electronic warfare, reconnaissance, artillery-reconnaissance, parachute-reconnaissance, radio-technical, bridging, and chemical defense battalions. The armies also controlled their own artillery, chemical, communications, vehicle and armor, combat engineering, medical-sanitary, fuel, and food depots, military hospitals, and maintenance and mobilization bases to support their maneuver units. They had one or two territorial training centers that functioned as reserve divisions for their respective armies. The centers were organized into reserve detachments for motorized rifle, tank, artillery, and antiaircraft troops, and specialist training groups for artillery-technical, antitank, reconnaissance, communications, combat engineering, maintenance, and rear support troops. Many reserve detachments were significant forces in themselves, often as large as motorized rifle regiments but lacking a full contingent of personnel. The low-strength Second Army itself was similar in organization and purpose to a territorial training center. It had one full-strength tank brigade, one artillery regiment, several combat support regiments and battalions, several reserve detachments and groups, depots, one military hospital, and one maintenance base.

The typical motorized rifle division had four motorized rifle regiments, one artillery regiment, one antiaircraft artillery regiment, one independent tank battalion, one independent artillery battalion, one antitank battalion, and several machine gun-artillery battalions. Reconnaissance, communications, combat engineering, maintenance, and supply battalions provided necessary combat support to the division.

A typical motorized rifle regiment had three motorized rifle battalions with ninety armored combat vehicles and one tank battalion with thirty tanks. Its artillery battalion had two to four batteries of nine artillery pieces. It had one antiaircraft artillery battalion, one antitank battery, and one or two machine gun-artillery batteries.

Air and Air Defense Forces

Air and air defense force units were rather evenly dispersed throughout the country. They operated approximately 300 combat aircraft, including over 160 MiG-21, 70 MiG-23, 40 Su-25, and 20 MiG-29 fighters and more than 100 L-29 and L-39 combat trainers. Two MiG fighter and three MiG interceptor regiments were operational. The air forces had two regiments of Mi-24 attack helicopters, two regiments of Mi-17, Mi-8, and Mi-2 multipurpose combat support helicopters, and one squadron of Mi-2 and Mi-8 transport helicopters. The air and air defense forces had over 22,000 personnel, about 75 percent of whom were conscripts.

The First Air Defense Division and Second Air Defense Division, deployed in Sofia and Burgas provinces, respectively, were composed of two interceptor regiments with eighteen aircraft each. They operated Soviet-made MiG-21, MiG-23, and MiG-29 fighters. A third air defense division controlled the strategic air defense network of approximately 280 Soviet-made SA-2, SA-3, SA-5, and more modern SA-10 surface-to-air missile launchers dispersed at about thirty sites throughout the country. In 1991 the division probably had four regiments, each composed of several battalions. Battalions provided central command and control for as many as ten launchers, with each launcher corresponding to a battery.

The Tenth Composite Air Corps in central Bulgaria was the largest air formation. It had more than 225 aircraft. Its principal mission was to provide air support, tactical reconnaissance, and mobility for the ground forces. It had two fighter-bomber regiments, one fighter regiment, one reconnaissance aircraft regiment, and four helicopter regiments, as well as large numbers of radar, maintenance, and communications support units under its command. Its aircraft included MiG-21 and MiG-17 fighters and MiG-23 and Su-25 fighter-bombers, Su-22, MiG-21, and MiG-25 reconnaissance variants, and over forty specialized Mi-24 attack helicopters and forty Mi-2, Mi-8, and Mi-17 combat and transport helicopters.

The Higher Aviation School of the air and air defense forces command also controlled two aviation training regiments and one aviation training squadron with over eighty L-29 and L-39 primary trainers and over eighty MiG-15, MiG-17, and MiG-21 armed combat trainers in northern Bulgaria (see Officer Education, this ch.). The Higher Aviation School also had a large number of logistics and other support units to train specialists for the service.

Naval Forces

The navy defended approximately 350 kilometers of coastline along the Black Sea. Its major bases were located at Varna (the headquarters), Atiya, Sozopol, Balchik, and Burgas. Naval forces included over twenty submarines and minor surface combatants that could be deployed in coastal defense operations. As recently as 1989, Bulgarian naval forces defended claims to their territorial waters in incidents with Turkish forces at sea. As in the case of the ground forces, the Ministry of National Defense announced some unilateral naval reductions in 1990. In all, five vessels were to be retired or sold abroad: two submarine chasers, two coastal patrol boats, and one submarine. They were basically obsolete and had little residual military value. This deletion was more than balanced by the addition of three Soviet Poti-class corvettes to the operational inventory. In 1990 the navy had about 10,000 personnel, half of them conscripts.

The navy had four components: the Black Sea Fleet, Danube Flotilla, Coastal Defense, and a shore establishment. The Black Sea Fleet was organized into submarine, escort ship, missile and torpedo boat, amphibious craft, and minesweeping squadrons and brigades. The Danube Flotilla operated patrol craft along the riverine border with Romania. Coastal Defense included amphibious landing and mine countermeasures forces. The shore establishment controlled naval bases, training facilities, and naval aviation, coastal artillery, and naval infantry units.

Bulgaria obtained its minor surface combatant crafts from the Soviet Union. Its main forces consisted of four Pobeda-class submarines, two Druzki-class frigates, five Poti-class corvettes, six Osa-class missile patrol boats, six Shershen-class torpedo boats, and three SO-1-class and seven Zhuk-class patrol craft. The navy received its Pobeda- (formerly Romeo-) class submarines from the Soviet Union beginning in 1972. Originally built in the 1950s, they were armed with eight 533mm torpedo tubes. The Druzki- (formerly Riga-) class frigates were built in 1957 and 1958. They were modernized extensively during the early 1980s. They had three 100mm guns, three 533mm torpedo tubes, and four five-tube antisubmarine rocket launchers. The navy acquired its first three Poti-class corvettes from the Soviet Union in 1975 and another three in 1990. These were lightly armed antisubmarine warfare platforms carrying four 406mm torpedo tubes and two antisubmarine rocket launchers. The Osa-class missile patrol boats carried four SS–N–2 surface-to-surface missile launchers. The Soviet Union built them in the 1960s and first transferred them to Bulgaria in the early 1970s. The Shershen-class torpedo boats had four 533mm torpedo tubes and were built and acquired at approximately the same time as the Osa-class boats.

The navy operated more than thirty mine-warfare countermeasures ships, including four modern Soviet-built Sonya-class oceangoing minesweepers acquired in the early 1980s. The other minesweepers, including the Vanya-class, Yevgenya-class, and several miscellaneous ships, were restricted to coastal or inshore operations. The inventory also included two Polish-built Polnocny-class medium landing ships. These amphibious ships each could transport and land six tanks and 150 troops. The navy had nineteen additional Vydra-class medium landing craft, each of which could carry 100 troops and 250 tons of equipment on their open tank decks.

Naval aviation, coastal artillery, and naval infantry were small support arms of the navy. Naval aviation consisted of one squadron of three armed and nine unarmed search-and-rescue and antisubmarine warfare helicopters. These Mi-14, Mi-8, Mi-4, and Mi-2 naval helicopters were obtained from the Soviet Union. Coastal artillery had two regiments with about 150 guns of 100mm or 130mm caliber. They were organized into several battalions with five batteries each. Coastal artillery units also operated an unknown number of Soviet SS–C–1 and more modern SSC–3 antiship missile launchers. Their mission was to direct fire against combatants offshore, supporting amphibious assaults on the Bulgarian coastline. The naval infantry force consisted of three companies of 100 troops each. Their small size limited them to guard duty and ground defense of important coastal installations against commando raids and other assault forces.

Border Troops

The Border Troops were part of the BPA. Composed of 13,000 troops in sixteen light infantry regiments, they resembled military units more than a police force. The mission was to defend the country's frontiers against illegal crossings. The Border Troops regulated the movement of people within a strip twelve kilometers wide along the border. They cooperated with other authorities to prevent smuggling, although contraband control was not primarily their responsibility (see Crime, this ch.). During wartime the Border Troops were to coordinate their actions with the ground forces as a first line of national defense. The majority of the Border Troops were deployed to guard frontiers with Greece, Turkey, and Yugoslavia, but they also defended the Romanian border. Several light patrol boats operated along the Danube River where it separated Bulgaria from Romania and along the Black Sea coast.

Construction Troops

Between 12,000 and 15,000 conscripts traditionally served as construction troops. They had their origin in the compulsory labor service established by the Bulgarian Agrarian National Union (BANU) government in 1920 (see Stamboliĭski and Agrarian Reform, ch. 1). Commanded by a general and organized into military units, this labor service built roads, railroads, and entire industrial enterprises. Although service in the Construction Troops satisfied military service requirements, these units were controlled by the Ministry of Construction, Architecture, and Public Services, and they received little or no military training. According to the chairman of the Movement for Rights and Freedoms, these units typically drafted Turks and other ethnic minorities considered unsuitable for service in combat units because of linguistic barriers or perceived political unreliability (see Turks, ch. 2; The Movement for Rights and Freedoms, ch. 4).

After the fall of Zhivkov, the Construction Troops received considerable attention. It was alleged that the Construction Troops had built over 20,000 apartments and houses for members of the BCP elite during the last ten years of the Zhivkov regime. High-ranking officers reportedly could requisition labor crews from the Construction Troops to work on their apartments or country homes. The Construction Troops often were reported as working in uranium mines, metallurgical industries, and other unsafe environments that did not attract enough civilian workers.

In 1991 the future of the Construction Troops depended on the status of professionalization in the armed forces. Opponents argued that these units were not a necessary component of professional armed forces, and that their functions should devolve to the civilian economy. Proponents insisted that the Construction Troops provided a low-cost labor force for important national projects, including factories, power plants, and other capital investment projects, as well as useful occupational training in the building trades for a large number of conscripts. In the first half of the 1980s, a reported 1.2 billion leva (for value of the lev, see Glossary) worth of labor came from this source for more than 700 projects. Similar debates surrounded specially designated railroad troops and transportation troops.

Civil Defense Troops

A strong emphasis on civil defense resulted from Bulgaria's participation in the Warsaw Pact and the BCP's efforts to mobilize the population. The civil defense program developed in the 1960s from the recognition that nuclear, biological, and chemical weapons delivered by long-range missiles and artillery ended the clear distinction between the front lines and civilian areas. Planning for civil defense was intended to meliorate the worst effects of weapons of mass destruction and to ensure continuity in communications, transportation, supply, and power generation during wartime.

The Ministry of National Defense operated the National Radiation and Chemical Defense Warning System and planned the overall direction and financing of civil defense activities. Civil defense committees attached to people's councils at the province or municipality level implemented civil defense plans for those jurisdictions. Civil defense organizations in manufacturing plants, enterprises, schools, and other collectives had similar responsibilities. Staffed with conscripts and organized into battalions, the civil defense troops trained the civilian population in individual and collective defensive measures, including dispersal and evacuation. They maintained firefighting, decontamination, civil engineering, salvage, rescue, and medical assistance programs and skills needed for the civil defense program. Despite these preparations for civil defense, construction of protective shelters for the population was a relatively low priority, primarily because of economic constraints. A network of hardened command posts for the military and civilian leadership was believed to exist.

Logistics and Arms Procurement

The Material-Technical and Rear Support Command had wide responsibility for logistical support to the BPA, ranging from routine supply operations to maintenance and arms procurement. Its base and depot network included petroleum-oil-lubricant (POL) depots, special fuel bases, POL and special fuel equipment maintenance battalions, central supply bases, food and general supply depots, central maintenance bases, central vehicle and armor-tank depots, vehicle and armor-tank maintenance bases, artillery depots, central artillery ammunition bases, and central missile maintenance bases.

One major directorate of the Material-Technical and Rear Support Command was responsible for military repair bases and factories. This directorate controlled general equipment repair factories, electro-mechanical factories, vehicle repair factories, and an institute for research and development in maintenance of weapons and equipment. In addition to this directorate, the command ran a military technology research institute, a laser technology laboratory, an electro-mechanical training equipment factory, a central artillery-technical test range, and a billeting service. It also operated several schools for maintenance specialist training (see Military Training, this ch.).

Despite the range of these activities, Bulgaria produced relatively few of its own armaments and other combat equipment. Defense production plants were located in Gabrovo, Karlovo, Kazanlŭk, Plovdiv, Sofia, and Varna, but the vast majority of arms and equipment came from the Soviet Union, with smaller amounts from Poland and Czechoslovakia. The Zhivkov regime also occasionally purchased military equipment from at least three NATO members, including the Federal Republic of Germany (West Germany). The exact nature and amount of weapons systems produced for domestic use remained largely unknown during that period, however. The Tundzha mortar and a few types of armored combat vehicles were produced domestically. Bulgarian shipyards did not produce surface combat ships or submarines.

Following the lead of the Soviet Union, Bulgaria announced a major program of defense industry conversion in 1990. The section of the Ministry of Industry, Trade, and Services responsible for arms production was renamed the Special Production and Conversion Department to reflect conversion to civilian manufacture. Bulgaria planned to convert an unspecified number of military plants and to require firms producing both military and civilian goods to double their output of the latter. By the end of 1990, defense plants were required to produce a total of 246 million leva worth of nonmilitary goods, increasing to 394 million leva in 1991, and to 1,130 million leva by 1995. In this period, their production mix was to change to 60 percent civilian and 40 percent military goods. Fully and partially converted military enterprises would manufacture textiles, capital equipment and machine tools, tractors and cultivators, durable consumer appliances, industrial and medical lasers, and canned food. The encouragement of joint ventures between Bulgarian and foreign firms was another element of the conversion program. Despite these changes in the defense industries, the government planned to retain complete authority over military production.

Military Budget

Bulgaria traditionally spent less on defense than other Warsaw Pact countries, but military spending was a greater burden on its economy than on those of its allies. During the late 1980s, the military budget amounted to more than 10 percent of the gross national product (GNP—see Glossary) because Bulgaria had the lowest GNP in the Warsaw Pact. Measured in terms of total government spending, the military budget typically accounted for more than 20 percent of the national budget. In contrast, BPA leaders complained that by 1990 defense spending had dropped to about 6 percent of state expenditures, a smaller proportion than that spent by the governments of Greece or Turkey.

Between 1986 and 1989, the military budget increased gradually from 1.67 to 1.8 billion leva. In January 1989, however, the State Council and the Council of Ministers reduced the appropriated defense budget for 1989 by 12 percent to 1.6 billion leva. The announcement cited restructuring in the armed forces and economic considerations as reasons for the reduction. The Ministry of National Defense stated its intention to absorb the cut by reducing expenditures on operations, maintenance, and procurement, which were the largest components of the military budget.

Military Personnel

Bulgaria traditionally had more troops in uniform per capita than the other Warsaw Pact countries. At one time, it had almost as many soldiers as Romania, a country with a population three times larger than Bulgaria's. Total personnel in the BPA were drastically reduced from 152,000 to 107,000 between 1988 and 1991, however. The Ministry of National Defense cut the officer corps by over 1,700 and general officers by 78. The military strongly opposed additional reductions on the grounds that they would seriously jeopardize national security. Military spokesmen pointed to the 300,000- to 350,000-soldier Turkish force in eastern Thrace and western Anatolia as the key factor in determining the appropriate personnel level for the BPA. The unilateral reduction between 1988 and 1991 occurred against a backdrop of sharp domestic political debate over reducing the basic two-year military conscription term to eighteen months.

Recruitment and Service Obligations

The standard two-year term of military service for most conscripts was reduced to eighteen months by the National Assembly in 1990. At the same time, the three-year term for sailors and other specialists was changed to two years. Bulgarian males entered the armed forces at the age of nineteen. Although the BPA was smaller than before, the new eighteen-month service term caused a turnover of one-third of all conscripts every six months, making universal conscription of nineteen-year-old males a necessity to maintain force levels. A population growth rate barely above zero exacerbated the manpower problem. In 1991 the minister of national defense noted an increased incidence of potential conscripts avoiding military service. He stated that 6,000 young men over seventeen years of age were known to have departed the country illegally for this reason, and another 3,500 failed to appear before the conscription commission and were presumed to be living abroad. The existing law on the armed forces prohibited men in this age category from leaving Bulgaria before performing their compulsory service. Although young men enrolled in a higher school or university could defer fulfillment of their military obligation until they had completed their education, draft deferments for other reasons were granted infrequently and reluctantly.

In 1991 political parties debated additional adjustments in the conscription system. The UDF and the BANU argued for a further reduction to a one-year term for most conscripts and six months for university graduates. They also called for extending contracts to some soldiers and noncommissioned officers (NCOs) to shift the BPA to a more professional force. Other aspects of military service discussed by the Commission on National Security of the National Assembly in 1990 were possible voluntary service by women and service in the national police force as an alternative to military conscription.

Supported by the BSP, the military argued that one year of military service was insufficient to provide required training for conscripts. It maintained that at any given time only 50 percent of the army would have completed basic training and be in a state of minimum combat readiness. Furthermore, shorter service would make the training of Bulgarian troops inferior to that of other armies in the region. Military spokesmen argued that the country could not afford the wages or the benefits required in a professional army, nor could it attract enough volunteers under the austere conditions of military service throughout the country. The army viewed the draft and mobilization as essential to ensure an adequate force in wartime. Some military leaders charged that the UDF and the BANU sought to reduce service terms in order to gain votes from servicemen who would gain early release. The military opposed alternative service on the grounds that the Construction Troops were the existing alternative to combat service.

Military Training

Military training began with mandatory premilitary training through the Organization for Cooperation in Defense, a mass organization with more than 10,000 affiliates in schools, cooperative farms, and enterprises throughout the country. Under its auspices, reserve officers and active-duty junior officers trained thousands of young men and women between the ages of sixteen and eighteen in a year-round program. In classroom and field exercises, trainees learned marksmanship, radio communications, scuba diving, and technical military specialties such as aircraft and vehicle operations and maintenance. For the last, the Organization for Cooperation in Defense had an inventory of more than seventy BTR–60 and MT–LB armored personnel carriers. Although the organization also sponsored sports competitions and summer camps less directly related to military service, the main goal of premilitary training was to reduce the time required to adapt young inductees to military life.

Military training followed the Soviet model because the Soviet-made weapons and equipment in the inventory required specialized training in operation and maintenance. Training, which also followed Soviet tactical concepts, moved in an annual cycle under the two-year service term. Adjustments in the training cycle were expected to compensate for the shorter eighteen-month service term. On the other hand, in 1990 elimination of political indoctrination requirements freed as much as 25 percent of conscript training time for military and physical training. Immediately after induction, conscripts began basic physical conditioning, training in handling and maintenance of small arms, drill, and general military indoctrination. They learned a range of individual skills required in small unit combat situations, including first aid, radiation and chemical decontamination, and camouflage techniques. After basic training, soldiers formed crews for training on larger weapons and equipment. They participated in exercises of increasing scale until the training cycle culminated in a large-scale combined arms maneuver held each year. In 1990 the minister of national defense called for more realistic training, especially for combat at night and in poor visibility conditions. Conscripts received specialist training in a variety of fields. Separate schools trained junior specialists in transport and rear services, tank and vehicle maintenance, POL handling, and military music.

The majority of NCOs were new inductees selected at induction for special training at service schools. NCOs served longer than the usual conscription period. In the early 1970s, special secondary schools were also established for NCO training. These schools were available to acceptable applicants who had completed the eighth grade. The course of study lasted three years and graduates were obligated to serve in the armed forces for ten years.

Military life was generally austere but not significantly different from conditions throughout the country. The greatest hardship was the requirement that conscripts serve outside their home provinces. In 1991 increasing criticism was leveled at the negative aspects of military service, especially the hazing of new conscripts. The press widely reported complaints from conscripts and parents that hazing often included intimidation and violence against young recruits by senior soldiers. In response, junior officers were assigned barracks duty to prevent such excesses. A general decline in military discipline also had become a problem in 1991. The press reported widespread cases of soldiers failing to wear proper uniforms or to carry proper identity papers, increased rates of absence without leave, and black market activities by soldiers. Misappropriation of money and property, theft of weapons and ammunition, and violent assault and murder were cited as increasingly common occurrences. The Plovdiv garrison alone reported 600 violations of military conduct rules during the last six months of 1990. Burgas, Stara Zagora, and other garrisons in southeastern Bulgaria were cited as particular problem areas. A spokesperson for the Ministry of National Defense voiced concern that the process of democratization had the unintended side effect of undermining order in the ranks of the BPA. The spokesperson accused the media and political parties of encouraging disciplinary violations and disobedience among conscripts without regard to the need to maintain the integrity and capabilities of the BPA. On the other hand, the military leadership tended to label all agitation for better living conditions as simply a failure of discipline.

Officer Education

The level of education of Bulgarian officers rose in the 1970s and 1980s. In the early 1970s, only 40 percent had degrees from higher military or civilian schools, but this figure rose to nearly two-thirds of the entire officer corps by 1980. Cadet programs in several higher military schools provided officers for the armed forces. These programs were equivalent to a civilian university curriculum. Applicants were required to have a secondary school education and to be single, in excellent physical condition, and under twenty-four years of age. Many applicants had completed their compulsory military service as conscripts and had decided to pursue a professional military career. The ground forces had three higher military schools for training combined arms officers, artillery officers, and reserve officers. The air and air defense forces had one Higher Aviation School that provided firsthand experience with aircraft besides its classroom training. The Higher Aviation School had three flight training regiments with supporting aviation engineering, communications, and radio-technical (radar) support battalions (see Armed Services, this ch.). The naval forces had a Higher Naval School to train officers for the service. Cadets in training to be line officers had four-year courses of study; those preparing for technical specialties such as artillery, aviation, and communications had five-year courses of study. Cadets received their commissions immediately after they graduated.

Selected officers could obtain advanced academic training. Mid-grade officers could apply for acceptance in the Georgi Rakovski Military Academy in Sofia. Graduation from the academy, which was similar to a Western war college or command and staff course, was a prerequisite for advancement into the senior officer ranks. Approximately one-third of all career officers completed that course. Most active-duty officers studied in one of several Soviet military academies. Completion of a two-year program in the Soviet Union and fluency in Russian were requirements for field-grade officers. In 1991 the minister of national defense raised the possibility of sending officers to study in Western military academies, but he cited the language barrier and the country's financial difficulties as obstacles. The General Staff had several other specialized academic institutes for the study of military science and history (see High Command, this ch.). It also operated the Military Medical Academy, which was established as a training and research center in the military aspects of the medical sciences, to upgrade training of military physicians and to provide medical services for the armed forces.

A professional military career was considered relatively prestigious in Bulgaria, although prestige began to wane in the post-Zhivkov era. Depending on whether nonmonetary benefits like housing and food were considered, an officer's pay was generally 25 to 50 percent higher than that offered in civilian positions with comparable responsibilities. Only in 1990 did the defense establishment begin to address problems familiar to military officers in all countries, however. For example, spouses frequently were unable to find work in the vicinity of military posts. In 1991 a special cash allowance to military families was being considered to cover these instances. Day-care and school accommodations often were scarce, and adequate housing unavailable. The quasi-official Georgi Rakovski Officer Legion was established in 1990 to promote a broad range of professional interests and address issues such as living standards within the Ministry of National Defense.

In the early 1990s, tenure became a vital concern to officers. In 1991 the minister of national defense announced that reductions in the armed forces would reduce the officer corps by nearly 15 percent. A military affiliate of the Podkrepa labor federation was founded in 1991 by a group of junior officers and NCOs (see Trade Unions, ch. 4). As an independent organization, it was seen as a more formidable adversary to the Ministry of National Defense than the Georgi Rakovski Officer Legion. Some of the Podkrepa affiliate's founders were dismissed from the service, apparently in retaliation for their activities.

Reserves and Mobilization

In 1991 Bulgaria had a force of approximately 500,000 in reserve for service in the event of mobilization. This figure included over 400,000 in the ground forces, nearly 50,000 in the air and air defense forces, and smaller numbers in the naval forces. Individuals were counted in the active reserves for the first five years after their release from military service. Their reserve obligation continued until age fifty for former conscripts and until age sixty for officers. The demand for labor in the civilian economy and a lack of training put a practical limit on the effectiveness of the reserves. Soldiers discharged in the latest five-year period represented the largest contingent in the reserves, and they could be mobilized after a short period of refresher training and physical conditioning. The deactivation of four motorized rifle divisions and increased emphasis on territorial training centers indicated that reserves could become a more important part of the force structure.

Ranks, Uniforms, and Insignia

The ground forces and air and air defense forces used the same system of ranks. The air and air defense forces and naval forces lacked an equivalent to the four-star army general rank in the ground forces. Below army general, there were three general-grade, three field-grade, and four company-grade officer ranks. In descending order, the ranks were colonel general, lieutenant general, major general, colonel, lieutenant colonel, major, captain, senior lieutenant, lieutenant, and junior lieutenant. Naval officer ranks included three admiral, four captain, and three lieutenant ranks. The ground forces and air and air defense forces had six enlisted grades, four sergeant and two private. The naval forces had equivalent petty officer and seaman grades.

Officers wore a service uniform consisting of a tailored blouse with patch pockets and trousers that tucked into high boots. A Sam Browne belt and sidearms were optional. The ground forces wore stripes and piping on caps and rank insignia that varied in color according to the branch of service (motorized rifle, tank, artillery, and others). Enlisted uniforms were similar in design but had less ornate trim. The air and air defense forces and naval forces had the same uniforms but could be distinguished by blue stripes and piping for the former and traditional naval blues and whites for the latter.

Rank insignia on uniforms consisted of stars or stripes on shoulder boards. Officer ranks were identified by varying numbers of stars and increasingly ornate shoulder boards with higher ranks. Those of company-grade officers were relatively plain; those of general officers were very ornate. Enlisted grades were denoted by increasing numbers of stripes. Privates and seamen wore no stripes and plain shoulder boards. The number and width of stripes increased with promotion to higher grades (see fig. 13; fig. 14; fig. 15).

Foreign Military Relations

For most of the postwar era, Bulgaria's strictly defined relations with the Soviet Union and the Warsaw Pact limited its relations with the military establishments of other countries. In the 1970s and 1980s, Bulgaria established military contacts with a few developing countries in the Middle East and Africa because of their relations with the Soviet Union. The collapse of the Warsaw Pact raised a question about Bulgaria's future external military ties. Options included continuing a bilateral relationship with the Soviet Union, establishing a multilateral security arrangement with neighboring Balkan countries or former Warsaw Pact allies in Eastern Europe, mounting an effort to join NATO, or withholding military commitments to other countries.

The Warsaw Pact

Geographically isolated from the strategically more important northern-tier countries of the alliance, Bulgaria participated in a few joint exercises of the Warsaw Pact along the central front opposite NATO in the German Democratic Republic (East Germany) and Czechoslovakia. Participation in that front usually was limited to small contingents. Small-scale maneuvers or command and staff exercises were held in Bulgaria in 1964 and 1972. Shield-82 was the first major Warsaw Pact exercise in Bulgaria. That exercise involved 60,000 allied troops and included units from the northern-tier Warsaw Pact countries for the first time. The majority of participants were Soviet soldiers, however. The use of air or sea transportation instead of ground transportation across Romania, which allowed no foreign troops on its territory, restricted participation by the northern-tier Warsaw Pact countries. Part of the rationale for the Varna-Odessa ferry completed in the late 1970s was to bypass this obstacle and provide direct Soviet-Bulgarian transport of equipment and troops. The Warsaw Pact conducted a major command and staff exercise for its Southwestern Theater of Military Operations in Bulgaria in March 1984. Union-84 included general staff elements from the Soviet Union, Hungary, Romania, and Bulgaria in simulated coordination of their respective ground and naval forces.

Military Cooperation and Exchanges

Bulgaria had fewer military contacts with developing countries than did its Warsaw Pact allies, instead stressing economic, agricultural, and technological exchanges. Military cooperation with developing countries occurred primarily as part of assistance programs to Soviet allies rather than as an independent policy.

Beginning in the late 1970s, Bulgaria developed military relations with several key countries in the Middle East and Africa. By the mid-1980s, friendship treaties were in effect with Angola, Ethiopia, Libya, Mozambique, and Syria—all of which were receiving substantial military aid from the Soviet Union. These treaties mentioned unspecified military cooperation between the two signatories. In the 1980s, the Bulgarian minister of national defense paid official visits and received military delegations of developing countries without further elaboration of those terms. During this period, Bulgaria also had limited military relations with several developing countries that were not Soviet client states, including India, Nigeria, and Zambia.

More recently, Bulgaria extended its policy of military cooperation to immediate neighbors. In 1987 and 1988, Bulgaria and Greece exchanged visits by the chiefs of their respective general staffs. In 1990 the National Assembly ordered several units of special troops deployed to the Persian Gulf. Over 270 troops, consisting of a medical team, chemical defense company, and rear services unit, supported the United States-led coalition that forced the Iraqi army to withdraw from Kuwait in February 1991. In November 1990, the Bulgarian General Staff sent a delegation to Turkey, signaling a decisive warming of relations with that traditional enemy. In 1991 a Bulgarian-Turkish nonaggression pact was discussed, but Bulgaria feared that a bilateral treaty would damage its close relations with Greece.

Arms Sales

During the 1980s, Bulgaria annually exported an estimated US$250 to US$500 million worth of arms and military equipment. On one occasion, Zhivkov personally boasted of having arms supply

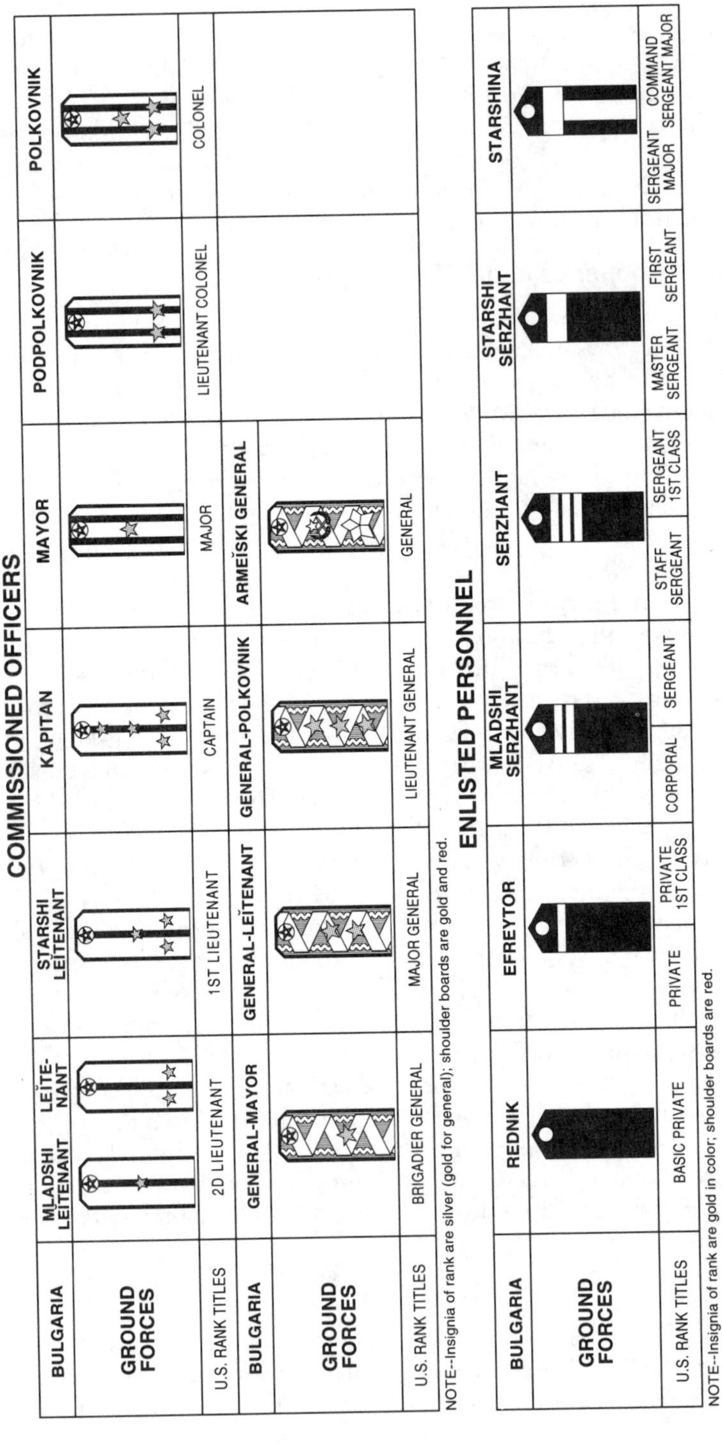

COMMISSIONED OFFICERS

BULGARIA	MLADSHI LEĬTENANT	LEĬTENANT	STARSHI LEĬTENANT	KAPITAN	MAYOR	PODPOLKOVNIK	POLKOVNIK
GROUND FORCES							
U.S. RANK TITLES	2D LIEUTENANT	1ST LIEUTENANT	CAPTAIN	MAJOR	LIEUTENANT COLONEL	COLONEL

BULGARIA	GENERAL-MAYOR	GENERAL-LEĬTENANT	GENERAL-POLKOVNIK	ARMEĬSKI GENERAL
GROUND FORCES				
U.S. RANK TITLES	BRIGADIER GENERAL	MAJOR GENERAL	LIEUTENANT GENERAL	GENERAL

NOTE--Insignia of rank are silver (gold for general); shoulder boards are gold and red.

ENLISTED PERSONNEL

BULGARIA	REDNIK	EFREYTOR	MLADSHI SERZHANT	SERZHANT	STARSHI SERZHANT	STARSHINA
GROUND FORCES						
U.S. RANK TITLES	BASIC PRIVATE	PRIVATE	PRIVATE 1ST CLASS	CORPORAL	SERGEANT	STAFF SERGEANT	SERGEANT 1ST CLASS	MASTER SERGEANT	FIRST SERGEANT	SERGEANT MAJOR	COMMAND SERGEANT MAJOR

NOTE--Insignia of rank are gold in color; shoulder boards are red.

Figure 13. Ranks and Insignia of Ground Forces, 1990

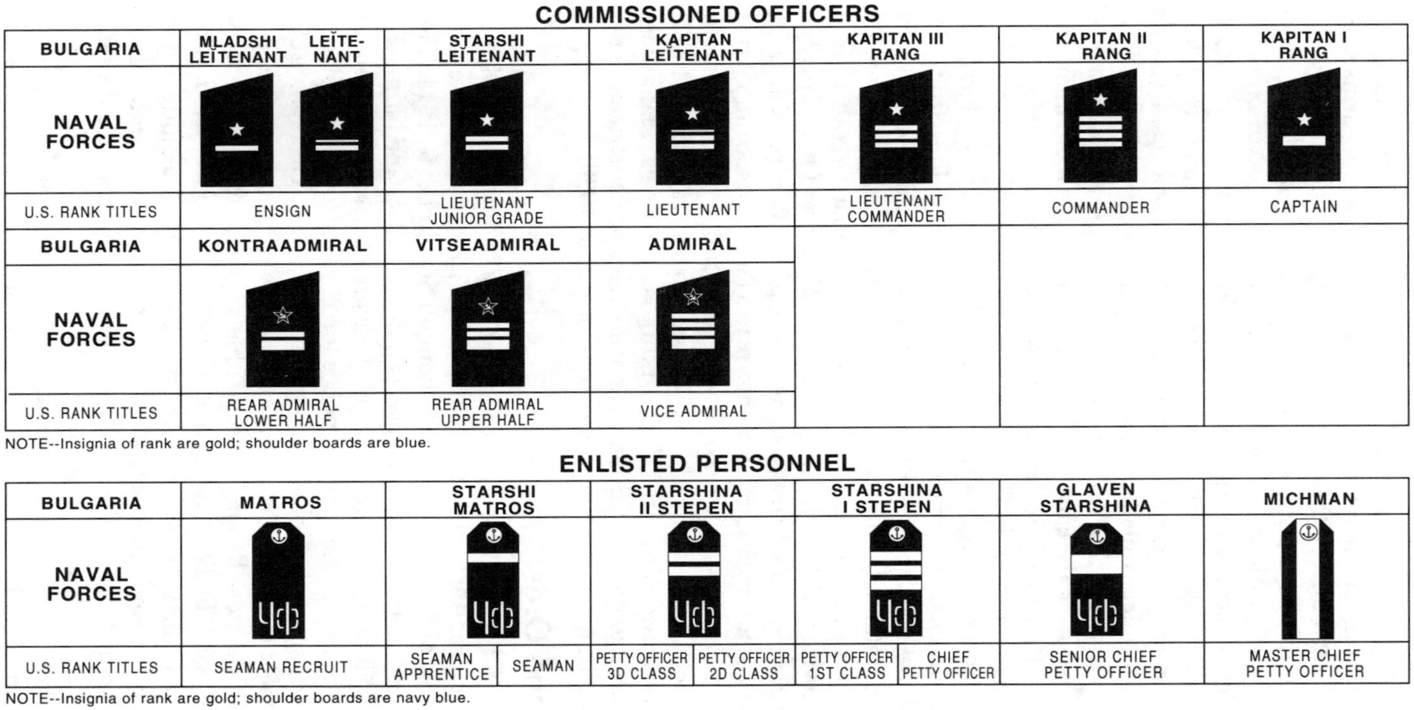

COMMISSIONED OFFICERS

BULGARIA	MLADSHI LEITENANT	LEITENANT	STARSHI LEITENANT	KAPITAN LEITENANT	KAPITAN III RANG	KAPITAN II RANG	KAPITAN I RANG
NAVAL FORCES							
U.S. RANK TITLES	ENSIGN	LIEUTENANT JUNIOR GRADE	LIEUTENANT	LIEUTENANT COMMANDER	COMMANDER	CAPTAIN

BULGARIA	KONTRAADMIRAL	VITSEADMIRAL	ADMIRAL
NAVAL FORCES			
U.S. RANK TITLES	REAR ADMIRAL LOWER HALF	REAR ADMIRAL UPPER HALF	VICE ADMIRAL

NOTE--Insignia of rank are gold; shoulder boards are blue.

ENLISTED PERSONNEL

BULGARIA	MATROS	STARSHI MATROS	STARSHINA II STEPEN	STARSHINA I STEPEN	STARSHINA	GLAVEN STARSHINA	MICHMAN
NAVAL FORCES							
U.S. RANK TITLES	SEAMAN RECRUIT	SEAMAN APPRENTICE	SEAMAN	PETTY OFFICER 3D CLASS	PETTY OFFICER 2D CLASS	PETTY OFFICER 1ST CLASS	CHIEF PETTY OFFICER	SENIOR CHIEF PETTY OFFICER	MASTER CHIEF PETTY OFFICER

NOTE--Insignia of rank are gold; shoulder boards are navy blue.

Figure 14. Ranks and Insignia of Naval Forces, 1990

261

relationships with thirty-six different countries. The Kintex foreign trade organization had responsibility for managing arms sales abroad. Beginning in the early 1960s, Bulgaria reportedly used its merchant ship fleet to deliver arms to socialist-oriented forces fighting civil wars in Algeria, Angola, Guinea-Bissau, and Mozambique and to leftist terrorist groups in Italy, Turkey, and the Middle East. Kintex allegedly was willing to accept narcotics from Turkish terrorists and other insurgent groups as payment for arms, a charge Bulgarian officials denied. A captured leader of the Italian Red Brigades asserted that Bulgaria was willing to provide weapons to his group during the early 1980s. One of Bulgaria's more infamous sales transferred sixty Soviet tanks to Nicaragua and trained seventy Nicaraguan pilots in 1983 and 1984, at the height of the Sandinista government's war against anticommunist rebels in that country.

Political change removed Kintex and its activities from the category of state secrets. In 1990 the trade organization revealed that it maintained contacts in fifty countries and sold them mainly small arms, ammunition, and tanks and combat aircraft retired from service with the BPA. The democratization of post-Zhivkov Bulgaria reportedly had the same downsizing effect on Kintex as it had on other defense-related enterprises (see Logistics and Arms Procurement, this ch.). According to one source, arms exports to the Soviet Union declined from billions to several hundred million leva between the late 1980s and the early 1990s. Plans were announced to continue Bulgaria's arms sales under stricter legislative scrutiny and government control in the 1990s.

Law and Order

The BCP gained control of the Ministry of Justice and Ministry of Internal Affairs in the Fatherland Front coalition after the overthrow of the wartime government on September 9, 1944. The party used these posts to increase its political power and ultimately to push all noncommunists out of the cabinet. In the subsequent reorganization of the national police force, party loyalists replaced officers suspected of having cooperated with the Gestapo. BCP cadres held every important national, regional, and municipal position in the new People's Militia that replaced the prewar local police force. The BCP also replaced the prewar court system with People's Courts, in which party members served as judges and jurors. With some modifications, the internal security and justice systems established in the mid-1940s remained in place for the next forty years, bolstering one-party rule.

The fall of Zhivkov in November 1989 and the end of the communist monopoly on political power brought overt pressure for democratic reform of the justice system. In 1991 some improvements were evident, but other problems persisted. The Ministry of Internal Affairs retained its broad responsibility for maintaining law and order, law enforcement, internal security, and foreign intelligence activities. Before 1989 it had been more powerful and important than the judicial system it was supposed to serve; in 1991 many still considered the ministry a reactionary and sinister force because of past involvement in repressive activities and indications of continued party influence within its ranks. However, a new union of its employees called for significant reforms, including the depoliticization and professionalization of its work force. Immediately after the Zhivkov ouster, substantial public pressure called for depoliticizing the ministry, which one high official described as the "armed detachment of the party." Early in 1990, a reorganization plan proposed drastic cuts in budgeting and personnel and a complete revision of the ministry's functions.

Bulgaria lost social stability between 1989 and 1991. Increased social tension, crime, violence, and civil disorder were the unintended consequences of greater freedom. A crisis of law enforcement followed in the wake of political relaxation and democratization. The police seemed unsure whether to enforce the laws of the legal system of the discredited Zhivkov regime. This uncertainty was reflected when the People's Militia, formerly an efficient and feared instrument of the communist regime, took no action to stop vandals and arsonists who attacked and burned the BSP headquarters in August 1990.

Crime

More than 700,000 crimes were reported in Bulgaria between 1970 and 1990. The People's Militia reported an annual rate of 570 crimes per 100,000 people in 1989. By 1989, homicides had increased by 30 percent, burglaries by nearly 40 percent, and rapes by 45 percent over the rates in the mid-1980s. In 1990, the incidence of crime again increased sharply. Compared with the 15,000 crimes committed during 1989, the People's Militia received reports of more than 4,600 crimes in Sofia alone during the first six months of 1990. Approximately 70 percent of these crimes were committed by repeat offenders, and a very high percentage were petty crimes against property. Organized crime was increasingly evident; more than ten criminal organizations reportedly operated in Sofia. They were involved in black-market activities and were reputed to have connections to organized crime in other countries.

In an effort to curb another aspect of the crime problem, the National Assembly appealed in 1990 for citizens to surrender their

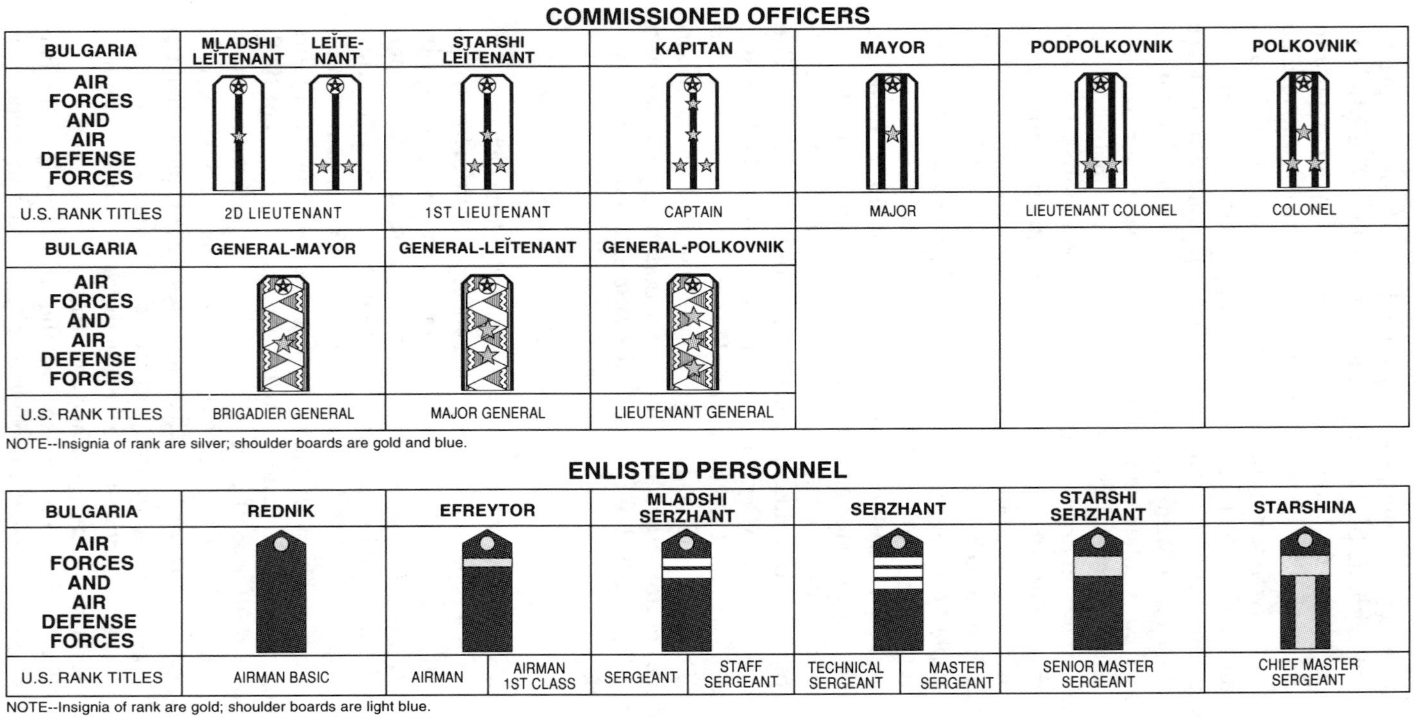

COMMISSIONED OFFICERS

BULGARIA AIR FORCES AND AIR DEFENSE FORCES	MLADSHI LEITENANT	LEITE-NANT	STARSHI LEITENANT	KAPITAN	MAYOR	PODPOLKOVNIK	POLKOVNIK
U.S. RANK TITLES	2D LIEUTENANT		1ST LIEUTENANT	CAPTAIN	MAJOR	LIEUTENANT COLONEL	COLONEL

BULGARIA AIR FORCES AND AIR DEFENSE FORCES	GENERAL-MAYOR	GENERAL-LEITENANT	GENERAL-POLKOVNIK
U.S. RANK TITLES	BRIGADIER GENERAL	MAJOR GENERAL	LIEUTENANT GENERAL

NOTE--Insignia of rank are silver; shoulder boards are gold and blue.

ENLISTED PERSONNEL

BULGARIA AIR FORCES AND AIR DEFENSE FORCES	REDNIK	EFREYTOR		MLADSHI SERZHANT		SERZHANT		STARSHI SERZHANT	STARSHINA
U.S. RANK TITLES	AIRMAN BASIC	AIRMAN	AIRMAN 1ST CLASS	SERGEANT	STAFF SERGEANT	TECHNICAL SERGEANT	MASTER SERGEANT	SENIOR MASTER SERGEANT	CHIEF MASTER SERGEANT

NOTE--Insignia of rank are gold; shoulder boards are light blue.

Figure 15. Ranks and Insignia of Air Forces and Air Defense Forces, 1990

unregistered firearms and ammunition. The People's Militia reported that 145 crimes were committed with firearms between 1985 and 1989 and that in that period 60 people were killed and more than 120 people were wounded by illegal firearms. In 1989 authorities seized nearly 800 illegal firearms, and 2,500 firearms were surrendered voluntarily. That year approximately 85,000 firearms had been registered in the country. In 1990 the government revoked a law allowing party members and government officials to carry weapons.

Smuggling of drugs, arms, and other contraband was a persistent problem during and after the Zhivkov regime. Allegations of official involvement in smuggling appeared frequently in the foreign press (see Arms Sales, this ch.). Government spokespersons denied these charges and routinely asserted that the geographical situation of Bulgaria at the crossroads of Europe and Asia made it a natural route for illegal trade. They pointed out instances in which customs officials arrested foreigners, particularly Turks and Yugoslavs, passing through Bulgaria with illegal narcotics bound for Europe. The press noted cooperation between customs authorities and the UN Commission for Narcotics Control in efforts to curtail international drug trafficking. The UN supported these efforts by funding construction of modern border checkpoints in Bulgaria. The International Criminal Police Organization (Interpol) also certified that Bulgaria had a good record in international law enforcement. In Bulgaria the Directorate of Customs and Customs Control of the Ministry of Finance was responsible for preventing drug trafficking; however, the People's Militia and Border Troops also were active in the counternarcotics effort.

The Judicial System

In 1991 the court system operated basically as it had before 1989. The administration of justice was based on the penal code of 1968 and several subsequent amendments to it, and on the constitution of 1971. In general, the courts had little independence and the Ministry of Justice had few powers under the former regime. In 1991, however, the National Assembly was considering draft laws on penal procedure, punishment, courts, amnesty, state secrets, and travel abroad. It sought to guarantee accused persons access to defense counsel during each phase of the legal process, to eliminate detention on suspicion, and to ensure that three judges and four lay jurors, called assessors, would preside over trials involving particularly grievous crimes in which the death penalty would be a possible sentence.

The court system consisted of municipal, provincial, and military courts; the Supreme Court; and public prosecutors at corresponding levels. The National Assembly elected the judges of the Supreme Court, its president, and the chief prosecutor to five-year terms. The chief prosecutor selected and supervised prosecutors to serve at the municipal and province levels and enforced compliance with legal standards by the government, its officials, and all citizens, prosecuting cases involving major crimes detrimental to the national interests or economy of Bulgaria. Judges at lower levels were elected to five-year terms by their respective constituencies. Conciliation committees in enterprises or municipal courts ruled on labor disputes. The arbitration court adjudicated civil cases and disputes between enterprises.

Under the penal code inherited from the Zhivkov era, crimes against the socialist economy or socialist property generally were punished more severely than crimes against persons. Major economic crimes, misappropriation, and serious malfeasance were punished rigorously. Directors and managers could be held criminally liable for the shortcomings of their enterprises. Six-year prison terms were levied for crimes such as conducting private economic activity while representing a state enterprise and receiving economic benefits for work or services not rendered. Illegally crossing national borders was punishable by a fine of 3,000 leva and a five-year prison term, with heavier penalties for recidivists. In the reform period, an increasing number of minor offenses were changed to receive administrative punishments such as fines up to 300 leva. These administrative proceedings represented rather arbitrary justice because the accused did not have the right to trial or legal counsel. The administrative proceedings were an expedient designed to alleviate a tremendous backlog of minor cases. Beginning in 1990, the dismantling of the state enterprise system called for shifting the emphasis of the criminal code from protection of state property to protection of the individual. This shift was attempted in the new constitution ratified by the National Assembly in July 1991. Independence of the judicial system, needed to standardize and clarify the administration of justice, received little attention in initial rounds of reform, however (see The Judiciary, ch. 4).

The Ministry of Internal Affairs

Under Zhivkov the Ministry of Internal Affairs had been charged with all aspects of internal and external security in peacetime. Given this assignment, the forces under the ministry had vast jurisdiction over society and were a feared and hated part of the communist government. For that reason, reorganization of internal security and intelligence operations was one of the first goals of the post-Zhivkov

*Troops disembarking from armored personnel carrier during military
exercises in Khaskovo District, 1985
Courtesy Sofia Press Agency*

regimes. The overthrow of Zhivkov revealed the activities of Department Six, the "thought police" division of State Security that had been in charge of monitoring the activity of dissidents. Liquidation of that department was announced within a month of Zhivkov's ouster; it also was blamed for the assaults on demonstrators that had received world publicity at the time of the 1989 ecological conference in Sofia (see The Ferment of 1988–90, ch. 4). The UDF and other political organizations called for a complete review of past investigations to identify violations of civil rights by the ministry, review accusations of physical abuse during detention, improve prison conditions, and overturn sentences applied after improper investigation. The remaining prestige of the ministry was demonstrated in December 1990, however, when it and the defense ministry were the posts most hotly contested between the BSP and the UDF in formation of the first multiparty cabinet. At that time, a civilian became head of the Ministry of Internal Affairs for the first time since 1944.

The Ministry of Internal Affairs controlled the People's Militia (police) and the special militarized Internal Security Troops known as the Red Berets. In response to public demands for reform, a new Independent Trade Union Organization of Militia Employees set forth reforms to improve the organization's public relations, which remained very poor in 1990. Declaring that membership in a party was incompatible with nonpartisan law enforcement, the union called for the depoliticization and professionalization of the militia through training programs, legal definition of its authority, and visible separation from influence by the BSP, with which the public still linked the militia. The force also sought to change its name from "militia" to "police." The Commission on National Security of the National Assembly supported this proposal, and the Ministry of Internal Affairs itself drafted a new law on the People's Militia for consideration by the National Assembly.

The People's Militia controlled several subordinate organizations, including the Territorial Militia, Road Militia, Commercial Militia, Central Investigations Department, Training Department, and Administration Department. The Territorial Militia provided law enforcement at the local level. Directorates for the Territorial Militia in each province of the country reported to the People's Militia at the national level. The Road Militia acted as a traffic enforcement authority similar to a highway patrol or state police force. The Commercial Militia investigated economic crimes, fraud, and thefts. The Training Department supervised the training of personnel for the People's Militia. It operated a special secondary school to train sergeants and a national academy to train officers. Candidates studied law codes, criminology, criminal procedure, and foreign languages.

The Red Berets were also part of the Ministry for Internal Security. They were a militarized, light infantry force responsible for preventing riots and other civil disturbances. Their 15,000 personnel were organized into fifteen regiments; they operated over 100 BTR–60 armored personnel carriers equipped for riot control. Together with the People's Militia and the secret police, the Red Berets were involved in the infamous Bulgarization campaign during 1984 and 1985 (see Bulgaria in the 1980s, ch. 1; The Turkish Problem, ch. 4). They were deployed in November 1990 to maintain order in Sofia during the general strike that toppled the BSP government.

The Penal System

Until 1990 the Ministry of Internal Affairs operated the penal system through its Central Prison Institutions Department and its Prison Service. The latter organization trained and administered prison guards. In 1990 the system included thirteen prisons and twenty-six minimum-security facilities housing 6,600 prisoners.

*Military personnel used in crowd control during Union of
Democratic Forces rally, Sofia 1990
Courtesy Charles Sudetic*

Major prisons were located in Bobov Dol, Pazardzhik, Plovdiv,
Sofia, Stara Zagora, Varna, and Vratsa. In 1990 authorities reported that the total prison population had declined by 10,000 as
a result of amnesties granted to political prisoners during the previous three years. The remaining prison population included a high
percentage of repeat offenders and prisoners convicted of serious
crimes. The institution at Pazardzhik reported more than 560 inmates, including more than 50 imprisoned for murder, 60 for rape,
140 for other crimes against persons, and the balance for crimes
against property. Offenders guilty of less serious crimes served time
in minimum-security facilities, including open and semi-open labor
camps. Prison strikes and demonstrations began with the Zhivkov
ouster, continuing and escalating through the first half of 1990.
Sparked by the release of large numbers of political prisoners, massive strikes elsewhere, and the suddenly volatile sociopolitical climate, the strikes became violent, and several inmates reportedly
immolated themselves to protest prison conditions. Red Berets were
called upon to reinforce Prison Service guards. By 1991 Bulgaria
had already implemented one stage of prison reform to improve
its international human rights image: prisons were put under the
Ministry of Justice instead of the Ministry of Internal Security.

269

Security and Intelligence Services

In 1990 the Bulgarian state security system was substantially revamped in response to opposition pressure to improve the sinister, oppressive reputation gained by agencies of the Ministry of Internal Affairs during the Zhivkov era. After encountering strong resistance from party functionaries accustomed to using their positions for personal gain, the realignment used the American security system as a model to create three services under a streamlined Ministry of Internal Affairs. The National Security Service (before mid-1991 called the National Service for Defense of the Constitution) was given responsibility for identifying and countering foreign intelligence, subversive, or terrorist activities affecting the security, territorial integrity, or sovereignty of the country. It had authority for domestic law enforcement in cases involving international criminal activity, organized crime, smuggling, political corruption, and illegal fascist or nationalist organizations. The new philosophy announced for conduct of these activities included independence from all political parties, oversight by the Commission on National Security of the National Assembly, and recruitment according to professional rather than political qualification. In 1990 the service was given the important new role of preventing violence during elections.

Unlike the catchall National Security Service, the other two intelligence agencies had very specific roles. The National Protection Service was formed from the Department of Security and Protection, which Zhivkov had turned into a massive organization with unspecified functions ranging from personal protection to supplying imported cars to high party officials. The new protection service was much smaller and was confined to physical protection of government officials and foreign dignitaries.

The third security agency, the National Intelligence Service, was responsible for counterespionage and monitoring activities in neighboring countries, roles filled by the State Security (Dŭrzhavna sigurnost, DS) prior to 1990. The National Intelligence Service announced a personnel cut of 20 percent in 1991, but even in the new atmosphere of disclosure little else was reported about its activity or staffing. After the collapse of the Warsaw Pact, the Bulgarian counterintelligence effort continued to be directed against the NATO countries adjacent to Bulgaria; counterintelligence against former Warsaw Pact allies remained forbidden under a mutual cooperation agreement. The work of the National Intelligence Service was supplemented by the Military Counterintelligence Service, which was moved from DS jurisdiction to the Ministry of National Defense in 1990. The military service reported to the General Staff. According to its chief, military intelligence was responsible for identifying and countering subversive actions, including terrorism, sabotage, and espionage. Besides foreign intelligence services, the activities of military intelligence were directed against domestic political extremism and crime.

After reorganization of the DS agencies, substantial public skepticism remained about the role of the secret services in monitoring Bulgarian society. Some Department Six agents remained active, and in 1991 the existence of still undisclosed Department Six files fueled much media speculation. Revelations that the KGB had overseen DS activity under Zhivkov brought speculation that KGB agents might still be active in Bulgaria after the Warsaw Pact ended. The Ministry of Internal Affairs claimed that only two agents remained in 1991, attached to the Soviet Embassy.

Terrorist and Espionage Activities

Bulgaria's involvement in international terrorism began in the early twentieth century when it provided sanctuary and a base of operations to the Internal Macedonian Revolutionary Organization (IMRO) for terrorist activities against Yugoslavia and Greece. In the 1920s and 1930s, IMRO became a virtual state within a state in southwestern Bulgaria, also known as Pirin Macedonia.

From the beginning of the first communist regime, the State Security service was involved in conventional intelligence collection, illegal technology transfer, and covert actions abroad. The more recent notoriety of the State Security began in 1978 when it was accused of murdering prominent émigré Georgi Markov in London. Once a protégé of Zhivkov, Markov had fled Bulgaria in 1969 and was frequently critical of his former mentor in Bulgarian language broadcasts for the British Broadcasting Corporation. He was stabbed with a poison-tipped umbrella in London, assumedly by a Bulgarian agent. During the same period, at least two similar assassination attempts were made on émigrés, and a number of Bulgarian dissidents received threatening letters. In 1991 President Zheliu Zhelev agreed to open a full investigation of the Markov murder, using State Security files.

Other incidents of State Security activity abroad received international attention. The Bulgarian Embassy in Egypt was closed in 1978 after authorities found evidence of a plot to incite the Egyptian population to overthrow President Anwar al Sadat. In the 1980s, Bulgaria engaged in retaliatory expulsions of Italian and Turkish diplomats on charges of espionage at a time when relations with both countries were strained. The most infamous incident was the State Security's alleged involvement in the attempted assassination of Pope John Paul II in 1981. In that case, the attacker, a Turkish radical, claimed that the Bulgarian and Soviet intelligence agencies had masterminded his plan in order to eliminate the Polish pope's political influence in Eastern Europe. Three Bulgarians identified as coconspirators were acquitted in 1986, but the incident caused the United States Department of State to place Bulgaria on its list of countries sponsoring terrorism.

A leader of the Red Brigades, an Italian terrorist group that kidnapped a U.S. Army general in 1981, later implicated Bulgaria in the kidnap plot. The terrorist asserted that the aim of Bulgarian intelligence was to destabilize Italy and gain information about NATO. The terrorists were ostensibly offered training, arms, and logistical assistance in this operation. A Bulgarian diplomat was expelled from Japan for spying on the Japanese biotechnology and genetic engineering industry in 1983. In 1990 the UDF asserted that it possessed documents detailing the connections between the ousted Zhivkov regime and international terrorists as well as the operation of terrorist training centers in Bulgaria. In 1991 the government of Prime Minister Dimitŭr Popov pledged to disclose additional information on intelligence activities under Zhivkov.

During the Turkish assimilation campaign of 1984–85, the DS, People's Militia, Red Berets, and the army were reported as using violence against ethnic Turks who resisted adopting Bulgarian names in place of their Turkish ones. As many as several hundred ethnic Turks may have been killed by secret police during this campaign. Additional hundreds of Turks were forcibly resettled, arrested, or imprisoned for refusing to cooperate with the assimilation measures. Bulgarian authorities blamed ethnic Turks for a bombing campaign in which thirty Bulgarians were killed in public places in 1984 and 1985. Although guilt was never established, the terrorist acts aroused ethnic feeling that supported the Bulgarization campaign. As the 1990s began, the Bulgarian civilian government had asserted control over all internal security agencies, inspiring the hope that a more open society would result.

*   *   *

English-language sources on Bulgarian national security, the armed forces, and law and order are relatively few. Stephen Ashley's 1989 article in *The Warsaw Pact and the Balkans,* edited by Jonathan Eyal, is the best treatment of the BPA and Bulgarian security. F. Stephen Larrabee's article "Long Memories and Short Fuses" sets a context for understanding the security environment in which the country found itself as the Warsaw Pact disbanded and traditional conflicts reemerged in the Balkans. A 1982 book by Ivan Volgyes, *The Political Reliability of the Warsaw Pact Armies,* remains a good overview of BPA force structure and personnel. Michael M. Boll's *The Soviet-Bulgarian Alliance* on Bulgarian security policies is useful but dated. Official Bulgarian data supplied for the Treaty on Conventional Armed Forces in Europe and *The Military Balance* provide detail on the organization, structure, strength, and disposition of ground forces and air and air defense forces. Milan Vego covers the naval forces in "Special Focus: The Bulgarian Navy" in the *U.S. Naval Institute Proceedings.* Given increasingly open coverage of national security issues in primary sources, translations of the Bulgarian press by the Foreign Broadcast Information Service and Joint Publications Research Service provide information on current developments. (For further information and complete citations, see Bibliography.)

Appendix

Table 1. Metric Conversion Coefficients and Factors

When you know	Multiply by	To find
Millimeters	0.04	inches
Centimeters	0.39	inches
Meters	3.3	feet
Kilometers	0.62	miles
Hectares (10,000 m²)	2.47	acres
Square kilometers	0.39	square miles
Cubic meters	35.3	cubic feet
Liters	0.26	gallons
Kilograms	2.2	pounds
Metric tons	0.98	long tons
....	1.1	short tons
....	2,204	pounds
Degrees Celsius	1.8	degrees Fahrenheit
(Centigrade)	and add 32	

Table 2. Area and Estimated Population of Provinces, 1987

Province	Area *	Population
Burgas	14,657	872,700
Khaskovo	13,892	1,044,400
Lovech	15,150	1,072,100
Mikhaylovgrad	10,607	668,200
Plovdiv	13,628	1,258,000
Razgrad	10,842	850,000
Sofia (city)	1,331	1,208,200
Sofiya	18,979	1,017,000
Varna	11,929	980,100
TOTAL	111,015	8,970,700

* In square kilometers.

Source: Based on information from *The Statesman's Year-Book, 1990–1991*, Ed., John Paxton, New York, 1990, 243.

Table 3. *Population of the Largest Cities, 1987*

City	Population	City	Population
Sofia	1,128,859	Sliven	106,610
Plovdiv	356,596	Shumen	106,496
Varna	305,891	Pernik	97,225
Burgas	197,555	Yambol	94,951
Ruse	190,450	Khaskovo	91,409
Stara Zagora	156,441	Gabrovo	81,554
Pleven	133,747	Pazardzhik	81,513
Dobrich (Tolbukhin)	111,037		

Source: Based on information from *The Stateman's Year-Book, 1990-1991,* Ed., John Paxton, New York, 1990, 243.

Table 4. *Urban Growth, Selected Years, 1946-87*

Year	Urban Population	Percentage of Total Population	Natural Urban Population Increase
1946	1,735,200	24.7	19,800
1956	2,556,100	33.6	25,500
1965	3,828,400	46.5	31,800
1975	5,067,000	58.0	58,100
1985	5,807,500	64.9	30,200
1987	5,959,400	66.4	29,000

Source: Based on information from Klaus-Detlev Grothusen (ed.), *Bulgarien,* Göttingen, Germany, 1990, 445, 447.

Table 5. *Birth Rates and Death Rates, Selected Years, 1946-87*

Year	Births Number	Birth Rate *	Deaths Number	Death Rate *
1946	179,200	26.5	95,800	13.7
1956	147,900	19.5	71,200	9.4
1965	125,800	15.3	67,000	8.1
1975	144,700	16.6	90,000	10.3
1985	119,000	13.3	107,500	12.0
1987	116,700	13.0	107,200	12.09

* Per 1,000 population.

Source: Based on information from Klaus-Detlev Grothusen (ed.), *Bulgarien,* Göttingen, Germany, 1990, 437, 440.

Table 6. Major Ethnic Groups, 1956 and 1965

	1956		1965	
Ethnic Group	Population	Percentage	Population	Percentage
Bulgarian	6,506,541	85.5	7,231,243	87.9
Turkish	656,025	8.6	780,928	9.5
Gypsy	197,865	2.6	148,874	1.8
Macedonian *	187,789	2.5	9,632	0.1
Armenian	21,954	0.3	20,282	0.3
Greek	7,437	0.1	8,241	0.1
Tatar	5,993	0.1	6,430	0.1

* Official census category. Figures do not represent actual size of this group.

Source: Based on information from Klaus-Detlev Grothusen (ed.), *Bulgarien*, Göttingen, Germany, 1990, 475.

Table 7. Protestant Denominations, 1975

Denominations	Membership	Clergy	Parishes
Pentecostal	5,000–6,000	36	43
Adventist	3,500	40	20
Congregationalist	2,600	24	26
Methodist	1,000	15	13
Baptist	700	7	10

Source: Based on information from Klaus-Detlev Grothusen (ed.), *Bulgarien*, Göttingen, Germany, 1990, 564.

Table 8. Employees in the State Economy by Sector, 1985, 1986, and 1987 (in thousands)

Sector	1985	1986	1987
Agriculture	878.8	848.1	821.5
Industry	1,411.1	1,403.0	1,422.3
Construction	360.6	359.2	359.1
Commerce	355.2	360.7	361.4
Transportation and communications	299.5	306.3	303.3
Education and culture	311.7	317.2	317.6
Health, welfare, and recreation	201.1	201.8	207.7
Administration	54.1	54.3	57.2
Science and research	82.1	83.0	85.8
Housing and community services	54.4	56.7	58.7
Other	86.2	86.2	89.0
TOTAL	4,094.8	4,076.5	4,083.6

Source: Based on information from *The Europa World Year Book, 1989*, 1, London, 1989, 567.

Table 9. Population Distribution as Related to Working Age,
Selected Years, 1956–87

Year	Under Working Age		Working Age *		Over Working Age	
	Number	Percentage	Number	Percentage	Number	Percentage
1956	2,136,700	28.1	4,486,800	58.9	980,200	13.0
1965	2,112,400	25.7	4,789,000	58.2	1,326,500	16.1
1975	2,061,400	23.6	5,058,100	58.0	1,608,100	18.4
1985	2,046,700	22.9	5,013,200	56.0	1,888,800	21.1
1987	2,029,300	22.6	5,004,500	55.8	1,942,400	21.6

* 16 to 54 for women; 16 to 59 for men.

Source: Based on information from Klaus-Detlev Grothusen (ed.), *Bulgarien*, Göttingen, Germany, 1990, 456.

Table 10. Number of Schools, Teachers, and Students by Kind of School,
Selected Years, 1951–88

School	1951	1961	1971	1981	1988
Trade schools					
Number	187	236	328	300	264
Teachers	1,564	2,835	8,454	9,435	7,457
Students	35,724	42,123	130,292	151,200	107,967
Schools for the handicapped *					
Number	11	20	116	129	128
Teachers	115	987	2,155	2,373	2,364
Students	976	8,090	16,870	17,420	16,764
Professional schools					
Number	175	231	246	234	248
Teachers	2,690	5,307	9,045	9,415	10,619
Students	61,591	93,944	152,919	97,575	115,036
General middle schools					
Number	129	144	134	112	74
Teachers	4,627	8,021	6,270	7,419	9,637
Students	113,259	158,004	100,949	97,089	167,845

* Includes schools for mentally handicapped, maladjusted, deaf-mute, blind, and speech-impaired individuals.

Source: Based on information from Klaus-Detlev Grothusen (ed.), *Bulgarien*, Göttingen, Germany, 1990, 502, 506, 508, 510.

Table 11. Investment Apportionment in the State Economy, Selected Years, 1949–88 (in percentages)

Category	1949	1960	1965	1970	1980	1985	1988
Industry	31.4	34.2	44.8	45.2	41.9	46.8	51.0
Agriculture	12.4	29.7	19.7	15.8	12.4	8.2	7.0
Construction	2.2	1.6	2.7	2.9	2.5	3.8	3.4
Transportation	16.5	5.4	6.1	7.8	9.7	8.5	9.7
Housing	22.9	19.2	16.9	15.8	20.2	19.5	17.3
Other	14.6	9.9	9.8	12.5	13.3	13.2	11.6

Source: Based on information from Bulgaria, Tsentralno statistichesko upravlenie. *Statisticheski godishnik na Narodna Republika Bŭlgariia, 1989,* Sofia, 1989, 38; and John R. Lampe, *The Bulgarian Economy in the Twentieth Century,* New York, 1986, 165.

Table 12. Average Annual Growth Rate of Net Material Product by Five-Year Plan, 1949–88 *

Five-Year Plan	Total Economy	Industry	Agriculture
First (1949–52)	8.4	20.7	-0.9
Second (1953–57)	7.8	12.7	4.9
Third (1958–60)	11.6	16.2	6.6
Fourth (1961–65)	6.7	11.7	3.2
Fifth (1966–70)	8.7	10.9	3.5
Sixth (1971–75)	7.8	9.1	2.9
Seventh (1976–80)	6.1	6.0	0.9
Eighth (1981–85)	3.7	7.0	-3.9
Ninth (1986–88)	5.5	5.6	1.2

* Official government figures. First, third, and ninth plans were abandoned or declared fulfilled before the full five years had elapsed. For definition of net material product—see Glossary.

Source: Based on information from Bulgaria, Tsentralno statistichesko upravlenie. *Statisticheski godishnik na Narodna Republika Bŭlgariia, 1989,* Sofia, 1989, 42, 43, 46; and John R. Lampe, *The Bulgarian Economy in the Twentieth Century,* New York, 1986, 144, 162.

Table 13. *Government Budget, Selected Years, 1980-90* [1]
(in millions of leva) [2]

	1980	1986	1988	1990
Expenditures				
Current expenditures				
Wages and salaries	1,162	1,729	1,778	2,316
Maintenance and operation	3,403	4,756	5,167	5,904
Defense and security	1,139	1,914	1,929	2,114
State subsidies	3,128	5,301	6,767	6,050
Interest	422	369	795	2,125
Social security	2,392	3,627	3,895	4,446
Total current expenditures	11,646	17,696	20,331	22,955
Capital investments	1,237	3,447	2,062	1,488
Total expenditures	12,883	21,143	22,393	24,443
Revenues				
Tax revenues				
Taxes on profits	2,302	6,440	8,110	9,734
Income taxes	945	1,372	1,538	1,721
Turnover and excise taxes	3,431	5,672	4,442	4,565
Customs duties	0	159	310	355
Social security contributions	2,753	3,325	3,628	4,027
Other	36	56	133	126
Total tax revenues	9,467	17,024	18,161	20,528
Nontax revenues				
Trade-related revenues	1,975	920	1,551	1,510
Other	1,574	2,197	2,092	2,010
Total nontax revenues	3,549	3,117	3,643	3,520
Total revenues	13,016	20,141	21,804	24,048

[1] Figures may not add to total because of rounding.
[2] For value of the lev—see Glossary.

Source: Based on information from World Bank, *Bulgaria: Crisis and Transition to a Market Economy*, 1, Washington: 1991, 28.

Table 14. *Ownership of Selected Consumer Products,*
1980, 1983, and 1987
(in percentages of households)

Item	1980	1983	1987
Radio	88	92	94
Refrigerator	76	88	94
Television	75	87	97
Washing machine	71	81	91
Automobile	29	34	39
Telephone	24	34	47

Source: Based on information from Klaus-Detlev Grothusen (ed.), *Bulgarien*, Göttingen, Germany, 1990, 470.

Table 15. *Conversion Values of the Lev to Major World Currencies, 1991*

Currency	Symbol	Per	Lev Value
Austrian schilling	ATS	1	1.5146
Belgian franc	BEF	100	51.719
British pound	GBP	1	31.417
Dutch gulden	NLG	1	9.4505
French franc	FRF	100	313.86
German mark	DEM	1	10.642
Greek drachma	GRD	100	9.718
Japanese yen	JPY	100	13.307
Swiss franc	CHF	1	12.489
United States dollar	USD	1	18.367

Source: Based on information from Bulgarian National Bank notification to domestic foreign-exchange bankers, June 3, 1991.

Table 16. *Distribution of Imports by Country, Selected Years, 1950–88* (in percentages)

Country	1950	1960	1970	1980	1988
Comecon countries *					
Soviet Union	50.2	52.6	52.2	57.3	53.5
East Germany	3.8	11.1	8.6	6.6	5.9
Other	31.6	20.3	15.3	18.8	17.3
Western countries					
West Germany	3.4	5.9	2.7	4.8	4.9
Other	1.3	7.7	16.5	8.6	10.6
Third World countries	n.a.	2.4	4.7	3.9	7.8

n.a.—not available.
* Comecon—Council for Mutual Economic Assistance (see Glossary).

Source: Based on information from Bulgaria, Tsentralno statistichesko upravlenie. *Statisticheski godishnik na Narodna Republika Bŭlgariia, 1989,* Sofia, 1989, 84–85; and John R. Lampe, *The Bulgarian Economy in the Twentieth Century,* New York, 1986, 152, 188.

Table 17. *Distribution of Exports by Country, Selected Years, 1950–88*
(in percentages)

Country	1950	1960	1970	1980	1988
Comecon countries *					
Soviet Union	54.4	53.8	53.8	49.9	62.5
East Germany	5.5	10.2	8.7	5.5	5.2
Other	32.0	20.2	17.2	15.4	16.9
Western countries					
West Germany	0.7	3.3	2.6	2.5	1.0
Other	7.2	9.1	11.6	13.3	5.3
Third World countries	0.2	3.4	6.1	13.4	9.1

* Comecon—Council for Mutual Economic Assistance (see Glossary).

Source: Based on information from Bulgaria, Tsentralno statistichesko upravlenie. *Statisticheski godishnik na Narodna Republika Bŭlgariia, 1989,* Sofia, 1989, 84–85; and John R. Lampe, *The Bulgarian Economy in the Twentieth Century,* New York, 1986, 152, 188.

Table 18. *Distribution of Major Imports by Commodity,
Selected Years, 1980–88*
(in percentages at constant prices)

Commodity	1980	1985	1987	1988
Machinery and equipment	45.4	47.2	43.5	43.5
Fuels, metals, and minerals	28.3	24.0	32.4	32.2
Consumer goods	7.2	6.8	5.4	5.7
Chemicals	6.7	6.6	6.4	5.6
Raw materials	5.9	6.2	5.4	5.6
Foodstuffs	2.9	5.0	4.1	4.3
Other	3.6	4.2	2.8	3.1

Source: Based on information from Bulgaria, Tsentralno statistichesko upravlenie. *Statisticheski godishnik na Narodna Republika Bŭlgariia, 1989,* Sofia, 1989, 83.

Table 19. *Distribution of Major Exports by Commodity,
Selected Years, 1980–88*
(in percentages at constant prices)

Commodity	1980	1985	1987	1988
Machinery and equipment	50.7	54.1	58.8	58.7
Processed foods	15.6	12.7	11.4	11.2
Fuels, metals, and minerals	12.7	10.4	8.8	8.2
Consumer goods	9.4	9.4	10.2	11.0
Foodstuffs	3.6	3.2	2.8	2.8
Chemicals	2.8	3.9	3.7	4.0
Construction materials	2.2	1.9	1.9	1.7
Other	3.0	4.4	2.4	2.4

Source: Based on information from Bulgaria, Tsentralno statistichesko upravlenie. *Statisticheski godishnik na Narodna Republika Bŭlgariia, 1989,* Sofia, 1989, 83.

Appendix

Table 20. Social Categories in Bulgarian Communist Party Membership, Selected Years, 1944-86
(in percentages)

Year	Workers	Farmers	Professionals and Intelligentsia	Women	Under 30
1944	26.5	51.9	8.0	n.a.	n.a.
1948	26.5	44.7	16.3	13.0	26.0
1954	34.1	39.8	17.9	1.3	n.a.
1962	37.2	32.1	23.6	21.3	15.6
1971	40.1	26.1	28.2	25.2	16.1
1976	41.4	23.0	30.2	27.5	15.0
1986	44.4	16.3	n.a.	32.7	11.9

n.a.—not available.

Source: Based on information from Klaus-Detlev Grothusen (ed.), *Bulgarien*, Göttingen, Germany, 1990, 183, 185.

Bibliography

Chapter 1

Anastasoff, Christ. *The Bulgarians.* Hicksville, New York: Exposition Press, 1977.

Bankowicz, Marek. "Bulgaria—The Limited Revolution." Pages 195–210 in Sten Berglund and Jan Åke Dellenbrant (eds.), *The New Democracies in Eastern Europe.* Aldershot, United Kingdom: Edward Elgar, 1991.

Bell, John D. *The Bulgarian Communist Party from Blagoev to Zhivkov.* Stanford, California: Hoover Institution Press, 1986.

_____. *Peasants in Power: Alexander Stamboliski and the Bulgarian Agrarian National Union, 1899–1923.* Princeton: Princeton University Press, 1977.

Berglund, Sten, and Jan Åke Dellenbrant (eds.). *The New Democracies in Eastern Europe.* Aldershot, United Kingdom: Edward Elgar, 1991.

Bokov, Georgi (ed.). *Modern Bulgaria: History, Policy, Economy, Culture.* Sofia: Sofia Press, 1981.

Bokova, Irina. "Bulgaria and Ethnic Tensions in the Balkans," *Mediterranean Quarterly,* 2, No. 1, Winter 1991, 88–98.

Bromke, Adam, and Derry Novak (eds.). *The Communist States in the Era of Detente, 1971–1977.* Oakville, Ontario: Mosaic Press, 1979.

Bromke, Adam, and Teresa Rakowska-Harmstone (eds.). *The Communist States in Disarray, 1965–1971.* Minneapolis: University of Minnesota, 1972.

Bukowski, Charles. "The Dilemma of Economic Reform and Political Legitimacy in Eastern Europe," *Coexistence,* 23, No. 3, 1986, 227–45.

Constant, Stephen. *Foxy Ferdinand: Tsar of Bulgaria.* New York: Franklin Watts, 1980.

Crampton, Richard J. *A Short History of Modern Bulgaria.* Cambridge: Cambridge University Press, 1987.

Debove, Alain. "The Turkish Minority in Bulgaria," *Nordic Journal of Soviet and East European Studies* [Oslo], 4, No. 3, 1987, 53–63.

Dellin, L.A.D. (ed.). *Bulgaria.* New York: Praeger, 1957.

Devedjiev, Hristo H. *Stalinization of the Bulgarian Society, 1949–1953.* Philadelphia: Dorrance, 1975.

Dimitrov, Ilcho (ed.). *Kratka istoriia na Bŭlgariia.* Sofia: Nauka i izkustvo, 1981.

Evans, Stanley G. *A Short History of Bulgaria.* London: Lawrence and Wishart, 1960.

Genchev, Nikolai. *The Bulgarian National Revival Period.* Sofia: Sofia Press, 1977.

Georgiev, Emil, et al. *Bulgaria's Share in Human Culture.* Sofia: Sofia Press, 1968.

Groueff, Stephane. *Crown of Thorns.* Lanham, Maryland: Madison Books, 1987.

Holden, Gerard. *The Warsaw Pact: Soviet Security and Bloc Politics.* Oxford: B. Blackwell, 1989.

Hristov, Hristo. *A History of Bulgaria.* Sofia: Sofia Press, 1985.

Jelavich, Barbara. *The Habsburg Empire in European Affairs, 1814-1918.* Chicago: Rand McNally, 1969.

————. *History of the Balkans.* Cambridge: Cambridge University Press, 1983.

Jelavich, Charles. *The Establishment of the Balkan National States, 1804-1920.* Seattle: University of Washington Press, 1977.

Kaplan, Robert D. "History's Cauldron," *Atlantic Monthly,* 267, No. 6, June 1991, 93-96.

Kinder, Hermann, and Werner Hilgemann. *The Anchor Atlas of World History,* 1. Garden City, New York: Anchor Books, 1974.

Lang, David. *The Bulgarians.* Boulder, Colorado: Westview Press, 1976.

McIntyre, Robert J. *Bulgaria: Politics, Economics, and Society.* London: Pinter, 1988.

Miller, Marshall Lee. *Bulgaria During the Second World War.* Stanford: Stanford University Press, 1975.

Mishev, Dimitur. *The Bulgarians in the Past.* New York: Arno Press, 1971.

Nicoloff, Assen. *The Bulgarian Resurgence.* Cleveland, 1987.

Oren, Nissan. *Bulgarian Communism: The Road to Power, 1934-1944.* Westport, Connecticut: Greenwood Press, 1971.

————. *Revolution Administered: Agrarianism and Communism in Bulgaria.* Baltimore: Johns Hopkins Press, 1973.

Parker, John. "The Macedonian Problem Solved?" *South Slav Journal* [London], 6, No. 4, Autumn 1983, 12-21.

Perl, Lila. *Yugoslavia, Romania, Bulgaria.* Camden: Thomas Nelson, 1970.

Rusinov, Spas. *Bulgaria: A Survey.* Sofia: Sofia Press, 1969.

Schöpflin, George (ed.). *The Soviet Union and Eastern Europe.* New York: Praeger, 1970.

Staar, Richard F. *Communist Regimes in Eastern Europe.* Stanford, California: Hoover Institution Press, 1988.

The Statesman's Year-Book, 1990–1991. (Ed., John Paxton.) New York: St. Martin's Press, 1990.

Wolff, Robert. *The Balkans in Our Time.* Cambridge: Harvard University Press, 1956.

Chapter 2

Amnesty International. *Bulgaria: Imprisonment of Ethnic Turks.* London: 1986.

Asenov, Boncho. *Religiiata v Bŭlgariia.* Sofia: Narodna Mladezh, 1987.

Boiadzhiev, Stefan. "Za prestŭpnoto prebroiavane v Pirinskiia krai prez 1946 g.," *Makedoniia* [Sofia], No. 11, 1990.

Bokov, Georgi (ed.). *Modern Bulgaria: History, Policy, Economy, Culture.* Sofia: Sofia Press, 1981.

"Brachnost, razhdaemost, smŭrtnost, estestven prirast na naselenieto i detska smŭrtnost," *Statisticheski izvestiia* [Sofia], No. 4, 1989, 12.

Bulgaria. Ministerstvo na obshtestvena prosvetata. *The School in the Republic of Bulgaria.* Sofia: Ministry of Public Education, 1991.

Delinski, Dimitŭr. "Strukturi za visoka efektivnost," *Rabotnichesko delo* [Sofia], September 1987, 1.

Dimitrov, G. *Kniazhestvo Bŭlgariia.* Sofia: Pridvorna pechatnitsa B. Shimachek, 1894.

The Europa World Year Book, 1989, 1. London: Europa, 1989.

Foreign Policy Institute. *The Tragedy of the Turkish Muslim Minority in Bulgaria.* Ankara: Foreign Policy Institute, 1989.

Genchev, Stoian (ed.). *Etnografski problemi na narodnata dukhovna kultura* [Sofia], Bŭlgarskata akademiia na naukite, 1989.

Grothusen, Klaus-Detlev (ed.). *Bulgarien.* Göttingen: Vandenhoeck und Ruprecht, 1990.

Hadjihristev, Argir. *Life-styles for Long Life: Longevity in Bulgaria.* Springfield, Illinois: Charles C. Thomas, 1988.

Iordanov, Borislav. "Shte izbegnem li insulta?," *Rabotnichesko delo* [Sofia], March 1987, 5.

Iordanov, Tianko (ed.). *Geografiia na Bŭlgariia.* Sofia: Bŭlgarskata akademiia na naukite, 1981.

Karakachanov, Krasimir. "Makedoniia ne zhelae da bŭde srŭbska banovina," *Makedoniia* [Sofia], No. 12, 1990, 4.

Khadzhiiski, Ivan. *Bit i dushevnost na nashiia narod.* Sofia: Bŭlgarski pisatel, 1974.

Khristov, Khristo (ed.). *Stranitsi ot bŭlgarskata istoriia.* Sofia: Nauka i izkustvo, 1989.

Kŭstanova, Kipriana. "Vŭzrastovi regulativni funkstsii na narodnata sotsialnonormativna kultura." Pages 224–26 in Stoian Genchev, (ed.), *Etnografski problemi na narodnata dukhovna kultura*. Sofia: Bŭlgarskata akademiia na naukite, 1989.

Laber, Jeri. *Destroying Ethnic Identity: The Turks of Bulgaria*. New York: Helsinki Watch Committee, 1987.

"Makedoniia dnes," *Vesti Makedoniia* [Skopje], Nos. 11–12, 1990, 1.

Marinov, Dimitŭr. *Etnografichesko (folklorno) izuchavane na zapadna Bŭlgariia*. Sofia: Nauka i izkustvo, 1984.

McIntyre, Robert J. *Bulgaria: Politics, Economics, and Society*. London: Pinter, 1988.

Mijalkovic, Sava. "Sofija—zatvoreni grad," *Borba* [Belgrade], September 23, 1986, 5.

Oppression and Discrimination in Bulgaria. London: K. Rustem, 1986.

Pamukchiev, Minko. "Intelektualen pazar, demokratizŭm i akademichna avtonomiia na VUZ," *Problemi na vissheto obrazovanie [Sofia]*, No. 2, 1990, 3–7.

Poulton, Hugh. *The Balkans: Minorities and States in Conflict*. London: Minority Rights, 1991.

———. *Minorities in the Balkans*. London: Minority Rights, 1989.

Stoyanov, Peter (ed.). *Churches and Religions in the People's Republic of Bulgaria*. Sofia: Synodal, 1975.

Todorov, Tzvetan. *Les morales de l'histoire*. Paris: Bernard Grasset, 1991.

Todorova, Maria. "Population Structure, Marriage Patterns, Family and Household," *Etudes Balkaniques* [Sofia], 1983, 63–68.

Vakarelski, Khristo. *Etnografiia na Bŭlgariia*. Sofia: Bŭlgarskata akademiia na naukite, 1979.

(Various issues of the following publications were also used in the preparation of this chapter: Foreign Broadcast Information Service, *Daily Report: East Europe;* Joint Publication Research Service, *JPRS Report: East Europe;* and *Kak Zhiveem* [Sofia]).

Chapter 3

Alton, Thad, et al. *Economic Growth in Eastern Europe, 1965, 1970, 1975–81*. New York: L.W. International Financial Research, 1982.

Bell, John D. *The Bulgarian Communist Party from Blagoev to Zhivkov*. Stanford, California: Hoover Institution Press, 1986.

Bulgaria. Tsentralno statistichesko upravlenie. *Statisticheski godishnik na Narodna Republika Bŭlgariia, 1989*. Sofia: Tsentralno statistichesko upravlenie, 1989.

"Bulgarian Investment Climate Improving," *Eastern Europe Business Bulletin*, August–September 1991, 3.

Cochrane, Nancy J., and Miles J. Lambert. "Agricultural Performance in Eastern Europe, 1988," *East European Agriculture*, 89, No. 38, August 1989, 1–27.

Crampton, Richard J. *A Short History of Modern Bulgaria.* Cambridge: Cambridge University Press, 1987.

————. "'Stumbling and Dusting Off,' or an Attempt to Pick a Path Through the Thicket of Bulgaria's New Economic Mechanism," *Eastern European Politics and Societies*, 2, No. 2, Spring 1988, 333–95.

Economist Intelligence Unit. *County Report: Romania, Bulgaria, Albania* [London], No. 1, 1992, 28–37.

Engelbrekt, Kjell. "Bulgaria's Industrial Crisis and the Coming Election," Radio Free Europe/Radio Liberty, *Report on Eastern Europe* [Munich], 1, No. 23, June 8, 1990, 1–4.

————. "Round-Table Talks on Economic Reform: Gradual Approach or Shock Therapy?" Radio Free Europe/Radio Liberty, *Report on Eastern Europe* [Munich], 1, No. 13, March 30, 1990, 1–3.

The Europa World Year Book, 1989, 1. London: Europa, 1989.

Feiwel, George R. *Growth and Reforms in Centrally Planned Economies.* New York: Praeger, 1977.

Gherardi, Sophie. "Bulgaria No Longer Able to Feed Itself," *Guardian Weekly* [Manchester, United Kingdom], 143, No. 26, December 9, 1990, 16.

Grothusen, Klaus-Detlev (ed.). *Bulgarien.* Göttingen: Vandenhoeck und Ruprecht, 1990.

Lampe, John R. *The Bulgarian Economy in the Twentieth Century.* New York: St. Martin's Press, 1986.

McIntyre, Robert J. *Bulgaria: Politics, Economics, and Society.* London: Pinter, 1988.

Nikolaev, Rada. "The Government's Economic Program," Radio Free Europe/Radio Liberty, *Report on Eastern Europe* [Munich], 1, No. 47, November 23, 1990, 6–10.

————. "Lukanov's Report on the Economic Crisis," Radio Free Europe/Radio Liberty, *Report on Eastern Europe* [Munich], 1, No. 38, September 21, 1990, 4–9.

Sachs, Jeffrey D. "Accelerating Privatization in Eastern Europe." (Paper presented at World Bank Annual Conference on Development Economics, 1991.) Washington: World Bank, 1991.

Semov, Marco, and Atanas Semov. "Bulgaria on the Threshold of Drama and Hope," *International Affairs* [Moscow], No. 1, January 1991, 13–22.

Sjoberg, Orjan, and Michael L. Wyzan (eds.). *Economic Change in the Balkan States: Albania, Bulgaria, Romania, and Yugoslavia.* New York: St. Martin's Press, 1991.

United States. Congress. 99th, 2d Session. Joint Economic Committee. *East European Economies: Slow Growth in the 1980s.* Washington: GPO, 1986.

World Bank. *Bulgaria: Crisis and Transition to a Market Economy.* Washington: 1991.

(Various issues of the following publications were also used in the preparation of this chapter: *Business Eastern Europe;* Foreign Broadcast Information Service, *Daily Report: East Europe;* and Joint Publications Research Service, *JPRS Report: East Europe.*)

Chapter 4

Bankowicz, Marek. "Bulgaria—The Limited Revolution." Pages 195–210 in Sten Berglund and Jan Åke Dellenbrant (eds.), *The New Democracies in Eastern Europe.* Aldershot, United Kingdom: Edward Elgar, 1991.)

Bell, John D. *The Bulgarian Communist Party from Blagoev to Zhivkov.* Stanford, California: Hoover Institution Press, 1986.

––––––. "'Post-Communist' Bulgaria," *Current History,* 89, No. 12, December 1990, 417–420.

Berglund, Sten, and Jan Åke Dellenbrant (eds.). *The New Democracies in Eastern Europe.* Aldershot, United Kingdom: Edward Elgar, 1991.

Binder, David. "Going Back: Bulgaria, 20 Years Later," *New York Times Magazine,* December 8, 1985, 154–55.

Bokova, Irina. "Bulgaria and Ethnic Tensions in the Balkans," *Mediterranean Quarterly,* 2, No. 1, Winter 1991, 88–98.

Bromke, Adam, and Derry Novak (eds.). *The Communist States in the Era of Detente, 1971–1977.* Oakville, Ontario: Mosaic Press, 1979.

Chiodini, Steven. "Bulgaria: An Eastern European Revolution in Suspension," *Harvard International Review,* 13, No. 1, Winter 1990–91, 47–49.

Bromke, Adam, and Teresa Rakowska-Harmstone (eds.). *The Communist States in Disarray, 1965–1971.* Minneapolis: University of Minnesota Press, 1972.

Crampton, Richard J. *A Short History of Modern Bulgaria.* Cambridge: Cambridge University Press, 1987.

Danevski, Valentin. *Political Parties, Movements and Organizations in Bulgaria and their Leaders.* Sofia: Sofia Press, 1990.

Devedjiev, Hristo H. *Stalinization of the Bulgarian Society, 1949-1953.* Philadelphia: Dorrance, 1975.

"Exodus," *The Economist* [London], 312, No. 7610, July 8, 1989, 36.

"The Experience of Being Bulgarised," *The Economist* [London], 297, No. 7424, December 14, 1985, 32.

Gati, Charles. "Gorbachev and Eastern Europe," *Foreign Affairs,* 65, No. 5, Summer 1987, 958-75.

Grothusen, Klaus-Detlev (ed.). *Bulgarien.* Göttingen: Vandenhoeck und Ruprecht, 1990.

Halpern, Joel Martin, and Barbara Kerewsky-Halpern. *Bulgaria's Time Bind: The Search for Democracy and a Viable Heritage.* (Universities Field Staff International, UFSI Reports, Eastern Europe, No. 12.) Indianapolis: 1990.

Larrabee, F. Stephen. "Long Memories and Short Fuses: Change and Instability in the Balkans," *International Security* [Cambridge], 15, No. 3, Winter 1990/91, 58-91.

Luers, William H. "The U.S. and Eastern Europe," *Foreign Affairs,* 65, No. 5, Summer 1987, 976-94.

McIntyre, Robert J. *Bulgaria: Politics, Economics, and Society.* London: Pinter, 1988.

Nelson, Daniel N. *Balkan Imbroglio: Politics and Security in Southeastern Europe.* Boulder, Colorado: Westview Press, 1991.

_____. "Political Dynamics and the Bulgarian Military," *Berichte des Bundesinstituts für ostwissenschaftliche und internationale Studien* [Cologne], 1990, No. 43, July 1990.

Oren, Nissan. *Revolution Administered: Agrarianism and Communism in Bulgaria.* Baltimore: Johns Hopkins Press, 1973.

"The Other Side of the Moon," *The Economist* [London], 297, No. 7425, December 21, 1985, 14.

Prins, Gwyn, et al. "After the Collapse of Communism," *Political Quarterly,* 62, No. 1, January-March 1991, 1-74.

Semov, Marco, and Atanas Semov. "Bulgaria on the Threshold of Drama and Hope," *International Affairs* [Moscow], No. 1, January 1991, 13-22.

Starr, Richard F. *Communist Regimes in Eastern Europe.* Stanford, California: Hoover Institution Press, 1988.

Statkov, Dimiter. "Monarchists and Nationalists in Bulgaria," *Swiss Review of Western Affairs* [Zurich], 41, No. 5, August 1991, 8-10.

Tzvetkov, Plamen S. "The Politics of Transition in Bulgaria," *Problems of Communism,* 41, No. 3, May-June 1992, 34-43.

Wolff, Robert. *The Balkans in Our Time.* Cambridge: Harvard University Press, 1956.

(Various issues of the following publications were also used in the preparation of this chapter: Foreign Broadcast Information Service, *Daily Report: East Europe;* Joint Publications Research Service, *JPRS Report: East Europe;* and Radio Free Europe/Radio Liberty Research Institute, *RFE/RL Research Report* [Munich].)

Chapter 5

Ashley, Stephen. "Bulgaria: Between Loyalty and Nationalism." Pages 109–53 in Jonathan Eyal (ed.), *The Warsaw Pact and the Balkans: Moscow's Southern Flank.* New York: St. Martin's Press, 1989 [Munich].)

Boll, Michael M. *Cold War in the Balkans: American Foreign Policy and the Emergence of Communist Bulgaria, 1943–1974.* Lexington: University Press of Kentucky, 1984.

_____. "The Soviet-Bulgarian Alliance: From Subservience to Partnership," *Parameters,* 24, No. 4, Winter 1984, 47–55.

Bulgaria. Ministry of Defense. *Republic of Bulgaria Data Provided in Accordance with the Data Exchange Protocol of the Treaty on Conventional Armed Forces in Europe.* Sofia: 1990.

Crampton, Richard J. *A Short History of Modern Bulgaria.* Cambridge: Cambridge University Press, 1987.

Dupuy, R. Ernest, and Trevor N. Dupuy. *The Encyclopedia of Military History from 3500 BC to the Present.* New York: Harper and Row, 1986.

Economist Intelligence Unit. *Country Profile: Bulgaria, 1990–91.* London: 1991.

Eyal, Jonathan (ed.). *The Warsaw Pact and the Balkans: Moscow's Southern Flank.* New York: St. Martin's Press, 1989.

Foss, Christopher, F. (ed.). *Jane's Armour and Artillery, 1989–90.* Surrey, United Kingdom: Jane's, 1989.

"High Command of the Bulgarian People's Army (BNA)," *Jane's Soviet Intelligence Review* [Surrey, United Kingdom], 2, No. 9, September 1990, 412–13.

Lambert, Mark (ed.). *Jane's All the World's Aircraft, 1990–91.* Surrey, United Kingdom: Jane's, 1990.

Larrabee, F. Stephen. "Long Memories and Short Fuses: Change and Instability in the Balkans," *International Security* [Cambridge], 15, No. 3, Winter 1990/91, 58–91.

McIntyre, Robert J. *Bulgaria: Politics, Economics, and Society*. London: Pinter, 1988.

The Military Balance, 1990–1991. London: Brassey's for International Institute for Strategic Studies, 1990.

Miller, Marshall Lee. *Bulgaria During the Second World War*. Stanford: Stanford University Press, 1975.

Nelson, Daniel N. *Balkan Imbroglio: Politics and Security in Southeastern Europe*. Boulder, Colorado: Westview Press, 1991.

_____. "Political Dynamics and the Bulgarian Military," *Berichte des Bundesinstituts für ostwissenschaftliche und internationale Studien* [Cologne], 1990, No. 43, July 1990.

Sharpe, Richard (ed.). *Jane's Fighting Ships, 1990–91*. Surrey, United Kingdom: Jane's, 1990.

United States. Arms Control and Disarmament Agency. *World Military Expenditures and Arms Transfer, 1989*. Washington: GPO, 1990.

Vego, Milan. "Special Focus: The Bulgarian Navy," *U.S. Naval Institute Proceedings*. (No. 114/3/1021.) March 1988, 52–54.

Volgyes, Ivan. *The Political Reliability of the Warsaw Pact Armies: The Southern Tier*. Durham, North Carolina: Duke University Press, 1982.

(Various issues of the following publications were also used in the preparation of this chapter: Foreign Broadcast Information Service, *Daily Report: East Europe* and Joint Publications Research Service, *JPRS Report: East Europe*.)

Glossary

Asia Minor—The Asian portion of what is now Turkey.

Bogomilism—A religious sect founded in Bulgaria and flourishing in the Balkans between the tenth and fifteenth centuries. It combined beliefs from several contemporaneous religions, most notably the Paulicians from Asia Minor (*q.v.*). The central belief was that the material world was created by the devil.

Cominform (Communist Information Bureau)—An international communist organization (1947–56) including communist parties of the Soviet Union, Bulgaria, Czechoslovakia, France, Hungary, Italy, Poland, Romania, and Yugoslavia (expelled in 1948). Formed as a tool of Soviet foreign policy, it issued propaganda advocating international communist solidarity.

Conference on Security and Cooperation in Europe (CSCE)—Originating at the Helsinki meeting that produced the Helsinki Accords (*q.v.*) in 1975, a grouping of all European nations (the lone exception, Albania, joined in 1991) that subsequently sponsored joint sessions and consultations on political issues vital to European security.

Conventional Armed Forces in Europe Treaty (CFE)—An agreement signed in 1990 by the members of the Warsaw Pact (*q.v.*) and the North Atlantic Treaty Organization (*q.v.*) to establish parity in conventional weapons between the two organizations from the Atlantic to the Urals. Included a strict system of inspections and information exchange.

Council for Mutual Economic Assistance (Comecon)—A multilateral economic alliance headquartered in Moscow until it disbanded in 1991. Members in 1991: Bulgaria, Cuba, Czechoslovakia, Hungary, Mongolia, Poland, Romania, the Soviet Union, and Vietnam. Also known as CMEA and CEMA.

Cyrillic—Alphabet ascribed to the missionary Cyril (ninth century), developed from Greek for recording church literature in Old Church Slavonic. Now the alphabet of Belarus, Bulgaria, Montenegro, Russia, Serbia, Ukraine, and several former Soviet republics in Central Asia, it is considered one of the three principal alphabets of the world.

Enlightenment—Intellectual and spiritual movement in Europe in the seventeenth and eighteenth centuries, concerned with the relationship of God, nature, reason, and man, often challenging the tenets of Christianity.

European Bank for Reconstruction and Development (EBRD)—
A bank founded under sponsorship of the European Community (EC) in 1990, to provide loans to East European countries (Bulgaria, Czechoslovakia, Hungary, Poland, Romania,
the Soviet Union, and Yugoslavia) to establish independent,
market-type economies and democratic political institutions.
Some forty-one countries were shareholders in 1991.

European currency unit (ECU)—The unit of account of the European Economic Community (*q.v.*), value of which is determined
by the value of the currencies of the member states, apportioned
by relative strength and importance of the member's economy.
In 1988 one ECU equalled about one United States dollar.

European Economic Community (EEC)—The ''Common Market'' of primarily West European countries, organized to
promote coordinated development of economic activities, expansion, stability, and closer relations among member states.
Methods included elimination of customs duties and import
regulations among member states, a common tariff and commercial policy toward outside countries, and a common agricultural and transport policy. A significant further reduction of
intraorganizational barriers was planned in 1992.

General Agreement on Tariffs and Trade (GATT)—An integrated
set of bilateral trade agreements among nations, formed in 1947
to abolish quotas and reduce tariffs. Bulgaria applied for membership in 1991.

glasnost—Russian term, literally meaning ''openness,'' applied beginning in the mid-1980s in the Soviet Union to official permission for public discussion of issues and access to information.
Identified with the tenure of Mikhail S. Gorbachev as leader
of the Soviet Union (1985–91).

gross national product (GNP)—The sum of the value of goods and
services produced within a country's borders and the income
received from abroad by residents, minus payments remitted
abroad by nonresidents. Normally computed over one year.

Helskinki Accords—Signed in 1975 by all countries of Europe except Albania (which signed in 1991) plus Canada and the
United States at the Conference on Security and Cooperation
in Europe (*q.v.*), a pact outlining general principles of international behavior and security and addressing some economic,
environmental, and humanitarian issues.

International Monetary Fund (IMF)—Established with the World
Bank (*q.v.*) in 1945, a specialized agency affiliated with the
United Nations and responsible for stabilizing international ex-
change rates and payments. Its main business was providing

loans to its members when they experienced balance of payments difficulties. Bulgaria became a member in 1991.

League of Nations—An organization for international cooperation established by the Allied powers after World War I. Discredited by failure to oppose aggression in the 1930s, it became inactive at the beginning of World War II and was replaced in 1946 by the United Nations.

lev (pl., leva)—The national currency unit of Bulgaria, consisting of 100 *stotinki.* Exchange rate to the U.S. dollar in 1991 was 18 leva.

Marshall Plan—In full, the European Recovery Program, a United States-sponsored program to rehabilitate European nations after World War II and prevent communist subversion of countries weakened by war.

net material product (NMP)—The total economic value of production in the productive sectors of a national economy (not counting administration, defense, finance, education, health, and housing) after depreciation has been deducted.

North Atlantic Treaty Organization (NATO)—An organization founded in 1949 by the United States, Canada, and their postwar European allies to oppose the Soviet military presence in Europe. Until the dissolution of the Soviet-led Warsaw Pact (*q.v.*) in 1991, it was the primary collective defense agreement of the Western powers. Its military and administrative structure remained intact after the threat of Soviet expansionism had subsided.

passenger kilometers—The total number of kilometers traveled by passengers by a given mode of transportation in a specified period of time.

perestroika—Russian word meaning "restructuring," applied in the late 1980s to official Soviet program of revitalization of the communist party, economy, and society by adjusting economic, social, and political mechanisms. Identified with the tenure of Mikhail S. Gorbachev as leader of the Soviet Union (1985–91).

Shia—A member of the smaller of the two divisions of Islam, supporting the claims of Ali to leadership of the Muslim community, in opposition to the Sunni (*q.v.*) view of succession to Muslim leadership—the issue causing the central schism within Islam.

Solidarity—An independent trade union founded in 1980 in communist Poland. For its defiance of the communist system, the union attained great political power through the loyalty of a large part of the Polish population. Under the leadership of Lech Wałęsa, it eventually formed the basis of the first postwar noncommunist Polish government.

Sunni—A member of the larger of the two fundamental divisions of Islam, opposed to the Shia (*q.v.*) on the issue of succession to Muslim leadership.

ton kilometers—The total number of tons of cargo conveyed via a given mode of transportation in a specified period of time.

Warsaw Pact—In full, Warsaw Treaty Organization, a mutual defense organization including the Soviet Union, Albania (which withdrew in 1961), Bulgaria, Czechoslovakia, the German Democratic Republic (East Germany), Hungary, Poland, and Romania. Founded in 1955, it enabled the Soviet Union to station troops in most of the other countries to oppose the forces of the North Atlantic Treaty Organization (NATO, *q.v.*) and was the basis of invasions of Hungary (1956) and Czechoslovakia (1968). Disbanded in 1991.

World Bank—Informal name used to designate a group of four affiliated international institutions: the International Bank for Reconstruction and Development (IBRD), the International Development Association (IDA), the International Finance Corporation (IFC), and the Multilateral Investment Guarantee Agency (MIGA). The IBRD, established in 1945, has as its primary purpose the provision of loans to developing countries for productive projects. The IDA, a legally separate loan fund but administered by the staff of the IBRD, was set up in 1960 to furnish credits to the poorest developing countries on much easier terms than those of conventional IBRD loans. The IFC, founded in 1956, supplements the activities of the IBRD through loans and assistance designed specifically to encourage the growth of productive private enterprises in the less-developed countries. The MIGA, founded in 1988, insures private foreign investment in developing countries against various non-commercial risks. The president and certain senior officers of the IBRD hold the same positions in the IFC. The four institutions are owned by the governments of the countries that subscribe their capital. To participate in the World Bank group, member states must first belong to the International Monetary Fund (IMF—*q.v.*).

Index

abortion: restrictions on, 78
Academic Freedom, Law on (1990), 112-13
acquired immune deficiency syndrome (AIDS), 107-8
Administration Department, 268
administrative subdivisions, 71, 194, 197
Adrianople, Battle of (718), 228
Adventist Church, 93
Afghanistan: military support to, 53; Soviet invasion of, xxxiii, 52, 55, 221
agrarians. *See* Bulgarian Agrarian National Union (BANU)
Agricultural and Cooperative Bank, 156
agricultural collectivization, xxxi, 46, 53, 53-54, 127, 129, 144-47; benefits of, 49; campaigns, 144-47; compensation for, 150-51; opposition to, 44; pace of, 47, 127, 129; peasant resistance to, 46, 147, 180; problems with, 180; reforms in, 132
agricultural cooperatives: increase in membership of, 39; voluntary formation of, 150
agricultural-industrial complex (*agropromishlen kompleks*—APK), 53-54, 132, 134, 147, 148
agricultural labor: percentage of, in labor force, 122; shortages of, xxxiv, 72, 82, 121, 147, 184
agricultural land: chemical damage to, 69, 70; as percent of total, 121
agricultural plots: private, 150; consolidation of, 147-48; size of, 40, 129-30
agricultural production, 150; attempts to increase, 128; attempts to industrialize, 132; decline in, 147; diversification of, 39; under five-year plans, 129; government control of, 39; growth of, 25, 27, 39, 129, 136, 147, 148; under Liapchev, 37; quotas in, 147, 148; under Stambolov, 25; target negotiation, 132; under Third Five-Year Plan, 49
agricultural products (*see also under individual crops*), 148-51; export of, 40, 148, 164; food, 150; grain, 121; industrial crops, 40; tobacco, 121, 148; vegetables, 121

agricultural reform, 33-35, 148; resistance to, 151; retreat from, 132; under Zhivkov, 55, 125
agricultural workers, 100; income of, 150; minimum wage for, 164; number of, 102; as party members, 197; as percentage of population, 101; shortage of, xxxiv, 102, 148
agriculture, xxx, 144-48; aid for restructuring, 168; under democratization, 118; under five-year plans, 128, 129; government intervention in, 27; income in, 123, 165; investment in, 47, 160; modernization of, 129; net material product growth of, 141; as percentage of net material product, 130, 144; policy, experiments with, 53; privatization in, 76, 129, 150; resources, 121
agropromishlen kompleks. *See* agricultural-industrial complex
AIDS. *See* acquired immune deficiency syndrome
air and air defense forces, 242, 246-47; aircraft of, 246; combat units of, 246; commanders of, 242; conscripts in, 246; deployment of, 246; number of personnel, 246; uniforms, ranks, and insignia, 257-58
air pollution, 70
Albania: Bulgarian occupation of, 229; in World War I, 31
Albanians: revolt against Ottoman Turks, 29
alcohol consumption, 107
Algeria: arms sales to, 262
Aleksandŭr, Ivan, 7
Alexander II: assassinated, 23
Alexander III: death of, 26; relations of, with Alexander of Battenburg, 23
Alexander of Battenburg, 230; deposed, 24; elected prince, 22-23; opposition of, to liberal faction, 23; opposition of, to Tŭrnovo constitution, 23; relations of, with Alexander III, 23
Alexander the Great, 4
Allied Control Commission, 43, 232; dismantled, 44, 176
Allied powers, xxx; attempts to achieve peace with, 42

301

DS. *See* State Security
Dubrovnik, 91
Duma, 212
Dŭrzhavna sigurnost (DS). *See* State Security
Dzhagarov, Georgi, 210
Dzhurov, Dobri, 185, 241

earthquakes, 64-67
Eastern Europe: trade with, 117, 160
Eastern Orthodox Church (*see also* Bulgarian Orthodox Church), 88-89; in First Bulgarian Empire, 80, 90
Eastern Rite Church. *See* Eastern Orthodox Church
Eastern Rumelia: union with, 23; war over, 229
EBRD. *See* European Bank for Reconstruction and Development
Ecoforum conference, xxxiv, 121, 184, 199, 267
economic association, xxxix
economic growth: under communist rule, 136; decline of, 135-36; under Ferdinand, 27; under New Economic Model, 136; under Stambolov, 26
economic planning (*see also* five-year plans), xxxi, xxxiii, 128; failures of, xxxiv-xxxv; hierarchy, 125; inefficiency under, 125; innovation discouraged under, 125; material balances in, 126; process, 126-27; Soviet model for, 47, 49, 125, 126; system, 125-27
economic policy, 127-38; assessment of, 118; of Chervenkov, 47; under communist rule, 118, 127-28
Economic Policy Commission, 167-68
economic reform, xxxi, 47, 123, 130-38, 166-69; under democratization, xxxv, xliv, 121, 187; goals of, 169; incentive for, 131, 184; mechanisms, 166-67; methods, 166; of 1965, 53; Poland as model for, 166-67; timing, 166; trade unions under, 204-5
economy: aid for restructuring, 168; crisis in, 54; effect of reparations payments on, 37; experimentation in, xxxiii, 117, 125, 130-38; indicators, 49; interwar, 39-40; market, 117; performance, 127-38; rehabilitation, postwar, 46; restructuring of, 127; role of Bulgarian Communist Party in, 117; Soviet inter-

vention in, 47; statistics, 118; structure, 123-27; units, larger, 132-34
economy, centrally planned, 124-25; advantages of, 124; criticisms of, 124-25; distribution problems under, 135; transition from, 164; under constitution of 1947, 45-46
Edinna sredna politekhnicheska uchilishta. *See* Unified Secondary Polytechnical Schools
education (*see also* schools), xxxiii, 109-13; communist indoctrination in, 110, 112; compulsory, 35, 110; curriculum, 110; employment in, 101; foreign aid for reforming, 113; for girls, 15; of Gypsies, 86; independence of, 37; level of, 61; under Liapchev, 37; and marriage, 98-99; political activity in, 112; postsecondary, 112; problems in, 111; reform of, 110, 112; religious, 89; restructuring of, 111; secular, 15; socialist, 111; Soviet model for, 47, 49; subsidies for, 165; of workers, 101
educational councils, 111
EEC. *See* European Economic Community
EFTA. *See* European Free Trade Association
Egypt: attempted coup in, 53, 271
Ekoglasnost, xxxii, 184-85, 202, 207, 211; demonstrations by, 184; founded, 207; membership of, 207; platform of, 207
election commissions, 195
election laws, 194, 195, 196
elections: campaigns for, 196; candidates for, 195; under communist rule, 177; communists in, 174; constituencies of, 197; eligibility for, 195; free, 186, 196; intimidations in, 35; multicandidate, 183; of 1919, 34; of 1931, 37; of 1938, 39; of 1944, 44; of 1946, 44; of 1990, 174, 186, 196, 100; of 1991, xxxvi, xxxviii, 194; nomination process for, 195; rigged, 44; Russian intervention in, 23
electoral procedures, 194-97
electric power: brownout schedule for, 140; generation of, 55-56, 121; shortages of, 55, 140; state ownership of, 40
electrification, 128
Electronic Materials Processing and Equipment Scientific-Production Combine, 142

Published Country Studies

(Area Handbook Series)

550–65	Afghanistan		550–87	Greece
550–98	Albania		550–78	Guatemala
550–44	Algeria		550–174	Guinea
550–59	Angola		550–82	Guyana and Belize
550–73	Argentina		550–151	Honduras
550–169	Australia		550–165	Hungary
550–176	Austria		550–21	India
550–175	Bangladesh		550–154	Indian Ocean
550–170	Belgium		550–39	Indonesia
550–66	Bolivia		550–68	Iran
550–20	Brazil		550–31	Iraq
550–168	Bulgaria		550–25	Israel
550–61	Burma		550–182	Italy
550–50	Cambodia		550–30	Japan
550–166	Cameroon		550–34	Jordan
550–159	Chad		550–56	Kenya
550–77	Chile		550–81	Korea, North
550–60	China		550–41	Korea, South
550–26	Colombia		550–58	Laos
550–33	Commonwealth Caribbean, Islands of the		550–24	Lebanon
550–91	Congo		550–38	Liberia
550–90	Costa Rica		550–85	Libya
550–69	Côte d'Ivoire (Ivory Coast)		550–172	Malawi
550–152	Cuba		550–45	Malaysia
550–22	Cyprus		550–161	Mauritania
550–158	Czechoslovakia		550–79	Mexico
550–36	Dominican Republic and Haiti		550–76	Mongolia
550–52	Ecuador		550–49	Morocco
550–43	Egypt		550–64	Mozambique
550–150	El Salvador		550–35	Nepal and Bhutan
550–28	Ethiopia		550–88	Nicaragua
550–167	Finland		550–157	Nigeria
550–155	Germany, East		550–94	Oceania
550–173	Germany, Fed. Rep. of		550–48	Pakistan
550–153	Ghana		550–46	Panama